D1466373

# Observing America's Jews

*Edited and with a foreword by* Jonathan D. Sarna

*Afterword by* Charles S. Liebman

# Marshall Sklare

## Observing America's Jews

BRANDEIS UNIVERSITY PRESS

*Published by University Press of New England/Hanover & London*

BRANDEIS UNIVERSITY PRESS
Published by University Press of New England, Hanover, NH 03755
© 1993 by Trustees of Brandeis University
All rights reserved
Printed in the United States of America     5   4   3   2   1
CIP data appear at the end of the book

Acknowledgment is made for permission to reprint the following material:
"The Jewish Religion in America": From *America's Jews* by Marshall Sklare Copyright ©
1971 by Marshall Sklare. Reprinted by permission of Random House, Inc.
"A Study of Jewish Attitudes Toward the State of Israel": Reprinted with the permission of
The Free Press, a Division of Macmillan, Inc. from *Jews: Social Patterns of an American Group*
by Marshall Sklare. Copyright © 1958 by The Free Press; copyright renewed 1986.
"The Sociology of Contemporary Jewish Studies," in *The Jew in American Society*: Published
by Behrman House, Inc. 235 Watchung Ave., W. Orange, NJ 07052. Used with permission.
Additional acknowledgments appear on p. 291.

# Contents

## Contents

# Editor's Foreword

The origins of this volume date back to a late Saturday night party in December 1990. Professor Marshall Sklare was there, regaling his friends with anecdotes; he looked healthier and more jovial than I had seen him since before his hospitalization. Thinking that he might, at last, be ready for a new project, I seized the opportunity to discuss with him a volume of his own articles. "You have collected everybody else's articles," I observed, thinking of his now-famous readers in American Jewish Sociology. "The time has come for you to collect your own."

Sklare expressed cautious interest in the project—he did not mention that years before he had proposed just such a volume to a major publisher—and he soon set to work. By late March he had prepared a tentative table of contents as well as sample introductions to three selections. "[T]he introductions will serve to supply background as well as to analyze how and why I came to write the article," he explained in a letter to his editor at University Press of New England. "Thus the volume can have something of the character of an intellectual biography." He also hoped that his introductions would tie the book together and "reduce the discontinuity that is characteristic of volumes of this type."

Unfortunately, circumstances forced Sklare to put the volume aside for several months. When he returned to it, he decided to prepare his general introduction, again with an eye toward intellectual biography. The result, to the delight of both his family and editors, was the autobiographical introduction published here for the first time. Tragically, this also turned out to be Marshall Sklare's last sustained piece of writing. As such, it stands as something of a personal testament, reflecting the forces that shaped his life, his faith, and his values.

Marshall Sklare passed away on March 1, 1992. At the time of his death, he was hard at work on this volume, drafting introductions to its various selections, re-editing some pieces for publication, and preparing to update footnotes and bibliographies. Not enough progress had been made, however, to publish this book along the lines that he had charted. So when I agreed to take over as editor, it was with the understanding that necessary changes would be made in an effort to bring the volume to press at an early date.

With the agreement of the family, the table of contents that Sklare had originally proposed was significantly altered. He himself expected to make some revisions, but I felt that many more changes were needed to provide readers with a comprehensive picture of his pioneering contributions to the study of American Jewish life. As a result, chapters from each of Sklare's best known books are now included in this volume, including his analysis of "the Jewish Religion in America" from *America's Jews*, his updated look at the Conservative movement prepared for the first revised edition of *Conservative Judaism: An American Religious Movement*, and his provocative survey of "The Image of the Good Jew in Lakeville," originally published in his *Jewish Identity on the Suburban Frontier*. To accommodate these additions, the entire volume was reorganized, and several shorter pieces had to be dropped. They, along with all of the books and articles that Sklare published during his productive and distinguished career, are now listed here as part of the "Bibliography of the Writings of Marshall Sklare."

The most painful decision that needed to be made concerned the chapter introductions that Sklare had originally planned for this volume. These, as indicated, featured prominently in his conception of the book, and they occupied him during the last days of his life. Only a few introductions, however, seem to have been committed to writing. To have included them and not others would have made for an uneven volume, while surviving notes did not permit us to reconstruct what background information about other articles he might have sought to convey, or what changes in the articles he intended to introduce. So, in the end, and not without a great deal of sadness, we abandoned Sklare's original plan, substituting a few short editorial headnotes for the discursive introductions that he himself would surely have preferred.

The last significant change in this volume concerns the afterword, entitled "Marshall Sklare: An Assessment." Professor Charles S. Liebman of Bar Ilan University, Sklare's distinguished friend and fellow social scientist, graciously agreed to write this essay on short notice. He offers a well-rounded exposition of the forces that shaped Marshall Sklare, the discipline that Sklare in turn shaped as the "dean" of American Jewish sociologists, and the influence of both the man and the field on American Jewish life as a whole.

It remains only to acknowledge the kind assistance that I have received in the completion of this volume. The staff of the Maurice and Marilyn Cohen Center for Modern Jewish Studies, founded by Sklare and now directed by Gary A. Tobin, extended a great deal of support; special thanks to Lawrence Sternberg, Sylvia Barack Fishman, and Sylvia J. Riese. Leonard Dinnerstein and Shelly Tenenbaum read the volume for the press; I am especially indebted to Shelly, who wrote her doctorate under Marshall Sklare, for suggesting that we include "The Image of the Good Jew in Lakeville" in this volume.

I hope that this volume brings some measure of comfort to Marshall Sklare's family, students, and friends and trust that they will accept the book as a tribute to a devoted and beloved teacher from a grateful student.

*Erev Rosh Hashanah, 5753*                                     Jonathan D. Sarna

# Author's Preface

This volume constitutes a selection of my articles, which have appeared during the past four decades. It also includes an introductory essay entitled "A Sociologist of the Jews: Some Autobiographical Remarks." In rereading this essay it struck me that it reads like a self-congratulatory statement—almost like a record of multiple success stories. This is not my intent—like all of us I have suffered disappointments and rejection. But perhaps it can be said that this volume is not the occasion to underline the negative.

I had long thought of preparing a volume of this type, but it was not until my colleague Jonathan Sarna gave me a "pep talk" that I started to get to work on this book. I am grateful to him for his interest and encouragement. I should also like to thank Jeanne West of the University Press of New England for her support and interest in the volume. I am also grateful to Lawrence Sternberg of the Maurice and Marilyn Cohen Center for Modern Jewish Studies. He was of assistance to me when I was director of the Center for Modern Jewish Studies, and he has continued his help after I retired from that position. The same holds true for Sylvia Riese. She has assisted me for almost a decade, and I am obligated to her for many kindnesses. I also want to thank Ofer Shiff and David Kaufman, graduate students in the Department of Near Eastern and Judaic Studies at Brandeis, who have assisted me in diverse ways.

Brandeis University has had the virtue of reuniting me with a friend from college days: Marvin Fox. While his help has had a personal dimension, it has also been an expression of his regard for the totality of Jewish studies. A leading authority in the field of medieval Jewish philosophy, he is blessed with the ability to understand and appreciate fields of study quite different from the one in which he specializes.

Marshall Sklare

*Observing America's Jews*

# A Sociologist of the Jews:
## Some Autobiographical Remarks

Our age is an age of confession. One has only to watch daytime television to realize the abundance of such material and how vulgar it can sometimes be. While I am a strong believer in the right of privacy, it is nevertheless evident that an autobiographical statement can be helpful in interpreting the work of an author. The remarks that follow are offered in that spirit.

I should explain that they are confined to material that is helpful in understanding my work as a sociologist of the Jews. I only touch upon such crucial matters as my relationship with my wife and children in a peripheral way. I have sought both to protect my privacy and at the same time to reveal aspects of my life that I deem helpful in interpreting my work as a sociologist.

Both of my parents were born in Chicago, the children of immigrants. All of my grandparents had been born in Lithuania, and all four came from Kovno or its environs.

My father was a businessman. He had been in a variety of enterprises until he married my mother and entered her father's firm. My father came from a poor family. His first job had been selling newspapers after school in the downtown office buildings of Chicago. His formal education ended when he graduated elementary school. He then began to work on a full-time basis; most of his earnings were contributed to his family. When his father died he took over the support of his mother. In his mature years he extended financial assistance to various relatives as well.

My mother's family was more secure financially, although the struggles of immigrant days always remained fresh in the minds of her parents. My mother was a homemaker and an expert in her craft. She was the type of housekeeper—now extinct—who would clean the apartment before the cleaning woman arrived. Her three sons, who benefited from her culinary skills, would jokingly tell her that she should go into business inasmuch as her baking far surpassed that of the Chicago firm of Sara Lee.

My father's conception of the duties incumbent on an adult Jew were quite simple: to give generously to Jewish causes, to join a synagogue, to belong to a Zionist organization, and to subscribe to an Anglo-Jewish weekly—in his case the *Chicago Jewish Sentinel*. Some years before my father died he was written up in the *Sentinel* as the individual who had been a subscriber for a longer period than anyone else in the city.

There was another duty that my father believed was required of an adult. It was incumbent on the individual to buy a "plot"—that is, a burial place in a Jewish cemetery. In his case it was Waldheim—a huge cemetery located immediately west of Chicago. Waldheim advertised itself as the world's largest Jewish cemetery—a boast that may have been true, although I traced it to the boosterism endemic to the Windy City.

My father had been raised in a very Orthodox home—a household that seemed to me to be more European than American. His mother, to whom he was very devoted, never felt any desire to learn English. Despite her intelligence, after about fifty years in America, her English vocabulary seemed to be limited to approximately one hundred words. To me she was always a romantic, even heroic, figure. She had resisted acculturation despite the attractions of Chicago, the importunings of her children, her daughters-in-law, and her grandchildren.

Although my mother's mother was somewhat traditional, her father— Meyer W. Lippman—had not resisted the acculturation process. In his old age, when he lived in a nursing home, he dictated his memoirs that traced his life from Kovno to his mature years in Chicago. He entitled the document "America I Love You."

Meyer Lippman had been raised in an Orthodox home but deviated from Orthodox norms soon after leaving Kovno. Meyer Lippman felt that Conservative Judaism was not only appropriate for himself but that it was the only religious approach that could succeed with his five children. Despite my father's very strict Orthodox upbringing he followed in the path of his father-in-law.

As a child I found it comforting to go to a synagogue where my grandfather was a substantial contributor and a person of some prominence and where my parents, as well as assorted aunts and uncles, belonged. I was enrolled in the congregation's Hebrew school and must have been more involved than most of my peers; I recall receiving a certificate attesting to the fact that I had a perfect record in respect to attendance at Junior Congregation services on Saturday morning. The pattern that I followed on the Sabbath was unorthodox but very rigid. It consisted of attending services in the morning, having lunch at home (it was not an elaborate lunch since my father worked on Saturdays), and then going to the movies in the afternoon. Going to the movies involved a considerable investment of time; it was the era of the double feature plus the short subject.

After we left the neighborhood and affiliated with a Conservative congregation in a new neighborhood, my attendance at services on Saturday morning became irregular. Also, I did not continue on to Hebrew high school. It was not that I rejected further Jewish study. Rather there was no tradition of continued Jewish learning in my nuclear family. Furthermore, the reinforcement of relatives was missing in the new neighborhood.

It was assumed that my secular education would continue well beyond elementary school. There was no question that, unlike my father, I would continue on to high school and then would go to college. However, despite my limited Jewish education I was never really alienated from my Jewish identity. In high school I was active in the Jewish Youth League of Chicago—clubs that were located in each of the city's high schools in which there were substantial numbers of Jewish students. After I became the president of the club at my high school I went on to become president of the citywide Jewish Youth League.

During my high school years something happened that affected the course of my life. One of my brothers was sickly and consequently had never attended Hebrew school. My parents felt something had to be done about his Jewish education. Accordingly my mother called the College of Jewish Studies of Chicago and asked for a referral to a private teacher. She was given the name of Seymour J. Pomerenze, a student in the College as well as a graduate student in the history department of the University of Chicago.

Pomerenze made a very strong impression on my mother. It was not only his personality but the fact that he was an orphan. His parents had died in the Ukraine in the wake of World War I. Although my mother was in many respects a thoroughly modern woman, she had great sympathy for orphans—a value that must have had its origins in Eastern Europe from which her parents had come. My mother was concerned that Pomerenze would have sufficient income to keep body and soul together. Also she felt the obligation to supply him with home-cooked meals to supplement the food served at the University's cafeterias. Thus she scheduled his appointments with my brother at mealtimes. Pomerenze readily availed himself of the opportunity to improve his diet.

My mother also sought to improve Pomerenze's economic situation. She arranged for Hebrew lessons with nieces and nephews. Another of her ideas to augment Pomerenze's income was for me to take lessons with him. I was agreeable—I was in awe of someone who was studying with some of the nation's most distinguished historians at the University of Chicago. But what should we study? It occurred to both Pomerenze and myself that this would be an opportunity for me to study Jewish history. I had always been interested in history, especially in American history, and had read far beyond the requirements of the high school curriculum. Although I was also interested in Jewish history, the only knowledge I had was the little that I had gleaned in Hebrew school. For all practical purposes I was a novice.

After dinner, and after Pomerenze had finished tutoring my brother, he turned his attention to me. If I recall correctly the text we used was *A History of the Jewish People* by Marx and Margolis. This book was short on interpretation but very long on facts. Despite its dryness—even aridity—it caught my attention.

Pomerenze was a crucial influence in my development not only because he introduced me to Jewish history but also because he stimulated me to enroll in the College of Jewish Studies of Chicago. The College was an agency of the Board of Jewish Education of Chicago. It was then located in the heart of the downtown area; it occupied space in a nondescript building serviced by a rickety elevator. Despite its physical limitations I found a home at the College. I began to take classes there while I was still a student in high school.

The College had an unusual faculty. It included such renowned figures as Shimon Rawidowicz, Shimon Halkin, and Nahum Glatzer. Furthermore, I was exposed for the first time to *Die Wissenschaft des Judentums*—"the science of Judaism." This approach to Jewish study involved learning about the religion and culture of the Jews throughout the ages—and doing so in a manner that met accepted scholarly standards. Since it was a period before Jewish studies were taught in American universities, the several Hebrew colleges located in the nation's largest cities were the only place (aside from the Reform and Conservative rabbinical seminaries) where one could approach Jewish study in the spirit of "the science of Judaism."

My closest connection to the faculty of the College was with the historian and philosopher Fritz Bamberger. He had been the director of the Board of Jewish Education of Berlin and had been in charge of a Jewish teachers college in that city. Bamberger arrived in Chicago just before World War II and brought with him a considerable library, including some rare items on Spinoza. He began to teach at the College of Jewish Studies and apparently found me to be an eager student; he offered to tutor me on a volunteer basis.

While my interest was modern Jewish history, Bamberger pointed out that I needed an understanding of medieval Jewish history. Thus Friday afternoons began to be spent in the combined living room and study of his apartment reading documents in Latin, Hebrew, and in other languages relevant to the study of medieval Jewish history. However, these wonderful pre-Sabbath afternoons did not last; in 1942 Bamberger became the research director of *Coronet* and later of *Esquire*. After a successful career in magazine research, Bamberger returned to the Jewish field and became an administrator at Hebrew Union College-Jewish Institute of Religion in New York City.

My feelings about the College can be understood by something that took place in the early months of 1943. The registrar of the College informed me that, assuming the successful completion of the courses for which I was enrolled I would graduate at the end of the spring semester. I pleaded with her to recalculate my credits—perhaps I had been given more credits than I had really earned. As a special favor she recalculated. After she did so, she was immovable: I must graduate. She not only told me that I would have the required number of courses but she told me to stop acting like a selfish child. She explained that graduating was good for the College inasmuch as it strengthened the College's case for the financial support that it needed so desperately. She told me to start acting like a *mensch*. This would involve participating in the commencement, inviting my relatives to attend, and giving my parents a little *nachas*. So I graduated from the College, even if reluctantly.

I was delighted when, in 1980, I was invited to return to the College to receive an honorary degree and to give the commencement address. I concluded my address as follows:

Much has changed since the 1930's and '40's. Perhaps even my recollections of the College are faulty—some of the shortcomings of the College may have receded into my unconscious, not to speak of my own inadequacies. But I hope that the graduates of 1980 will be able to *shep naches* from their experience at the College as I have done. . . . May their *nachas* increase from year to year, and may the College go from strength to strength. May it introduce new generations of students to the study of the culture of the Jews from its earliest periods until the present day. May its students be reluctant to graduate and eager to continue their study of Jews and Judaism. And may the class of 1980 find their education at the College liberating, making them exemplars of what the Jewish version of a liberal arts education should be.

I should explain that when I use the term "the College," I am referring to the College of Jewish Studies of Chicago (the College's present name is the "Spertus College of Judaica") despite the fact that I attended Northwestern University for my undergraduate education and continued graduate study at the University of Chicago. Classes at the College were held in the late afternoons, in the evenings, and on Sunday afternoons (there were no classes at the College on Sunday morning since many of us taught that morning at a Hebrew or Sunday school). To my friends and me, it was "*the* College" despite the fact that we attended one or another of Chicago's leading universities. I for one was proud to be enrolled in an obscure school tucked away in a decrepit office building. I suspect that we felt that "the College" was our college in a way that we did not feel that Northwestern or the "U. of C." was ours.

What was the reason for this? Was it sympathy for the underdog—a college that had no endowment and no campus? Was it a feeling that both Northwestern and the U. of C. were, in the final sense, Christian schools? Or was it the fact that at the time Northwestern had a quota for Jews? I conceded that the University of Chicago was friendlier to Jews than Northwestern, and I did indeed feel more comfortable in Hyde Park, where the U. of C. was located than in bourgeois Evanston, where Northwestern had its college of liberal arts.

Interestingly enough, it never occurred to me to request that either Northwestern or the U. of C. accept any of the credit I had accumulated at the College. To be sure a transfer of credit might have been difficult to arrange given the fact that at the time hardly any Jewish courses were given at either university. But I think that the reason was a more subtle one. I must have conceived of the College in the context of the sacred and the universities in the context of the secular. Although I was studying liberal arts at the universities, I must have felt that they were connected (in some vague way to be sure) with making a living. Except for a small group who might become professional Jews, most of us at the College would derive no worldly profit from our studies there. We were studying "for the sake of Heaven."

But how would I make a living? On a conscious level I was not very concerned with the problem of a career. However, my parents, and especially my father, were strongly concerned. Business, including the lumber company that my grandfather had established, held no attraction for me.

The alternative was to practice a profession. Given my lack of interest in medicine and my facility with language and debating, my parents began to see me as a future lawyer. I thought I would put an end to such talk by saying that my political convictions would not allow me to become a lawyer for the capitalists. I told them that the only type of lawyer I could consider becoming would be a labor lawyer (or, more exactly, a lawyer who worked on behalf of labor). Instead of insisting that I become a "normal" lawyer my father reacted positively to the idea of labor law, which I was using only as a ploy to get him off my back. He knew of a young labor lawyer in Chicago, Arthur Goldberg by name, who was rising to wealth and prominence. My father saw no reason why his son could not do as well.

Despite my parents' anxieties, I succeeded in deflecting the question of career for some time. During college days I taught Sunday School and Hebrew School at one or another Chicago congregation. But Zionism was my chief extracurricular activity. I became active in Avukah—the college student Zionist federation—and rose to become president of the Midwest region. In regard to academics I majored in modern European history at Northwestern. I developed a strong interest in sociology after I took an introductory course in that subject and ended up taking a minor in sociology. I was particularly attracted to Paul Meadows, then a junior member of Northwestern's sociology department. He was a sociologist who made extensive use of historical data. Furthermore, he treated my interest in Jewish things as a legitimate intellectual activity and did his best to wade through the papers I wrote for him on Jewish topics. In these papers I sought to relate the theories he developed in class to my Jewish interests.

After Northwestern I continued my education at the "U of C," or, as it was immodestly known, "*the* University." Majoring in sociology I wrote an M.A. thesis on the assumptions and programs of American Jewish organizations seeking to combat anti-Semitism. My adviser was Herbert Blumer, a well-known social psychologist. Despite his Jewish-sounding name Blumer was not

Jewish. Like Paul Meadows, he accepted my Jewish concerns. He never gave me the feeling that my interests were any less legitimate than those of students in the department who were in the mainstream.

Louis Wirth was the one Jewish member of the University's famed sociology department who was identified as a Jew. He had written a doctoral dissertation that had been published by the University of Chicago Press under the title *The Ghetto*. It remained in print for many years. Studying the ghetto had been suggested to Wirth by members of the faculty. In his book Wirth traced the phenomenon of the ghetto from medieval Venice to contemporary times, and he focused on the development of Jewish immigrant neighborhoods in Chicago. Wirth was an opponent of Zionism and—it was said—was proud of the fact that he had married a Gentile woman. Wirth was not assimilated—he was only an assimilationist. But in my view the latter was worse than the former. Although I took some work with Wirth, including his well-known course on the sociology of knowledge, I never felt free to discuss Jewish matters with him.

After the completion of my masters degree I spent three years of full-time work in the field of Jewish education. I had decided that despite my intellectual approval of being a *chalutz* in Palestine, *aliyah* was not for me. I think I must have been looking for an alternative—some kind of Jewish pioneering in the United States. To be sure, draining the swamps in Palestine was dangerous work, but Jewish education had its difficulties. While parents were generally appreciative of my efforts, many were less than firm in their Jewish identity. Furthermore, the schedule of the Reform congregations in which I served as a principal afforded relatively few hours to build the kind of Jewish identity and knowledge that I envisioned. Most parents were ready to settle for a minimalist standard.

My work was well received by the rabbis of the congregations I served and by the staff of the Board of Jewish Education of Chicago. But those who counseled me sought to deter me from pursuing a career in Jewish education. In essence they told me that I was too talented to become a Jewish educator and that I would not be satisfied with the status accorded a Jewish educator. They advised me to become a rabbi. As a rabbi I would occupy a higher status and earn a better salary. I found it discouraging that even individuals who occupied leading positions in Jewish education had such a negative view of their field. I had expected that they would seek to recruit me to enter their profession.

My parents were in complete agreement with those who discouraged me from becoming a Jewish educator and who suggested that I become a rabbi instead. My father maintained that I would be able to do more for the Jewish people as a lawyer than as a rabbi—I would have the wealth to support Jewish causes, and I could become the president of a synagogue. My parents knew

the hardships and heartaches of the rabbinate, but they felt that if I must become a professional Jew the rabbinate offered a much better future than Jewish
education.

My father in particular was incensed at the idea of having what he termed a
*melamed*—usually translated as a "Hebrew teacher"—in the family. My parents
supported the idea of giving their children a Jewish education, but they never
conceived that a child of theirs would want to make a career in that field. My
father was not an East European Jew in any meaningful sense, but he seemed to
have inherited the lack of regard for the *melamed* that was common in Eastern
Europe. Since I was not attracted to the idea of my becoming a rabbi, I soon
reached a standoff with my parents. I decided that the better part of wisdom
would be for me to let matters ride and to proceed to study for a doctorate.

Both my wife, Rose, and I agreed that a change of place was indicated, and
we decided to move to New York where I would enroll at Columbia University.
My wife was able to locate a position at a leading New York publishing house
and thus to continue with the career that she had started in Chicago. I secured
a part-time position at the Jewish Education Committee (JEC) of New York.
My job was interesting, and it allowed me to retain my image of myself as a
*chalutz*. The JEC was the leading agency of its type in the nation, and its staff
was composed of some of the best people in Jewish education. However, my
work soon expanded well beyond my original commitment, and it became apparent that if I was to complete my doctorate in a reasonable period of time I
would have to become a full-time student. Thus I subsequently resigned from
the JEC.

At Columbia I had an opportunity for the first time of taking courses on
Jewish subjects in a university setting. I enrolled in the courses given by Salo
Baron and took a minor in Jewish history. I had met Baron when he came to
Northwestern to deliver a lecture on "The Jews and Modern Capitalism." It
was a dazzling performance (I later learned that this was one of Baron's standard lectures, which he had given at universities many times before). Afterward
I met with Baron at his hotel. He discouraged me from going into Jewish history. I later learned that this was standard operating procedure for him. Baron
did not foresee the growth of Jewish studies at American universities; it was his
practice to advise graduate students to enter the rabbinate so that they would
have a vocation. They could practice Jewish history as an avocation. I did not
spend very much time with Baron at Columbia—he was heavily engaged in
his scholarly activities, especially in the preparation of the new edition of his
multivolume *Social and Religious History of the Jews*. In any case, since I was majoring in sociology, it was appropriate for me to expend most of my energy in
that department.

The two leading members of the sociology department were both Jewish
(or, as some thought, only of Jewish ancestry). They were Paul Lazarsfeld and
Robert K. Merton. Although Merton fascinated me, his interests did not par-

allel my own. Again I was attracted to a junior member of the department—in this case Seymour Martin Lipset. He was later to become one of the most widely known members of his profession. Although Lipset's background was quite different from my own I felt that we shared common interests. This was not altogether obvious; while in later years Lipset's Jewish interests became strongly evident, at the time he had not written anything about Jews. But in any case it was apparent that I had chosen a first-rate individual to supervise my dissertation. I also located another member of the sociology department—the late Herbert Hyman—who, although not identified with Jewish matters, seemed to have an open mind on the subject.

The topic I chose for my dissertation was an analysis of the growth and development of Conservative Judaism in the United States. I felt that, although there had been some writing on the history of Conservative Judaism, the available material did not provide much in the way of insight into the dynamics of the movement. But before I committed myself to the subject I first had to be clear in my own mind that I could be objective about a religious movement in which I had been reared and to which my wife and I were committed. After due consideration I concluded that I would be capable of overcoming any biases that the subject might present.

The dissertation was a success—the examining committee accepted it without revision. A leading member of Columbia's anthropology department, who was on the examining committee, even asked me if he could retain his copy for a few more days. He confessed that he had not completed his reading of the manuscript. The request was unusual, and I concluded that the dissertation must have some value if a member of the committee who had already discharged his responsibility was still interested enough to want to complete his reading. In fact, after approving the dissertation the members of the examining committee recommended that I should prepare the manuscript for publication. Lipset volunteered to recommend it to friends in the publishing world.

My first book, entitled *Conservative Judaism: An American Religious Movement*, went through several editions and later appeared as a paperback. It served to help establish me in the world of scholarship. It was favorably received by reviewers. To be sure, some of the leaders of Conservative Judaism—especially Conservative rabbis—were unhappy with my approach. They felt that it denigrated Conservative Judaism. However, some years after the publication of *Conservative Judaism* I had a meeting on an entirely different matter with one of the nation's leading Conservative rabbis. As I entered his commodious office he greeted me as follows: "Young man, how dare you tell the truth about Conservative Judaism!" It was a remark that was to delight me for years to come.

Since our first child was on the way, the matter of career choice could no longer be deferred. I had given up the thought of making a career in Jewish education, but it took me years to learn how to sleep on Sunday mornings without feelings of guilt. The result of my years at Columbia was that I developed an image of myself as a professional sociologist, and I began to look for a faculty post where my interest in the sociology of the Jews could be pursued. We wanted to remain in New York City but I could not find a full-time position in the area. As a result I turned to research as an occupation and located a position on the staff of the American Jewish Committee (AJC). I served initially as a study director in its Division of Scientific Research. To be sure the division had a rather pretentious name, but the AJC was an exceptional Jewish organization in that it maintained a permanent research staff. Many years later, the AJC would encounter financial difficulties, but at the time it was a vibrant organization with a large staff of talented specialists. Two of the best had their offices adjacent to my own—Milton Himmelfarb and the late Lucy Dawidowicz.

The executives of the AJC had some reservations about me, particularly when the director of the division left the agency and the question arose as to whether or not I should be appointed his successor. The "front office" was familiar with my strong Zionist orientation; since the AJC described itself as a non-Zionist Jewish organization, their views and mine did not coincide on this issue. The AJC was also familiar with my religious views; from their viewpoint, my views were strongly rightist. Nevertheless my promotion was approved. I always felt that I owed the promotion to the agency's executive vice president, the late John Slawson. He had a deep respect for scholarship, and he trusted me to avoid needless embarrassment to the agency.

For all of its attractions, working for the AJC had its drawbacks. Frequently, long-range projects had to be put aside in order to initiate short-range studies that dealt with anti-Semitic incidents or with problems to which the agency had to respond. Furthermore, the traditional focus of the agency's work was anti-Semitism. While I continued with the research program in this area, my abiding interest was in research on the problem of Jewish identity. The agency did sponsor work in this area, but every such project required considerable justification and continuing persuasion.

Perhaps the most discouraging aspect of my position was that material to be published had to be checked for any possible negative repercussions. While I accepted the necessity for doing so in the light of the agency's public relations, the longer I was at the AJC, the more unhappy I became with the process. While material on the authoritarian personality and on anti-Semitic behavior posed no problems, material on Jewish identity and Jewish attitudes was suspect. It was feared that it might be used against the Jews by unfriendly individuals or organizations. It was obvious that if I joined the faculty of an academic institution, these restraints would disappear. However, the downside was that money for the type of research I was interested in would be very difficult to come by.

In 1965, I took a leave of absence from the AJC in order to accept a Fulbright professorship at the Institute of Contemporary Jewry of the Hebrew University. Freed from administrative responsibilities and working in the quiet of Jerusalem, I completed several AJC projects, including a manuscript on the "Lakeville Study" in which the Jewish identity of some 432 Jewish residents residing in a prestigious Midwestern suburb was analyzed. The study was published by Basic Books in 1967 under the title *Jewish Identity in the Suburban Frontier: A Study of Group Survival in the Open Society*. The book appeared under my name as well as that of Joseph Greenblum who had made a significant contribution to the analysis of the data.

All books are not created equal. A second edition of *Jewish Identity in the Suburban Frontier* was published by the University of Chicago Press in 1979 in hardcover and in paperback. While I had succeeded in convincing the AJC that the majority of the data we collected could be published without negative results, I felt the book never received the attention it deserved. Although I recognized that this feeling is a classic complaint of authors, I had hoped that the AJC would use its influence with the media to get the book wider coverage than it received.

John Slawson had been loath to respond favorably to my request to be granted a leave of absence in order to accept the Fulbright. He predicted that I would not return to the agency. He was right. For some years I had been a lecturer at the School of Social Work at Yeshiva University where I taught courses on the sociology of American Jewry. Offered a professorship at "Y.U.," and having completed thirteen years of service at the AJC, I decided that it was time for a change.

My four years as a professor at Y.U. were productive. The social-work students were all graduate students. It was good to be teaching individuals who were on the road to maturity. Furthermore, while the students at the Y.U. School of Social Work had all received a bachelor's degree, I did not have to invest the large amount of time with them characteristic of graduate-school teaching. There was a strong emphasis—apparently common to schools of social work—on fieldwork. The student's performance in the fieldwork part of the curriculum was crucial for academic success. As I saw it, this emphasis served to limit the amount of time and effort that went into the student's intellectual development. However, the emphasis worked to my advantage. The students were not demanding—they seemed to save most of their energy for the challenge of the fieldwork. Thus I could do my own research and writing without undue distractions. Furthermore, my colleagues did not ask me to carry a heavy burden in respect to committee work. Although I enjoyed good personal relations with them I always had the feeling that they did not trust a sociologist to be overly involved in social-work matters.

While at Y.U., I wrote a book entitled *America's Jews*. This was part of a Random House series entitled "Ethnic Groups in Comparative Perspective." It was an important book for me. While short in length, it gave me an opportunity to write a widely ranging volume covering many aspects of American Jewish life. It also helped to provide material for students interested in learning about the subject. If used in conjunction with one of the readers I prepared, *America's Jews* provided supplementary classroom material for courses on American ethnic groups and for instructors who wanted to give a course on the sociology of the American Jew but were not specialists in the subject.

I was eager that the teaching of Jewish studies in the college curriculum would include the study of contemporary Jewry as well as the study of Jews and Judaism in past ages. There was no question that teaching about Jews and Judaism was geared to the study of the past and that there were relatively few resources for the study of contemporary Jewry. One of the ways I sought to remedy this situation was by preparing a series of readers. The first was published in 1958 by The Free Press under the title *The Jews: Social Patterns of an American Group*. It became fairly well-known among sociologists since it was one in a series of readers published by The Free Press and edited by leading sociologists. The first paragraph in the preface quoted a statement about contemporary Jewish studies made by Dr. Louis Finkelstein, then president of the Jewish Theological Seminary of America. Subsequently the statement became widely quoted:

Some years ago, I undertook to prepare a comprehensive work describing the whole phenomenon of Judaism. It was to include a history of the Jews, a description of their present condition, a discussion of their contribution to civilization . . . and an outline of their beliefs and practices as Jews. . . . What surprised me . . . was the dearth of information about Jews today. There are probably a hundred people, and more, whose profession it is to discover all that can be known about Jews in Jerusalem in the first century; there does not seem to be one who has the same duty for the Jews of New York in the twentieth century. So it comes about that we understand Judaism in the first century better than we understand Judaism in the twentieth.

When I started the project that led to the publication of *The Jews: Social Patterns of an American Group*, I was not at all sure that I could produce a book comparable to the other volumes in the series published by The Free Press. There was no body of standard literature in the field of contemporary Jewish studies. I read through a host of theses, dissertations, and research reports. I had to ask authors to produce articles for the volume instead of relying on previously published material. My requests were generally well received, but in some cases authors had turned their attention elsewhere and had no interest in contributing to the volume. Others had heavy commitments and could not promise a manuscript within a reasonable period of time. In cases where the material was particularly valuable and the author was otherwise occupied I myself prepared an article based on the author's original study. After the publication of *The Jews: Social Patterns of an American Group*, I prepared three subsequent volumes of readings: *The Jew in American Society*, *The Jewish Community in America*, and *American Jews: A Reader*. Instead of merely reprinting articles, I followed the practice of writing an introduction to each article. The introductions were meant to serve as guidelines for both student and teacher.

In 1969 I accepted a professorship at Brandeis University. Brandeis had a very large Jewish studies department that included some of the leading people in the field. The original idea was that I would have a joint appointment with sociology, but that did not come to pass. While the sociology department was nationally rated, it was strongly influenced by the radical politics of the period. For the first time I was interviewed by students—undergraduates who were sociology majors and by graduate students enrolled in the department. My ideas apparently did not find favor in the eyes of the students, and they did not make a good impression on me.

It was gratifying to join a department of Jewish studies. It was also good to be in a setting that encouraged sociability. While the Y.U. faculty were scattered throughout the New York metropolitan area, most members of the Jewish studies department (known as the Department of Near Eastern and Judaic Studies or NEJS) lived in one of two adjoining suburbs—Brookline and Newton. While some of the older members of the department retained a type of European formality, the younger members of the department had been influenced by the informality characteristic of American academic life. And Brandeis was a small-enough institution that relationships with members of other departments, as well as with officers of the University, could proceed on an informal level.

To be sure I was still in a minority at Brandeis. Many of my colleagues in the social sciences had little interest in Jewish matters. Some of them even seemed to resent the fact that they had joined the faculty of a "Jewish" school. But even more to the point was the fact that not every member of the NEJS Department was comfortable having a sociologist in their midst, particularly a sociologist who was a specialist in the field of contemporary Jewish studies. Apparently they feared that the department would endanger its moorings in the humanities and in classical Jewish studies. And when I succeeded in raising money for a center of modern Jewish studies at Brandeis, I sensed that there were some members of the department who were not gratified at the development.

I had long had the idea of a research institute on contemporary (or "modern") Jewish studies. It was obvious that the field required a systematic program of research that could only eventuate if there was a permanent research institute. But I hesitated to push the idea. My experience at the AJC had shown me what a drain administration could be on the resolve to continue with one's personal scholarly endeavors. However, there was sentiment at Brandeis to establish a center for modern Jewish studies. The chairman of the NEJS department, who also doubled as director of the Lown School, was Marvin Fox, whom I had first met at Northwestern when I was an undergraduate. While an authority on medieval Jewish philosophy, Fox had a strong belief in the unity of all subjects in the field of Jewish studies. He became a strong advocate for a center for modern Jewish studies. It was decided to go ahead with the idea. I took on the task of locating foundation support.

The Revson Foundation evidenced interest, but they wanted assurances that the idea was practical. Accordingly, they gave the University a grant to hold a planning conference. The planning conference—held in 1979—was well received. The papers delivered at the conference were published in a volume that I edited entitled *Understanding American Jewry*. Subsequently, the Revson Foundation made a substantial gift to the University for the establishment of a center for modern Jewish studies. The gift carried the stipulation that the University would have to raise three dollars for every dollar contributed by the Foundation. We achieved this goal, assisted by a gift from Maurice Cohen and his wife, Marilyn. Maurice Cohen was a longtime supporter of the University who had a strong interest in Jewish studies. The center was named the Maurice and Marilyn Cohen Center for Modern Jewish Studies.

I retired from Brandeis at the end of the Fall semester, 1990. The University gave me a farewell party. I was not very happy with the idea of such a party—I felt it might be painful to listen to speeches that of necessity would sound like funeral orations. To my surprise I enjoyed the event. Marvin Fox was in the chair, and in his usual efficient and disciplined manner he saw to it that however flattering the speeches, they were kept to a decent length. I was extolled as a veritable *chalutz*—the "father" of the sociological study of the American Jew. None of the speakers were bold enough to call me the "grandfather" of the sociological study of the American Jew!

A cynic once remarked that flattery is mouthed for the purpose of establishing one's right to favors in the future rather than as gratitude for past favors. Perhaps I also enjoyed the event because it was difficult to be cynical. The speakers included colleagues, students, former students, former Brandeis administrators, and Rabbi Samuel Chiel, the rabbi of the synagogue to which we belonged. It was difficult to think of what I could do for the speakers in the future.

As I sat next to Rose, listening to the extravagant praise of my work, it occurred to me that she deserved much of the credit for whatever I had accomplished. If it was not altogether clear to me why I had such a consuming interest in the sociology of the Jews, it certainly must have been difficult for her to understand. She married me on speculation as it were—the belief that despite my being an oddball sociologist I would somehow manage to assume the responsibilities of being a husband to her and a father to our children. While it is not for me to evaluate to what extent I have succeeded as a husband and father, I hope that my wife feels that her very risky speculation has paid dividends. It is altogether proper that this aspect of my life, being private, was not alluded to during the retirement party. But I cannot conclude these autobiographical notes without making mention of this important aspect of my life.

# A Wife's Response

W hen the series editor of this volume asked me to read and perhaps edit Marshall's autobiographical remarks, I was pleased at the opportunity. This was an early draft written by Marshall shortly before he died and we both knew that Marshall liked to polish his manuscripts before submitting them for publication. However, when I read the manuscript I could hardly touch a word. Whenever Marshall asked me in the past to read a draft of something he was writing, I always felt that his early drafts read better than most of the final manuscripts I had received in my years in publishing.

Instead I decided to shed some light on the question Marshall posed when he wrote ". . . it is not for me to evaluate to what extent I have succeeded as a husband and father." I have one qualification that enables me to make such an evaluation: Marshall and I were married to each other for almost forty-five years.

I first met Marshall Sklare in the summer of 1941 at the Avukah Camp in Grand Junction, Michigan. It was a student-run Zionist camp and Marshall was in charge of the educational program. I had occasion to describe this fortuitous meeting in a piece I wrote in December 1953:

I first heard his warm, full laughter around a campfire on a shivering Michigan night in June. He sat beside me, alone, in a large circle of college students. In the center a strand of fire pirouetted in the black air and disappeared in the wind. The tense, gutteral voice of the visiting lecturer swelled and softened as he related a humorous incident. I was watching an angry robot leap from the campfire when I heard him laughing with the others. He was a large stocky man, about twenty, wearing a brown leather jacket and khaki slacks. When I faced him he was racing his fingers through his cropped black hair, shoulders shaking in lusty appreciation of the joke. Then I saw a vast plain—his forehead—a high arena that was taut and clear like the skin on a tympany. A small dent in the center was the only relief. It was a forehead that had never known the wrench of two pairs of hands, polar opposites. It radiated an uncluttered warmth it had always known.

His deep grey eyes, set far apart, were reading my face for recognition as we exchanged names and schools. He had completed his junior year at Northwestern and I at Chicago Teachers College. We began to talk and I noticed that his bass voice was not accustomed to the bubble of first-meeting chatter. We talked of many things, of the starch-heavy food, of the self-effacing professor, of the fire, of Heine. I watched his full, sensuous lips offset by a plain straight nose, carved in the middle like a young pugilist. We spoke rapidly, the words heatedly tripping over each other. And between the words a sonata was gradually unfolding.

We renewed our relationship in August of 1946, two weeks before Marshall was to be best man at his younger brother's wedding. He expressed some concern about what he would say when he toasted the bride and groom. During the wedding festivities he called me at home to tell me his toast had been well received. He also mentioned that he had been seated next to a young woman his family wanted him to meet. Not only was she very smart, but as an added bonus—she spoke Russian. He laughed as he related the story and then said that he preferred to speak to me.

A week later Marshall asked me whether I would like to fly to Manhattan for our honeymoon. I thought it was an original way to propose marriage but I nonetheless agreed that Manhattan was a great place for a honeymoon. I had fallen deeply in love with this man with the hearty laughter and the oddball (his word) idea of becoming a sociologist of the Jews.

We were married on June 8, 1947, at noon at the Stevens Hotel in Chicago. It was an intimate wedding with close family and friends. We walked down the aisle to the music of a string quartet. Later, Marshall borrowed a violin from one of the musicians and serenaded me with part of a Mozart sonata.

When we decided to move to New York so that Marshall could study for his doctorate at Columbia, Marshall's parents and my mother, who was widowed, were deeply saddened. It was not usual for young couples of our generation to leave Chicago and family. My parents-in-law felt rejected; my mother felt abandoned. Finally Marshall's father made the pronouncement that turned everything around: "Chicago is not big enough for Marshall!" Both mothers laughed, nodded vigorously in agreement, and that issue was settled. At least for a while.

Our lives in New York were busy with career building and raising a family. Marshall received his Ph.D. from Columbia in the winter of 1953 and his career took off immediately. As Seymour Martin Lipset noted at the Brandeis Memorial Service for Marshall, "What can you say about a man whose doctoral dissertation [*Conservative Judaism*] became a classic in the field?" Marshall engaged in research, he taught, he wrote books, and he was invited to lecture by universities and synagogues throughout the United States.

Together we conceived and raised three wonderful children—Daniel, Judith, and Joshua. I polled my children, now grown: "Was Dad a successful father?" They each answered with a resounding "Yes!" Despite his hectic work schedule, Marshall was always there for them. They came to him with their problems, their tears, and their victories. He would talk to them for hours if need be. He transmitted his values of charity, honesty, integrity, and love of Judaism to them. He was a strong supporter of the day school movement as another effective transmitter of the culture. And when the Solomon Schechter School opened its school in Queens, we enrolled our children. I believe it gave them a base for their own Jewish identity.

Our move to Boston was a happy one. Marshall enjoyed his work at Brandeis and the warm relationship with colleagues and graduate students. He wrote some pivotal books and realized his dream of establishing a center of modern Jewish studies. We made some very close friends who became our extended family. And my career in publishing took off in an interesting direction.

We watched our children grow to adulthood and establish careers. On June 28, 1978, our son Dan married Judy Ben-Zev and on August 31, 1980, our daughter Judy married Ken Gould. Marshall embraced the new members to our family wholeheartedly. They are now raising their own families and we have been blessed with eight beautiful grandchildren. I look forward to our son Josh getting married and raising a family though I am deeply saddened that Marshall will not be there to share the joy.

As for Marshall and me, the spark that ignited that night around the camp-fire in Grand Junction, Michigan, continued to grow and drew us together into a single line of light. No matter what the time or the circumstance, Marshall was there with his nobility, his generosity, his keen insights, his laughter, and his love.

"Yes Marshall, you were a supremely successful husband and father. I hope that I told you so often enough when you were alive! And I hope you knew how much your grandchildren, your children, and I loved you and needed you!"

*Newton, Massachusetts*                                           Rose Sklare
*August 12, 1992*

# American Jews and
# American Judaism

# Jewish Acculturation and American Jewish Identity

## I. Introduction: From Self-Segregation to Acculturation to Assimilation

From its inception, American sociology has been interested in racial, ethnic, and religious groups. This interest originally stemmed from two sources: (1) the fact that a substantial proportion of the American population have been identifiable as members of minority groups, and (2) the belief that the relationship between the dominant group and the minorities may pose problems for American society.

What has been the approach of social scientists to the presence of minority groups in American society? If we study the work of early American sociologists on the subject of ethnicity, we notice that the regnant school of thought is that ethnic groups (generally referred to as "immigrant groups") would go through a three-stage process. They would start at the stage of self-segregation, progress to the stage known as acculturation, and end with assimilation. Assimilation would mean that they no longer constituted a significant entity in the society, though to be sure individuals might retain some ancestral memories as well as continue to use family names that would indicate that their country of origin was not dominated by Anglo-Saxon culture.

In sociological writing the word *ghetto* has frequently been used to describe the first stage—the stage known as self-segregation. This usage is unfortunate because the term *ghetto* should only be employed to describe situations of imposed segregation. For the majority of American ethnic groups, segregation has been elective rather than imposed, though to be sure groups have not always had perfect freedom to decide where they would live and what occupations they would follow.

The sociologists of yesterday assumed that after some years of self-segregation, and certainly by the time the second generation would come to maturity, ethnic groups would progress to the stage of acculturation. Acculturation would involve taking on many of the culture patterns of the majority, although continuing with some culture patterns inherited from self-segregated immigrant parents.

The final part of the process was assimilation, namely, the merging into the general society of members of a minority group. Sociologists of an earlier era did point out that the cycle of self-segregation to acculturation to assimilation would not proceed automatically: it could be interfered with by the presence of prejudice and discrimination. As they saw it, prejudice and discrimination would not only make it difficult for individuals to assimilate, but would create psychological pressures as well—individuals would hesitate to assimilate since by so doing they could be accused of cowardice, of deserting their fellow ethnics who had suffered rejection by American society.

It was also felt that the movement from self-segregation to acculturation to assimilation needed to be a gradual process. If all individuals moved precipitously from one stage to another, resistance to the final step of assimilation would emerge on the part of the dominant group. A differential rate of assimilation within the minority community was thus desirable; it would have the advantage of not exceeding the absorptive capacity for assimilation on the part of the dominant group. It was assumed that those who were well-educated would assimilate before those who were ill-educated, and that those who were members of the middle and upper classes would assimilate before those who were members of the working class.

To be sure there were those who had reservations about the validity of this cycle. Marcus Hansen, for example, a historian at Harvard, advanced another conception that was later to be given wide currency by Will Herberg. Hansen contended that the assimilation of the third generation was not inevitable. He suggested that the grandson of the immigrant, feeling himself to be fully an American, might wish to remember and even to perpetuate what his second-generation father had wanted to forget. Nevertheless the dominant theory was that the trend to assimilation was irreversible. The great society would swallow up all ethnic subcommunities, particularly those that were white and had originated in Southern, Central, or Eastern Europe.

## II. Assimilation as an Incorrect Prediction

It is apparent to us today that the early conception of an orderly cycle from self-segregation to acculturation to assimilation was an incorrect prediction. One of the reasons for the incorrect prediction appears to be that ideology played a considerable role in its formulation. Sociologists who were members of the dominant group tended to be committed to Wasp culture. They viewed the cycle as a natural phenomenon, given what they conceived to be the nature of the relationship between minorities and dominant groups. Overall they regarded assimilation as desirable—desirable for both the dominant group and the minority group.

Sociologists who were members of minority groups did not, as a rule, advance a different view. Generally they were marginal members of their particular ethnic group. In most cases they were eager to be assimilated. Hence they had no objection to what one sociologist has termed "Anglo-conformity." In sum, neither scholars who came from the dominant group nor those who originated from various minority groups looked very hard for evidence that would cast doubt on the cycle of self-segregation to acculturation to assimilation.

Today it is clear that American Jewry, as well as a variety of other white ethnic groups, has not gone through the orderly cycle of self-segregation, acculturation, and assimilation that earlier generations of sociologists had predicted. Some American Jews, for example, can even be characterized as occupying the position of self-segregation. Furthermore, the self-segregation group is presently composed of members of the second and third generation as well as members of the first generation.

There are other aspects of the theory that reality has not validated. The acculturated group includes not only members of the second generation but of the third and fourth generations as well. Furthermore, some members of the first generation are acculturated rather than self-segregated.

In respect to assimilation, it is evident that while some Jews have assimilated, assimilation has not proceeded as predicted. Jewish identity is far from disappearing. If anything, the Jewish community as an organized entity has gained in visibility in recent decades rather than diminished in visibility. In fact this lecture series constitutes evidence of the fact that the cycle is far from completed. The lecture series is based on the assumption that the Jews are a living entity in American society rather than a historical curiosity. The existence of this series suggests that earlier social scientists made an imperfect prediction of what would occur in the future. We should remember that this prediction had its source in a belief in the melting-pot ideology. And it was reinforced by a less-than-perfect understanding of the dynamics of ethnic-group life.

## III. The Pervasiveness of Acculturation

If I were asked where on the cycle most American Jews are presently located, the answer would have to be that they are on the level known as acculturation. Acculturation of course spans a wide spectrum. There are considerable differences among Jews in respect to where they are located on the acculturation scale. Furthermore, many are more highly acculturated than they know.

My belief is that if we were to examine a variety of indicators of acculturation, it could be demonstrated that considering the culture that Jews brought with them, they have taken giant steps in incorporating various aspects of American culture. In some cases they have sought quite deliberately to blend

American culture with values and patterns of Jewishness that they wish to retain. While we are not able in one essay to analyze who is at what level of acculturation, we can address ourselves to the more modest task of delineating how it is that Jews acculturated with such great speed and drive. What are the factors that transformed a group that spoke a different language from the dominant group, that had a style of dress different from the dominant group, and whose very religion was in opposition to the religion espoused by the dominant group?

1. The first matter that is involved in understanding the speed of Jewish acculturation in the United States is the fact that the United States has no medieval past. There is no history here of the Jew existing as a pariah people. There were, to be sure, some legal restrictions against Jews in some of the constitutions of the states that composed the original Union. However these were removed during the early part of the nineteenth century and were not of great importance even when they were on the statute books. We should also remember that there was, and still is, considerable interest in the conversion of Jews to Christianity. John Adams and John Quincy Adams, for example, were highly interested in such conversion, though to the best of my recollection this interest was not alluded to in the *Adams Chronicles* as presented on TV.

Even if there has been interest in converting the Jew, this would not involve conversion to a religion that has dominated the American continent for hundreds of years. American Christianity, whether Protestant or Catholic, was itself new to these shores. It had no status here as an ancient or medieval religion. Furthermore, it is not always intimately connected with the great monuments of the American past or with the great events of American history. As we have seen, the Jew can celebrate the Bicentennial without compromising his Jewish identity.

In acculturating, then, the American Jew does not have to do violence to his Jewish past. He does not have to leave a ghetto. He does not have to be a traitor to his ancestors. In sum, the acculturation of Jews could proceed without feelings of overwhelming guilt and conflict. The acculturation of the Jews could proceed without their feeling that they must deny and bury their heritage. I do not mean to minimize the family conflicts that were engendered by acculturation—there were to be sure some serious rifts between the first and second generation. Nevertheless, we must stress that the acculturation of the Jews could proceed without their feeling that such acculturation was a price exacted if the Jews were to have the same rights as others.

2. A second factor involved in the thrust and speed with which Jews acculturated is the fact that the history of the Jews is a history of acculturation. That is, Jews have lived in a variety of countries and hence in a variety of cultures. They are experienced in adjusting to a dominant culture. Their experience became evident when, in modern times, the ingathering of Jews took place in Palestine. It is even more evident today in the State of Israel, despite all of

the efforts that have been made to absorb and integrate all of the segments of Israel's Jewish population.

It has frequently been said that the history of the Jews is a history of acculturation. If Jews have been influenced by cultures that were unfriendly to them, it is to be expected that the influence of American culture would be especially strong, for, as we have noted, American culture had no medieval past. Even though there has been considerable prejudice and discrimination against Jews in the United States, on the whole such manifestations have not resulted in a feeling of embitterment on the part of Jews.

Contrast Jewish experience with that of others. Many immigrant groups that came to the United States had no familiarity with living as a minority and adapting to a dominant culture. The Jews, on the other hand, had a wealth of experience in that form of accommodation that we know as acculturation. They also had a great deal of experience with both segregation and self-segregation.*

3. In explaining the speed of Jewish acculturation, we must assign a role to the fact that the Jews lacked a homeland. All of the immigrant groups who came to America came from a homeland. To be sure, in some cases that homeland was under the domination of a foreign power—the English in the case of the Irish, and the Russians in the case of the Poles. Nevertheless, the Irish and the Poles felt that their country was *their* homeland. In fact, although they lived on American soil, some of the Irish and Poles sought to use the United States as a base to defeat the foreign nations that ruled their homelands.

The Puerto Ricans are a classic contemporary case of the easy availability of a homeland, with the consequent slowing of acculturation. This is ironic since Puerto Rico is a part of the American Commonwealth, though to be sure there are separatists who would like to end Puerto Rico's ties with the United States. Furthermore, Puerto Rico itself has undergone considerable acculturation to the American way of life.

If the constant movement of Puerto Ricans to and from their homeland is at one end of the spectrum, the Jews are located at the opposite end of the spectrum. The Jews are a group that had very little interest in returning to the countries from which they came. Accordingly, their emigration rate has been minimal. The German Jews who came here in the nineteenth century, and who gloried in German culture, generally did not return to Germany. Furthermore, very few of the German refugees who came in the 1930s availed themselves of the opportunity to return to post–World War II Germany.

The Jews from Eastern Europe who came in the 1880–1914 period showed the same lack of enthusiasm for emigration. A few of the ultra-Orthodox did return, and there was a small circle of Jewish radicals who repaired to Russian soil when tsarism was destroyed, as well as a decade earlier when social

* Salo Baron's theory that Jewish survival is more likely in a multicultural society than in one dominated by a single culture is an important point, but I will not deal with it systematically here. It involves a full-scale examination of how pluralistic American culture has been.

reform was in the Russian air. However, the vast majority of Jewish socialists, communists, and anarchists were not motivated to return to Russian soil; they had the good sense to continue to preach their radicalism from the safety of New York, Philadelphia, and Chicago, and later from Los Angeles and Miami. Finally, the East Europeans who came to the United States during and after World War II had little interest in returning to their former homes. They would have to return to communities that were, in effect, cemeteries, and in many cases they would have to live in countries dominated by communist regimes. Understandably they did not wish to be reminded of the Holocaust every day of their lives.

4. If a homeland to which the Jews felt strong bonds was absent, there was another significant factor that was influential in speeding Jewish acculturation. This is the factor of upward social mobility, by which I mean the rise in class position. The Jews are well-known to students of American society as a group that moves up much more rapidly than other groups. Indeed, in two generations Jews have reached the lofty class level occupied by denominations located at the top of the Wasp group. Depending on the area of the country, these denominations are most commonly the Presbyterians, the Episcopalians, and the Congregationalists. It should be remembered that the Jewish advance is all the more remarkable since it occurred in the face of prejudice and discrimination.

The reason why such rapid upward mobility took place so quickly is a large and difficult question. What we are interested in is that the rise of many Jews to the middle and the upper class has had the effect of speeding acculturation. The rise brought with it new relationships with Gentiles, it depleted neighborhoods and areas of the city where a distinctive Jewish life-style had established itself, and it gave the Jews new aspirations. Some would say that it also gave them new pathologies.

5. The next factor that must be examined is the question of values. There has been, and there still is, a great deal of loose talk to the effect that many Jewish values are the same as American values. Such talk is sometimes a thinly disguised device to improve intergroup relations and to demonstrate that Jews have been model citizens. Nevertheless, it is correct to say that certain American values and certain Jewish values (if properly modified) can overlap. That is, if certain Jewish values are modified they are capable of a smooth articulation with American values. In cases where such overlap was possible and where the benefits were substantial, Jews were motivated to modify their value structure. When they did so their acculturation was speeded enormously.

The example that is most frequently adduced is the value of education. California, with its multitiered system of higher education, represents the ultimate in the American belief in the value of education, the rightness of education, and the availability of education to all who wish to use it as an avenue of upward social mobility.

Jews too believe that education is a social good. However, in traditional

Jewish culture the education that is prized is education in the realm of the sacred. Secular education is viewed as distinctly inferior to sacred education and should only be pursued after the individual has achieved mastery in the area of the sacred. Furthermore, in traditional Jewish culture education is prized only for males. There is very little emphasis, if any, on providing equal educational opportunities for women.

We must remember that some of the Jews who came to the United States had already encountered secularism before they arrived here. Those who did not were soon touched by it. Thus the ground was prepared for shifts in attitude that would create value homophyly. Jews speedily relinquished the idea of the primacy of sacred education, and, at a later period, also accepted the idea that females as well as males should be educated. Thus Jews began to take advantage of the educational opportunities that were afforded them. They did so much more extensively and more intensively than any other ethnic group coming from the European continent. Secular education led to a great deal of acculturation—a degree of acculturation more extensive than most Jews realized.

6. Another factor that has worked to speed the acculturation of the American Jew is that the element of European Jewish society that we may designate as the *proste* (the crude and common Jew) came here in very large numbers. Indeed the *proste* came to dominate the Jewish community. Some have contended that America is the revenge of the *proste yidn* upon the *scheine yidn*.

There is little question that immigration to America was a selective process. Although it did not reach down to the very lowest levels of Jewish society, America was inordinately attractive to those at the lower levels of Jewish society, whether in Western or Eastern Europe. Up to 1914 in Eastern Europe, emigration to America or to other Western lands (or, as an alternative, to the large cities in Eastern Europe) was especially attractive to individuals in modest economic circumstances and in relatively modest status positions. It is apparent that many of the immigrants who came to the United States lacked the strong ideological commitments of those who stayed behind. This was especially true in the area of religious commitments.

All of these characteristics of the pre–World War I immigrants became apparent after the Russian Revolution. The Russian Revolution involved a radical restructuring of society and meant that those who had been firmly rooted in the Jewish upper class, and in the upper reaches of the Jewish middle class, were now declassed. The old status hierarchy was shaken to its very foundation. After the Russian Revolution there arrived on American shores elements of the elite of the Russian Jewish community, including those strongly committed to various ideological causes, which included Orthodoxy, Zionism, Hebraism, and Yiddishism. The victory of the Bolsheviks also resulted in the migration of radicals who faced imprisonment or worse if they remained in the Soviet Union.

The domination of the *proste* was noticed as early as the eighteenth century. Haym Salomon, who in recent decades has achieved a place in American Jewish history that he did not occupy in his own lifetime, wrote to his relatives in 1783 advising them to stay in Europe. "Your *yichus* (ancestral reputation) is worth very little here" was the way he put it. Even those who came here with the most impeccable *yichus* had to achieve social position by virtue of achievement rather than ascription. Jacob Schiff is perhaps the best example. Upon his arrival he did not automatically occupy the role that his singular *yichus* entitled him to. Rather it was his financial genius, his great generosity, his communal devotion, and his imposing manner that made him the leading figure in the American Jewish community.

By definition *proste yidn* had few inhibitions. They were eager for acculturation. Lacking the conservatism that comes from an aristocratic background, they were prepared to move rapidly on all fronts: economic, educational, and cultural. They did not arrive here wedded to a style of life to which they were deeply committed. They were open to the new, and they were eager to achieve the recognition that they could not attain in Europe.

7. The final factor in our analysis of rapid acculturation is the persecution that the Jews have endured, together with their exclusion from society. Because of this history the Jews could not bring themselves to rebuff the invitation to participate in American culture. However, when Jews came to perceive that full participation in American culture would involve melting into the melting pot, they sought to retain their Jewish identity and to call a halt to further acculturation.

The fact, then, that the Jews had so long been outside of society meant that they were inordinately attracted to American culture. Thus for Jews America was more than a place to make money. It was a kind of promised land, a kind of holy land. The term *goldene medinah* did not only have the meaning that the streets were paved with gold and that America was a land of great economic opportunity. The phrase *goldene medinah* had the additional meaning that America is a place that gives the Jew an equal chance (or at least some chance), a place that does not subordinate him, and a place that is open to his talents. Jews who used the phrase *goldene medinah* were quite aware of American prejudice and discrimination. Nevertheless, they viewed America as a veritable paradise in comparison to the countries from which they had come.

## IV. The Problematics of Assimilation

Now that we have analyzed the factors responsible for the speed and impact of acculturation on the American Jew, we need to turn to the question of why acculturation was not followed by assimilation. We should, of course, bear in mind that individual Jews did assimilate. In the eighteenth and nineteenth centuries, such assimilation was common in the South, in the Middle West, and, later, in the Far West. In our own day assimilation has also occurred in places of high Jewish concentration, including the Middle Atlantic and New England states. If assimilation did occur in many individual cases, why did it not become a mass phenomenon? Why has the loss of Jewish identity been more the exception than the rule?

1. Perhaps the most frequently adduced reason for the lack of mass assimilation is the hostility of non-Jews. There is little question that Gentiles, whether Wasps or ethnics, were not particularly eager to assimilate the Jew, and that some of this lack of eagerness can be traced to the factor of prejudice. The attitudes of middle- and upper-class Wasps is especially important in this connection. (Jews who were candidates for assimilation were not interested in assimilating into minority groups whose acculturation was less than their own and whose social status was limited.) The ambiguities of the Wasps were quite evident. On the one hand, they encouraged assimilation by rewarding those who wished to subordinate their Jewish identity. On the other hand, when they realized what mass assimilation would mean, they were not so sure that it should be encouraged.

We must reckon, then, with the ambiguous stance of the Wasp and the possibility that the attitude of Gentiles was a factor in discouraging assimilation. At the same time, however, we must recognize that any effort to account for Jewish survival purely on the basis of Gentile attitudes is necessarily incomplete and one-sided.

2. It is apparent that demographic factors have been an important influence in making the American Jewish community viable. Although Jews are less than three percent of the total population of the United States, the American Jewish community is the largest community in the millenial history of the Jewish people.

An important point about the size of the community is that it is concentrated in a relatively few urban centers. To be sure, Jews now frequently reside in the suburbs rather than the central city, but even in suburbia there tends to be areas of Jewish concentration. The point that needs making is that the American Jewish population is sufficiently large and concentrated to maintain a variety of Jewish institutions, to offer a variety of services, and to be a sufficiently large group to be visible. Indeed, given the size of the Jewish community American Jewry has had high visibility. Finally, although intermarriage is a very serious problem, the size of the Jewish community is such that intermarriage is not a foregone conclusion; the marriage market is large enough to ensure endogamy for all those who want it.

3. A factor that is seldom mentioned in any analysis of American Jewish survivalism is that anti-Semitism in the United States has not been strong enough to motivate assimilation. There are a variety of responses to anti-Semitism in the modern era. These responses are as varied as the feeling that it is dishonorable to assimilate as long as there is anti-Semitism and the reaction that the

parent owes it to his child to assimilate so that the child will have the chance for a less stressful and embattled life.

As we have noticed in our analysis of acculturation, anti-Semitism in the United States was quite different from what it was in Europe. Furthermore, the Jewish reaction to anti-Semitism in the United States was different than on the European continent. The American Jewish attitude has generally been that anti-Semitism was more temporary than permanent, that anti-Semitism is, in fact, un-American. It violates American values, it contradicts the American creed, and in the final analysis is subversive.

Given all of these beliefs about anti-Semitism, it is not surprising that Jews felt no strong desire to capitulate to anti-Semitism by assimilating. Rather, their reaction has been to fight anti-Semitism, a reaction that has given rise to Jewish intergroup-relations agencies on both the national and the local level. Furthermore, the reaction of fighting against anti-Semitism has motivated programs even in Jewish organizations that are not specifically established for the purpose of combating anti-Semitism. American Jews have felt that they have both the right and the duty to fight anti-Semitism. At the same time they have felt that anti-Semitism would not necessarily doom them to remain at the bottom of the class level of the society. One could be both Jewish and successful. One could find economic opportunities in fields that had not been preempted by Gentiles. One could obtain an education despite the quotas that were in existence at some of the elite private universities.

4. Another factor that needs to be analyzed is that of the existence of pluralism. As we have pointed out, the idea of the melting pot has a long history. On the other hand, there were always pluralists who felt that the melting pot was unsatisfactory and even illegitimate. Social workers such as Jane Addams came to understand the danger and the illegitimacy of demanding that immigrants strip themselves of their heritage. And if some of the strongest advocates of the melting pot came from the Jewish group itself, as in the case of Mary Antin, the most persuasive argument for pluralism was, appropriately, developed by a Jew—the late Horace Kallen.

The new pluralism, or the "new ethnicity" as it is generally known, is not a direct descendant of Kallen's pioneer efforts to develop a justification for pluralism. In any case, the new pluralism is an important factor in assisting the continuance of Jewish survivalism. There are some students of American society, Jews included, who are worried about what the new pluralism may bring. They fear that it could ultimately be used to justify a restriction of Jewish educational opportunity and professional advancement, and more generally, promote a fragmentation of our society. Be that as it may, the current acceptance of pluralism (as well as the earlier existence of a pluralistic philosophy) must be considered an important aid in making assimilation only one option and in suggesting that the option of survivalism within the framework of acculturation is an acceptable and viable alternative for American Jewry.

5. The next factor that I would like to develop may strike you as rather quixotic. It is that one of the reasons why Jews have not assimilated is that they score very low on any scale of religiosity. On the whole, American Jews have been strongly secularistic in their mode of life.

Indeed, until the growth of cults in the 1970s, there were very few American Jews who displayed the behavior that we saw in Europe: the need to believe, the need to find a religious philosophy without which the individual feels he cannot continue to live. Franz Rosenzweig is a notable case in point, and he is the quintessential example of the wondering Jew who ends up choosing Judaism.

The relatively few American Jews who did have a deep need to believe tended to be repelled rather than attracted by Christianity. If Judaism was impossible for them Christianity was doubly impossible. Furthermore, most recently Christianity has been tainted for Jews by something that did not exist during Rosenzweig's time, namely, the fact that the Holocaust took place in Christian countries and that Nazism was able to flourish in what was ostensibly a country whose population was Christian, both Protestant and Catholic.

All of us know that at the present time there exists an organization with the name Jews for Jesus. We also know about young Jews who have become followers of Reverend Moon. We know that there are young Jews who have been converted to the Hare Krishna movement and to other Eastern religious cults. Thus some young Jews have been caught up in recent developments on the American religious scene. However, by and large Jewish secularity has persisted and has functioned as a protective mechanism, insulating the adult Jew from attempts to convert him either to Christianity or to religions that historically have had no encounter with Judaism.

6. In explaining the lack of mass assimilation we must consider the nature of Jewish culture. If we do so, it soon becomes obvious that despite the impact of secularism there is a fair amount of agreement among Jews that Jewish culture is both suprasocial and social. Thus Jewish culture is not comparable to other ethnic cultures, though, to be sure, some of these cultures—such as that of Greek Americans—are strongly intertwined with religion.

The suprasocial nature of Jewish culture means that it can retain a hold upon individuals for more than sentimental reasons. Furthermore, it can appeal to individuals who have had no contact with the homeland culture. Elderly East European Jews of the first generation may be sentimental about their Jewishness as they think back to the life of the *shtetl* or to that of larger communities in Eastern Europe. But for those who lack such bonds, the factor of the suprasocial nature of Jewish culture means that Jewish culture can still function to contain assimilation. As I have emphasized, secularity is strong among Jews. As a result, the suprasocial character of Jewish culture may have limited impact on some Jews. A case could be made for the fact that given Jewish secularity, the suprasocial nature of Jewish culture might result in alienation rather than in attraction. However, given the thrust of American culture—a culture where religion operates as a significant factor in the social system—I would contend that the suprasocial nature of Jewish culture attracts more Jews than it repels.

Although very little is said about it publicly, it is apparent that not only is there the feeling that Jewish culture is suprasocial but many Jews, including those who are quite secular in orientation, believe that Judaism is superior to Christianity. The point, which has been made publicly in literally thousands of sermons and speeches before Jewish audiences, is that Christianity is an off-shoot of Judaism. Listeners do not take this statement as a simple historical judgment. Rather they take it to mean that Christianity "needed" Judaism—that Christianity could not establish itself without extensive borrowing from a superior religion—Judaism. And the view of Christianity held by many Jews is that Christianity did not gain the upper hand because it was superior to Judaism. Rather it "won" because it was inferior—because it was imposed by officials of the state, because it appealed to a large mass of gullible individuals who were receptive to the miracles that it promulgated, and more especially to the belief in the divinity of a Jew named Jesus. Christians can therefore be viewed as intellectually naive, religiously unsophisticated, and as adhering to a religion geared to the masses. All of this is seen in contrast to Judaism, which stresses demanding ritualism and high standards of learning. And in the view of some Jews, Judaism's glory is that it has prophets who were mere humans but who saw through sham and hypocrisy and had the courage to denounce the evils that existed in their society.

7. In addition to the belief that Jewish culture is suprasocial there is a related phenomenon: the feeling that to be a Jew is to be a member of an elite people. It would take us far afield if we were to try to trace the process by which the Jewish group developed a belief in its own eliteness. Eliteness is rarely discussed publicly because of the fear that it will be resented by Gentiles and boomerang against Jews. But it is constantly present and constantly reinforced. Thus the awarding of the Nobel Prizes in 1976 served to underline in Jewish minds that the eliteness of the Jews still persists. As a consequence, if you assimilate you enter into a group that is not superior to the Jewish group. On the contrary, the belief is that the Gentiles are inferior. Is it the Jews or the Gentiles who produced the three titans of the modern age: Freud, Einstein, and Marx?

Jewish eliteness has a variety of implications. It means that as high as one may climb in the class or status structure of the nation, there are enough Jews of similar accomplishment with whom to form a clique. However high one's brow level, there are enough Jews to interact with. Finally, being Jewish is taken to mean that one automatically becomes a member of an elite by virtue of being born Jewish.

These points about Jewish eliteness become quite apparent if we take the example of the Poles and the current rash of Polish jokes that has infested the nation. The Polish joke is based upon the fact that the Pole is inferior, is at the bottom of the heap, and belongs to a group that is the very antithesis of an elite group. From this perspective, the Pole who has attained elite status is conflicted about his identity. What does he have in common with his fellow Poles? Even if he accepts his identity as a Pole, he suffers under the burden of being an exception. He has achieved elite status despite the inferiority of his group. Jews experience something quite different—namely, the feeling that one may have achieved eliteness precisely because of one's Jewishness.

8. In our discussion of how the Jews acculturated so quickly, I made the point that acculturation is speeded because of the lack of ties with the land from which one came. However, there is now a new homeland—the State of Israel. Despite all of the problems it has encountered and all of the demands it has placed upon American Jewry, there is great pride in its existence. It has been a vital factor in retarding assimilation. Very few Jews reacted to the establishment of the State in the way in which Arthur Koestler did. For him the establishment of a Jewish state meant that he could honorably assimilate. There was now a Jewish homeland; those who wish to retain their Jewishness could repair to the homeland, leaving Jews in the Diaspora free to assimilate. The Jews of America have not taken their cue from Koestler. Indeed, the emergence of the State of Israel has been a factor in heightening Jewish identity rather than in diminishing it.

An additional point must be made about Israel, namely, that Jews of diverse backgrounds can relate to it. Jews of very diverse patterns of Jewish identity can find something in Israel to which they can relate. From the standpoint of Jewish identity, Israel can function as a kind of Rorschach. Since it itself contains so many diverse patterns of Jewish identification, there is always something in Israel to validate the most diverse types of Jewish identity.

9. In our analysis of acculturation I discussed the concept of America as a *goldene medinah* and highlighted the fact that this concept was a spur to acculturation. If one carries the concept of the *goldene medinah* far enough, however, one not only acculturates but positions oneself close to that of the assimilationist.

From this perspective it is fortunate that attitudes to America have undergone modification during the last decade or two. In its most radical form, there has emerged the feeling that America is imperfect, corrupt, polluted, declining, and a threat to world peace. These feelings had a strong impact on young Jews during the late 1960s and the early 1970s. Their elders did not develop a similar allergy to America. As has been evident during the Bicentennial, they are still capable of considering the establishment of the country an event worthy of celebration. But the dethronement of America has affected wide circles in the Jewish community in the sense that it has placed a heavy shadow over the theory behind the melting-pot ideology.

The dethronement of America has a sad aspect to it. Nevertheless, it has assisted the building of Jewish identity and the awakening on the part of some of a greater Jewish consciousness. No longer must everything Jewish be measured against how it conforms to American culture. Take the position of Classical Reform Judaism in the United States. Classical Reform fitted Judaism to America because what was American was superior. For example, for all practical purposes the left wing of Classical Reform proceeded to change the Jewish Sabbath to Sunday since Sunday was the Sabbath of all civilized men. Given the end of America as the *goldene medinah*—the ideal culture to which all decent men should aspire—no longer can a case be made for shifting the Jewish Sabbath to Sunday. In fact the number of Reform congregations that hold their main service on Sunday are now so few in number that they are sociological oddities.

10. The last point that I should like to make about the resistance to mass assimilation is that American Jewry has gone so far as to test the climate for assimilation. The test found that America was unreceptive. Such unreceptiveness is not simple anti-Semitism or even the patterns of group exclusivity that we analyzed earlier. Rather it has been a resistance traceable to the feeling on the part of the Gentile that he wishes to remain the kind of Gentile that he is.

The testing of the Gentile took two forms. One was led by Eastern European Jews and the other by German Jews. In the case of German Jews the test was the establishment of the Ethical Culture movement. For the East European Jews it was the promotion of a variety of leftist movements. The interesting thing about both tests is that they did not involve assimilation in the classical sense. They made the demand upon the Gentile that he meet the Jew halfway. In the case of Ethical Culture the demand was that the Gentile give up his loyalty to Christianity. In the case of Jewish leftism the demand was that the Gentile give up his belief in capitalism.

It soon became obvious that Gentiles were not prepared to move in either of these two directions. It became apparent that Jews could only assimilate if they were prepared to meet Gentiles on Gentile turf. Interestingly enough, Jews in the United States have considered this a form of capitulation and they have had no strong desire to capitulate. Finally, some Jews committed to Ethical Culture and to radicalism have retained links—however attenuated—with the Jewish community.

## V. Summary

The conventional wisdom has been that American ethnic groups would move through three stages: (1) self-segregation, (2) acculturation, and (3) assimilation. Most American Jews have reached the second stage and have done so with great speed. Many are more acculturated than they know. The factors that have transformed a group that spoke a different language from the dominant group, that had a style of dress different from the dominant group, and whose very religion was in opposition to the religion espoused by the dominant group, into a subcommunity that is so "American" as the Jews include the following:

1. America had no medieval past.
2. The Jews had a history and familiarity with acculturation.
3. The Jews lacked a homeland.
4. The Jews were able to climb the class ladder very quickly.
5. The factor of value homophyly operated to speed acculturation.
6. America was dominated by *proste yidn* rather than *scheine yidn*.
7. America and American culture was overwhelmingly attractive, given the history of the Jew as an object of persecution and exclusion.

While many Jews have acculturated, the majority have not moved to the final position on the cycle: assimilation. What has kept American Jews from moving beyond the stage of acculturation to that of mass assimilation? The following factors are the most significant:

1. The attitude of Gentiles to Jews.
2. The size of the American Jewish community has been sufficiently large and concentrated to make Jewish life possible.
3. The comparative weakness of anti-Semitism and the ability of the Jew to penetrate those areas of the culture that he was interested in without having to pay the price of conversion to Christianity or the denial of Jewish identity.
4. The rise of a new pluralism that seeks to supersede the older philosophy of the melting pot.
5. The secularism of the Jew has operated as a protection against conversion at the time that American society—with all of its secularity—has retained a religious base. This religious base has served to retard assimilation.
6. The retention, despite secularization, of the belief that Jewish culture is suprasocial as well as social.
7. The fact that there is a widespread belief that to be a Jew is to be a member of an elite people.
8. The emergence of the State of Israel and the impact that it has had upon Jewish identity.
9. The end of America as the *goldene medinah*, a process that may be painful to view but that provides the possibility of the strengthening of Jewish identity.
10. The rebuffing by Gentiles of Jewish-led movements that were assimilationist in effect if not in intent and that would have spelled the end of Jewish identity.

Prognostication is a dangerous art. We need not burden ourselves with the making of predictions about the American Jewish future. What is evident in the contemporary Jewish community is that while there is considerable inter-marriage and numerous instances of assimilation, considerable efforts are being made to stand fast and halt the cycle at the second stage—namely, accultura-tion. There is also the contemporary phenomenon of efforts to strengthen Jewish identity. Frequently these efforts to take the form of a process that we may call "reculturation"—the return to Jewish forms and culture (or, more technically, what are considered to be Jewish forms and culture). In some cases reculturation also includes the creation of new Jewish forms and culture. Some of these new forms are controversial and, in the minds of critics, even dan-gerous. Such controversy is inevitable, and under specifiable conditions it can even have a salutary effect.

Centuries ago an anonymous Jew placed a graffito on the Arch of Titus, which was erected in Rome to celebrate Titus' capture of Jerusalem in the year 70. The graffito consists of three Hebrew words: *Am Yisrael Hai* (the Jewish people still live). Today, Jews not only live in the very city that Titus destroyed, but they have established a new Jewish Commonwealth. And in addition to the State of Israel there is the impressive example of Jewish survival in the United States. It is evident that Jews continue to exist as a recognizable and—despite their comparatively small numbers—highly significant segment of American society.

# The Jewish Religion in America

---

Jewish tradition teaches that the Jews became a group only by their having embraced the Torah. Thus in classical perspective religion is recognized as the foundation of group identity. American Jews seem to follow this tradition. Increasingly they have come to understand their group identity in religious terms. However, they have not arrived at this position purely out of respect for tradition. Their feelings have also been influenced by factors such as the desire to survive as a group; the belief that survival can best be assured by a group identity that is based on religious commitments; and the impact of a culture that assumes that all men have a religion and believes that religion is good, and that regards separatism on the basis of a religious commitment as justifiable, even admirable. Finally, the ever-present need to explain Jewish identity to the general community has created an additional incentive for affirming religion as the foundation of such identity.

## Observance and the Jewish Home

If Jews increasingly have come to think of themselves as religionists, this does not mean that they are prepared to act accordingly. There are in fact some very formidable obstacles to their making a serious religious commitment. A substantial segment of those who arrived in the United States during the great wave of East European immigration were at best nominally Orthodox. They had already felt the impact of secularization before they left Europe and the process gained considerable momentum in the United States. Thus the experience of many native-born Jews—even those who are members of the second or third generation—has been to grow up in a household where the hold of secular values was strong.

Secularization brought the usual challenges that members of other religions experienced. But its impact was sharpened by certain problems traceable to the special character of Judaism. For example, in traditional Judaism the arena of the sacred is extremely wide. Under the influence of secularization the

American Jew was challenged to fashion a sacred-secular dichotomy. As a consequence he exempted much of what had formerly been considered holy from the operation of sacred norms. Furthermore, many Jewish observances were disharmonious with the environment—they had been fashioned in the East and consequently were at odds with Western culture. Additionally, while the thrust of Jewish religious culture is sacramental, the thrust of American religious culture is moralistic.[1] As acculturation proceeded, Jews began to doubt the necessity of upholding the *mitzvot*. Furthermore, Judaism is distinguished by the lack of any real system of differential religious obligations as between laity and clergy—identical behavior is expected of both layman and rabbi. Under the influence of secularism, however, a distinction came to be recognized. The rabbi became a religious specialist charged with observing norms from which the layman was excused.

As the impact of these processes was felt, the need to define oneself as an individual who upheld religious values despite apparent secularity became more pressing. Consequently, the designations *Reform* and *Conservative* emerged; as a reaction, the term *Orthodox* also entered the popular vocabulary. Reform came to stand for a Judaism in which a sacred-secular dichotomy had been implemented and the area of the sacred narrowly defined; where Western culture was observed and religious practices in conflict with that culture were either discarded or were reshaped to conform with norms of the larger culture; where sacramentalism was downgraded and moralism (or "prophetic Judaism") upgraded; and where rabbi and layman were accorded different roles. Orthodoxy came to stand for a Judaism that maintained strong continuity with tradition. Conservatism came to stand for a Judaism located at some loosely defined point between Orthodoxy and Reform.

Whether accurately or not, the majority of American Jews would describe their grandparents as Orthodox. But they would not describe themselves as Orthodox, and increasingly they would not describe their parents as being such. In Boston, for example, 44 percent consider themselves to be Conservative, 27 percent to be Reform, and 14 percent to be Orthodox.[2] With the possible exception of New York City, where the Orthodox group is generally assumed to be somewhat stronger, these figures seem to be typical for most communities in the Middle Atlantic and New England states. In the South, the Middle West, and the West, the percentage considering themselves Reform tends to be higher.

In explaining why Reform and Conservatism have made such strong gains, some Orthodox spokesmen maintain that their success is based on a formula of making Judaism easy. They contend that Reform and Conservatism attracted those who were looking for a Judaism that would demand the least amount of sacrifice. But if we view the problem from a more sociological perspective it appears that the crucial issue is Judaism's sacramental emphasis and the inability of many a modern Jew to embrace the totality of the Jewish sacred system.[3]

Instead of receiving all that has been handed down to him, such a Jew seeks to discover what *mitzvot* he can still adhere to out of the vast sacramental heritage. Whatever the particular results of such a confrontation, the *mitzvot* that many a contemporary Jew finds meaningful may not conform to the criteria internal to the religious system. Thus the tenets that were hallowed in traditional life may conflict sharply with contemporary culture, and those that were formerly of secondary importance may now achieve primacy because they fulfill important needs.

In sum, then, the modern Jew selects the *mitzvot* that are subjectively possible for him to identify with. He is guided by a new personalism rather than by an old prescriptionism. Of course his personalism is not truly individualistic: it is influenced by the prevailing culture, by his class, by his education, his spouse, his children, his parents, his friends, his neighbors, his community. These influences help ensure that selection from the sacramental heritage will not be a random one and that a limited number of observance-patterns will emerge that will be characteristic of entire population segments.

An analysis of any single observance or set of observances would illustrate the problem that individuals have, on one hand, in identifying with Jewish tradition and, on the other, of maintaining a feeling of identity should they choose to neglect or reject the observance. For example, the dietary laws are a striking illustration of Judaism's sacramental tradition. They invest the routine and mundane act of eating with sacred significance, and they provide the believer with recurring opportunities to show his obedience to God's will. Having no hygienic or other instrumental purpose, their sole justification is that they are pleasing in God's sight. Furthermore, their observance affects the individual in the most profound ways. Observance of the laws may influence choice of friends, neighborhood, occupation, and spouse. Finally, they give the home an indisputably Jewish character.[4]

There is no simple answer to the question of what constitutes full observance of *kashrut* (the system of dietary laws), for there are considerable variations in strictness even among observant Jews who seek to follow the system both outside as well as inside the home. But it is indisputable that certain basic aspects of the system are observed by only a minority. In as conservative a community as Providence, only 32 percent say that they use separate dishes in the home for milk and meat.[5] Even this modest figure does not characterize a cross section of the community. While 53 percent of the first generation use separate dishes for milk and meat, only 25 percent of the second and 16 percent of the third generation do so. Unless there is a sharp change on the part of younger people (we must remember that by now a significant percentage of them have been reared in homes where the laws were disregarded to a greater or lesser extent), it can be assumed that in the future *kashrut* will be observed by an even smaller minority of Jews.

While basic aspects of the dietary laws are disregarded by many, other observances are followed by a clear majority. The best examples are the Seder on Passover and the lighting of the *menorah* on Hanukkah. In Providence, for example, some 79 percent attend a Seder each year, and 74 percent light the *menorah*. Furthermore, there are no strong differences between the generations with respect to these observances. Why, then, do some home observances live while others die, or are retained only by a special group? Observance seems to result from the pull of two forces: the pervasive impact of the modern, Christian, and secularist environment, and the desire to express Jewish identity and continuity in familiar forms. But which forms? Five criteria emerge in explaining the retention of specific home rituals. The highest degree of retention will occur when a ritual: (1) is capable of effective redefinition in modern terms; (2) does not demand social isolation or the adoption of a unique life-style; (3) accords with the religious culture of the larger community while providing a "Jewish" alternative when such is felt to be needed; (4) is centered on the child; and (5) is performed annually or infrequently.

To review these criteria in detail:

1. *Capable of effective redefinition in modern terms*. We might expect that neither Hanukkah nor Passover would be attractive to the American Jew. These holidays center around the celebration of a miracle: in the case of Hanukkah, the cruse of oil normally sufficient for one day that lasted for eight days; in the case of Passover, the exodus from Egypt accomplished by divine intervention. However, the miraculous elements inherent in both holidays are capable of redefinition: both holidays are interpreted to symbolize man's unquenchable desire for freedom. The focus is no longer on God's benevolence but on the struggle of the ancient Jewish people and their heroic leaders to overcome slavery in the case of Passover and religious intolerance in the case of Hanukkah.

As the dietary laws attest, not all reinterpretations are equally successful. One familiar reinterpretation of the dietary laws is that they have hygienic significance. But the idea has had little appeal for individuals who live in a publicly enforced sanitary environment, and who, furthermore, conceive of food prohibitions as primitive taboos.

2. *Does not demand social isolation or the adoption of a unique life-style*. If the Jew were to observe the full routine of traditional rituals, he would find himself following a separate and highly distinctive life-style. Valuing his acculturation and disinclined to lead a distinctive way of life, he is attracted to those rituals that demand minimal separation and deviation from the general community. By way of contrast Hasidim seek to retain even those aspects of culture, as for example East European Jewish dress, that have no basis in *halachah*. Among the reasons why such dress is retained is that it constitutes a distinctive style and thus serves to separate Jews from Gentiles, and Hasidic Jews from other Jews.

3. *Accords with the religious culture of the larger community while providing a "Jewish" alternative when such is felt to be needed*. This criterion refers to con-

vergent characteristics in each of the major American religions that form the basis of the "tri-faith" culture that has been noted by many commentators. The aspects of Hanukkah observance currently emphasized—the exchange of gifts and the lighting and display of the *menorah* in the windows of homes—offer ready parallels to the general mode of Christmas observance as well as provide a "Jewish" alternative to the holiday. Instead of alienating the Jew from the general culture, Hanukkah helps to situate him as a participant in that culture. Hanukkah, in short, becomes for some a Jewish Christmas.

4. *Centered on the child.* Both the Passover Seder and the lighting of Hanukkah candles have traditionally been among the most child-centered observances in the Jewish calendar. Not only is the Passover Seder a personal religious experience for adults but it also has the purpose of conveying to the next generation the experience of the Exodus. While the ritual of Hanukkah is not explicitly child-centered, its mode of celebration inclined in this direction even before the encounter with America; witness *dreydl* (spinning-top) games[6] and the giving of Hanukkah *gelt* (money) in Europe. In essence, then, the recitation of the Haggadah and the lighting of the *menorah* constitute religious acts performed by adults to satisfy personal religious requirements as well as ritual occasions that are made doubly meaningful by the participation of the young.

While the retention of these rituals may be stimulated by the child's eagerness, the motivation of the parent does not rest on his child-centeredness alone. These occasions appeal to the parent because they accord with his desire to transmit Jewish identity to his offspring. Hanukkah and Passover, which provide ready-made forms and techniques for involving the child at major points in their celebrations, carry the imputation and the hope that when the child becomes a parent he will be performing these rituals for himself and for *his* children.

The mood of a child-centered holiday must be appropriate. Passover and Hanukkah have special appeal in this connection, for both commemorate joyous occasions. Their tenor is in keeping with the norms of optimism, fun, and gratification that the general culture holds with respect to the atmosphere in which children should be reared. And the parent feels that having provided his child with "positive" associations with Jewishness, the child will have no cause to reject his heritage.

5. *Performed annually or infrequently.* The fact that both Passover and Hanukkah are annual rather than weekly or daily occasions undoubtedly serves to maintain their observance. Sabbath rituals and customs—such as the lighting of candles, the preparation of a special meal, the attendance at the meal by all members of the family, the recitation of *Kiddush*—involve a kind of regimen. While they are not to be compared with the significance of the decision to avoid work and other proscribed Sabbath activities, they do make regular demands on each member of the family. Thus their appeal is primarily to the more pious. But the lighting of the *menorah* (even if done faithfully on eight

successive evenings) and the holding of a Seder (even if it includes the reading of all of the Haggadah—the book read at the Seder) are unusual occasions. Coming once a year they are a relief from the routine.

Infrequently performed rituals harmonize more with the secular component in modern American life than daily or weekly rituals. Secularization affects the scope of religion. It restricts the application of religion to fewer and fewer areas of the individual's life. It results in limitations on the regular and routine performance of religious observances. Given the pervasiveness of secularization, the yearly ritual will persist more than the seasonal, the seasonal more than the monthly, the monthly more than the weekly, the weekly more than the daily. Secularization undercuts the emphasis of Jewish sacramentalism on the sanctification of the routine and imperils the continuation of those rituals that do not celebrate an extraordinary occasion.

In summary: the observance of religious ritual in the American Jewish home is geared to the celebration of selected aspects of certain occasions on the Jewish calendar, observance is personalistic in orientation, and holidays are emphasized rather than the sanctification of routine. The resulting pattern reflects a home that has been strongly affected by secular culture.

## Worship

In traditional Jewish society, worship takes place in the home. Women pray at home as well as at the synagogue, and although it is considered preferable for men to pray with a congregation or quorum of ten adult males (*minyan*), convenience may dictate that on weekdays adult males recite morning, afternoon, or evening prayers in private at their homes (or if more suitable, at their places of work). While this tradition has survived among some Orthodox Jews and undoubtedly reinforces the Jewish character of their homes, worship has increasingly come to be centered in the synagogue. (A *minyan* may of course be convoked in the home, but at present this is common only during the initial period of mourning for the dead.) An analysis of synagogue attendance will give us greater insight into the religious habits of the American Jew, as well as provide an introduction to the sociology of the American synagogue.

Many investigators have collected statistics on the question of attendance at worship. Their findings all point in the same direction: Jews attend religious services very infrequently. Furthermore, Jewish behavior is not a simple response to the prevailing culture, for Gentiles attend church much more faithfully than Jews attend synagogue services. Even if we grant that at times comparisons across religious lines may be misleading, it is undeniable that attendance statistics underline the heavy impact of secularization on American Jewry. In Boston, for example, some 39 percent of the Jewish population worship only on High Holidays, while another 23 percent attend less often or never (see Table 1). Since we may safely assume that those who pray in private attend

TABLE I
*Frequency of Synagogue and Church
Attendance in Greater Boston*
(percent)

| Frequency of synagogue or church attendance | Jewish | General |
|---|---|---|
| More than once a month | 17 | 65 |
| Once a month or every few months | 21 | 11 |
| Only on High Holy Days | 39 | 6 |
| Less often or never | 23 | 18 |
| Total | 100% | 100% |

NOTE: Because in this survey the general population includes Jews, the extent to which the 6 percent who attend services "only on High Holy Days" represent Jewish respondents in the "general" population is unclear. It is possible that this figure includes some Gentiles who construed the question to refer to holidays such as Christmas and Easter.
SOURCE: Axelrod et al., *Boston*, p. 139.

public worship frequently, we are justified in concluding that the experience of worship on a daily, weekly, monthly, or even seasonal basis is unknown to the majority of Boston's Jews.

The pattern of attendance that is restricted to High Holiday worship is a very striking phenomenon. Why does the person who is basically a nonworshipper feel compelled to come to the synagogue on these particular days? Have the High Holiday services in some way become defined as exercises that are obligatory upon the individuals who are ethnic survivalists? Or, to put it another way, is absence from synagogue unacceptable to the nonworshipper because he would feel that by staying away he was betraying the group, that he was disowning his ancestors in general and his immediate forebears in particular? The hypothesis requires further study. What does seem apparent is that the High Holidays suggest the operation of one of our criteria for ritual retention: the greater persistence of certain annual and infrequently performed rituals. Their endurance also underlines the break with prescriptionism: according to traditional norms attendance at weekly Sabbath services is highly important, and the commandment to observe the Sabbath is in no sense inferior to the requirement to observe the High Holidays. In any case a full explanation of the significance of High Holiday attendance must await the results of an inquiry on this singular phenomenon.

Some 17 percent of Boston Jewry may be considered regular attendees inasmuch as they go to services more than once a month. While in a distinct minority regular attendees constitute a crucial group—it is they who keep the system of Sabbath services alive. Their attendance is also important in maintaining the daily services that are conducted in some congregations. Paralleling the case of *kashrut*, they exercise a subtle influence over their less devout peers: their maintenance of the services constitutes a kind of indirect pressure upon those who acknowledge the desirability of attendance but do not themselves come to worship. And by maintaining the system they also provide the Jewish public with a structure to which they may return when they feel the need to do so. On the other hand, by maintaining the system they alleviate whatever guilt feelings are experienced by their less devout peers.

The contrast between Jewish attendance and attendance among the total population in Boston is sharp: while only 17 percent of the Jews attend regularly, 65 percent of the population at large do so. Thus there is nothing comparable in the general population to the very considerable percentage of Jews who appear year after year for one, two, or three services. But there is one similarity between the Jews and Bostonians in general: the proportion who rarely or never attend. Some 18 percent of the total population are in this category in comparison to 23 percent of the Jews.

While the large number of Catholics in Boston (more specifically the large number of Irish) may serve to raise non-Jewish attendance figures over what they would be in other communities of similar size, there is nothing to suggest that the religious behavior of Boston Jewry is particularly deviant. In New York City only 19.8 percent attend once a month or more.[7] Furthermore, regular attendance is much more common in the first generation than in later generations. Thus while 33.8 percent of foreign-born Jews are regular attendees, only 11.6 percent of the native-born fall into the same category. But even foreign-born Jews are less faithful worshippers than the most secularized of the non-Jews: 51.7 percent of the group designated as "Other Protestants" are regular worshippers.[8] And the "Other Protestants" are no match for the Irish, some 87.9 percent of whom go to church once a month or more.

## The American Synagogue

From the attendance statistics of New York City, Boston, and numerous other communities we might expect that the American synagogue is a struggling institution that is banished to the periphery of Jewish life and located predominantly in neighborhoods where the foreign-born reside. Nothing could be further from the truth. The American synagogue is a vital institution; it is by far the strongest agency in the entire Jewish community. Many hundreds of new synagogues—Reform, Conservative, and Orthodox—were built as a consequence of population movement after World War II. The process continues. As new Jewish neighborhoods and suburbs develop, new synagogues are established or old synagogues are transferred to new locations. Not only have synagogues been built in areas where Jewish life is intensive but sooner or later they are organized even in places that attract the more marginal Jewish families.[9] The number of synagogues, the value of their buildings, and their location in all areas where the Jewish population totals more than a handful of families all attest to the predominance of this institution in American Jewish life.[10]

We already know that only a minority of American Jews can bring themselves to patronize the synagogue with any degree of regularity in connection with its function as a house of prayer. Yet the continuing construction of new buildings, as well as the prosperity of established institutions suggests that the American synagogue must be more than a house of prayer. To help us discover its real nature, we must first know what proportion of America's Jews are affiliated with a synagogue.

There are no reliable nationwide statistics on affiliation. The most notable aspect of synagogue affiliation is that it varies greatly with the size of the Jewish population. In small communities affiliation commonly reaches well over 80 percent, despite the high intermarriage rates characteristic of such communities. In Flint, Michigan, for example, where the Jewish population is under 3,000, a total of 87 percent of the Jews in the community are affiliated with a synagogue.[11] In communities of intermediate size (10,000 to 25,000 Jewish population), the level of affiliation is lower—commonly over 70 percent are synagogue members. Thus in Providence the figure is 77 percent, in Springfield it is 76 percent, in Rochester, N.Y., 71 percent, and in Camden, it reaches the exceptionally high figure of 82 percent.[12] In large Jewish communities the rate of affiliation is much lower, commonly running at about 50 percent of the Jewish population. Thus in Detroit 49 percent are affiliated while in Boston the figure is 53 percent.[13] New York is *sui generis*—while no study is available observation suggests that the affiliation rate is measurably lower than it is in any other large city.

Unlike the observance of many *mitzvot*, which as we have seen tend to be concentrated in one segment of the population, synagogue membership is widely diffused. Irrespective of community size, membership is common in all segments of the population, with the following exceptions: it is somewhat more concentrated among the prosperous as well as among those with children between the ages of five and fifteen. Significantly, the rate of affiliation among the foreign-born is no higher than among the native-born. Even in the large cities where the rate of affiliation is so low, most non-members have belonged to a synagogue at one time or another. Former members include, for example, the widow who resigned after her husband's death and who now lives in reduced circumstances, or the prosperous family that dropped out after their children had a Bar Mitzvah or Confirmation. Furthermore, some of those who have never been affiliated will do so in the future. This is the case with many young marrieds who will join when they move from city apartments to suburban homes, or when they have children old enough to enroll in a Sunday or Hebrew School.

Whatever criticisms former members may have, and whatever the situation of those who have never affiliated, it is hard to find a principled opponent of the American synagogue.[14] Those who are outside of the synagogue are not firm opponents of the institution. Absence from the membership rolls does not generally represent a clear commitment to any rival institution. It does mean of course that the individual has been strongly influenced by the secularization process. But any critical observer would be quick to point out that most synagogue members have been vitally affected by the same process.

The lack of principled objection to the synagogue and the affiliation of diverse segments of the population must be added to our previous findings about wide differences in affiliation rate between smaller and larger communities. There is little to suggest that Jews in smaller communities are more sacred in their orientation than their metropolitan cousins. In fact a case can be made for precisely the opposite conclusion: that they are more secular in orientation, and much less traditional in their thinking. Why then do those who reside in smaller communities affiliate with greater frequency?

The smaller the community, the clearer is the threat of assimilation and the clearer it is that the future of Jewish life rests upon the personal decision of each individual Jew. The decision to affiliate with a synagogue, then, means to vote yes to Jewish survival. And the smaller the community, the more literal the voting metaphor: since every individual in the small community is asked to join, he is forced into casting his ballot. A refusal to join means placing himself in the assimilationist camp unless of course he has provided clear-cut evidence to the contrary by becoming intensely involved with some alternative Jewish agency. The larger the community, the less chance of solicitation by significant others, the less pressure to make a decision for survival, and above all, the more remote the threat of assimilation.

Clearly in the largest communities, especially in New York, synagogue membership does not have high symbolic significance. Since many people lack the feeling that Jewish identity requires synagogue membership, nonaffiliation does not mean a vote for assimilation. Conversely, one's resignation from a synagogue is not interpreted as meaning disloyalty to the group. In the metropolis, then, the synagogue must appeal on the basis of its instrumental as well as symbolic functions. However, a substantial proportion of the population finds the synagogue unessential to its needs. These people have little interest in the classical functions of the synagogue—religious services and study by adult males of Jewish texts. Nonclassical functions that the synagogue has added also do not attract them. Their children may be too young or too old for Hebrew School or Sunday School. Furthermore, they are not interested in the social activities provided by the synagogue, for they already are a part of a satisfying clique. Generally their group is entirely Jewish and dates back to friendships that were cemented in adolescence or early adulthood. Others are not attracted to the synagogue's social activities because they have a rich social life within their family circle. Finally, in the largest communities a host of organizations and causes of a specifically Jewish nature are available outside of the orbit of the synagogue.

Whether situated in a large or small community the synagogue is focused upon Jewish survival. It need not have been so—conceivably the synagogue in America could have followed a different course and insisted that as a religious institution it was an end in itself rather than a means for Jewish survival. Such a stance would exclude those who were strongly secular in orientation or at least require that they accept a subordinate position. But there is religious justification for the synagogue moving in the direction it has: in Judaism the preservation of the Jewish people as a group is an act of religious significance.

The American synagogue has accepted the secular Jew on his own terms; the institution has been more concerned with transforming him than with erecting barriers to his admission. In most congregations membership is open to all; no test of the applicant's religious attitudes or observance of *mitzvot* is required. While in many Reform or Conservative congregations an applicant for membership is generally sponsored by a member of the synagogue or by one of its officials, this is only for the purpose of screening those who have an objectionable moral reputation. The exceptions to the rule are certain Orthodox congregations that are interested in an applicant's observance of *mitzvot*. Such institutions prefer to restrict their roster to those whose behavior is in conformity with certain selected religious norms.

Since the typical American Jewish congregation is formed by local initiative rather than by the authority of a central body, every synagogue is free to determine its own program and ritual.[15] Furthermore, because the polity—the form of religious organization—among American Jews is congregational rather than episcopal, each synagogue is the equal of all others. Residents join together to hold religious services and to establish a school for their children. They raise the funds necessary to build an edifice and to hire a professional staff. The synagogue is organized in the form of a corporate body that holds periodic membership meetings at which the affairs of the institution are discussed and officers and board members elected. The board is responsible for determining the policies of the institution, although on strictly religious questions, as well as in certain other areas, the advice and consent of the rabbi is commonly solicited.

The prototype of the contemporary American synagogue is the "synagogue center." This is the synagogue that compromises with the culture while serving the need for Jewish identification. Recognizing the impact of acculturation, this type of synagogue expands its program far beyond the traditional activities of prayer and study. It seeks encounter with the Jew on his own secular level, and it strives to reculturate him. The content and procedures of religious services are adapted to give them greater appeal, with Reform synagogues, Conservative synagogues, and Orthodox synagogues each handling the problem of cultural adaptation in characteristic fashion. Although traditionally there is no sermon during the weekly Sabbath service, part of the process of adaptation involves the introduction of this feature. Thus the sermon has become a standard feature of the weekly service in Reform, Conservative, as well as in some Orthodox congregations. The sermon is employed as an instructional as well as a hortatory device.

All synagogues sponsor some kind of program of adult Jewish study, although its character, and the importance attached to it, varies greatly from congregation to congregation. With the exception of some Orthodox synagogues, women are free to participate in the program. In many places the traditional textual approach to study has been modified or supplemented. New kinds of courses have been introduced. But Jewish learning for children rather than for adults constitutes the real focus of the congregation's educational efforts. With the exception of certain Orthodox synagogues, all congregations sponsor a Jewish school. While the majority of those who attend are of elementary school age, most schools aim to retain their youngsters after the high point of the educational experience: Bar Mitzvah, Bat Mitzvah, or Confirmation.

For the less committed, the opportunity for Jewish education is a strong inducement to affiliate. In most newer neighborhoods of the city and in the suburbs, the only available Jewish religious schools are those conducted under congregational auspices. Some congregations make membership mandatory for enrollment, while others adjust their tuition fees to provide a financial incentive for membership.

Another important motivation for affiliation is the desire of secular-minded Jews to attend religious services on the High Holidays. While daily services, Sabbath services, and festival services are open to all, the demand for seats on the High Holidays is so large that admission is commonly restricted to ticket holders. In some congregations tickets are distributed only to members while in other synagogues they are sold to the public, but at a higher price than that made to members. Since most High Holiday services today are conducted under the auspices of a synagogue, the institution is in a position to attract individuals who might not ordinarily be interested in an affiliation. The phenomenon of "mushroom synagogues"—opened during the High Holidays by private entrepreneurs—is on the wane, and the phenomenon is rarely encountered in more prestigious neighborhoods. It has been replaced by the practice of established congregations that hold overflow services for the High Holidays, or of Reform congregations that conduct services on a double shift.

Most congregations sponsor a variety of clubs for high school youth, young adults, young marrieds, adult women, adult men, and the elderly. These organizations provide the synagogue member with another tie to the congregation. They are particularly crucial for individuals who are not strongly involved in the classical functions of prayer and study. Generally the organization composed of adult women (the "sisterhood") is the most vital of these clubs. Membership in the clubs is so widespread that in the intermediate-size Jewish community they enroll far more members than any other Jewish organization. In Providence, for example, 53.2 percent of all men age fifty to fifty-nine are members of a synagogue-affiliated club, as are 55 percent of the women.[16] Recreational and associational opportunities are not limited to the synagogue affiliates, however. There are congregational socials and parties, dinner dances, specialized activity groups, and fund-raising drives. All strive to increase the interaction among members. In the New York area in particular many synagogues provide a variety of athletic facilities.[17]

The contemporary synagogue is a large institution by traditional standards. While older Jewish neighborhoods in the largest cities may contain a dozen or more small congregations in addition to two or three large ones, an average synagogue in a newer neighborhood of a metropolis or suburb will generally enroll over 500 families. Congregations of this size have many members who confine their participation to specialized activities, or who participate very irregularly. Given the large size of most congregations and the specialized, irregular, or even nonparticipation of members, the printed word becomes a vital part of congregational life. Thus most congregations publish a bulletin at regular intervals. The bulletin contains the time of services and the topic of the weekly sermon, the schedules of the clubs, information about adult education lectures and courses, and news of the school. Of equal if not greater significance are the personals columns of the bulletin. Births and deaths are announced, donors are listed, names of active workers are publicized, and significant milestones in lives of members and their families are featured, including birthdays, wedding anniversaries, graduations, and promotions.

While synagogues of the more traditional variety contrast sharply with the synagogue-center type of institution, it is the synagogue characteristic of modern Israel that places the contemporary American synagogue in boldest relief. The core of the program of the Israeli synagogue is the traditional activities of prayer and study. Worship activities are centered on the three daily services and the Sabbath service. Some men remain after the daily services or come early for the purpose of studying various sacred texts. They do this either by themselves, in pairs, or in groups. Most synagogues are small. Each has its officials, its leaders, and its congregants. However, individuals think of themselves as praying at a particular synagogue rather than being affiliated with it in any formal sense. Most synagogues do not have a professional staff—rabbis are employed by a central authority rather than by a particular congregation. While attendance and participation at services and in the study circles ebbs and flows, and although at certain holidays worshippers appear who are absent at other occasions, the interaction of the group of men who pray and study together constitutes the foundation of the institution.

Unlike the United States, then, the synagogue in Israel offers little other than the classical functions of prayer and study of the sacred system by adult males. Unlike the United States, its existence and prosperity is not interpreted as a promise of Jewish survival at a time when the acculturation process is so advanced as to make survival difficult to ensure. And unlike the United States, the Israeli synagogue is not perceived as an emblem of Jewish identity or as the guarantor of the Jewish future. Rather, the nationhood of Israel is viewed as assuring Jewish survival. In essence, then, the synagogue in Israel has little symbolic significance; it exists as an end in itself rather than as a means to an end. Because it does not occupy the unique role that it does in the United States, the Israeli synagogue is a much weaker institution. It reaches a much smaller proportion of the population than its American counterpart.

Even if the American synagogue is generally a means to an end rather than an ultimate value, it is still a religious institution. As such, it is subject to evaluation by a unique yardstick—the yardstick of spirituality. Critics of the synagogue, while conceding that it makes a valuable contribution to Jewish life, are prepared to argue that it is nonetheless more of a liability than an asset. Some maintain that the American synagogue protects the individual from the demands of the Jewish religion as much as it exposes him to them. In a scathing indictment of the American synagogue Rabbi Eugene Borowitz, a leading Reform thinker, has commented:

. . . the average synagogue member . . . comes . . . to join the synagogue because there are few if any socially acceptable alternatives to synagogue affiliation for one who wants to maintain his Jewish identity and wants his children to be Jewish, in some sense, after him. Though this is not the only motive or level of concern to be found within the synagogue today, the Jew who does not rise above such folk-feeling unquestionably and increasingly represents the synagogue's majority mood. More than that, however, it must be said that he also represents the synagogue's greatest threat. . . . His newfound affluence and his need for status within the community have made the big building with the small sanctuary, the lavish wedding with the short ceremony, and the fabulous Bar Mitzvah celebration with the minimal religious significance well-established patterns among American Jewish folkways. . . . What does it say of Jewish life in America when Reform Judaism appeals because it demands so little but confers so much status? when people blandly proclaim that they are nonobservant Orthodox Jews; when Conservative Judaism makes a virtue of not defining the center so that it may avoid alienating those disaffected on either side.[18]

Borowitz believes that the synagogue should become a more sectarian institution, that it should be transformed to become an end rather than a means, and that it should relinquish its function of providing identity for the secular-minded, ethnically oriented Jew. Proponents concede that this policy will mean that many who presently belong will feel compelled to sever their affiliation (or, if not, have it severed for them), but their eventual assimilation is viewed as the price that must be paid for the survival of Judaism. Proponents hope that the loss of the masses will be compensated, at least in part, by the affiliation of those who—they claim—have remained outside or at the margin of congregational life because of an understandable distaste for the American synagogue. As Borowitz sees it:

Clarifying Jewish faith might bring many to the conclusion that they cannot honestly participate in Judaism and the synagogue. . . . No one wishes to lose Jews for

Judaism, but the time has come when the synagogue must be saved for the religious Jew, when it must be prepared to let some Jews opt out so that those who remain in, or who come in, will not be diverted from their duty to God. As the religion of a perpetual minority, Judaism must always first be concerned with the saving remnant, and so long as the synagogue is overwhelmed by the indifferent and the apathetic who control it for their own nonreligious purposes, that remnant will continue to be deprived of its proper communal home.[19]

More ethnically oriented religionists have proposed less drastic remedies. One such idea is the *havurah*, a local group composed of individuals who belong to congregations but find such institutions to be so lax and undemanding that they require other avenues to express their Jewishness. It is claimed that banding together and forming a fellowship or *havurah* will protect and advance the spiritual life of those individuals who are ready for a richer religious diet than the synagogue makes available:

> The *havurah* is certainly *not* intended either to supplant the congregation or even to downgrade it. There is no doubt that the congregation serves many vital functions . . . [but it] insufficiency inheres . . . in the heterogeneous character of the constituency. And the main aspect of that insufficiency lies in the fact that belonging to congregations is often no more than an innocuous gesture. . . . Rabbis assume that the vast majority will attend only three times a year. Little—often nothing—is actually required besides the payment of dues. No commitment is asked; none is generally given.
>
> Now, while this may appeal to the escapists and the irresponsible, it does not appeal to those who are looking for a place in which they can take their Judaism seriously in the company of likeminded Jews. Thus, *commitment* is the key to one of the essentials of *havurah*.[20]

The American synagogue is considerably more differentiated than its critics assume. Population size and density permitting, a variety of congregations are commonly established. Even when such congregations are similar in ideological preference they cater to different segments of the community. Such population segments are generally distinguishable by secular differences such as class position and level of general education, but frequently they are also separated by differences relating to Jewishness: levels of acculturation, differing conceptions of spirituality, and contrasting degrees of observance of the *mitzvot*.

Lakeville, for example, is served by four Reform synagogues. All of the congregations are distinctive. One of them—the Samuel Hirsch Temple—is highly individual in its approach. In its conscious effort to break with the synagogue-center type, it has been called a synagogue for people who do not like to join synagogues. For a long time the congregation resisted constructing a synagogue building, because the leaders did not want to become involved in the type of activity that a building would entail. Furthermore, the Samuel Hirsch Temple in Lakeville has banned all clubs, and thus it does not have a sisterhood or men's club. The congregation has sought to confine its program to the traditional activities of worship and study, though these activities are of course conducted in a style that differs markedly from the traditional approach.[21]

Differences in the Reform group are paralleled and even accentuated among traditionalists. Far Rockaway, New York, for example, is a community that is as Orthodox in reputation as Lakeville is Reform. Beneath its seeming uniformity there is great diversity among the many small synagogues in the area, and considerable difference between the two largest institutions: the White Shool and Congregation Shaaray Tefila:

The White Shool has developed primarily as a synagogue for the young layman who was once a yeshiva bochur [student in a school for advanced Talmudical learning]. . . . It is unique as an American synagogue in that it numbers among its congregants about thirty-five ordained, non-practicing rabbis. The congregation has no chazan [cantor] but instead uses a battery of its own unusually gifted baaley-tefilah [prayer-leaders] who "work" in rotation. . . . [The rabbi] not only gives more classes . . . than the average rabbi, but he offers them on a generally much higher level. In some areas—such as Gemorah [Talmud]—he may give shiurim [classes] on the same subject to different groups at different levels . . . like the European Rav, the largest part of the rabbi's time is given over to learning Torah and preparing shiurim . . . while a relatively small portion is devoted to the social duties and obligations which take up ninety per cent of the average American rabbi's time.

Shaaray Tefila is tailored . . . to serve the total Jewish community rather than being primarily geared to the intensively Torah-educated Jew. Shaaray Tefila's decorous, dignified service, led by a capable chazan, gives the synagogue and its divine worship an air of sacred reverence and respect for the Almighty. Many White Shool'ers, however, whose own synagogue breathes an atmosphere of an informal camaraderie prevalent in a "second home," feel uncomfortable in the dignified atmosphere of Shaaray. . . . On the other hand, most Shaaray'ites would feel ill at ease in the White Shool, where a considerable amount of conversation goes on during the service. The White Shool, to them, is an "overgrown shtibel" [an intimate setting for prayer and religious study] and far too undecorous.[22]

As we noticed earlier those who wish to change the American synagogue are tempted to do so either by going outside of the synagogue or by somehow convincing established institutions of the error of their ways and seeing to it that they implement higher standards of spirituality. But another option is open to the elitists: they are free to establish their own synagogues. This option is afforded by the congregational structure of American Judaism, guaranteeing as it does the independence of the local synagogue. If this option is exercised, the burden of proof will then be on the elitists, for they will be compelled to demonstrate the superiority of their institutions over the standard American synagogue center. Since the individual Jew is able to exercise freedom of choice, such new congregations will find themselves competitors in the open market of affiliation. The American Jew, then, is free to remain unaffiliated, to retain his present affiliation, or to establish a new institution that offers him a more congenial spiritual atmosphere.

# Notes

1. On the usage of the term "sacramental," see Marshall Sklare and Joseph Greenblum, *Jewish Identity on the Suburban Frontier: A Study of Group Survival in the Open Society* (New York: Basic Books, 1967), p. 46. Some of the paragraphs that follow are adapted from Chapter III of this work.

2. Morris Axelrod, Floyd J. Fowler, and Arnold Gurin, *A Community for Long Range Planning—A Study of the Jewish Population of Greater Boston* (Boston: Combined Jewish Philanthropies of Greater Boston, 1967), p. 119. Most of the balance of 15 percent have no preference or consider themselves nonreligious.

3. The low status occupied by Orthodoxy until recent years is an additional consideration. This factor has apparently operated only among Ashkenazim.

4. It is apparent that individuals who were reared in observant households are seldom prepared to neglect the dietary laws altogether. And when they do violate them, they are aware of their violation, sometimes acutely so. Frequently, they are prepared to concede to the demands of Orthodox Jews who maintain that the laws should be observed on public occasions.

5. Sidney Goldstein and Calvin Goldscheider, *Jewish Americans: Three Generations in a Jewish Community* (Englewood Cliffs, N.J.: Prentice-Hall, 1968), p. 201. The true figure may be somewhat lower. Given the nature of community, the sponsorship of the study, and the affect surrounding *kashrut*, it seems likely that respondents would overstate their religiosity.

6. *Dreydl*: a spinning top on the four sides of which are engraved the Hebrew initials of the phrase "a great miracle happened there."

7. Note that in Boston this category is defined as more than once a month.

8. In evaluating cross-religious comparisons (particularly in the case of New York City), it should be noted that Orthodox Judaism does not require regular synagogue attendance on the part of women.

9. Note the case of Park Forest, Ill. See Herbert J. Gans, "The Origin and Growth of a Jewish Community," in Marshall Sklare (ed.), *The Jews: Social Patterns of An American Group* (New York: The Free Press, 1958).

10. So great is the stress on the building of synagogues that it has drawn the attention of students of art and architecture. See, for example, Avram Kampf, *Contemporary Synagogue Art: Developments in the United States 1945–1965* (New York: Union of American Hebrew Congregations, 1966).

11. Albert J. Mayer, *Flint Jewish Population Study: 1967* (Processed, Flint, Mich.: Flint Jewish Community Council, 1969), p. 45.

12. See Sidney Goldstein, *A Population Survey of the Greater Springfield Jewish Community* (Springfield, Mass.: Springfield Jewish Community Council, 1968), p. 93.

13. Albert J. Mayer, *Jewish Population Study—Series II* (Detroit: Jewish Welfare Federation of Detroit, 1964–1966), p. 24; and Axelrod et al., *op. cit.*, p. 136.

14. In Springfield, where inquiry was made into reasons for nonaffiliation, the most frequent response was the cost of synagogue membership. Only about one out of ten went so far as to say their reason for nonaffiliation was a lack of interest.

15. In recent years the congregational unions such as the Union of American Hebrew Congregations (Reform), the United Synagogue (Conservative) and the Union of Orthodox Jewish Congregations of America (Orthodox) have taken greater initiative in forming new congregations.

The most notable exception to the freedom of the local congregation to determine its own affairs are synagogues affiliated with Young Israel (Orthodox). Title to the property of a Young Israel synagogue is vested in the national movement. The purpose of the arrangement is to prevent a congregation from instituting religious practices that violate Orthodox norms.

16. Sidney Goldstein, *The Greater Providence Jewish Community: A Population Survey* (Providence: General Jewish Committee of Providence, 1964), p. 141.

17. One important aspect of the synagogue center (very much emphasized in the writings of Mordecai M. Kaplan, for example) is the conception that nothing Jewish should be alien to the synagogue—that the synagogue should offer its facilities to all Jewish organizations that make a contribution to Jewish survival and that it should seek to facilitate the work of such organizations. But inasmuch as there are inherent strains in the relationship of the congregation to the community, this is more easily said than done.

18. Eugene B. Borowitz, *A New Jewish Theology in the Making* (Philadelphia: The Westminster Press, 1968), pp. 45–46.

19. *Ibid.*, pp. 53–54.

20. Jacob Neusner and Ira Eisenstein, *The Havurah Idea* (New York: The Reconstructionist Press, n.d.).

21. See Sklare and Greenblum, *op. cit.*, pp. 97–178.

22. Michael Kaufman, "Far Rockaway—Torah-Suburb By-the-Sea," *Jewish Life*, 27, No. 6 (August 1960), 25–28.

# The Conservative Movement:
## Achievements and Problems

———————

[*Conservative Judaism: An American Religious Movement* originated as Marshall Sklare's doctoral dissertation at Columbia University, written under the direction of a then very young assistant professor named Seymour Martin Lipset. The Free Press published the dissertation as a book in 1955, and it became an instant classic. It pioneered the socio-logical study of American Judaism and introduced both methodologies and theoretical paradigms that continue to influence students of the subject to this day.

When Sklare began his work, Conservative Judaism was the newest and fastest grow-ing movement in American Judaism. He endeavored to explain this popularity in socio-logical terms, describing the rise and development of Conservative Judaism, the nature of Conservative Jewish worship and education, the new-style Conservative rabbi, and the problem of Conservative ideology in terms of the "changing needs and values" of the American Jewish community. As he put it, "the signal contribution of Conservatism would seem to be that of offering an acceptable pattern of adjustment to the American environment for many East European-derived Jews." In his preface to the third edition of the book (1985), he described the "essence" of what Conservatism has grappled with through the decades as "the problem of accepting and living with received tradition and, at the same time, meeting the need for change."

Sklare took a fresh look at Conservative Judaism early in the 1970s, adding a chapter entitled "Recent Developments in Conservative Judaism" to the paperback edition of his book published in 1972. This chapter, under a different title, is reprinted here. As a third-generation Conservative Jew, Sklare detected a pervasive crisis of confidence in the movement, a sense of anomie, a loss of direction, and as a result, growing fears for the future. He also took the occasion to comment on the revitalization of American Orthodox Judaism, which critics charged that he had earlier underestimated.

To mark three decades since the publication of *Conservative Judaism*, the journal *American Jewish History* devoted a special issue (December 1984) to a retrospective on the book and the Conservative movement as a whole. Four scholars offered new per-spectives on the work, and Sklare himself provided commentary as well as a brief history of how the volume evolved. In a rare display of pride, he revealed, in the course of these remarks, that *Conservative Judaism* was selected, in 1963, for the White House library, a 2,500-volume collection of books deemed "most essential for an understanding of our national experience." "This mark of recognition," he admitted, "is one that is actually very meaningful to this author."—JDS]

C onservative Judaism has flourished during the past two decades. Conservatism's prosperity is particularly noteworthy standing as it does in such stark contrast to developments in Protestantism and Catholicism; Conservatism has experienced none of the reductions-in-force that have characterized the Christian community. To be sure, most recently the budgets of Conservative institutions have had to be scrutinized, plans for certain programs have had to be deferred, and the viability of some Conservative synagogues located in changing Jewish neighborhoods has had to be reevaluated. But retrenchment, when it occurred, has been on a minor scale.

The recent prosperity of Conservatism also suggests that Conservative Judaism is much more than a temporary resting place on the road from Orthodoxy to Reform. Rather Conservatism has come to occupy a permanent place in Jewish life. In fact, the group's progress in the 1950's and '60's was so rapid that Conservatism overtook Orthodoxy and Reform and went on to achieve primacy on the American Jewish religious scene. Considering the recency of its establishment, the victory of Conservatism was remarkable.

## I. The Primacy of Conservatism

Religious prosperity during the past two decades has not been confined to Conservatism alone—Orthodoxy and Reform have also made progress. But if Jewish religious groups have fared better in the secular city than Christian groups have, it is apparent that Conservatism has fared particularly well. Thus, during recent years more American Jews have come to consider themselves "Conservative" than either "Orthodox" or "Reform."

The trend to Conservatism is particularly evident in cities of substantial Jewish population, especially cities located in the Northeast. For example, a survey conducted in 1965 in Boston found that 44 percent of the Jews of that community thought of themselves as Conservative, some 27 percent thought of themselves as Reform, and 14 percent as Orthodox.[1] In smaller cities in the same geographical areas the triumph of Conservatism has been even more overwhelming. Thus a survey conducted in 1963 in Providence, R.I., discovered that as many as 54 percent of the Jews of that community thought of themselves as Conservative, while only 21 percent thought of themselves as Reform and 20 percent as Orthodox.[2] Furthermore, Conservative strength has become evident even in the Midwest, which has long been a center of Reform. For example, in 1964 as many as 49 percent of Milwaukee Jews considered themselves Conservative in contrast to only 24 percent who considered themselves Reform.[3]

Statistics for New York City are unavailable; the presumption of most observers is that Orthodoxy is stronger in New York than elsewhere. Nevertheless, it is apparent that even in the New York metropolitan area more Jews would describe themselves as Conservative than as either Orthodox or Reform.[4] And inasmuch as some 64 percent of American Jewry is concentrated in the Northeast, Conservatism's predominance in the Middle Atlantic and New England states means that it has won a plurality in the nation. Thus while Reform remains strong in the South, the Middle West, and the West, Conservatism's growth in the East, together with its penetration into all areas of the nation, has resulted in its primacy. The victory of Conservatism is particularly remarkable if we bear in mind that until recently it was generally assumed that the dominance of Reform was inevitable. Reform is, after all, the form of Judaism most in tune with the norms of the general society.

The new predominance of Conservatism is still imperfectly reflected in synagogual affiliation, for not every individual who describes himself as Conservative is affiliated with a synagogue. In Boston, for example, some 39 percent of those who describe themselves as Conservative are unaffiliated.[5] The problem of unaffiliation cuts across all groups; there are also unaffiliated Reform and Orthodox Jews. But the presence of unaffiliated Conservative Jews has in one sense been especially advantageous to Conservatism—it means that there is a large pool of individuals to draw upon for future expansion.

Conservatism has made good use of its reservoir of potential recruits. The last two decades have witnessed a noticeable increase in the number of Conservative synagogues as well as a sharp rise in the membership of those Conservative synagogues which are located in areas of expanding Jewish population. Furthermore, the type of synagogue that the Conservative movement pioneered in—the "synagogue center" that offers social and recreational activities in addition to the classical functions of prayer and religious study and that conceives of itself as the central Jewish address in the geographic area that it serves—has become predominant on the American Jewish scene.[6] As a consequence Reform and Orthodoxy have come to look to Conservative models in fashioning their own religious institutions.[7]

The rising influence of Conservatism can be traced, in part, to the suburbanization that has occurred during the past two decades among Jews living in the largest cities. Suburbanization brought with it the problem of the maintenance of Jewish identity, and it was to the synagogue that the new Jewish suburbanite tended to look for identity maintenance. The net result was that the synagogue emerged in the 1950's and '60's as the crucial institution in Jewish life. And Conservatism exemplified the type of synagogue that was most appealing to the new suburban Jew.

The vitality of individual Conservative synagogues had actually been clear prior to the development of the newer suburbs. During the 1940's there were

any number of Conservative synagogues that had surpassed their Reform competitors. But Conservatism's predominance was not apparent at the time; the
past achievements of Reform lived on in the monumental temples that had
been constructed in the 1920's and earlier. In the newer suburbs, however, the
predominance of Conservatism became visible to all.

Philadelphia provides the clearest example of the process. In the 1950's Beth
Sholom, one of the leading Conservative congregations of the city, decided to
remove to suburban Elkins Park. The congregation chose no less a personage
than Frank Lloyd Wright to be the architect of its new edifice.[8] Considering
Wright's imperial manner and demands the decision was an act of daring. But
Beth Sholom was amply rewarded: the edifice that Wright designed was visible
for miles, and it immediately established itself as the most striking synagogue
in Philadelphia. It was so definitive a statement that no Reform or Orthodox
congregation in the area felt capable of exceeding it. Even today Beth Sholom
remains the most widely known of the nation's newer suburban synagogues;
it is a magnet for tourists, architects, and of course for devotees of the Wright
mystique who wish to study the master's only synagogue.

Prior to the 1950's the emerging strength of Conservative Judaism on the
local level was not reflected on the national scene. While the United Synagogue
of America—the union of Conservative congregations—had been established
as early as 1913, it remained a paper organization for many years.[9] The only
group that visualized Conservatism in national terms were the rabbis, organized as the Rabbinical Assembly of America. However, in the past two decades
a sharp change has occurred: the laity have transmuted their loyalty to local
congregations into attachment to a national movement.

The rapid development of the United Synagogue, which now has a membership of 832 congregations, is an index to the new sense of constituting a
movement. During the 1950's and '60's the United Synagogue emerged as an
important Jewish agency. In contrast to its older status as a paper organization,
the United Synagogue currently maintains some seventeen field offices in addition to its national headquarters. The conventions of the United Synagogue,
held every two years at the Concord Hotel, have grown in size to the point
where they tax the facilities of what is the largest kosher hotel in the country. The United Synagogue would long have surpassed its Reform counterpart—the Union of American Hebrew Congregations established in 1873—
but for the fact that it has been under the control of the Jewish Theological
Seminary of America. Fearful of the centrist and left-wing influence of the laity
and of many congregational rabbis, Seminary officials—all of whom belong
to Conservatism's right wing—have discouraged aggressive growth. Their influence over the United Synagogue is symbolized by the fact that the agency
makes its national headquarters in the buildings of the Seminary.[10]

Despite discouragement from influential quarters the feeling of constituting
a distinctive movement has become an increasingly pervasive sentiment in

Conservatism. The growth of the United Synagogue is not the only sign of this development—the establishment in 1959 of the World Council of Synagogues is another illustration of the same trend. The organization's name bears no relationship to reality, for the World Council consists of the Conservative congregations of the United States and Canada plus only a handful of synagogues located in other countries. The World Council is consequently barely more than a paper organization, but it nevertheless serves an important symbolic function: its existence serves to imply that Conservative Judaism is characterized by great force, wide scope, and permanence. Furthermore, the existence of the World Council conveys the message that Conservatism is more than simply an American idiosyncrasy—a group of local congregations that happen to have evolved a common synagogual pattern at a single point in time.

The symbolic significance of the World Council has been complemented by the establishment of other Conservative agencies whose unanticipated effect has been to add to the feeling that Conservative Judaism is a movement. Ramah—a chain of Conservative summer camps conducted under the supervision of the Teachers Institute of the Seminary—is the best example of the process. While the idea had long been discussed on the national level, Ramah is a grass-roots development initiated by a group of Conservative laymen and rabbis from Chicago who opened a camp in the woods of Northern Wisconsin in 1947. The purpose of the enterprise was to train an indigenous Conservative leadership—both lay and rabbinical—and thereby to assure the perpetuation of the movement. As Rabbi Ralph Simon—the spiritual leader of Congregation Rodfei Zedek of Chicago and the chairman of the camp's program committee—phrased it, the purpose of Ramah was to "bring out and develop those qualities in boys and girls which will best prepare them for leadership in the American-Jewish community."[11]

During the first year only some 89 youngsters enrolled; in its early period Ramah was an obscure experiment. However, Ramah developed rapidly during the 1960's, and by 1970 it had grown to a network of seven camps. In addition, there were programs in South America and Israel, as well as other activities such as a day camp and a training camp. In 1970 Ramah enrolled 2,833 youngsters in its seven American camps, 350 in an Israeli program and 52 in a special training program. The staff totalled 1,321 individuals.

The extent to which Ramah has succeeded in fulfilling its original objective need not concern us here. For our purposes what is significant about Ramah is that it brings Conservative youngsters who come from many different areas together in a setting where they necessarily constitute a community. As a consequence Ramah campers develop close associations with each other—associations that flow from their common Conservative origins. Inevitably the feeling of a shared Conservatism is nurtured.

Ramah also serves to bring Conservative adults into a closer bond. Visiting Day, for example, serves as an opportunity to meet peers from other congre-

gations. Again, the feeling of a shared Conservatism is reinforced. The effect
of Ramah, however, goes much beyond the campers and their parents. The
Ramah ideal is that every camper graduate to a staff position. With the exception of Israeli specialists who are hired to enrich the camp program, the
majority of the staff are in fact ex-campers or individuals who are otherwise
connected with Conservatism. The staff constitutes a kind of Conservative
society in miniature, and interaction is intense. The "Ramah marriage" has
become a well-known phenomenon in Conservative circles.[12]

In summary, the recent development of Conservative Judaism is characterized by: (1) the emergence of Conservatism as the favored religious self-
designation of the American Jew and the consequent achievement by Conservatism of primacy on the American Jewish religious scene; (2) the emergence
of Conservative synagogues, particularly in suburban areas in the East, as the
leading congregations in their communities; (3) the emergence of national
agencies that reflect the strength of Conservatism on the local level; and (4) the
emergence of a sense of constituting a movement—a sense of a shared Conservatism on the part of the Conservative laity.

These developments appear to portend a brilliant future for Conservatism.
The continued growth of Conservative Judaism seems assured: in the large
metropolitan centers there are significant numbers of unaffiliated Jews who
identify themselves as "Conservative." All that seems necessary to further augment the primacy of Conservatism is that such individuals be induced to acti-
vate a commitment that they already hold.

## II. The Problem of Conservative Morale

Despite brilliant achievements and excellent prospects for future growth,
the morale of the Conservative movement is on the decline. Seemingly, present-
day Conservative leaders are less satisfied with their movement than they have
a right to be; they are less sanguine about its future than the facts would appear
to indicate. Paradoxically, during the period when the movement was overshadowed by Reform and Orthodoxy, Conservatism's élan was high. But when
Conservatism came into its own, morale began to sag.

Doubts about the movement are most frequently expressed by the rabbis.
As religious professionals they have a heightened interest in Conservatism, a
special sensitivity to its problems, and a sophisticated set of standards by which
to judge its success. The following statement illustrates the doubts that are felt
by some Conservative rabbis:

During these past decades we have grown, we have prospered, we have become a
powerful religious establishment. I am, however, haunted by the fear that somewhere along the way we have become lost; our direction is not clear, and the many
promises we made to ourselves and to our people have not been fulfilled. We are in

danger of not having anything significant to say to our congregants, to the best of our youth, to all those who are seeking a dynamic adventureous faith that can elicit sacrifice and that can transform lives.[13]

This statement emanates from an esteemed leader of Conservatism, Max Routtenberg. As the rabbi of the Kesher Zion Synagogue in Reading, Pa., from 1932 to 1948, Routtenberg helped to establish Conservatism in Eastern Pennsylvania. After a period during which he served as a leading official of the Seminary and Rabbinical Assembly, Rabbi Routtenberg went on to become the spiritual leader of B'nai Sholom of Rockville Centre, N.Y. He was instrumental in developing B'nai Sholom into an important suburban synagogue in the prime area of Long Island. In 1964 Routtenberg was elected to the presidency of the Rabbinical Assembly. He was viewed by his colleagues as a kind of ideal Conservative Jew. He succeeded in combining the scientific methodology that he encountered as a student at the Seminary with the approach to learning that he had assimilated during his earlier years at a *yeshivah*. Furthermore, Routtenberg was a man of the world—he sought in his person to combine Jewish and Western culture. However, in his presidential address to the Rabbinical Assembly from which we have quoted, Rabbi Routtenberg spoke in accents far different from those that characterize the man of success.

Why this disparity between achievement and satisfaction? Why the decline in morale among Conservative leaders? The proper starting point for an analysis of these questions is the world of Orthodoxy. More specifically it is the attitude of Conservatism toward Orthodoxy.

The founders of Conservatism believed that Orthodoxy was fated to disappear. While some Orthodox Jews might persist, Conservatism held that such individuals would be relatively few in number and insignificant in social status. The founders of Conservatism did not relish the passing of Orthodoxy; they had strong sentimental ties with their Orthodox childhood, they had friends and relatives who had remained Orthodox, and they admired Orthodoxy's persistence in the face of seemingly overwhelming odds. However, while conceding Orthodoxy's historic contribution, they were convinced that it had run its course. As Rabbi Routtenberg put it:

I think back to the period when my fellow students and I, at the *yeshivah*, decided to make the break and become Conservative rabbis. . . . We were breaking with our past, in some cases with our families who had deep roots in Orthodoxy. We broke with beloved teachers who felt betrayed when we left the *yeshivah*. It was a great wrench . . . but we had to make it. . . . We loved the Jewish people and its heritage, and as we saw both threatened we set out to save them. We saw the future of Judaism in the Conservative movement.[14]

Orthodoxy, then, was viewed as a kind of *moshav z'kainim*—a home for the aged, and for those old in spirit. Accordingly, Conservatism felt destined to supplant Orthodoxy. Furthermore, Conservatism was seen as a contemporary expression of what was most vital and creative in the Orthodoxy of old—that is, in the Orthodoxy of the premodern era. As a leading Conservative rabbi has put it:

In spite of the claims made in other quarters it is we [Conservative Jews] who are the authentic Jews of rabbinic Judaism. . . . Many of those who attack our movement as "deviationist"—a term totally repugnant to the authentic Jewish tradition—and who demand unswerving adherence to the written letter of the Law are actually the Sadducees of the twentieth century. Had they lived in the days of Hillel, Rabbi Johanan ben Zakkai, Rabbi Akiba, Rabbi Meir or Rabbi Judah Hanasi, they would have condemned every creative contribution that the Sages made to the living Judaism of their age.[15]

In a sense, then, Conservatism is conceived by its elite as twentieth-century Orthodoxy. Or, to put it another way, if Orthodoxy had retained the ability to change, it would have evolved into Conservatism.

The Conservative movement's understanding of its relationship to Orthodoxy has been best expressed in the many books, articles, and addresses of the man whom we have just quoted: Robert Gordis. Gordis is considered by his colleagues to be the most powerful mind in Conservatism. From 1931 until his recent retirement into academic life, Gordis served as the rabbi of Temple Beth El of Rockaway Park, N.Y. He also taught on a part-time basis at the Seminary as well as at other institutions. Gordis recalled his traditional upbringing with great affection. But at the same time he stressed Orthodoxy's rigidity and resistance to change. He maintained that Conservatism had adopted what was best in Orthodoxy. And although Gordis avoided making a painful declaration that Orthodoxy was doomed to a lingering senility, the conclusion was inescapable.

In recent years it has become clear that Conservatism is incorrect in its diagnosis of Orthodoxy and especially in its prognosis of Orthodoxy's future. Unaccountably, Orthodoxy has refused to assume the role of invalid. In fact, Orthodoxy has transformed itself into a growing force in American Jewish life. It has reasserted its claim of being *the* authentic interpretation of Judaism.

Having achieved a new sense of élan, Orthodoxy has proceeded to implement a policy of strict non-cooperation toward Conservatism. Orthodox policy has called for the rejection of all changes proposed by Conservatism— even changes that might be acceptable if they emanated from a different quarter. Furthermore, the tolerance of individual Orthodox rabbis toward Conservatism, characteristic of the 1920's and '30's, has become only a dimming Conservative memory, especially on the Eastern seaboard. While the Orthodox rabbi of yesterday might successfully resist a Conservative takeover of his congregation,[16] he was prepared to conclude that Conservatism represented the wave of the future. Today's Orthodox leaders, however, proceed on the assumption that Conservatism is a hollow shell—that its seemingly strong syna-

gogues are peopled by weak Jews who are fated to assimilate, that only Orthodoxy will have the tenacity to survive the temptations of the open society.

The Orthodox offensive against Conservatism has been waged on two
fronts simultaneously: Israel and the United States. Orthodox leaders in the
United States have stimulated their colleagues in Israel to attack Conservatism.
Inasmuch as Orthodox leaders in Israel are in firm control of their country's
religious establishment, have considerable political leverage, and are not inhibited by a tradition of church-state separation, they have been able to implement anti-Conservative policies inconceivable in the United States. Accordingly, Conservative rabbis have been disqualified from performing any rabbinic
functions in Israel. The few Conservative institutions that have managed to
gain a foothold in Israel are barely tolerated. The fugitive position occupied
by Conservatism in Israel has been a particularly bitter blow for the American
movement. To Conservative leaders it appears that instead of being rewarded
for its long history of support for the Zionist cause, Conservatism is being
penalized.[17]

The full story of the renaissance of American Orthodoxy has yet to be written. One scholar has ably analyzed the disorganization of the older Orthodoxy
as well as the new spirit of confidence that emerged after World War II.[18] Nevertheless, the reasons for the resurrection of what was seemingly a dead religious
movement are still imperfectly understood. If by the 1960's the editors of the
*American Jewish Year Book* were struck by the renewal of Orthodoxy and commissioned a study of it (they termed Orthodoxy "a vital but hitherto neglected
area of American Jewish life"), Conservative leaders had noticed the resurgence
a decade earlier. However, they were unsure of what their response should
be, for the Orthodox renaissance played havoc with their understanding of
the balance of power in the American Jewish community as well as with their
prognosis of the American Jewish future.

To Conservative leaders each new Orthodox success seemed to provide
another instance where the laws of religious gravity had been repealed. Orthodoxy did not satisfy itself with serving those Jews who continued to reside
in decaying central-city neighborhoods. Rather it began a push outward. It
proceeded to establish congregations in the better residential areas. In the Midwood area of Brooklyn, for example, the giant East Midwood Jewish Center—
which had once dominated the neighborhood—found itself surrounded by a
network of smaller Orthodox synagogues whose dynamism recalled its own
exuberant past. In Boston there was the example of the Orthodox synagogues
of Roxbury, Dorchester, and Mattapan. Unaccountably, when these areas became black, their Orthodox synagogues refused to die. Rather, the synagogues
relocated in new neighborhoods. And some of the congregations were not satisfied to establish themselves even in such solid middle-class areas as Brookline
and Brighton. Rather they proceeded to relocate in Newton, the most desir-

able Jewish area in Boston. It had always been assumed that Newton—with its upper-class reputation—was a Conservative and Reform preserve.

During the 1950's and '60's the *yeshivot* multiplied in number, size, and fundamentalism; the Orthodox rabbis became ever more intransigent; the influence exercised by Orthodoxy in Israel became clearer; and Orthodox synagogues established themselves in upper-class and upper-middle-class areas. Even Hasidism was transformed from an antediluvian curiosity into a movement that—it was said—had much to teach modern man. The net result was that the Conservative understanding of the American Jewish present, together with the Conservative expectation of the American Jewish future, became confounded. The ground was prepared for the development of a kind of Conservative *anomie*. The problem was particularly aggravated in the case of one segment of the Conservative elite—the rabbis. Many rabbis had a deep sympathy with Jewish traditionalism. Thus on the one hand they admired and identified with the Orthodox advance, but on the other hand they were filled with dismay and hostility toward this totally unexpected development.

## III. The Crisis in Conservative Observance

While the renewal of Orthodoxy has been an important cause of the decline in Conservative morale, developments internal to the Conservative movement have also been an important influence. Conservatism is a religious movement. As such it is subject to evaluation from the vantage point of suprasocial achievement. Thus, Conservative Jews may measure the progress of their movement in terms of its success in bringing man closer to God, or as Rabbi Routtenberg phrases it, by its ability to "transform lives." If they are strong religionists, Conservative Jews not only have this option but they are impelled to embrace it. That is, they must give preference to suprasocial achievement and disregard, or even disvalue, such social achievements as monumental synagogue buildings and prosperous congregations.

All religious traditions have several yardsticks to measure suprasocial achievement. But each religious tradition tends to stress a particular yardstick. The one that predominates in Judaism is that of the performance of the *mitzvot maasiyot*, the commandments of the Jewish sacred system. True to this thrust, Conservatism uses a ritualistic yardstick in gauging its effectiveness. While at times Conservatism has been attracted to the moralistic ethical yardstick in measuring religious growth, it has nevertheless remained close to the sacramental approach of rabbinic Judaism.[19]

Conservative Judaism believes that it possesses a unique approach to the *mitzvot*, and especially to the problem of maintaining their observance. Conservatism holds that it is possible to advocate change in *halachah* (Jewish law) and simultaneously to be loyal to *halachah*. Change is seen as essential. From the Conservative standpoint the maintenance of observance has been immensely complicated, if not rendered impossible, by what is regarded as Orthodoxy's ossification. While the modern Jew must be responsive to the requirements of *halachah*, such loyalty cannot reasonably be expected unless *halachah* is responsive to the needs of the modern Jew. Thus in the Conservative view Orthodox authorities who refuse to sanction change, much less stimulate it, bear part of the responsibility for the lamentable decline of observance. As Rabbi Simon put it in a presidential address to the Rabbinical Assembly: "We have felt that Reform Judaism abandoned Halachah while Orthodoxy permitted Halachah to abandon us."[20]

As Conservatism sees it, certain *mitzvot* are outmoded or even offensive to the modern spirit. In the interest of promoting observance, as well as out of a desire for intellectual honesty, such *mitzvot* should be declared null and void. Furthermore, emphasis must be placed on the promotion of the essential requirements of the sacred system. Minutiae of the Jewish code can safely be disregarded. *Mitzvot* that are "fences around the Torah" rather than central to the Torah itself may be allowed to fall into disuse. Change can be effected by proper interpretation of the halachic system, and, where necessary, by legislation.

The essence of the Conservative position, then, is liberalization. While Conservatism believes that liberalization is its own justification, it also holds that liberalization makes possible the promotion of observance. As religious authorities come to differentiate between major and minor, between what is required and what is elective, between what is in keeping with the modern temper and what is offensive to it, between what can be reinterpreted in the light of new needs and what is beyond rescue, the ground for a renewal of observance of the *mitzvot* is prepared.[21] In addition to liberalization, the Conservative platform has two additional planks. One is "innovation," the development of new observances or procedures that are required when there is a need to substitute for, modify, or extend the traditional *mitzvot*. The other is "beautification," the requirement that the *mitzvot* be practiced in as esthetic a manner as possible— "the Jewish home beautiful." In sum, the Conservative position is that liberalization—in combination with innovation and beautification—will succeed in averting the evil decree of non-observance.

The dominant Orthodox position on the *mitzvot* differs radically from the Conservative stance. From the Orthodox perspective, liberalization is seen as severely limited, due to restraints internal to the halachic system. But even more to the point, liberalization is viewed as self-defeating. From the dominant Orthodox perspective, the net result of seeking to make the *mitzvot* more modern and appealing, more rational, more internally consistent, and more discriminating as between major and minor requirements of the Jewish code will not be more observance. Rather it will be lessened observance and ultimately complete non-observance.

If liberalization is viewed not only as subversive but as counterproductive, innovation is also rejected. (To be sure there has been some acceptance of innovation when promulgated by the Israeli rabbinate.) And while beautification is viewed as more acceptable than is liberalization and innovation, it too is under suspicion: the essence of observance should be the desire to serve God rather than the appeal to the esthetic sense.

The crucial aspect of the Conservative position on observance is not its acceptability to Orthodoxy, however. It resides in its success in promoting religious growth among the Conservative laity, specifically in advancing their observance of the *mitzvot*. Judged from this vantage point Conservatism has been an abysmal failure: there has been a steady erosion of observance among Conservative Jews. And despite a strong desire to encourage observance, Conservatism has not succeeded in arresting the decline in observance among its adherents, much less in increasing their level of conformity to the Jewish sacred system. The belief among Conservative leaders that the movement's approach to *halachah* had the power to maintain observance, as well as inspire a renewal of observance, has proven to be illusory.

The decline in observance is in part traceable to the changing composition of the congregations. Overall, religious observance among Jews in the United States has tended to decline with each succeeding generation. Thus, observance has dropped as the membership of Conservative congregations has come to be composed of Jews of more advanced generation. To be sure, in each Conservative synagogue there are some families that are as observant as those of the preceding generation. Furthermore, there are cases in Conservative congregations of increased performance of the *mitzvot*: for example, men who recite *Kiddush* on the Sabbath more regularly than did their fathers, and women who light Sabbath candles more faithfully than did their mothers. But such instances of retentivism and growth have not been frequent enough to offset the sharp trend toward diminished observance.

In recent years it has become increasingly clear that Conservative Jews have broken with *halachah* as a system. Not only has this meant a steep decline in observance but it has also brought about a new personalism. Resulting incongruities include the fact that lesser observances, such as the lighting of the menorah on Chanukah, have become more widespread than major observances, such as the lighting of candles on the Sabbath.[22]

Conservatism's defeat on the ritual front can be demonstrated in almost every area of Jewish observance. Sabbath observance is a case in point. After World War II there was a good deal of optimism in Conservatism in respect to Sabbath observance. The influences that seemed to portend a renewal included the rising prosperity of Conservative Jews and the increased popularity of the five-day workweek. The new life-style of the suburban Jew, which stressed the building of a meaningful pattern of identity for one's children, constituted an additional factor. And the need for surcease from the increasingly hectic pace of life appeared to offer new justification for Judaism's stress on the sanctity of Sabbath rest.

Encouraged by these prospects the Conservative rabbis pushed for liberalization. In 1950 the Law Committee of the Rabbinical Assembly proceeded to make a daring innovation. On a split decision it voted to permit travel on the Sabbath—travel specifically for the purpose of attending services. It also voted to permit the use of electricity on the Sabbath.[23]

What these decisions were saying was that the traditional concept of prohibited work was outmoded and counterproductive. Thus, driving an automobile was not intrinsically bad, and if the machine was employed to transport the individual from his home in the sprawl of suburbia to the synagogue on the Sabbath, it was a positive good. In any case the emphasis should not be on prohibitions as much as on positive acts that would promote the holiness of the seventh day: attending services, lighting candles, "making" *Kiddush*, reciting the blessing over bread, and serving special Sabbath meals. Furthermore, such an emphasis would inevitably lead the congregant to refrain from following his accustomed routine on the Sabbath. Thus the emphasis on positive acts constituted a more profitable approach to building Sabbath observance than would harping upon a detailed list of prohibited activities.

In addition to the technique of liberalization the Conservative approach to building Sabbath observance stressed the role of beautification. Thus the congregational gift shops conducted by the Sisterhoods were stimulated to promote the sale of candlesticks, *Kiddush* cups, *challah* covers, *challah* knives, Sabbath napkins, and other such items. Finally, innovation was utilized. Innovation was in fact a long-standing Conservative tradition in respect to Sabbath observance—the instituting of late Friday evening services had been one of the movement's most significant innovations.[24]

The available evidence suggests that the Conservative strategy of liberalization, innovation, and beautification has been a failure; it underlines the fact that the majority of Conservative Jews do not follow even the most basic Sabbath observances. To cite the example of Conservative-dominated Providence, R.I., only 12 percent of those who designate themselves as "Conservative" attend services once a week or more. And what is even more serious, attendance at Sabbath worship declines with each generation: while some 21 percent of the first generation attend, only 2 percent of the third do so.[25] The lighting of Sabbath candles fares somewhat better, in part because the ritual is a woman's obligation. But despite the fact that lighting the candles is required of the Jewish woman, it is observed in only 40 percent of Conservative households. And while the ritual is observed in 52 percent of first-generation households, it is followed in only 32 percent of third-generation households.[26]

*Kashrut* constitutes another problematic area of observance for Conservative Jews. Thus only 37 percent of Conservative households in Providence buy kosher meat. Furthermore, in only 27 percent of the households are separate dishes utilized. And true to the pattern we have already encountered, observance declines in each generation; while 41 percent of the first generation maintain two sets of dishes, only 20 percent of the third generation do so.[27]

If anything, the level of observance in Providence tends to be higher than among Conservative Jews in the nation-at-large—a result that is due to the fact that Jews in the Middle Atlantic and New England states are more traditionalistic than those who reside in other parts of the country. However, it might be contended that since a communitywide survey includes respondents who do not have sufficient commitment to join a synagogue, it is to be expected that their level of observance would be well below the ideal norms. But the fact is that there is not a Conservative synagogue in the country where the overwhelming majority of congregants practice the *mitzvot* according to the Conservative regimen.

The observance of the membership of the Har Zion Synagogue of Philadelphia illustrates the problem. Har Zion is located in the city where Conservatism has made its deepest impact. And if Beth Sholom of Elkins Park is Conservatism's architectural showcase, Har Zion is its religious standard bearer. Har Zion's preeminence is traceable to the influence of powerful laymen, but more especially to Simon Greenberg who served as its rabbi from 1925 to 1946. A strong personality, talented organizer, and determined opponent of left-wing thinking in Conservatism, Greenberg developed Har Zion into a model of Conservative traditionalism. He was so successful that he was invited to join the staff of the Seminary and exercise his influence on the national level. However, despite his removal to New York, Har Zion continued to look to Greenberg for inspiration.

A recent study of this model congregation has uncovered the fact that despite its seeming traditionalism the level of observance of the *mitzvot* is strikingly low. Sabbath candles are lit in only 52 percent of Har Zion households. The practice of *kashrut* is limited to a minority: only 41 percent purchase kosher meat, and only 33 percent utilize separate dishes for meat and dairy foods. A bare majority—only 51 percent—attend services other than on the High Holidays, and only a segment of this group—perhaps a quarter—are regular Sabbath worshippers.[28]

For understandable reasons the Conservative elite have avoided publicizing the painful evidence that is contained in the congregational and communal surveys. Aware of how far its followers deviate from Conservative norms, the movement has felt in recent years that it can do little more than provide a source of information and inspiration for those who might somehow find their way back to the *mitzvot*.[29] While a "National Sabbath Observance Effort" was sponsored by the United Synagogue in the early 1950's when there was hope of a renewal of observance, the campaign has not been repeated.

In recent years it has become increasingly clear that the problem of observance constitutes a permanent crisis in Conservatism—that the religious derelictions of Conservative Jewry are much more than a temporary condition traceable to the trauma of removal from the closed society of the *shtetl* to the open society of the American metropolis. The elite are losing faith in their belief that through liberalization, innovation, and beautification the mass of Conservative Jews can be persuaded to return to the observance of the *mitzvot*. In lieu of a solution to the crisis the movement has sought to ensure the observance of the *mitzvot* in public: in the synagogue, at the Seminary, at Ramah, and during the tours and pilgrimages of the United Synagogue Youth (USY). Although such conformity is gratifying to the elite—particularly to the older men who were reared in Orthodoxy and who have a strong need to justify their defection—it does not serve to erase the suspicion that the movement has been a failure. And Conservatism's failure in the area of the suprasocial is heightened by its brilliant achievements in the social arena: its success in building synagogues, in promoting organizational loyalty, and in achieving primacy on the American Jewish religious scene.

There is one final aspect to the observance crisis—the disillusionment among the Conservative elite with the very possibility of liberalization. The cause of this disillusionment is not so much Orthodox intransigence as the fact that whatever the validity of liberalization in theory, the principle has proved to be difficult to implement in practice within the Conservative movement itself. During the 1950's and '60's, sharply divergent opinions on almost every halachic problem were encountered in the Rabbinical Assembly. Consensus could not be arrived at. Important halachic opinions of the body's Committee on Jewish Law and Standards were seldom unanimous: they commonly consisted of a majority and a minority opinion. The result was that in an effort to achieve a workable approach to liberalization, Conservative rabbis were accorded the privilege of following the minority opinion if they were so inclined. However, such latitudinarianism succeeded in promoting further dissension rather than in building greater unity. By 1970 an impasse had been reached with the result that the majority of the members of the Committee on Law and Standards proceeded to resign. In an effort to salvage the decades of effort in the field of Jewish law, a special committee, with Rabbi Gordis as chairman, and Rabbi Routtenberg as cochairman, was appointed.[30] But whatever the outcome there is no possibility of a return to the old Conservative faith in the principle of liberalization.

## IV. The Next Conservative Generation

Although Conservative Judaism was not a creation of the young, its rise in the 1920–1950 era was closely connected with its appeal to young marrieds who were in the process of establishing independent households and developing a pattern of Jewish living that would be distinctive to their generation. Younger Jews who wished to retain continuity with their past and at the same time integrate into American middle-class culture found Conservative Judaism to be the perfect solution to their dilemma. Conservatism was traditional yet flexible, Jewish yet American. Its religious services were based on the Hebrew liturgy but also included prayers in English. Its rabbis appeared as authentic representatives of an age-old tradition yet were accepting the culture of the larger environment. Conservatism stood for religious observance without rejecting the less observant.

The élan of Conservative Judaism during the period of its rise was in no small measure due to the fact that the elite of the movement felt that their formula was precisely the one acceptable to younger age groups in the Jewish population—groups whose connection with traditional Jewish culture was less firm than their own. In 1949 a leading Conservative layman in the Midwest, Julian Freeman, neatly summarized the appeal of Conservatism when he commented: "A generation ago the young architect, the young engineer, the young doctor, the young lawyer, the young businessman saw in Conservative Judaism a chance for religious self-expression integrated with the best of thinking in the world at large."[31]

The present-day Conservative elite, however, is no longer so confident that its formula will be attractive to the younger generation. There are two aspects to this crisis of confidence. One is the problem of Jewish continuity—the problem of whether the battle against assimilation can be won. This question—most commonly perceived in terms of the threat of intermarriage—began to preoccupy the Jewish community in the 1960's. *The American Jewish Year Book* published its first study on the intermarriage problem in 1963, and the following year *Look* magazine published its famous article ominously entitled "The Vanishing American Jew."[32]

The ensuing discussion deeply affected the Conservative movement. Although the intermarriage rate was highest among Reform-affiliated Jews, its incidence among the offspring of Conservative-affiliated families was frequent enough to generate considerable anxiety. The confluence of individual instances of intermarriage and communal discussion of the problem soon produced a feeling of anxiety. It seemed to many that the very physical survival of the group was at stake. The threat inevitably spilled over into feelings about the prospects for Conservatism: if group continuity was in doubt, how much less was there a future for Conservative Judaism?

In addition to pessimism about whether the battle against intermarriage could be won, in recent years Conservatism has lost its older confidence in being in possession of a formula that can win the support of younger Jews. Despite interest in the *shtetl* and the East European milieu, many younger Jews—

including those reared in Conservative congregations—have little connection with the Jewish culture of the immediate past. Inasmuch as Conservatism assumes some continuity with the East European past and some familiarity with Jewish culture generally, it has been deeply affected by such Jewish deculturation. If the mission of Conservatism has been to show how it was possible to practice selected aspects of Jewish culture in an American milieu, the result of Jewish deculturation has been that the movement no longer has its older foundation of Jewish culture on which to build its synagogual loyalties. Rather than having an assured constituency as before, Conservatism finds itself placed under the uncomfortable necessity of winning adherents to its cause, and having to do so without the undergirding of cultural compulsions. Thus, if Conservative leaders seem less assured by Conservative prosperity than they have a right to be, in one sense they are justified in their insecurity.

To win a constituency rather than merely to inherit a constituency is difficult enough—particularly if a movement has the feeling that years of devoted labor and sacrifice entitle it to a loyal following. But Conservatism labors under the further doubt that it can prevail in its battle to win the loyalty of young people. The reason for Conservative pessimism resides in the disjunction between its cultural system and that of younger American Jews. Many Conservative young people not only lack Jewish culture but they have been influenced by youth culture—some are card-carrying members of the "Woodstock nation," others are fellow travelers, and still others have inchoate sympathies with the counterculture. While the problem of enlisting the loyalty of such young people is encountered by all Jewish religious movements, the issue is a particularly knotty one to Conservatism, with its stress on cultural reconciliation and the blending of Jewish and general culture.

Despite the fact that the so-called *havurot* originated among Conservative young people, Conservatism has not been notably successful in enlisting the loyalties of those who are part of the youth culture, who have little connection with East European culture, or who are antagonistic to the type of American culture on which the movement is based. The most notable demonstration of the difficulties involved in Conservative efforts at cultural reconciliation took place—appropriately enough—in the communitarian setting of Ramah—specifically at the Ramah Camp in Palmer, Mass., during the summers of 1969 and 1970.[33] The greening of the Ramah program was inspired by Rabbi Raphael Arzt, a member of one of Conservatism's first families and the son of Rabbi Max Arzt, a veteran Seminary administrator and a beloved figure in the Conservative movement. What Raphael Arzt sought to do was to integrate the Ramah program into youth culture. He sought thereby to provide a Jewish alternative for campers of high school and college age who were attracted to youth culture.

There has been considerable controversy in Conservatism as to what actually happened at Palmer: the extent of drug use, the degree to which campers

absented themselves from religious services, the extent of laxity about the
dietary laws, the amount of non-attendance at classes, and the implications
of an English-language presentation of "Hair." Some claim that the outcome
of the Palmer experiment was a greater Jewishness, while others contend that
Palmer resulted in heightened alienation.[34] Whatever the case, the movement
decided not to open Palmer in 1971. Palmer represented the first closing in
Ramah's history; it was understood that the experiment was not to be continued at any other Ramah camp.

Sensitive leaders in Conservatism are aware of how deeply the movement is
rooted in an older American middle-class culture that is currently out-of-favor
with a significant segment of Conservative youth. The problem was presented
to the Rabbinical Assembly by Rabbi Edward Gershfield in an address that
celebrated the organization's seventieth anniversary. According to Gershfield:

Our services of readings in fine English, correct musical renditions by professional
cantors and choirs, and decorous and dignified rabbis in elegant gowns arouse
disdain and contempt in our young people. They want excitement and noise, im-
provisation and emotion, creativity and sensitivity, informality and spontaneity. On
the other hand, they feel guilty about the spending of large sums of money for
synagogue buildings rather than for social services (generally for non-Jews). And
they are "turned off" by the very beauty and decorum that we have worked so hard
to achieve.
    Of course, the youth do not wish to go into the reasons why these aspects of our
life have been created. They are impatient with our explanations that most people
are not dynamic and creative, and look to religious leaders for directions and instructions; that we who have managed to survive the rigors of youth appreciate
regularity and stability in life, that we honestly want to endow our heritage with
dignity and beauty, and that a congregation of a thousand persons cannot have a
prayer service in a coffee house to the accompaniment of a guitar . . . we seem to be
doomed to having to watch as our youth relive the same self-destructive impulses
that we have seen long ago, and have thought could not happen again. Our appeals
to reason and history . . . go right past them and we are for the most part helpless.[35]

As Gershfield intimates, the fact that the American culture for which Conservatism has stood is under attack is profoundly upsetting to the movement. In
the years immediately ahead it will become apparent whether Conservatism
has retained sufficient flexibility to deal with such cultural challenges.

In summary, the immediate reasons for the drop in Conservative morale
at the very zenith of Conservative influence include the emergence of Orthodoxy, the problem of Conservative observance, and the widespread alienation
among Conservative young people from the American culture to which their
movement has been strongly attached. But on a deeper level the Conservative
crisis—if that be the word—represents a questioning of whether the Jewish
people and its "chain of tradition" can long endure on the American conti-

nent. Since Conservatism's future is predicated upon such survival, its fears are understandable. *Yisrael v'oraita chad hu*—the Jewish people and its tradition are indissolubly linked. There cannot be an authentic Jewish people without the continuity of Jewish tradition, even as there cannot be meaningful continuity of Jewish tradition without the maintenance of the integrity of the Jewish group. It is to this momentous issue that the Conservative movement, in its present mature phase, has been moved to address itself.

## Notes

1. Morris Axelrod, Floyd J. Fowler, and Arnold Gurin, *A Community Survey for Long Range Planning* (Boston: Combined Jewish Philanthropies of Greater Boston, 1967), p. 119.

2. Sidney Goldstein and Calvin Goldscheider, *Jewish Americans* (Englewood Cliffs, N.J.: Prentice-Hall, 1968), p. 177.

3. Albert J. Mayer, *Milwaukee Jewish Population Study* (Milwaukee: Jewish Welfare Fund, 1965), p. 48.

4. According to a recent study by Louis Harris and Bert E. Swanson, *Black-Jewish Relations in New York City* (New York: Praeger, 1970), some 35 percent of New York City Jews are Conservative, 21 percent are Reform, 16 percent are Orthodox, and 28 percent are "nonaffiliated" or "not sure" (p. xiii). It is not clear how the question on religious self-identification was asked by the Harris organization. Whatever the exact size of the Conservative plurality, it would have been appreciably increased if the study had included Jews residing in New York suburban areas.

5. Axelrod et al., p. 143.

6. See Marshall Sklare, *Conservative Judaism: An American Religious Movement* (New York: Schocken Books, 1972), pp. 135–45. Hereafter abbreviated: Sklare, *CJ*.

7. On the American synagogue, see Marshall Sklare, *America's Jews* (New York: Random House, 1971), pp. 126–35.

8. See Mortimer J. Cohen, *Beth Sholom Synagogue: A Description and Interpretation* (Privately Published, 1959).

9. See Sklare, *CJ*, pp. 218–19.

10. On the Seminary and the power of the "schoolmen" see Sklare, *CJ*, pp. 161–95.

11. See Abraham J. Karp, *A History of the United Synagogue of America, 1913–1963* (New York: United Synagogue of America, 1964), p. 76.

12. The effect of another youth-oriented agency, U.S.Y. (United Synagogue Youth), has also been to reinforce the feeling of a shared Conservatism.

13. Max J. Routtenberg in Rabbinical Assembly, *Proceedings*, XXIX (1965), p. 23.

14. *Ibid.*

15. Robert Gordis in Rabbinical Assembly, *Proceedings*, XXIX (1965), pp. 92–93.

16. See Sklare, *CJ*, pp. 58–60.

17. Sklare, *CJ*, pp. 192, 219–20.

18. See Charles S. Liebman, "Orthodoxy in American Life," *American Jewish Year Book*, LXVI (1965), pp. 21–97.

19. On the problem that such sacramentalism creates for the modern Jew, see Marshall Sklare and Joseph Greenblum, *Jewish Identity on the Suburban Frontier* (New York: Basic Books, 1967), pp. 45–48.

20. Rabbinical Assembly, *Proceedings*, XXXII (1968), p. 160.

21. On reinterpretation see Sklare, *CJ*, pp. 124–26.

22. See, for example, Goldstein and Goldscheider, *op. cit.*, p. 203.

23. See Sklare, *CJ*, pp. 237–38.

24. See Sklare, *CJ*, pp. 102–09.

25. Goldstein and Goldscheider, *op. cit.*, p. 194.

26. *Ibid*,, p. 203. See Axelrod et al., *op. cit.*, p. 131 for the somewhat higher figures in Boston.

27. Second-generation Conservative Jews in Providence locate themselves between the relatively observant first generation and the highly unobservant third generation. However, the second generation tends to be positioned closer to the third generation than to the first.

28. For the Har Zion study see Samuel Z. Klausner and David P. Varady, *Synagogues without Ghettos* (Processed, Center for the Study on the Acts of Man, University of Pennsylvania, 1970). I am grateful to Dr. Klausner for making these figures available to me.

29. See, for example, the following publications of Conservatism's Burning Bush Press: *The Jewish Dietary Laws* by Samuel H. Dresner and *The Sabbath* by the same author. Rabbi Dresner is singular in that he is a veteran Conservative leader of Reform background—he came to the Seminary from Hebrew Union College, the Reform rabbinical school. Since he embraced the *mitzvot* by an act of will rather than by virtue of family inheritance, Dresner has been especially well qualified to provide information and inspiration to the exceptional individual in Conservatism who is interested in returning to the *mitzvot*.

30. See Robert Gordis, "Toward a Revitalization of Halakhah in Conservative Judaism," *Conservative Judaism*, Vol. XXV, 3 (Spring 1971), pp. 49–55.

31. See Sklare, *CJ*, p. 90.

32. On the rate of intermarriage and the Jewish response see Sklare, *America's Jews, op. cit.*, pp. 180–206.

33. See Stephen C. Lerner, "Ramah and Its Critics," *Conservative Judaism*, Vol. XXV, 4 (Summer 1971), p. 14.

34. A doctoral dissertation by Uri Farrago in the Department of Sociology at Brandeis University discusses the Palmer experiment.

35. Rabbinical Assembly, *Proceedings*, XXXIV (1970), pp. 90–91.

# The Greening of Judaism

---

[This review-essay, a critique of the first volume of the *Jewish Catalog*, may well be Marshall Sklare's most controversial piece of writing. It was occasioned, he recalled in an unfinished note prepared for this volume, by his surprise at the *Catalog's* warm reception:

I noticed that reviews of the *Catalog* were almost uniformly laudatory. Despite its obvious contempt for the establishment, the *Catalog* soon became a standard textbook in Reform and Conservative Jewish schools. The fact that Jewish scholars, teachers, rabbis, and others were so loath to subject the *Catalog* to critical analysis stimulated me to prepare the article.

Sklare had witnessed the long gestation of the *Jewish Catalog*; the editors and many of the contributors had been his students at Brandeis. Here he parted company with their effort at "communal self-help," and wondered aloud at the warm approval that the *Catalog* won from the very "establishment" that it affected to reject.

The tone of his article won him few friends. In an exchange of letters printed in *Commentary* of March 1975, not one respondent supported him, whereas Irving Greenberg, Trude Weiss-Rosmarin, William Novak, Michael Berenbaum, and others sided with the *Catalog* against him. "I am both mystified and distressed by the sacralization of the *Catalog* evident in the responses of some of my critics," Sklare admitted in his brief reply. He never appeared in *Commentary* again.—JDS]

Seldom does the appearance of a book become a major public event, and rarer still is the book that can be singled out as marking a turning point of any kind in public experience; but this, within the world of American Jewry, has been the happy fate of a 319-page volume entitled *The Jewish Catalog: A Do-It Yourself Kit*,[1] a book that within a few months of its publication in 1973 was already being referred to as a classic. The instant recognition accorded to *The Jewish Catalog* by the American Jewish community has been matched by a phenomenal sales record for a work that devotes itself entirely to the question of how to live a Jewish life and that was published by a house with a well-earned reputation for the seriousness of its titles. As of last July, 95,000 copies of the *Catalog* were in print, and a sixth printing had been ordered. In Jewish publishing, this is bestsellerdom with a vengeance.

# I

In physical appearance *The Jewish Catalog* bears a close resemblance to two of its models, both of them quintessential products of the counterculture of the late 60's, *Living on the Earth* by Alicia Bay Laurel and the famous *Whole Earth Catalog*:[2] it is a large-format paperbound work featuring a carefully contrived design and typography, with diagrams, line drawings, and photographs freely interspersed in the text. And like its models, too, *The Jewish Catalog* aims to provide practical information of a self-help nature: in this case, on how to live as a Jew. As the two original conceivers of the *Catalog* have put it:

> Like the *Whole Earth Catalog* we wish to be a clearing house for ideas, materials, and personal resources, if not as an actual catalogue store, then at the very least in a "where-to-get-hold-of-it" way. We also want, in many cases, to be a "how-to" book as well. . . . For certain topics which we deem important or desirable to describe, we will include more than a simple mention of the tool and where to get hold of it, but in addition present a recipe, or a blueprint, or instructions to enable a person to do certain things right from the book.[3]

In line with these principles, the *Catalog* is organized into four sections: "Space," "Time," "Word," and "Man/Woman." The first section opens with "Symbols of the Home," a chapter largely concerned with the history, significance, and laws relating to *mezuza*, the small reticule containing parchment inscribed with verses from Deuteronomy that observant Jews affix to doorposts of the home. The chapter includes detailed instructions on how one can make these objects for oneself rather than purchasing them. This is followed by a chapter on "Kashrut: Food, Eating, and Wine-Making," which has material on setting up a kosher home and an extensive recipe section with directions for preparing *cholent, tzimmes, felafel, houmos*, gefilte fish, matzah balls, *kreplach*, cabbage rolls, and chicken soup. Next comes an entire chapter on "Hallah," followed by "Candles and Candle-Making," "Kippah" (largely devoted to the art of crocheting skullcaps), "Tallit" (with particular attention to the tying of ritual fringes and with instructions for making your own *tallit*, or prayer-shawl), "Tefillin," "Shofar" (here too the emphasis is on how to make your own), "Lulav and Esrog," and, finally, "Jewish Travel."

The second section of the *Catalog*, "Time," begins with a chapter on the Jewish calendar and includes detailed instructions on the blessing of the new moon. This is followed by a chapter on the Sabbath, with directions for the proper observance of the day. Then comes "The Festivals: Some Home Customs and Rituals," featuring material on the building of a *sukkah*, the construction of a *dreidel*, a *menorah*, and a *grager*, and the baking of matzah. "Berakhot" tells you what blessings to pronounce upon eating, or upon performing given precepts, or when petitioning or expressing gratitude to God. In "Weddings," a description of marriage laws and customs takes the reader from the highly traditional to the highly innovative, and in "Tumah and Taharah—Mikveh," a detailed analysis of traditional laws relating to ritual pollution and uncleanliness is accompanied by a description of the actual rites of purification. The section on "Time" concludes with "Death and Burial."

The third section, "Word," covers "Scribal Arts" (a treatise on the making of Hebrew letters and a guide to Hebrew calligraphy, with the aim of enabling the reader to prepare his own Hebrew documents, especially the marriage certificate, or *ketubah*); "Gematria"; "Music," particularly the Hasidic variety; "Film"; "The Jewish Press and Periodicals"; and, finally, "Creating a Jewish Library," a lengthy and sophisticated bibliography of adult books and children's books, a listing of Jewish bookstores, and instructions on collecting a well-rounded personal library of Judaica.

The "Man/Woman" section of the *Catalog*, something of a hodgepodge, begins with a chapter entitled "How to Bring Mashiah [Messiah]," followed by "A Guide to Jewish Women's Activities," and "Using the Jewish Establishment—A Reluctant Guide," the latter being a listing of local and national Jewish organizations and institutions from which various kinds of assistance may be obtained and a subject guide to resources offered by Jewish organizations. Then come chapters on "Hakhnasat Orchim—Hospitality" and on "Communities." "Where to Learn in Your Ghetto" has a list of American universities offering eight or more courses in Jewish studies, as well as of seminaries, *yeshivot*, and Hebrew colleges. "Teachers" offers the names of Hillel directors, a number of Hasidic *rebbaim*, some professors of Jewish studies, some Orthodox, Conservative, and Reform rabbis who hold pulpits, and individuals who function as unofficial spiritual leaders to the Jewish young. The *Catalog* ends with a chapter entitled "A First Step: A Devotional Guide," stressing meditation and prayer and closing with the novel formula: "May His blessed Name be with you until you get to Him."

Even such a cursory rundown as this of the *Catalog*'s thirty-one chapters will give some idea of the scope of the editors' concerns and of the curious amalgam they have effected between the detailed exposition of Jewish law on the one hand and the ethos of the "Whole Earth" movement on the other, with its stress on the nonconforming and the homemade. So unexpected does this amalgam seem that the *Catalog* has been taken as representing something new on the American Jewish scene. Yet the fact is that the *Catalog* did not spring full-blown from the minds of the young people who conceived it. They themselves came out of a particular social-religious milieu within American Jewry and the *Catalog* is saturated with the attitudes and values of that milieu. It is a milieu whose "feel" is captured perfectly in the photograph that covers the end papers at the front and back of the *Catalog*, depicting a group doing an Israeli dance. A young man who catches our eye is sporting a skullcap, a girl nearby is wearing a sweatshirt imprinted with a large peace symbol and the word "Peace" underneath. The credits indicate that the "National Ramah Commission, Camp Ramah, Wisconsin" is responsible for the photo. To understand *The Jewish Catalog*, one has to know something about Ramah.

## II

Ramah came into existence in 1947 at the initiative of Rabbi Ralph Simon of Chicago, who envisioned it as the key to the survival of Conservative Judaism as a movement. The existing leadership of Conservatism had been reared in Orthodoxy, but it was clear that the next generation would have to come from the ranks of Conservatism itself. Ramah would address this situation by developing an indigenous Conservative leadership, and it would do so outside the traditional educational apparatus of the Conservative movement.[4] From the beginning Ramah had the backing of the Teachers Institute of the Jewish Theological Seminary, whose faculty saw the informal setting as a powerful tool for creating emotional commitments, furthering learning, and strengthening personal relationships that could later be transformed into institutional, religious, and ethnic loyalties.[5]

During its first year the pilot camp in the woods of northern Wisconsin was attended by a total of 89 youngsters, almost all of them from the Midwest (some staff members came from the East and were students at the Seminary). Thereafter the growth of Ramah was spectacular—several times in the succeeding years Ramah was so flooded with applicants that it could not build or purchase needed physical facilities rapidly enough. By 1970 Ramah included a network of seven camps in which 2,833 youngsters were enrolled, plus a program in Israel in which an additional 350 were registered; staff numbered 1,321, with another sizable group attending a training program from which future staff would be recruited.

Several camps stressing Jewish culture or the Hebrew language existed before Ramah, among them the Massad camps and the largest Jewish camp in the nation, Cejwin (located in Port Jervis, New York). But none managed to establish quite the reputation Ramah did for combining intellectual seriousness and Jewish commitment with just the right admixture of flexibility to temper these with the latest fashions in the progressive liberal culture. On the intellectual front, each Ramah had a "professor-in-residence"—generally a member of the faculty of the Seminary—and a large number of instructors in Hebrew, classical texts, and Jewish culture. Every camp also had a library featuring standard Jewish texts and reference materials. Drawing its clientele from the newly affluent, suburban congregations of the Conservative movement, Ramah regarded itself as the Ivy League of summer camps, and in fact developed a kind of elitist view of its role in training a new generation of leaders.

Ramah's sense of self-assurance, bolstered by its success in drawing ever-increasing numbers of campers, was no doubt a factor in the camps' atmosphere of openness toward new trends in middle-class life, from the 50's craze for folksinging to the 60's craze for blue jeans and beards. Given the proclivity of Conservative Judaism to reject or disregard those aspects of Jewish law or custom it finds unacceptable, there were few developments in the past decades in the realm of personal behavior that Ramah felt it necessary, doctrinally, to dismiss outright. In most cases it was able to turn all such potentially challenging developments to its own purposes, even claiming authentic Jewish precedent for them. And the process worked in the opposite direction as well, as Ramah demonstrated an unerring ability to utilize age-old Jewish symbols and practices in a way that gave them an "anti-establishment" tone.

A seemingly insignificant and perhaps amusing example of this is the use made of the *kippah*, or skullcap. According to the etiquette of Conservative Judaism, which demands the striking of a compromise between the exigencies of religious custom and the accepted practices of "polite" society, a male should have a *kippah* in his pocket to be available for prayer, for saying a blessing, or for studying sacred texts. Some Ramah campers, however, began to wear a *kippah* at all times, causing their parents, and a number of leading Conservative rabbis, definite embarrassment. The wearing of the *kippah* was a kind of provocation, directed against the "uptight" Jewish establishment with its excessive fear of seeming out of place in American life, or too "different," and the provocation was compounded by the fact that the Ramah *kippah* came in a variety of colors and patterns—anything but the standard demure black or navy. Most desirable of all was a hand-crocheted *kippah* produced at camp itself, preferably by a girlfriend who would work the Hebrew name of the intended recipient into the design. Similarly with the Ramah *tallit*, huge in size compared to the standard Conservative prayershawl, its material a symphony of bold colors and abstract designs.

Perhaps the major thrust of the Ramah "experience," as its participants liked to call it, was to instill in all concerned—campers, faculty, and staff—a sense of the sufficiency of that experience as a paradigm of Jewish life (and hence indirectly to call into question any other mode). Early in the history of Ramah it was recognized that the camps were performing as important a service for the staff as for the campers. The ideal was to become part of the Ramah family—every camper graduating to a staff position, and thus helping further to complete the closed circle. One reason for the large size of Ramah's staff was this emphasis on being part of a family—a family that had a regular reunion every summer.

Within the Conservative movement a continuing discussion took place over the years as to whether Rabbi Simon's ambitions for Ramah were being realized. Was Ramah providing the synagogues with an indigenous leadership, or was it separating itself from the movement and cultivating a feeling of alienation from, and superiority toward, the local synagogues among its campers and staff? Ramah administrators did not encourage inquiry into this question, pointing rather to the undeniable fact that many of the students at the Jewish Theological Seminary were alumni of Ramah and that the Jewish literacy of young people who had spent a few summers at Ramah exceeded anything the Conservative movement had been able to produce elsewhere. Still, the question lingered in the air and then gained added urgency in 1969 when the fragile mixture of elements that was Ramah's way of life suddenly became volatile.

The scene of the "explosion" was the Ramah camp in Palmer, Massachusetts, situated within easy driving distance of Harvard Square, the East-Coast center of American youth culture. Although to this day there is controversy over what actually occurred at Palmer,[6] the presence of marijuana was obviously of central importance. Campers absented themselves from daily services, and the cutting of classes was common; there were charges that the observance of *kashrut* was lax. A time-honored Ramah tradition—the presentation in Hebrew of a successful Broadway musical—was also observed in peculiar fashion, with older campers selecting *Hair* and then proceeding to present it in English. Just before the 1971 camp season, it was announced that Palmer would be closed for the summer. Some blamed poor registration, but this—the first closing in Ramah's history—was widely interpreted as a sign that eclecticism had its limits.

## III

So powerful was the Ramah experience in the lives of young Jews that many a camper must have wished that a means existed for transferring that experience to, and making it encompass, all of his life—to be in camp all year 'round, as it were. The commune movement of the 60's provided the sought-for means. In the mid-60's, groups of young Jews, frequently led by Ramah alumni and influenced by the communal ideal in the counterculture, came together on college campuses to set up communal housekeeping cum Jewish living and study. The *havurot*, as they came to be called (from the Hebrew for "fellowship"), were joined by Orthodox and Reform young people—Orthodox students who found themselves out of sympathy with Orthodoxy's political conservatism and hostility to the counterculture and Reform students who wanted to be more Jewish than the Reform norm and less politically active (the decline of political activism was a potent factor in the growth of the *havurot*, as of communes in general). And the *havurot* were also joined by students from nonreligious homes whose latent ethnic loyalties had been brought to the surface by the anti-Israel position of the New Left, the rejection by blacks of Jewish participation in the civil-rights movement, the new emphasis on pluralism, and the burgeoning Jewish Studies programs. But the core of the *havurot* remained young Jews from the Conservative movement, and the core of the core were graduates of Ramah.

*The Jewish Catalog* is a product of the havurah that is located in the Boston area, named Havurat Shalom. The editors, in fact, dedicate the *Catalog* to their *havurah*, which they see as the source of their strength and inspiration. They describe Havurat Shalom as the "'*alter zadeh*' of the Jewish commune movement . . . a community of people who study, pray, retreat, fight, talk, sing, dance, and love each other." And the *Catalog* opens with a full-page photo of Havurat Shalom's sanctuary (it is empty). This sanctuary is unlike any standard American synagogue, for while it has an ark and an eternal light, we do not see a reader's desk or a platform and pulpit. Even more startling is the absence of pews or benches—the floor is bare except for a liberal scattering of large pillows. To the typical American Jewish worshipper the scene must look bizarre—he associates sitting on the floor or a low place with mourning and death. But this is not how the members of Havurat Shalom feel. For them sitting on the floor is good because it is the way man sat before civilization imposed its constraints upon him.

Like the photograph of the group doing an Israeli dance at Camp Ramah, the photograph of the sanctuary at Havurat Shalom conveys a particularly good sense not only of the mix of elements that is the *Catalog* but of the relative weight the *Catalog* assigns to the various components in that mix. The biases and emphases of the *Catalog*, in other words, reflect its lineage with the utmost fidelity.

The attitude of the *Catalog*'s editors to Jewish religious law, or *halacha*, is the first and most obvious case in point. The regulation of the everyday life of the individual Jew, with a view toward enhancing the spiritual dimension and infusing it with meaning, has been the intent of every code of Jewish law from the Mishnah in the second century, to Maimonides's great twelfth-century code, the *Mishneh Torah*, to the *Shulkhan Aruch* of the sixteenth century, to such current handbooks as Hayim H. Donin's *To Be a Jew.*⁷ In that respect *The Jewish Catalog* follows in a long and venerable tradition, and its editors do not hesitate to lay claim to a link of honor in this historical chain.

At the same time, however, the editors exempt themselves from the central feature of Jewish religious law—its normativeness. According to Savran and Siegel, in the Master's Essay cited above, "The *halacha* is there to inform and set guidelines, to raise questions, to offer solutions, to provide inspiration—but not to dictate behavior." What they see in the *halacha*, instead, is the beauty of an ancient and primitive, *therefore* uniquely valuable, body of thought. "Because of its age, origins, and the traditions and mysteries surrounding it, Torah has assumed forms which are timeless and powerfully evocative—elements which are missing from contemporary life. As Tillich says, we are living in a time of broken myths."

The value of Jewish religious law, then, aside from its innate "mystery," lies in the uses to which it can be put in an age beset with rampant "alienation," a time of "broken myths." These uses are not limitless, the creators of the *Catalog* realize; indeed, they are quick to criticize the incompleteness of *halacha*, its weakness in the area of "political and social involvement," and the absence in Judaism as traditionally practiced of "song, dance, crafts, drama, poetry, folk-tale, legend. . . . It has taken the 'discovery' of these values by the contemporary culture to raise the full conscious awareness of their existence within Judaism." One such new awareness, the *Catalog* says, attaches to the *shofar*:

Certainly one of the strangest pieces of ritual paraphernalia is the *shofar*. Even though there are several other religious objects that never seem to lose their poten-tial for surprising and amazing people, in some ways the *shofar* still stands alone. The smoothly curved ram's horn has an aura of the primitive about it; for people saturated with sophisticated technology, the *shofar* appears to be a throwback to hoary antiquity. And perhaps this is precisely why the *shofar* is so exciting and stir-ring—it brings us back to places inside ourselves that are very basic and primitive, very near the root of our being. Since the *shofar* is used mainly around the time of the year when it is most important to be in touch with ourselves, finding those places is crucial.

Here, and in many similar passages, the editors reveal the indebtedness of the *Catalog*—an indebtedness they are the last to deny, although they do not appear to recognize just how pervasive, and ultimately compromising, it is— to the regnant pieties of American youth culture. This indebtedness extends from the kinds of language they use to the principles of selection they have fol-lowed, the emphasis they consistently place on the primitive and ritualistic as opposed to the abstract and intellectual, their stress on folk religion and on the mystical and the occult, and their preoccupation with handicrafts and cookery, which they justify with appeals to "art," on the one hand, and criticisms of the "impersonal, sterile, and alienating aspects of modern urban life" on the other. According to Savran and Siegel:

The *Catalog* addresses itself toward a rounding-out of Jewish experience, bringing back the physically oriented side of Tradition and life that has been relegated to a few specialists. Basic areas of Jewish life like Bar Mitzvah, Weddings, and Burials have become so "prefabricated" as to alienate those with any real feeling for the event being celebrated. The individual must physically involve himself in the sym-bols and structures of Traditional Judaism in such a way that he feels a personal meaning.

Thus, in most areas of life discussed within the pages of the *Catalog*, the relevant Jewish law is scrupulously reported, where applicable. But the domi-nant stress quickly shifts to the experiential side of the subject in question, the side connected with issues of personal style, of taste, of aesthetic pleasure. In-deed, if there is a single characteristic of Jewish life to which, in the "mind" of the *Catalog*, all others are subordinated, it is not the broadly metaphysical or philosophical (God does not figure largely in these pages), not the ethical or the social (society can hardly be said to exist for the editors, except as a machine of oppression), not even the devotional, properly speaking (there is a great deal of material on the accoutrements of prayer, significantly less on prayer itself), but the aesthetic. As the editors of the *Catalog* put it, in explaining this focus:

The tolerance for impersonal, "professional," alienated services is diminishing. Instead, more and more people are making their own clothes, fixing their own cars, cutting their own hair, creating their own toys, growing their own food, building their own houses, planning their own vacations. The personal response to the environment has been a component of Jewish life for centuries. The craftsman, though generally poor, was accorded considerable respect if not status. . . . Art had no independent realm. It existed in embroidery, illumination, scroll work, construction, filigree. Cooking, of course, was an art of its own contained within the private confines of the home. Similarly for study, music, and dance. It is these aspects which must be re-evaluated in the light of present developments and raised to the level of articulation.

Hence, the *Catalog* devotes an entire section to wine-making. Hence too it is contemptuous of such innovations as the Meal Mart chain of kosher prepared-food stores that are so heavily patronized in Brooklyn, where many Orthodox housewives find it necessary to work to supplement their husbands' earnings and so cannot spend the time at home necessary for the preparation of Sabbath dishes; for the *Catalog* the only Sabbath worthy of the name is one that includes homemade *hallah* and cake, as well as homemade wine, homemade chicken soup, homemade gefilte fish, homemade *cholent*, homemade *kugel*, homemade *tzimmes*, and homemade *kreplach*. And it goes without saying that if the *Catalog* recommends a strict regimen of home-cooked dishes, it is even more insistent on the lighting of homemade candles. The *Catalog* is in fact infatuated with candle-making, devoting an entire chapter to the subject and expressing its regret that Judaism has no daily ritual requiring the lighting of tapers and so few occasions that call for really substantial amounts of wax.

There are moments, however, when the *Catalog* seems not merely indebted to the youth culture in its interpretations of Judaism but subordinate to it. A small but revealing example is the *Catalog*'s treatment of one of Judaism's sacred symbols, the eternal light that is placed in the synagogue above the Holy Ark, in commemoration of a Scriptural directive to the children of Israel to cause a lamp to burn continuously in the tabernacle. After duly discussing its function in the synagogue, the *Catalog* comes up with something entirely new, a use for the eternal light in the home. According to the *Catalog*, "It is not inappropriate to set up a *ner tamid* [eternal light] in your house—to be used for times of prayer and meditation, for *Shabbat* and *yom tov* or for all times as a continual reminder of God's presence." One is touched by this pietistic gesture, but it soon becomes clear that what is wanted here is simply a light show, after all: "[attach] to each section one of a string of variously colored lights on a random-flashing sequence chain. Make sure to insulate against electrical fires."

Another example of the sacrifice of the normative to the aesthetic is the

*Catalog*'s meticulously detailed instructions for the baking of Passover matzah at home. An oven used for this purpose must be able to reach a temperature of 2,000–2,500 degrees Fahrenheit—unheard of in a home oven. The editors are aware that unleavened bread prepared in the home according to the *Catalog*'s instructions would in fact be leavened bread in the eyes of Jewish law. However, from the *Catalog*'s standpoint the important thing is that those participating in the preparation would presumably have had the experience of reliving a primal event in the history of their people.

Subordination to the youth culture can take more serious forms in the *Catalog* as well. Here, for example, is what the *Catalog* says about the *mikveh* or ritual bath:

[The *mikveh*] simulates the original living water, the primal sea from which all life comes, the womb of the world, the amniotic tide on which the unborn child is rocked. To be reborn, one must re-enter this womb and "drown" in living water. . . . We emerge from the *mikveh tahor* [pure], having confronted our own death and resurrection.

Actually, however, the purpose of the *mikveh* in Jewish life is not to force a confrontation with death and resurrection. The concept of *mikveh* has evolved over the ages; in contemporary life *mikveh* is centered on the question of the promotion of family purity. Yet about this the *Catalog* has relatively little to say.

Its downplaying of the family points to the most telling distortion of all— the fact that the *Catalog* has almost nothing to say about the entire social and ethical dimension of Judaism in general, what is referred to traditionally as the "commandments between man and his fellow man." In *To Be a Jew*, which represents the traditional conception of Judaism, Rabbi Donin makes this subject a cornerstone of his discussion of the Jewish way of life, in a chapter entitled "Kindness: A Means and an End," which he subdivides into "Acts of Kindness"; "Laws of Charity"; "Laws Relating to Slander, Revenge, and Deceit"; "Laws Pertaining to Work and Wages"; "Kindness to Animals"; and "Acts of Justice."

For Rabbi Donin, Jewish life without this dimension is totally unimaginable, and he gives it the kind of attention that *The Jewish Catalog* devotes only to such matters as the manufacture of wine, candles, and skullcaps. And not only is the *Catalog* weak in the area of human relations, when it does treat of this topic the emphasis throughout is on what the individual can get rather than give. Thus, the *Catalog* offers advice on how to live cheaply in Israel by deceiving and otherwise "ripping off" naive Israeli residents. In "Using the Jewish Establishment—A Reluctant Guide," it lists the available resources of the organized American Jewish community and gives suggestions for obtaining scholarships, fellowships, free medical and psychiatric care, interest-free loans, and the like, without a word on a reciprocal obligation to contribute to the life of one's fellow Jews.[8]

## IV

In sum, the *Catalog* is rich in ironies, a work in which a genuine familiarity with Jewish sources and Jewish practice has been put at the service of the latest cultural and aesthetic predilections, with results that are funny, vulgar, charming, and meretricious all at once. And by no means the smallest irony is the wholehearted approval the *Catalog* has won from the very Jewish "establishment" it affects to reject.

Throughout the 50's and 60's Jewish leaders, lay and rabbinic, had agonized over the "alienation" of the young, their seemingly inevitable assimilation to secular American society, and their ready acceptance of intermarriage. The New Left, the counterculture, drugs, Eastern mysticism—all seemed to combine among the college-age generation of Jews and to promise further erosion in their loyalty to the Jewish community. In the words of Rabbi Irving Greenberg, an Orthodox leader who made something of a specialty of the issue, writing in 1968: "All of the studies point to one fact. By and large college is a disaster area for Judaism, Jewish loyalty, and Jewish identity."[9] Fear of what was happening on the campus prompted the Council of Jewish Federations and Welfare Funds to establish a "Committee on College Students and Faculty," which sought to increase the availability of money for work on the campus. But there was little optimism about the results of such investment: alienation was seen as running rampant, and political and cultural radicalism was believed to have made particularly serious inroads in the ranks of Jewish students.

Given this situation, it is not so surprising that the publication of a document like *The Jewish Catalog* should have met with overwhelming delight among the leaders of the American Jewish community. The appearance of the *Catalog*—it was felt—showed that everyone's worst fears had not been realized: Jewish youth had not turned its back on its heritage after all. Jewish youth was not assimilating; on the contrary, Jewish youth was becoming fervently observant, albeit in a new style, congruent with the age. Indeed, the countercultural style of the *Catalog* only seemed to endear it further to the heart of the "establishment." For here, it was said, were young people who were as "with it" as anyone could wish, and who yet were consumed with a love for things Jewish. (Some even intimated that it was all too good to be true; the Jewish community really did not deserve such wonderful young people—a judgment in which the creators of the *Catalog* heartily concur.)

Rabbi Greenberg's reaction was typical. In a review written jointly with his wife Blu, he noted a few errors in the interpretation of Jewish law and listed several suggestions for a revised edition but went on to say that "everything [in the *Catalog*] is presented with great charm, saving humor, and a very human dimension." According to the Greenbergs, "One of the most heartening phenomena on the North American scene during the past few years has been the resurgence of interest by Jews in living Jewishly," a resurgence exemplified by the *Catalog*. Their return to Judaism has come none too soon, "for Jewish life is being swiftly flattened between the hammer of the open society and the anvil of vacuity in much of organized Jewish life." [10]

As we have seen, the reality is rather more interesting than what the Greenbergs construe it to be. There has been no "resurgence of interest" in the sense they suggest simply because, in the segment of American Jewry for which the *Catalog* speaks, interest never waned; one need only examine the application figures for Camp Ramah to confirm this observation. Nor is it correct to regard the young people associated with the *Catalog* as existing somehow outside of, or apart from, "organized Jewish life." For it was organized Jewish life—specifically, one highly organized part of it within the Conservative movement— that was responsible for their education and that, on the evidence of *The Jewish Catalog*, clearly succeeded in instilling in them its salient values, including its sense of the elasticity of Jewish tradition in adapting to contemporary styles of experience and its attitude of superiority toward the conventional institutional forms of American Jewish life; as is always the case with the young, the *Catalog* merely takes these attitudes to their logical extreme. And finally, if there is "vacuity" in American Jewry, it too is reflected, in appropriately up-to-date form, in the very pages of *The Jewish Catalog* itself.

## Notes

1. Compiled and edited by Richard Siegel, Michael Strassfeld, and Sharon Strassfeld, Jewish Publication Society of America.
2. See Sonya Rudikoff, "The Whole Earth People," *Commentary* (July 1972), for a description of these books and an analysis of the culture they represent.
3. "The Jewish Whole Earth Catalog: Theory and Development," by George Savran and Richard Siegel, Unpublished Master's Essay, Graduate Center for Contemporary Jewish Studies, Brandeis University, 1972.
4. See Marshall Sklare, *Conservative Judaism: An American Religious Movement* (New York: Schocken, 1972), p. 259.
5. On Ramah, see Stephen C. Lerner, "Ramah and Its Critics," *Conservative Judaism*, 25, No. 4 (Spring 1971), pp. 1–28.
6. See Sklare, *op. cit.*, pp. 279–81.
7. Basic Books.
8. An apparent exception to the rule is the chapter entitled "Hospitality," but this, it turns out, was written not by a student but by the oldest contributor to the *Catalog*, Rabbi Richard J. Israel, director of the Hillel Foundations of Greater Boston.
9. "Jewish Survival and the College Campus," *Judaism*, 17, No. 4 (Fall 1968), pp. 259–81.
10. "Do-It-Yourself Judaism: *The Jewish Catalog*," *Hadassah Magazine* (May 1974), pp. 14–15, 37.

# American Jews and Israel

# Jewish Attitudes toward
# the State of Israel

## with Benjamin R. Ringer

[This study, completed in 1948, was not published until one decade later when Sklare included it in *The Jews: Social Patterns of an American Group*, his pathbreaking reader in American Jewish sociology. In a revealing introductory note, he observed that the attitudes of American Jews toward the State of Israel was "an important aspect of American Jewish life," and that this article constituted "one of the few empirical studies of the subject."

Sklare was one of the first students of American Jewish life to appreciate Israel's significance. In his study of the Jewish community of "Lakeville" (carried out between 1957 and 1959), he devoted a whole chapter to the subject—"The Lakeville Jew and Israel"—in which he probed the subject generationally and across the Jewish spectrum. In 1965–66, he himself spent a year in Israel as a Fulbright lecturer at the Hebrew University. Then early in 1968, just after the Six-Day War, he returned to "Lakeville" to re-examine the relationship between the community's Jews and Israel in the wake of what had happened. His analysis, included as the second article in this section, helped to shape subsequent thinking about the war and its meaning.

By the time Sklare published his textbook entitled *America's Jews* (1971), Israel had become central to his analysis of American Jewish life. He made this clear in the book's final paragraph. "The creation of the State of Israel," he wrote, "has had a profound effect on the American Jew, particularly on his psychological makeup. It has given him a heightened sense of morale—morale that enables him to abide newer challenges on the American scene to Jewish status and security. . . . Paradoxically, the effort by Israel's enemies to destroy the young state has resulted in a reinforcement of the linkage between America's Jews and their old-new homeland."—JDS]

In the Spring of 1948, immediately after the new State of Israel was established in Palestine and soon after it had been recognized by the United States, the American Jewish Committee conducted a number of studies designed to assess the reactions of American Christians and Jews to these important events.[1] Among Christians, the investigation focused upon how much was known about these happenings, upon attitudes toward selected aspects of the Palestine situation, and upon the relationship of such attitudes to feelings toward Jews in general. Among Jews, the investigation also focused on the extent of knowledge about the Palestine situation and on reactions to the establishment of the State of Israel. In addition, an effort was made to determine whether the establishment of a Jewish State provoked conflicts in political loyalties.

The present article is concerned with only one phase of the larger study. It is confined to an analysis of the reactions of a sample of the Jewish population of Baltimore who were interviewed in May 1948. We shall also compare the attitudes of our Jewish respondents with those of white Gentiles residing in the same community.

## I. Methodology

The particular survey with which we shall be concerned was the second of two conducted in Baltimore by the American Jewish Committee (AJC) in cooperation with the National Opinion Research Center.

The first survey took place in November 1947, and was designed to investigate attitudes toward minority groups. Interviews were conducted with a probability sample of 1,200 residents of Baltimore, 18 years of age and older. About 800 members of the sample were white Christians. Some 77 were Jews— a number corresponding proportionately to the distribution of Jews in the total population.

After the establishment of the State of Israel, AJC decided to return to Baltimore for a second survey in May of 1948. Among other things, it wished to discover how the establishment of Israel had affected attitudes toward Jews. Therefore, AJC was interested in reinterviewing the same group of white Christians who had served as respondents for the survey conducted the previous November. Due to a variety of reasons such as refusal to be interviewed again, change of address, and inability of the interviewer to find the respondent at home even after three visits, only 556 of the original 800 were in fact reinterviewed.

Another of the research objectives of the 1948 survey was to examine in detail the response of Jews to the establishment of Israel. In particular, knowledge was desired about the extent to which Jews with varied backgrounds differed in their attitudes toward Israel. It was therefore decided that not only should the original Jewish respondents be reinterviewed, but also a group of new respondents be added. (In keeping with their representation in the population, only 7 percent of the November sample were Jews, a group that was too small for the elaborate analysis that was planned.) The May sample of Jews was thus greatly enlarged[2] and consisted of a total of 230 respondents, only 50 of whom had been interviewed in the first survey.[3] Because of the enlarged sample, data on changes in Jewish attitudes are available for only a minority of the Jewish respondents. Consequently, this paper will touch only incidentally upon the problem of attitude change; we shall instead concentrate on the uniformities and differences found within the May sample.

## II. Information and Interest

The 1948 survey was conducted during the period in which the recently established State of Israel was being attacked by the surrounding Arab nations. Most Jews in our sample responded to the strife with considerable interest. When asked, "What do you consider the most important trouble spots in the world today?," the one most frequently mentioned was Palestine. Virtually all—94 percent—made it one of their choices. This was more than twice as many as selected the next most frequent choice, Russia, a nation that was mentioned by only 41 percent. Among Christians the reverse was true. Russia was mentioned more frequently than was Palestine. Seventy-one percent chose Russia, and only 43 percent voted for Palestine. Thus, among Jews Palestine occupied the center of the world stage while among Christians it was Russia.

Not only were most of the Jewish respondents aware of the fighting in Palestine, but in addition they did not keep this awareness to themselves. They made the conflict a topic of conversation; they discussed it with other persons. This is evident in their response to the following question: "Do you ever talk with other people about the Palestine situation?"[4] Eighty-four percent replied that they did. More than one-third (37 percent) said they brought it up frequently in conversation, and almost half (47 percent) said they talked about it occasionally.[5]

In view of this widespread concern and discussion, it was not surprising to find that most Jews displayed more than a casual acquaintance with what was taking place in Palestine. They understood, for example, who the various participants in the conflict were and what role England played in the situation. To study the level of their general knowledge about the Palestine situation, we constructed an index from the following four items:

1. Knowledge of fighting taking place in Palestine.[6]
2. Which people are fighting each other in Palestine? (Correct answer: *Jews and Arabs.*)
3. Has any of the above countries—that is, United States, England, or Russia—been active in governing Palestine for the past thirty years or so? (Correct answer: *England.*)
4. Do you happen to know what is the name of the new Jewish State? (Correct answer: *Israel.*)

More than three-quarters of the Jewish sample answered all four items correctly; every Jewish respondent was able to answer at least two. Most Jews thus possessed a real knowledge of some of the major features of the Palestine situation. Indeed, they had a much better understanding of the events than did most Christians. Among the non-Jewish sample only one-third answered all four items correctly. Another third answered three correctly. The remaining one-third responded correctly to only two, one, or none of the questions.[7]

The familiarity of most Jews with certain major features of the Palestine situation did not mean that they were experts on its varied details. Few were as well informed on specifics as they were on items of more general information. Only 54 percent could identify correctly the Jewish organizations or individuals who were in favor of setting up a Jewish State; even fewer (35 percent) knew which organizations or individuals were *opposed* to setting up a Jewish State. Only 43 percent could correctly identify the *Irgun*.[8]

These differences in level of information did not occur at random. They varied with such factors as level of education, age, sex, income, and place of birth. Those who had completed high school or who had gone to college scored higher on the index of general knowledge and were better informed on the questions about detailed knowledge than were those with fewer years of formal education. Men were better informed than women; the native-born knew more than the foreign-born; and those under thirty-five were more knowledgeable than were those over thirty-five. In addition, people with higher incomes ($70 per week or more) were better informed than were those with lower incomes (less than $70 per week).[9] It is important to note, however, that even among the relatively less-informed groups, a significant number had kept up with the events and politics relating to the new Jewish State. Thus, among Jewish respondents who had *not* completed high school, more than two-thirds (69 percent) were high on the general knowledge index. This is in decided contrast to the Christians, among whom only 51 percent of those who *had* completed high school or more scored high on the same index.

## III. Support

The Jews in our sample hardly approached the Palestine situation as might a detached observer who seeks information for "scientific purposes." In other words, their concern and interest were not devoid of emotional content. Thus, they made no pretense at neutrality, and their partisanship for Israel was clearly expressed. For example, virtually all respondents endorsed the establishment of the State of Israel. Approximately nine out of ten replied "Approve" to the following question: "The Jews have set up a new Jewish State in part of Palestine. Do you approve or disapprove of this action by the Jews?" A similar number thought the United States had been right in recognizing the new State ("The United States has just recognized the new Jewish State in Palestine. Do you think that this was the right thing to do or the wrong thing to do?").

In the eyes of most, past support of Israel was not enough; they felt that the crisis situation that beset the new country necessitated a continuing effort.

Furthermore, they were desirous of support by the United States Government. They both wanted and expected the government to approve of Israel and to help it in its fight with the Arabs. For example, in answer to the question, "Do you think the United States Government should help the Jews in Palestine, should help the Arabs, or should help both or neither?," 62 percent favored helping the Jews, no one favored helping the Arabs, 16 percent favored the government not helping either group, and 14 favored helping both.

In seeking the assistance of the United States Government, our Jewish respondents were not looking for a way to relieve themselves of responsibility. On the contrary, they were convinced that providing Israel with the needed assistance was first and foremost an obligation of the Jewish community.[10] The obligation they saw as theirs, and its fulfillment they viewed as imperative— all this irrespective of the general tide of opinion and of the specific attitude of the United States Government. Asked the question, "Even if the United States does not help the Jews in Palestine, do you think that the Jewish people in the United States should or should not help them?," 95 percent signified that they should. Asked further, "In your opinion, would the Jews in the United States be right or wrong to try to help the Jewish State even if the United States were against helping it?," over seven out of ten felt that they would be right.[11]

How did Baltimore Jewry propose to help Israel? By what manner and means? The answer is primarily through *economic* means and only secondarily through *military* means. Virtually all would have Jews send money (91 percent) as well as food and clothing (93 percent). Somewhat fewer would approve of American Jewry sending munitions (80 percent). And fewest—but still the majority—would favor sending fighting men (51 percent).

Similar kinds of assistance would be welcomed from the United States Government, although fewer respondents expected from it the specific forms of aid they expected from Jews. Greatest support was for the sending of money (62 percent) and for the sending of food and clothing (59 percent). About half (51 percent) would have the United States Government ship arms and ammunition, but only a minority (23 percent) would have the government take military action by sending soldiers. Most Jews, in other words, while wanting economic and other forms of assistance, did not expect or want the United States to go to war for the sake of Israel.

## IV. Personal Involvement and Commitment to Jewish Life

Although the attitudes of most respondents reflected a *common* direction, consensus with regard to the *strength* or *intensity* of pro-Israel sentiment was absent. Thus, Baltimore Jewry did not share a uniform sense of urgency or a common desire to participate personally in the conflict. In fact, only a minority were completely preoccupied with the situation and totally committed to the cause. We have already noted that only somewhat over a third (37 percent) said they made the Palestine situation a frequent topic of conversation. It was also found that only a minority were so concerned with the situation that they could see themselves as personally joining the struggle. We have reference in this connection to the 38 percent who answered "Yes" to the pointed but "iffy" question, "If you could, would you yourself like to be fighting in Palestine?"

What accounted for these variations in involvement?[12] Why were some people much more concerned than others? One of the primary factors was found to be the strength of the individual's ties with Judaism and/or Jewishness. Included in the questionnaire were a number of queries thought to be indicative of such ties, and from these items an index of Jewish identification was constructed. The items were as follows:

1. Do you attend services at a Temple or a Synagogue? How often?
2. Are you a regular member of either a Temple or a Synagogue?
3. Are you a member of any Jewish organization?
4. Is Yiddish spoken in your home a good deal, fairly often, or hardly ever?

People who attended services regularly or fairly often, who were synagogue members, who were affiliated with a Jewish organization, and who spoke Yiddish at home a good deal or fairly often, or who could qualify on any three of these four criteria, were considered as having a strong or *high* Jewish identification. The rest were considered to have a relatively *low* Jewish identification.[13]

Comparing individuals manifesting high Jewish identification with those manifesting low identification, we found that the former went further in their support of Israel than the latter. They were more personally involved in the conflict and were more willing to have the United States Government send arms and men to Israel. This tendency is apparent in Table 1.

It is interesting to note, however, that commitment to Judaism and Jewish life, while making for greater personal involvement, did not increase the likelihood of a pro-Israel orientation. It affected the *intensity* but not the *direction* of a Jew's response to Israel. Virtually all, irrespective of level of commitment, showed some favorable sentiments toward Israel: it was right for the United States to have recognized the new Jewish State in Palestine, and Jews should help Israel even if the government was neutral or negative (see Table 2).

Thus, it is apparent that merely being Jewish was enough to evoke pro-Israel sympathies; however, it is equally apparent that something more was generally needed to transform these sympathies into active involvement with and support for Israel. A firm attachment to Jewish life and the sharing of strong sentiments and feelings about Jewishness played an important part in producing this involvement and support.

The importance of "sentimental ties" is further underscored when we look at the part played by "intellectual ties." Merely having an intellectualized concern with Israel did not in itself have any effect on involvement. This conclusion

TABLE 1
*Commitment to Jewish Life Intensifies Involvement
with Israel and Support of Military Assistance*

|  | Level of commitment to Jewish life | |
|---|---|---|
|  | High | Low |
| % who share a high level of personal involvement with Palestine situation.[14] | 50% | 33% |
| % who agree that: | | |
| U. S. Government should send *arms and ammunition* to help the Jews in Palestine | 61% | 46% |
| U. S. Government should send *soldiers* to help the Jews in Palestine | 34% | 16% |
|  | (77) | (153) |

TABLE 2
*Commitment to Jewish Life Has No Effect on
Sharing a Pro-Israel Orientation*

|  | Level of commitment to Jewish life | |
|---|---|---|
|  | High | Low |
| % who agree that: | | |
| It was right for the United States to recognize the new Jewish State in Palestine | 90% | 90% |
|  | (77) | (153) |
| Even if the United States does not help the Jews in Palestine, the Jewish people should *help* them. | 96% | 96% |
|  | (76) | (151) |

is apparent when the relationship between level of information and involvement is examined. We see no connection between the two. Knowing more about Israel did not make for more involvement (see Table 3).[15]

However, if the informed person was in addition deeply committed to Jewish life, then his being knowledgeable about Israel did make a difference. It increased the likelihood of his being intensely involved with the country. It was, therefore, only in the absence of commitment to Jewish life that knowledge failed to exert any influence on level of involvement. Apparently among the less committed, knowledge about Israel was merely part of a more general interest in world affairs. It was not, as in the case of the highly committed, an expression of a special concern with Israel (see Table 4).

Thus, commitment to Jewish life played an important part in the relation-

TABLE 3
*Knowledge Has No Effect on Level of Involvement*

|                                                                              | Level of knowledge about Palestine situation | |
| ---------------------------------------------------------------------------- | :----------: | :----------: |
|                                                                              | High         | Low          |
| % who share a high level of personal involvement with Palestine situation    | 39%<br>(178) | 38%<br>(52)  |

TABLE 4
*Knowledge of Palestine Situation Intensifies Involvement*
*Only among Those Highly Committed to Jewish Life*

|                                                                     | Level of commitment to Jewish life | |
| ------------------------------------------------------------------- | :----------: | :----------: |
|                                                                     | High         | Low          |
| % who are highly involved in Palestine situation among those having: |              |              |
| High level of knowledge about situation                             | 52%<br>(54)  | 33%<br>(124) |
| Low level of knowledge about situation                              | 43%<br>(23)  | 35%<br>(29)  |

ship between knowledge and involvement. It functioned as a condition that had to be present if knowledge was to intensify involvement with Israel. In the most simple terms, the Jew first had to have his "heart" in Jewish life if his "intellect" was to draw him closer to Israel.

## V. The Problem of "Dual Loyalty"

In view of the sympathies that our respondents manifested for the State of Israel, one might wonder whether such attitudes posed any special problems in regard to their relationship to the United States. The question of "dual loyalty" has on occasion been raised. Queries such as, "How does the Jew reconcile his interest in Israel with his loyalties as an American citizen?," and "To what extent does he perceive any conflict between the two?" have been asked.

The data suggest that our respondents felt little, if any, incompatibility between their ties to the two countries. It was evident from our interviews that even those individuals strongly involved with Israel saw no conflict between their support of that nation and their allegiance to the United States. To them the issue of a Jewish State was distinct from the issue of the national identification of the American Jew. As one woman much concerned with the Palestine situation said:

As far as I'm concerned, America is my home, but Jews should have a place they can call their home. I have no desire to leave America . . . but Jews should have a little place to call their own.

And, when a Jewish homeland was considered by Jewish respondents to be a necessity in order "to give displaced persons a chance to live and rehabilitate themselves," respondents felt even less strain upon their identity as Americans. The replies would indicate that a Jew may give wholehearted support to the establishment of a Jewish State, and to helping ensure its viability, while he reaffirms his allegiance to America.

Even our respondents' replies to the question that asked whether it would be right for Jews in the United States to try to help the Jewish State even if the United States were against helping the country revealed a reluctance to admit any incompatability between support of Israel and allegiance to the United States. Although the question would seem to raise that possibility and to require a choice between loyalties to the two countries, most of our respondents did not interpret the query in that light. Even though they answered that Jews would be right to help, they were not affirming greater loyalty to Israel than to the United States but were expressing their unwillingness to accept the premise that continued support of Israel might conflict with their allegiance to the United States. To them the statement that the United States would be against helping the new State did not imply that any basic issues of loyalty would be at stake or that any legal sanctions might be applied against Jewish help to Israel. It seemed simply a matter of course that Jews should help other Jews. Such action could not be harmful to the United States even if American policy was one of neutrality:

We must help our own. Every family or group knows this. We are not hurting our government by treachery, but we definitely are helping those who are oppressed and needy.

In other words, help for other Jews would do no harm to America. Jews are in need, and there is no conflict between loyalty to the United States and assistance to one's brethren.

However, a small group of respondents did consider that a conflict in loyalties might be involved if the United States opposed help to Israel. Why their perception of the situation differed from that of the others cannot be explained. Unfortunately, our data do not provide us with the kind of detailed information about the selective perceptions of our respondents that such an explanation would require. We do know, however, that in virtually all of the cases where a conflict was perceived, loyalty to the United States was reaffirmed. Though sympathetic to Israel, such respondents felt that under these conditions continued support might be construed as an act of disobedience to the United States Government and should as a consequence be stopped:

It would be wrong if the assistance placed this country in jeopardy. Our first loyalty is to the United States.

It's wrong if it's an act against the government. I wouldn't want them to.

Naturally, if the government would not want them to, it would be bad. I hope they will do their best for the Jewish people.

A similar reaffirmation of ties to America was observed in still another connection. Virtually all persons in our sample, despite their desire to help Israel, felt that their roots were in the United States and their primary loyalties to America. Few would sacrifice their ties to America for those to Israel. Indeed, even if given the opportunity, few would consider leaving the country. When asked "Would you yourself like to go to Palestine to live if you could, or would you rather stay in this country?," only 5 percent said they would prefer living in Palestine.

Thus, for most Jews Israel and the United States stood for two different kinds of commitments and ties, neither of which clashed with the other and both of which were essential to their total image of themselves as American Jews. However, should they be faced with a situation where they would have to choose between the two countries—a situation that they were anxious to avoid—loyalty to the United States would prevail.

## VI. Nonsupport and Fear of Heightened Anti-Semitism

As we have already seen, most of our respondents expressed support for the new State of Israel. Examination of the interviews of the small group of deviants who felt differently revealed a number of grounds on which they based their opposition. We have already commented on one of the more frequent: fear that support of Israel might bring the Jew into conflict with the United States Government. Closely allied with this as a major reason for nonsupport was the fear of a possible hostile reaction on the part of American Christians—not necessarily the government itself—to Jewish assistance of Israel.[16] This is seen in responses to the question, "Do you think that the Palestine situation may cause more anti-Semitism in the United States, or will it make for less anti-Semitism, or won't it affect anti-Semitism in this country?"

While the nonsupporters of Israel were no more convinced than were its supporters that the conflict would affect domestic anti-Semitism—only about half in each group foreseeing any domestic repercussions (see Table 5)—among those who *did* predict an effect, nonsupporters were much more pessimistic about the direction that such an effect would take. They firmly believed that the conflict would intensify anti-Jewish sentiments.[17] The supporters of Israel

TABLE 5

*Expectation That Arab-Israel Conflict Will Affect Domestic Anti-Semitism
Is Not Significantly Correlated with Attitude toward Aid for Israel*

| | The United States Government | | Even if the United States does not help the Jews in Palestine, Jewish People in the United States | |
| --- | --- | --- | --- | --- |
| | Should help Jews | Should not help Jews or don't know [18] | Should help them | Should not help them or don't know |
| % who feel that Arab-Israel conflict will have an effect on domestic anti-Semitism | 51% (175) | 53% (53) | 52% (219) | 40% (10) |

TABLE 6

*Among Those Who Predict an Effect, Nonsupporters Foresee an Increase
in Anti-Semitism while Supporters Foresee a Decrease*

| | The United States Government | | Even if the United States does not help the Jews in Palestine, Jewish People in the United States | |
| --- | --- | --- | --- | --- |
| Direction of predicted effect of Arab-Israel conflict | Should help Jews | Should not help Jews or don't know [18] | Should help them | Should not help them or don't know |
| Increase in domestic anti-Semitism | 38% | 68% | 44% | 100% |
| Decrease in domestic anti-Semitism | 62 | 32 | 56 | 0 |
| | 100% (89) | 100% (28) | 100% (114) | 100% (4) |

held the opposite view. They were confident that the Palestine situation would serve to lessen anti-Semitism (see Table 6).

Not all proponents of aid who expected repercussions, however, shared these convictions. Some expressed fears similar to those voiced by the opponents of aid. They too were worried that the conflict might increase anti-Semitism. The presence of these anxieties was closely related to the *degree* and *kind* of support proffered by those who were pro-Israel (see Table 7).

Respondents who approved limited assistance to Israel were more pessimistic about the probable impact of the conflict on the domestic situation than were those who approved more extensive aid. Specifically, those who would have American Jews offer money, food, and clothing but not fighting men were more fearful of anti-Jewish repercussions than were those who would even support the sending of fighting men.

Those respondents who did not favor giving aid or who favored limited

TABLE 7

*Among Those Who Predict an Effect, Presumed Direction of Effect*
*Is Related to Kind of Support for Israel*

| Direction of predicted effect of Arab-Israel conflict | Even if the United States does not help Jews in Palestine, Jews in America should help them by sending food, clothing, and money | |
|---|---|---|
| | And also by going there to fight | But not by going there to fight |
| Increase in domestic anti-Semitism | 35% | 57% |
| Decrease in domestic anti-Semitism | 65 | 43 |
| | 100% | 100% |
| | (68) | (44) |

help tended to worry that non-Jews would blame the Arab-Israel conflict for disturbing the peace of the world, and as one respondent stated:

If there is trouble in this world, they will blame it on the Palestine situation.

They feared that the impatience or even anger of the non-Jew would be directed not only at Israel but also at Jews in other parts of the world, including the United States. Anti-Semitic sentiments could, accordingly, be expected to rise.

To offset or to minimize these repercussions from the conflict, these respondents would have American Jews assert their independence and separateness from the Jews of Israel. Some would do this by having American Jews refrain completely from helping Israel. Others were less extreme. They wanted American Jews to do something for Israel but would avoid having those things done or given which to their way of thinking might jeopardize their security and blur their identity as Americans in the eyes of the non-Jew. They would, therefore, confine aid to the philanthropic level—food, clothing, and money.

On the other hand, those who favored all kinds of aid for Israel were inclined to see the matter from an entirely different frame of reference. To them the crucial thing was that a small nation was meeting the challenge posed by powerful aggressors and that a struggle for independence and survival was being waged by Jews for their own nation. They felt that the courageous behavior of Israeli Jews was bound to evoke the admiration of non-Jews. As one respondent commented:

The Palestine situation will cause more respect when they [the Christians] see Jews fight for a country.

As a result, they were convinced that Israel's struggle with the Arabs, far from stimulating anti-Semitism in America, would reduce it by enhancing the stature of the Jew. And, since the battle Israel was waging would benefit Jews in America and elsewhere in the world, it was entitled to full-fledged and unreserved support, including the sending of volunteers.

While it would appear from the above that the kind of aid a respondent

TABLE 8

*Among Those Who Predict an Effect, Level of Involvement
with Israel Affects Direction of Predicted Effect*

| Direction of predicted effect of Arab-Israel conflict | Level of involvement with Israel | |
|---|---|---|
| | High | Low |
| Increase in domestic anti-Semitism | 28% | 58% |
| Decrease in domestic anti-Semitism | 72 | 42 |
| | 100% | 100% |
| | (49) | (69) |

endorsed was more a result than a determinant of his conception of the probable impact of the conflict on the domestic situation, it is equally apparent that the conception was itself largely a product of the respondent's basic attitude toward Israel. He projected into the future that which corresponded to his present feelings and concerns. If he was deeply attached and involved with Israel, then he was disinclined to see anything bad resulting from its struggle with the Arabs (see Table 8). He stressed the identity of interests of world Jewry and Israel and pointed to the various benefits that would accrue to all Jews from the conflict. He felt, therefore, that Jews were obligated to provide all-out support for Israel. On the other hand, if the respondent was relatively uninvolved with Israel, he was inclined to distinguish between the interests of Israel and those of other Jews and to entertain the notion that the conflict might have harmful consequences for the Jew in America. He would, therefore, minimize these effects by having American Jews provide Israel with nothing more than philanthropic assistance.

## VII. The Effect of Israel on Jewish Identification

Having examined reactions to assisting the newly founded State of Israel, we may next inquire into the impact of the fighting upon the feelings of Jews with respect to the problem of Jewish identification. Our respondents were asked, "Since the fighting in Palestine has been going on, do you feel any closer to the Jewish people as a whole, or don't you feel any closer?" Half of them reported that they now felt closer; half reported that they did not. Those who maintained that they did not could be classified into two distinct groups. About half, or 24 percent of the total sample, claimed that they had always felt close to other Jews, and presumably could not be moved to feel any closer. The remainder indicated that they had not in the past, and did not now, feel any strong bond with other Jews.

Respondents who said that they now felt closer were asked to explain why. Frequently they indicated that they commiserated with the Jews fighting for a homeland:

There are so many homeless Jews with no future.

They've been persecuted. They should have a homeland.

They're in distress and still having bloodshed after all these years.

Other answers seemed to express something in addition to sympathy, perhaps pride:

It's wonderful that the people are fighting for a country.

They're fighting for something they believe in and a worthy cause.

A number of comments could not be easily classified in terms of sympathy or pride. An example is the statement, "They're fighting for their very existence." Because many comments were of this unrevealing nature, it was not possible to ascertain the relative prevalence of specific sentiments behind a statement of greater closeness to the Jewish people. Actually, the wording of the comments suggests that "feeling closer" did not always represent intimate identification with the Jews who were fighting or who wanted a homeland. "*They've* been persecuted" or "*They're* fighting" indicates that considerable distance was still felt between the Jew safe in America and the Jew persecuted in Europe or fighting in Palestine.

There is evidence, however, that a certain proportion of those claiming that the Palestine fighting had drawn them closer to other Jews did experience greatly intensified feelings of identification. For, although these individuals were less likely to manifest strong Jewish identification than those claiming they had always felt close to the Jewish people (32 percent with strong Jewish identification as compared with 46 percent),[19] they were as highly involved in the Palestine fighting. Thus, of those who now felt closer to the Jewish people, 43 percent claimed that they would be willing to go to Palestine to fight. A similar proportion, 40 percent of those who said they had always felt close, were willing to make the same commitment.

Besides examining the effect of the Palestine conflict upon group identification, the study also inquired into its effect upon specific behavioral commitments to Jewish life. Respondents were asked whether they had joined any Jewish organizations during the preceding year. Out of the 230 persons interviewed, 28 people or 12 percent said they had. Of the 28, a total of 15 had joined Zionist or pro-Zionist organizations. A total of three had joined an anti-Zionist organization, and the remaining 10 joined groups that could be best classified as "non-Zionist." It is noteworthy that people who said they felt closer to Jewry as a result of the Palestine fighting were more likely to have joined Jewish organizations than were those who claimed that their feelings in this connection had not changed.

## VIII. Summary

Pro-Israel sentiments were almost universally found among our respondents. The intensity of their sentiments, though, varied with the extent of their commitment to Jewish life. Those with the strongest attachment to Jewish life and Judaism were most likely to have a deep personal stake in Israel and to be vitally concerned with its fate. In addition, commitment to Jewish life played a crucial role in the relationship between level of information about Israel and involvement with the country. It had to be present if increased knowledge was to draw a person closer to Israel.

Being pro-Israel posed no threat, insofar as most of our respondents were concerned, to loyalty to the United States. The two countries stood for two different kinds of commitments and ties, neither of which clashed with the other and both of which were essential to our respondents' total image of themselves as American Jews. However, if a choice between the two countries had to be made, then loyalty to the United States would prevail.

A major worry expressed by the small minority who did not favor aid to Israel, and also by those only mildly pro-Israel, was that domestic anti-Semitism might be aggravated by the Arab-Israel conflict. This anxiety muted their enthusiasm for Israel and bolstered their resistance to helping the new country. The more ardent pro-Israel respondent felt differently. He expected the conflict to reduce anti-Semitism in America, and he would have American Jews provide all-out support for Israel.

Finally, the fighting in Israel seemed to have intensified the feelings of identification of a number of Jews. It made them feel closer to the Jewish people as a whole.

## Notes

1. Samuel S. Flowerman was the director of AJC's Division of Scientific Research at the time. Other members of the staff connected with "The Palestine Study" included Eunice Cooper, Helen Dinerman, Patricia Kendall, Thelma Herman MacCormack, Dean Manheimer, Marion Strauss, and Ruth Landes.

2. For each of the original seventy-seven, interviewers were instructed to query two additional people of the same age group. Where a block contained only Jewish families, additional respondents were obtained from the adjacent block. When both Jewish and non-Jewish families occupied a block, interviewers asked the original respondents where other Jewish families lived on that block and selected the additional respondents from among these. When an original Jewish respondent was not available, another person of the same sex and age was substituted. The use of this type of quota method to expand a sample involves a number of methodological problems, but it was felt that the procedure did ensure a representation of Baltimore Jewry adequate for our purposes.

3. Because of reasons similar to those noted for the non-Jews, twenty-seven of the original respondents could not be reinterviewed.

4. Since the study was conducted so soon after the State of Israel was established, the term "Palestine" was still very much in use and was therefore employed in the interview. In our analysis of the data, however, we will frequently use "Israel."

5. It is interesting to note that our respondents, though they made the Palestine situation an important topic in their conversations with other people, did not depend primarily on these conversations for getting news about the conflict. They turned to the formal media of communications, principally the press. This is evident in their response to the following question: "Do you get most of your news about Palestine from the newspaper, radio, magazines, or where?" Their most frequent choice was the newspaper—66 percent selecting this medium. Their second and third choices were radio (41%) and magazines (9%), respectively. "Talking to people" was the fourth choice—only 6 percent mentioned it. (The various percentages exceed 100 since some mentioned that they utilized more than one news source.)

6. Respondents were considered to have knowledge that fighting was taking place in Palestine if they replied "Palestine" to either of the following two questions: "15. What do you consider the most important trouble spots in the world today?" or "16. (If Palestine not mentioned above [in answer to Question 15]): Are there any places where fighting is going on?" or if they answered "Yes" to the following question: "17. (If Palestine not mentioned in answer to Question 15 or Question 16): How about Palestine—is there fighting going on there?"

7. The Jewish and Christian respondents were each divided into two groups: (1) those possessing *high* knowledge (correct on all four items), (2) those possessing *low* knowledge (correct on three or less).

8. *Irgun Zvai Leumi* ("National Military Organization"), widely regarded as a terrorist group.

9. The close relationship between education and the two factors of income and age raised the possibility that the latter's correlation with level of information might be spurious, that it might be solely a function of education—age and income having no independent effect on level of information. Unfortunately, there were not enough cases to permit our testing this by controlling for level of education.

10. This concurred with the trend of Christian opinion. Gentiles too were more willing to recommend aid by Jews than by the United States Government.

11. We have no way of knowing whether the Jewish population of Baltimore was more pro-Israel than was that of other cities; however, it is apparent that a pro-Zionist orientation was fairly widespread among Baltimore Jewry. For example, more than half of the sample, 57 percent, stated that they had favored a Jewish State even before the advent of Hitler. Half of our respondents belonged to Jewish organizations classified as Zionist or pro-Zionist.

12. The "involvement" with which we are concerned refers to favorableness toward and closeness of ties with Israel. It is not to be confused with saliency of interest in matters bearing on Israel. Possession of a highly salient interest in Israel does not necessarily require a very favorable attitude toward the country. For example, members of the American Council for Judaism, though preoccupied with Israel, are among its severest critics. Obviously, such persons would not score high on our involvement index (see footnote 14), although they might score high on an interest or even on our general knowledge index.

13. Strength of identification was highly correlated with nativity, education, and age. Foreign-born Jews were much more likely to manifest strong Jewish iden-

tification (57%) than were native-born (21%); the less educated were more likely to fall into this group (46%) than the better educated (21%); and people over thirty-five (52%) rather than people under thirty-five (12%).

14. The Index of Personal Involvement was composed of the two previously mentioned items: "If you could, would you like to be in the Palestine fighting, too?," "Do you ever talk with other people about the Palestine situation?" along with a third: "Since the Palestine fighting has been going on, do you feel any closer to the Jewish people as a whole, or don't you feel any closer?" Those who had at least two of the following responses: "Yes" for the first question, "A great deal" for the second, and "Yes, closer" for the third were defined as having a *high* personal involvement in the Palestine situation.

15. It is interesting to note that among non-Jews there was a positive correlation between knowledge about the Palestine situation and support of Israel.

16. There were several other reasons offered by respondents for opposing aid to Israel. One, voiced by only a few, was expressed in terms of "Realpolitik." Israel was too small to expect to survive in a world of larger and more stable nations:

> I don't think a Jewish State has any right to be. It's based on incorrect reasoning on the part of Jews that they can maintain a small nation on the same footing as the nations are today.

In addition, there were a few who disapproved of the new State because they felt that Jews were properly a religious and not a national group:

> Jews are a people of a certain religion and not nationality. The Jews in Europe who are enslaved should be allowed into many countries.

While thus "rationally" opposed, these people tended, nevertheless, to want to help the Jews in Palestine. Furthermore, they could understand and sympathize with the desire of American Jews to help the Jewish State in spite of their opposition to its establishment:

> From a . . . brotherly-love standpoint, they [the Jews] would be right to help the Jewish State.

Their position was analogous to that taken by those Christian liberals who objected to a Jewish State for political or intellectual reasons but who nevertheless sympathized with Jewish aspirations for statehood.

17. Among non-Jews, factors such as a low level of prejudice, high educational level, and high level of information went hand-in-hand with interest in the Palestine situation and support for Israel. On the other hand, a high degree of prejudice and low educational level went hand-in-hand with lack of interest in Palestine and opposition to Israel.

*No evidence was found to support the hypothesis that the Palestine situation was causing an increase in anti-Semitism.* In fact, there is some evidence—requiring further validation—that the reverse may have been true. There is also no evidence to support the hypothesis that the Palestine situation resulted in any basic feeling among Christians that Jews were lacking in loyalty to the United States. Here, too, the reverse seems to hold. Most Christians expressed confidence in the national loyalty of American Jews. Among the least prejudiced, it appeared that esteem for Jews increased with improved Jewish fortunes in the war between Israel and Arab nations.

18. This is taken from our questionnaire item: "Do you think the United States Government should help the Jews in Palestine, should they help the Arabs, or should they help neither?" We have also reclassified the original responses to fit

our revised version. Included in our category, "Should help Jews," are those who responded in the following manner to the original question: "Help Jews" or "Help both Jews and Arabs." Since no one chose "Help Arabs," our category, "Should not help Jews or don't know," includes only those who in response to the original question said, "Help neither" or "Don't know."

19. Those who claimed that they did not feel close to the Jewish people were least strongly identified as Jews. Only 21 percent manifested strong Jewish identification.

# Lakeville and Israel:
# The Six-Day War and Its Aftermath

T he response of American Jewry to the Crisis in Israel in April–May of
1967, to the Six-Day War that followed, to the Israeli victory, and to
the State of Israel from that time to the present, is as yet imperfectly
understood. While a veritable flood of books has appeared about the War—
the events that preceded it, the strategy on which it was based, and even the
attitudes of Israeli soldiers engaged in the struggle—no comparable literature
has emerged on events in the American Jewish community and on the attitudes
of American Jews. In fact, we do not as yet have even a simple chronicle of the
response to the War in a single American community.

The story of American Jewry and the Six-Day War will, of course, be a subject of scholarly inquiry in the years ahead, especially on the part of historians
who will seek to reconstruct the past by the use of documentary sources. But
the events are too momentous, and their significance for the understanding of
Jewish identity too crucial, to await the ultimate verdict of historians. Much
can be learned by studying what is readily available, especially by probing the
feelings and actions of both average citizens and community leaders. In fact,
data about such feelings and actions, if gathered close enough to the period
in which the events took place, may provide the type of understanding that is
difficult to come by from more conventional historical sources.

In the early months of 1968 we returned to Lakeville—where fieldwork had
been conducted a decade earlier on the problem of Jewish identity—to learn
something about the response to the Israel Crisis, to the War, and to its aftermath. Lakeville, located in the Middle West, is a suburb of Lake City, one of the
leading industrial and commercial centers of the nation. Lakeville's history as a
suburb goes back to the turn of the century, when it attracted members of the
Gentile upper class who proceeded to build very commodious, even luxurious,
summer homes, and estates in the community. As transportation improved,
Lakeville became their year-round place of residence. Shortly before World

War I the industrialist who was the most widely respected member of the Jewish community of Lake City, by both his fellow Jews and Gentiles, bought an estate in the area. His choice signified both to the Jewish upper class as well as to the Jewish middle class that Lakeville and the adjoining communities were to be the preferred locations for Jewish suburbanites.

Lakeville grew slowly in Jewish population during the 1920's, most of the new residents being upper-class and upper-middle-class German Jews. During this period the first Jewish religious institution was established: the Isaac Mayer Wise Temple. The Great Depression saw few Jewish newcomers, but soon after World War II a heavy migration of Jews from Lake City took place. Lakeville attracted the more prosperous and the more highly educated of the new Jewish suburbanites of the 1940's, '50's, and '60's. But although on the whole wealthier, better educated, more urbane, less traditionally Jewish, and less ethnocentric than the average new Jewish suburbanite of Lake City, the majority of Jewish newcomers were different from the Jewish old-timers in the community. For one thing, they were from East European stock, rather than from the more acculturated German-Jewish one.

The influx of new Jewish residents had profound implications for Lakeville's Jewish institutional structure. Many new Jewish groups were established, including branches of most of the major national Jewish organizations. Even the Isaac Mayer Wise Temple was transformed. The Classical Reform Jews who had established the institution were displaced, and they proceeded to establish the David Einhorn Temple. Einhorn grew out of a religious school established in the community by the American Council for Judaism. Two other Reform congregations were founded in the post–World War II era. The Max Lilienthal Temple serves the younger and newer suburbanites of East European lineage whose income is on the modest side by Lakeville standards. The Samuel Hirsch Temple is noted for its image as the "thinking-man's" temple; it ranks higher than any of the other congregations in the proportion of its members who are college graduates, and it includes families of both East European and German-Jewish stock. Conservative Judaism is represented in Lakeville by the Solomon Schechter Synagogue, a large and vigorous institution. Efforts to establish an Orthodox synagogue in Lakeville have been unavailing.*

There have been no startling changes in Jewish institutional life in Lakeville since the community was originally studied a decade ago. In the attitudinal area change has been slow as well: there is nothing to suggest that prior to May–June 1967 feelings of Jewish identity were in strong movement, either in a positive or negative direction. People do feel that there has been a gradual increase in the frequency of intermarriage. But they also feel that there is greater interest in Jewish education for both adults and the young.

* For details about the community and the findings of the original study see Marshall Sklare and Joseph Greenblum, *Jewish Identity on the Suburban Frontier: A Study of Group Survival in the Open Society*, New York: Basic Books, 1967.

The Crisis, and the Six-Day War that followed, altered the picture of orderly communal evolution and attitudinal change. All observers in Lakeville attest to the fact that no event during the past decade has had an impact upon feelings of Jewish identity comparable to that of the War. Yet there is no agreement about what the impact was, why it occurred, the extent of its duration, and its eventual result.

A definitive assessment of these challenging questions must await the mounting of a full-scale sociological assault. The present effort is in the nature of a reconnaissance: a series of relatively unstructured interviews with seventeen Lakeville residents, eleven of whom were among the 432 persons interviewed in the original sample.

A reconnaissance effort, by definition, is only a beginning, although if successful it may contribute measurably to present understanding as well as to the strategy of future research. But first there is the problem of evaluation. Should Lakeville's response be considered on the high or the low side when we think in terms of the nation at large? In evaluating Lakeville's response we must bear in mind that the community does not have the reputation of being a hotbed of pro-Zionist sentiment. For example, in contrast to some less statusful suburbs and inner-city Jewish neighborhoods where the most popular Jewish women's group is Hadassah, in Lakeville, Women's ORT occupies this position. Furthermore, there has been a very small but recognizable segment of the community identified with the American Council for Judaism. As we have noted, some years ago this group was strong enough to establish a religious school in the community, and as an outgrowth of this school the David Einhorn Temple was established. While the connection between Einhorn and the ACJ is quite different today from what it once was (the Temple now belongs to the Union of American Hebrew Congregations), the fact that such an institution was established means that there was a group of residents whose family background included a non-Zionist or anti-Zionist tradition. Lakeville has its Zionists of course (including some who are leaders of Zionist organizations), as well as an extremely large group who are pro-Israel. Yet while there are Lakeville residents who have made large financial contributions to Israeli causes, Lakeville is not the type of community where one would look for a maximum response to the Six-Day War (unless of course one is prepared to argue that the maximum response occurred in precisely the wealthier, more acculturated Jewish communities). Thus if we find that a given impact occurred in Lakeville, it would be fair to infer that this impact was at least as strong in the country at large.

## Concern and Interest

Our respondents remember being very anxious during the days in April–May 1967 when the crisis was developing. Their anxiety was greatly heightened by the doubts that they had concerning the ability of Israel to withstand the might of the Arab armies. Such doubts can best be illustrated by the two respondents who found themselves under cross-pressures to shift from a feeling of anxiety to a feeling of confidence. In both cases the impetus was provided by Israelis. In the first instance the Israeli was a houseguest of one of our respondents who had come to the United States on a fund-raising mission for a specialized Israeli institution. In the other case the cross-pressure was provided by a neighbor, a *yored* [an emigrant from Israel], who had recently settled in Lakeville after reputedly having made a "killing" on the stock market.

Both of our respondents were more troubled than reassured by what these Israelis told them, namely, that there was nothing to worry about and that Israel would be able to take care of its enemies without much trouble. Our first respondent—the one with the houseguest—reported that in spite of his great esteem for his visitor he became hostile to him on the basis that he was so lacking in feeling as not to experience the anxiety the respondent himself felt. The respondent with the *yored* for a neighbor had other problems. While the *yored* lived in luxurious style, he had rebuffed our respondent when the latter had approached him for a donation to a Jewish charitable cause. Our respondent felt that his neighbor was an insincere person who was putting up a brave front since he refused to acknowledge how difficult was the situation of beleaguered Israel and how much his help was needed.

If the two respondents who were under cross-pressures did not have their fears relieved, our respondents as a whole were left undisturbed with their anxieties. If the optimism of the two Israelis was typical of the mood in Israel at the time—as we think it was—then our respondents' fears may in part be traced to their very distance from Israel and Israelis; were they more involved they would have been less worried. But even more must be at stake. The man on the fund-raising mission who told his host to stop aggravating himself was resented. Thus a psychological reaction probably occurred, namely, that if the Israelis are bearing the brunt of the struggle, the least that we comfortably situated American Jews can do is worry. Those who would deprive us of this function will make us feel like bad Jews whereas we wish to consider ourselves to be good Jews. However, in spite of their anxieties our respondents were able to carry on with their normal routines. Only one reported psychosomatic symptoms.

*The feeling of our respondents was unambiguously pro-Israel. There was no doubt in their minds as to which side was right. Support for Israel seems to have increased as the Crisis deepened, undoubtedly because it evoked unconscious feelings.*

We shall have occasion to return to the problem of unconscious feelings; at this point we only wish to highlight the strength of pro-Israel sentiment. The depth of support for Israel during the Crisis and War can perhaps be gauged from the reactions of a respondent whom we shall call Robert Himmel. Himmel is a board member of the Einhorn Temple and a longtime member of the

American Council for Judaism. He traces his lineage to pioneer German Reform stock. Himmel now considers himself "pro-Israel and anti-Zionist." His justification for supporting Israel during the Crisis and War was that: "It is the only democracy out there [in the Middle East]. It is important for the United States from a strategic point of view." When Rabbi Elmer Berger came out with a statement critical of Israel during the period of the Crisis and War, Himmel reacted strongly. He wrote Berger a long and blistering letter (he instantly put his hands on the correspondence). Himmel did not object to the content of Berger's statement: "What Berger said was right but it was bad timing. I hate negativism. If he couldn't say anything good about Israel why couldn't he have kept his big yap shut?"

Our respondents felt so highly involved that their appetite for news during the Crisis and the War was well nigh insatiable. While they do not ordinarily listen to news broadcasts on transistor radios, such devices were pressed into service. One woman took her radio with her when she kept an appointment at her hairdresser. There was some radio listening in business offices, a most unusual procedure for our respondents. One woman reported an almost insatiable hunger for news comparable to what she had experienced when President Kennedy was assassinated.

Many of our respondents watched the debates at the United Nations far into the night. As they saw it, the hero of the drama that unfolded there was Abba Eban. All were entranced by Eban. His presentation was felt to be both logical and stirring, his case airtight, his mind colossal, his oratory magnificent. One respondent felt that Eban far surpassed Churchill at his best. All felt Eban to be the perfect Israeli and the perfect representative of Israel. Their overwhelming enthusiasm for Eban would suggest that they saw him as their representative as well, and they were gratified that he provided them with a model they could so readily identify with. None of our respondents seem to be aware that their feeling that Eban is the perfect Israeli is not shared by all Israelis.

If Eban was judged to be a Jewish superman, the representatives of the Arab states were regarded with contempt. Their presentations were seen as fraudulent, their motives as sinister, their corruption complete. The speeches of the Arab representatives—and those of their Communist allies—only confirmed our respondents in their pro-Israel opinions.

## American Loyalties versus Support for Israel

Our respondents were not only united behind Israel but the Crisis and War was a case where they did not experience any strain between their national loyalties and their support for a foreign country. Or better, they strove not to perceive any such strain. The fact that Gentiles did not press for such a strain was very helpful to them.

The desire not to perceive any strain is exemplified by a respondent who was thrilled at the Jewish response to the Crisis and who was firm in his support of Israel. He then added "I'm a firm believer that what affects other countries affects us as well," as much as to say that any right-thinking American would have supported the Israeli cause out of the national interest.

In the present instance the possibility of a strain was provided not by anti-Semites, not by the general public, and not even by the American government, but, surprisingly, by the government of Israel when it made the decision to attack the *U.S.S. Liberty*. But even this incident did not, in most cases, affect the feeling of our respondents that good Americanism and good Jewishness were one and indivisible. Some interpreted the incident, in which thirty-four U.S. sailors died, as the type of accident that is inevitable in a fast-moving war. They suggested that if it had been known that the *Liberty* was an American ship there would not have been an attack. Others, however, viewed the attack as deliberate—as a move by the Israelis to preserve their sovereignty and security. These respondents felt that the *Liberty* had no right being where it was (some interpreted the *Pueblo* incident along much the same lines). Many of these respondents supported the Israelis in their action, while others showed under-standing even if they did not support it. But whether the action was viewed as deliberate or accidental, there are those who remember being concerned at the time about the Gentile response. There is, for example, the man who recalls being "concerned that bigoted people might fasten on the incident and try to make the most out of it."

The strongest criticism of Israeli actions in respect to the *Liberty* came from a respondent who considered himself a firm supporter of Israel rather than from a present or former member of the ACJ. This respondent felt that the action was deliberate. He recalls his sentiment at the time: the incident was a "catastrophe." The Israelis had no right to proceed as they did because it meant hurting their staunchest supporter, the U.S. Government: "the Israelis should remember you don't bite the hand that feeds you." But in actuality this respondent was much more concerned with the welfare of American Jews than with the relationship between the two governments: "you don't complicate the position of American Jews who want to support Israel." In spite of his feelings against Israel for its action against the *Liberty*, there is no reason to suspect that this respondent shifted to a lower level of support. His strong reaction can be accounted for by the fact that, having considered himself pro-Israel for many years, he began to perceive a strain between his loyalties as an American and as a Jew.

## Ensuring an Israeli Victory

The story is told of an ultra-Orthodox Jew who, in the midst of the siege of Jerusalem during the War of Independence, went around the city proclaiming: "Jews, do not rely on miracles! Recite Psalms!" While prayers and Psalm saying are traditional Jewish responses to impending catastrophe, there is little reason to suspect that they were much in evidence in Lakeville during the Crisis and War. We did not probe our respondents on this score, but none volunteered information that would suggest any increase in personal devotions. (It is entirely possible, however, that prayers and Psalms were recited during the Crisis and War in various congregations during the course of their regularly scheduled services.)

If personal devotions were something that the Lakeville Jew was incapable of, he was able to perform a traditional act of another sort: the giving of money. In fact the giving of money is not only viewed as an act of solidarity with Israel but as having helped to ensure an Israeli victory.

Strange as it may seem, our respondents even today connect their own actions with the Israeli victory. If the winning of any war ever depends upon superior financial means, the Six-Day War was not such a war: by the time the first public (if not private) fund-raising meetings could be convened, victory was a foregone conclusion. But sober businessmen long experienced in problems of procurement, of manufacturing, and of transportation, acted as if the money they contributed one day could somehow miraculously be turned into the sinews of war the very next day. Because they wanted to believe in such a miracle, the emphasis was not upon pledges—the usual form of Jewish fund-raising—but on a different approach: the giving of cash. And when the imminence of the Israeli victory forced another justification for the fund-raising, and especially for the giving of cash, the following approach was articulated: "Since the costs of the War have been so great, Israeli resources have been completely depleted. Unless we help, Israel will become bankrupt, and the victory will be in vain." American Jewish money, then, would keep Israel from losing the peace.

The agency charged with the responsibility of organizing the drive for contributions to Israel from Lakeville Jews is the United Jewish Welfare Federation and Council of Lake City (JWF). This organization sponsored a drive for the Israel Emergency Fund. However, since grass-roots sentiment was so strong, drives were started on local initiative. Thus some of the religious institutions in Lakeville proceeded to organize campaigns; such campaigns, of course, were soon coordinated into the plans of the JWF. Nevertheless, the synagogue drives were more spontaneous than the JWF campaign, and at the outset they were relatively free from professional control. Although the largest gifts were given through JWF channels, it was the synagogue drives where grass-roots sentiment was apparent in its most pure and unsophisticated form. Thus, these drives hold a special interest for us.

Four of the five synagogues in the Lakeville area sponsored such drives. A detailed report on one of them—the drive sponsored by the Samuel Hirsch Temple—is presented below. This meeting eventuated from an extraordinary session of the Temple board, which had been convened on the evening of June 5th in response to the news that war had just broken out that morning in Israel. The information below is from an interview with the congregation's spiritual leader, Rabbi Samuel Aaron:

At the meeting Monday night the immediate thought was to raise money. It was clear that the money would be for the Emergency Fund but there was some complication with the [Israel] Bonds people, who wanted in. However, it was the feeling that they should not be in and some compromise was arranged in that Bonds were not sold from the rostrum but the chairman announced that officials of the Bond campaign were in the audience, that they had blanks, and that if anybody wanted to purchase Bonds he should see these men and women in the audience.

The Monday night planning meeting was attended by Joe Cohen, who is on the staff of the JWF. Cohen came to the meeting late, tired from the many meetings that he had already attended. There was a decided lack of rapport between him and Rabbi Aaron and it was necessary for peace to be made between the two men. Apparently some people at the meeting lined up on the side of Cohen but more seemed to line up on the side of Rabbi Aaron. Cohen wanted to hold the Wednesday meeting in usual Jewish fund-raising style, to call cards, to announce donations in order of magnitude and to do all the things that go on at these affairs. Aaron felt that this was completely inappropriate and that Cohen did not understand the nature of the crisis and the mood of the people. Cohen wanted a big-name speaker. Rabbi Aaron burlesqued his approach as follows: "We'll even get you a guest speaker who died in the War." The people at the Monday night meeting who wanted to do it the Cohen way were those people who were old JWF people and not really active Temple people. It was finally decided there would be no calling of cards, that people could get up in any order in which they wished to, that they would not need to announce any amounts, and that they could say anything they wanted and not only announce a gift. It was also decided that no refreshments would be served. No guest speaker was to be invited.

Some 500 families belong to the congregation. It was decided to send a telegram to each. When these were ordered there was immediately a problem at the local Western Union office: there was not sufficient manpower to deliver the telegrams. The youth [of the Temple] helped out, although some were in school and Aaron is not quite sure how all the telegrams got delivered. There was some annoyance at the telegram approach. Some people resented being disturbed by deliveries made in the middle of the night. There were some people who were against the idea of the telegram itself, and perhaps some who objected to the expense connected with it.

About 500 showed up on Wednesday night. In trying to estimate what percentage of the families of the congregation were represented, Aaron arrived at the figure of 55 percent. The people who had arranged the meeting had hoped for more. However, this was the largest meeting that had ever been held in the building. It attracted more people than on any other occasion in the history of the congregation except for the High Holidays.

The president of the congregation opened the meeting. Part of his job, he felt, was to justify the convoking of this extraordinary gathering. Aaron said "he is not a *farbrenter* Zionist" and therefore he had to put the meeting in context for the audience but even more for himself. The spirit at the meeting and the spirit during the week at the congregation was fantastic. More than on any other occasion the congregation was unified.

There was some problem at the Wednesday night meeting because the feeling of threat had been dissipated and by that time the Israeli victory was quite clear. Aaron took the approach at the meeting that even if the War would be won the disruption of the economy would be tremendous and that economic troubles might make Israel go down in the end. Money was therefore needed not so much to win the War but to keep the country alive.

Aaron is not sure how much money was actually raised at the meeting but it was an extremely large amount. The JWF was contacting people simultaneously and there was some confusion. They were also skimming off the cream by talking to the really big donors, so that from this point of view the meeting could be viewed as an anti-climax. It was not an anti-climax for any of the women, however, for they had not been contacted by the JWF.

The entire meeting was cash oriented. A great many checks were handed in; people not only wanted to pledge money but they actually wanted to give cash at the meeting. Several people got up and said that they had arranged for a bank loan so that they could give the cash. Another man got up to say that Baron Rothschild in Paris has sold his race horses to raise cash. Aaron found this example of "privation" hardly inspiring.

The entire meeting on Wednesday night lasted only one hour and ten minutes. People stood around afterward. They were reluctant to go home. Everyone told Aaron, who was the principal speaker, that his presentation was wonderful. He felt it was not, that it wasn't as good as it should have been.

There are intimations in this interview that giving is seen as a religious act. Hence the criticism of those who would secularize or in some other way corrupt it. It is difficult to say whether other respondents feel the same way as Rabbi Aaron. What we do find in quite a number of interviews is the mention of heroic acts of giving—of individuals who could not afford to give what they did. Not all such acts are known personally to our respondents—some are the result of second- or third-hand information. But some of those that are known at first-hand may strike the observer as less than heroic. For example, one of our respondents who is in the banking business was amazed to find that individuals came in to his bank to arrange loans so that they might make their Emergency Fund donations in cash. However, while the loaning of money in order to give charity deviates widely from the philanthropic norms of our culture, it actually says little about what proportion of his wealth the individual is giving away.

We avoided probing the respondent too deeply about the size of his own donation to the Emergency Fund, lest rapport be interfered with. But in only a single case is there even a possibility that a family might have temporarily had to deny themselves something to which they were accustomed. There is also a case among our respondents of a family that thought it might be necessary to cancel their summer vacation because of their Emergency Fund contribution. However, they finally decided to go through with their plans.

All of our respondents who gave to the Emergency Fund had enough ready cash to cover their gifts. None say that they had to resort to bank loans or to the selling of securities in order to meet their obligations. Respondents did not claim that they personally gave in a heroic manner: few if any who participated in the Emergency Fund campaign claim that their giving was of such a magnitude as to make a noticeable dent in their personal assets.

Focussing exclusively on the question of the magnitude of the gift, however, creates the danger that we lose sight of the significance of gift giving. This is particularly so in the case of first-time givers. One of the most interesting types of first-time givers is the kind whose previous non-giving is based on a lack of contact with Jewish life rather than on ideological considerations or psychological makeup. An example of such a non-giver who became a first-time giver is Mrs. Mildred Fried. Of all of our respondents Mrs. Fried is closer to being assimilated than any of the others interviewed. Thus she lacks any of the points of contact that Mr. Himmel, the anti-Zionist, has with Jewish life. Mrs. Fried follows no religious practices in her home, does not belong to a synagogue or a Jewish organization, and has not given her children a Jewish education. A salaried professional woman, she has been criticized by Jewish and Gentile colleagues for working on Yom Kippur, but she feels that she would be perpetrating a fraud if she remained at home. In contrast to most of our other respondents, Mrs. Fried has a number of close friends who are Gentile. In spite of all this Mrs. Fried leads an underground Jewish life. While she has never disapproved of the idea of intermarriage, she was secretly pleased when her daughter married a Jewish boy. While she has never given her Gentile friends any reason to suspect she is ethnocentric, she feels that "there is a certain 'ego' in being Jewish. Gentiles can't keep up with Jews."

Mrs. Fried was as emotionally involved as any of our respondents with the Crisis and the War. She was glued to the TV set, watching the UN debates far into the night and relishing each word of Abba Eban. She has saved the newspapers of June 6–11: "This is history, and this I wanted to keep." She made a contribution to the Emergency Fund. This is the first time she can remember doing anything for Israel. Giving a contribution was more complicated in her case than in others. Not appearing on any membership list of a synagogue or Jewish organization, she received no telegram summoning her to a meeting, and she had to go out of her way to find out where contributions should be sent.

Mrs. Fried's desire to donate to the Emergency Fund was not an uncomplicated act of generosity but was intimately connected with the meaning that the struggle had for her. According to our record:

The five days after the first day of the struggle Mrs. F. described as "pure ecstasy." Israel was performing miracles. She was deeply touched by what was happening. She felt that no more does the Jew march to the ovens. Now he has something to fight for.

Later in the interview Mrs. Fried told us about a letter she had received from her son who was at graduate school:

"Bill wrote to me how proud he was to be a Jew at this time. He had told me before that he could not understand why the Jews walked to the gas chambers." Mrs. F. says that her boy believes in fighting back. He could not understand his grandfather and previous generations who lived by "backing away." Her implication was that while she had tried to explain this to Bill, she could not really understand it herself. Now no more explanations are needed.

The interview concludes on the following note:

Mrs. F. emphasized that the Six-Day War was an enormous event in human history. "We have never fought back before. We always picked up our bundles and ran. Now we can fight back."

Mrs. Fried's donation, then, is intimately connected with her desire to assist those who, according to her understanding, were putting an end to Jewish behavior with which she could not identify—behavior that she had always been ashamed of.

Among the leaders of the David Einhorn Temple we find a different situation, for there we encounter cases where people have been approached year after year to contribute to Israel but have refused to do so, presumably because of ideological considerations. One of the leaders whom we interviewed persisted in non-giving and refused to make a contribution to the Emergency Fund. But we also interviewed other leaders of the Temple who made a first-time contribution to Israel. Unlike Mrs. Fried, both non-givers as well as first-time givers seek to justify their respective actions. According to non-givers, money given to the Emergency Fund would continue the tradition of the United Jewish Appeal that draws no distinction between philanthropic and political purposes; it uses its funds for the illegitimate purpose of stimulating *aliyah* to Israel, including the *aliyah* of American Jews. Thus, according to one board member of the Einhorn Temple, the JWF utilized the Six-Day War to raise funds far beyond anything they had previously conceived of, the JWF was "hysterical" and played upon the emotions of Jews, and the JWF never specified how the funds being given to the Emergency Fund were going to be used.

While this particular non-giver was well defended, he left us with the impression that he was not happy with his lack of giving. Two of his fellow board members—contributors to the Philanthropic Fund of the ACJ—had, on the other hand, donated to the Emergency Fund. These men were obviously happy that they made a decision for Israel. Their decision, however, was more a break with principles than a sacrifice of substance. While both are substantial businessmen, one stated that his contribution was $50, and the other did not reveal his gift. We infer it was also a pittance. Yet such token giving had deep significance for these men, for they were doing their bit to assure an Israeli victory. One man repeated his old resentments against the JWF: "They send the money to Israel and it comes back here for propaganda purposes." But he felt that money contributed to the Emergency Fund was different: "It is being used for economic needs in Israel."

The Einhorn Temple held no fund-raising meetings for the benefit of the Emergency Fund. Yet the question of how the group should respond to the Crisis agitated the leadership of the Temple. Some wished to do nothing while others went so far as to suggest that a fund-raising meeting be held. A compromise was arranged: a letter was sent out under the signature of the president and the rabbi, stating that if a member wished to make a donation he should contact the temple office where he would be supplied with a list of Israeli causes. One member resigned from the Temple as a result of the letter.

One board member of the Einhorn Temple remained staunch in his criticism of the philanthropic response of the Jewish community. He felt that people were exploited and as a consequence far too much money was made available to the Emergency Fund. On the whole, however, our respondents were thrilled at what was done. They have knowledge of some of the sums given by the big givers, and they highly approve of such generosity. Those who gave do know people who did not give and they also cite cases of friends, relatives, neighbors, or business associates who did not give enough. But in the main our respondents feel that the level of generosity was extraordinary. The most critical is Abraham Weinberg, a strong supporter of Israel and of all the laymen whom we interviewed the most devout, the most highly involved in Jewish life, and the most concerned with giving his children an intensive Jewish education. On his own initiative Weinberg organized a parlor meeting for the benefit of the Emergency Fund. About $5,000 were raised among his neighbors at this meeting, but he told us: "They felt it was tremendous but I feel that the response was lukewarm. People were surprised and worried by their generosity."

One special aspect of this particular parlor meeting requires mention at this point. When the meeting was being organized there was a question concerning a Gentile who resided on the block. Since this man was particularly friendly with his Jewish neighbors he constituted a problem: if he was not invited he might feel insulted, but on the other hand, if invited he might feel compelled to give and thus be forced into participating in an act of Jewish solidarity. It was decided that he should be invited but that he be instructed that he was to come as a guest and thus was not to make a contribution. The man came but refused to act as instructed. He made a contribution of $100. He also gave an additional gift of $25 on behalf of his son.* He said he admired the Israelis and supported what he called their fight against the Arabs and against Communism.

*A number of our respondents did the same thing—wanting their children to participate, they made donations in their name.

Though money represented the dominant mode of response, there were other reactions as well. Little if anything was done by our respondents in terms of political activity, but one declared: "If it would have been necessary I would have contacted my Congressman." Others echoed the same sentiment. A further question was whether children should be encouraged to go to Israel to help. Our respondents were generally passive in this regard. There were one or two who had a problem, however, for their children took the initiative and said that they wanted to go during the Crisis. The tendency of these parents was to temporize. Thus Mr. Weinberg's oldest son wanted to go, but he prevailed upon the boy to finish the term at college. In one family, however, there was an offer of support when a child indicated a desire to go to Israel. This is the Fried family—the most alienated among our respondents. But their youngster did not get to Israel: in spite of the approval of his parents, he was prevented from pursuing his objective of rendering personal assistance to Israel because of circumstances irrelevant to our present study.

## The Mass Media and Attitudes in the General Society

The problem presented by the Gentile on the block leads us to a consideration of the relationship between minority and majority. We have already discussed this problem in terms of the possible conflict between divergent loyalties, especially as these were highlighted by the Israeli attack on the *U.S.S. Liberty*. Here we shall be concerned about what the respondent perceived to be the attitude of Gentiles with whom he associated, of the mass media, and of society at large.

Most of our respondents report that they were happy, even delighted with the coverage given to the conflict in the mass media. Even media they expected to be hostile gave a fair presentation. The only critical reaction they can remember was to be found in letters-to-the-editor columns where occasional anti-Israel sentiments could be encountered. While anti-Israel material was absent, the mass media contained considerable anti-Arab and anti-Russian comment. As one respondent put it: "It was clear that the Gentiles were with us against the Arabs."

If our respondents perceived the mass media as friendly, their contacts with Gentiles—on whatever level these occurred—reinforced the impression that the general community supported their position. *Most respondents reported an unambiguously positive reaction.* However, the wife of one respondent—a woman who works in an office where most of the employees are Gentile—reports that on the first day or two of the War the reaction was not too positive: "Then it abruptly changed for the better when the Israeli victory became apparent." Respondents were very pleasantly surprised to see the reaction of Gentiles. The respondent who appears to be the most surprised of all (he says he was "rather startled") is the board member of the Einhorn Temple whose negative comments about the Emergency Fund were quoted earlier.

Our respondents have different theories about why the Gentiles were sympathetic. One feels it was a case of Israeli cowboys against Arab Indians. Others introduce the theme that the anti-Soviet views of the public made them unusually receptive to a pro-Israel point of view. Yet another respondent says that while he feels Gentiles were basically pro-Israel, he suspects that Jews heard as much pro-Israel sentiment from Gentiles as they did because "it was said for the benefit of the listener."

One respondent is thoroughly distrustful of the Gentile response. This is Rabbi Aaron, who ordinarily spends little time in interfaith work but who was drawn into such activities during the Crisis and War as well as during the months that followed:

On June 7th Reverend James, the minister of a Presbyterian Church in the area (and one of the brightest and most pro-Jewish of the ministers in the area), had the idea of circulating a petition to support Israel. This petition was never published, however, because not enough signatures of other ministers could be gathered. If only some of the ministers signed, it was felt that the publishing of the petition would do more harm than good. At the time of the blockade the rabbis in the area sought to promote a petition supporting the Israeli position, to be signed by ministers in the area. Aaron had been given about 15 names to call. He called all 15 and about eight or nine said yes. Other rabbis did not achieve such a high percent of assent. Since there was no clear consensus, this petition was dropped. Ministers who would not sign the petition generally responded by saying that the matter was a political one in which they could not interfere as ministers of the Gospel.

In addition to Reverend James, the other person who came to the fore during the blockade and crisis was the Unitarian minister in Lakeville. He sent a letter to his membership asking them to contribute to the Emergency Fund. It is Aaron's impression that this letter was signed by the president of the Unitarian Church as well as by the minister. This is the Church in which there are many Jewish-Gentile intermarriages and many people of Jewish lineage. The mood in the Church, as Aaron put it, was to show that "We Jewish Unitarians are doing our part."

The latest aspect of the Christian response is a gathering which had been held in the winter sponsored by the rabbis for the purpose of convincing Christian ministers that they had a long-range obligation to support Israel. It was first thought that the meeting should be held at the new sanctuary of the Isaac Mayer Wise Temple, but there was some question as to whether this was a good idea. The problem was whether the sanctuary was too showy and demonstrated too much wealth, and would therefore reinforce Gentile stereotypes.

Aaron is not quite sure how the meeting was financed, as this group has no treasury. He estimates the cost of the meeting was about $1,000. He wonders whether a Zionist group picked up the tab. The main speaker was the nationally known Rabbi Jacob Benjamin of New York, who spoke on the theological commitment of Jews to the State of Israel. He was followed in the afternoon session by a local man, Rabbi David Rose, who spoke about the Christian reaction to the Crisis and the War. Rose put the cards very much on the table, stressing that there was much less support from Christian leaders than the Jewish community expected. He stressed the great disappointment and shock the Jews experienced when they found what the Christian reaction was. Most of the ministers sat on their hands. The specific purpose of the meeting was to light a fire under these ministers. It was quite obvious that none was lit.

The meeting was predominantly a Protestant meeting, for only three or four Catholic priests were present. Aaron summarized his reaction by saying that: "We Jews are dealing with a deep-seated and potentially very dangerous anti-Semitism in this ministerial group."

Except for Rabbi Aaron, then, our respondents perceive that Gentiles supported their own position toward the War. *Furthermore, our respondents feel the victory of the Israelis improved the status of American Jewry.* Perhaps the single deviant in this regard is the nongiver of the Einhorn Temple, quoted earlier. The most doctrinaire of the anti-Zionists whom we interviewed, this man stated: "Gentiles do not think that we American Jews are connected with Israel in any way." But other Einhorn board members took a very different view. One reported that: "the stature of the Jew rose." A Gentile associate with whom this man has done business for many years told him over the long-distance phone with obvious approval: "You Hebes really taught those guys a lesson." Another board member, who had resigned from the ACJ because "they fight Zionism unintelligently," found that Gentile business associates considered the Israeli victory to be his victory. He became more respected in their eyes because of the Israelis' feat of arms. This was the general view: that the American Jew had achieved new respect in the eyes of the Gentile because of the Israeli victory.

## The Problem of Long-Range Impact

Perhaps the most frequently asked question about the Crisis and the War is its long-range impact on the attitudes of American Jews. Does it represent a decisive turning point in feelings about Jewish identity in the restricted area of attitudes toward Israel and/or in the more general area of attitudes toward self? Does it portend a renaissance in American Jewish life, or will its impact—whatever it is estimated to be—gradually be dissipated by the inevitable march of other events that turn out to have greater meaning and relevance in the life of the individual?

These are difficult questions to answer on several counts—they require us not only to prognosticate but also to provide a definitive answer to the problem of what exactly it was that happened to American Jewry during the Crisis and War. In approaching this issue we shall first discuss the desire of our respondents to experience the victory at first-hand and to strengthen their ties to the country by visiting Israel in the aftermath of the Six-Day War.

### 1. Visiting Israel

In the original study we did not ask a question about visiting Israel: a decade ago travel to Israel was still an exceptional experience. Asking now about visiting, our assumption was that most of our respondents (particularly those who were over 40 and who were in the upper-middle or the upper class) would have visited Israel at least once during the intervening decade. But we were surprised at how few had done so. *We were particularly surprised that as late as February of 1968 not a single one of our respondents had visited Israel since the War.* Furthermore, with a single exception—a family we shall call the Melvin Whites—none had at the time any definite plans to visit Israel.

The lack of any compelling desire to go to Israel during the summer of 1967 or in subsequent months is highlighted by the case of Philip Green. Mr. Green, who is in his early sixties, is a wealthy owner of a wholesale electric supply house. He lives in a very comfortable ranch house situated on one of Lakeville's best streets. As is apparent from the following extract from his interview, Green experienced as strong a pro-Israeli reaction during the Crisis and War as any of our respondents. In respect to the Six-Day War, Green said:

"I was never so vehement about anything in my life. I was practically ready to go over to fight." Green doesn't know why he reacted in the way he did, but he knows that he had never felt anything like this before. He went to a fund-raising affair at the Isaac Mayer Wise Temple, where he is a longtime member. He gave more than he had ever given before. At the fund-raising affair he made a contribution in the name of each of his children. He wanted them to participate in some way.

Green—the only one of our respondents who spontaneously mentioned the phantasy of fighting for Israel—has never been to Israel and has no plans for going. When asked about travel plans he seized upon the President's recommendations against nonessential foreign travel:

In respect to travel Green feels he is an American as well as a Jew and therefore the welfare of this country has to be considered. Thus, if travel to Israel has to be deferred because of the balance of payments, so be it.

Green's apathy about travel suggests that there was in his case, and by extension in others', a strong unconscious element in the reaction to the Crisis and the War. Like others, he could not explain why he reacted in the way he did.

The Melvin Whites are the exception—they are the only family that has made definite plans to visit Israel. This youngish family lives in a luxurious home on a heavily wooded site; it was once the estate of a member of the "400." Mr. and Mrs. White travel abroad regularly, sometimes with their three sons. Indeed they are the most fashionable people we interviewed in Lakeville: they travel more, play more, spend more, and seem to have better connections than any of our other respondents. Their style-of-life conveys a strong "JFK" image. To quote from the interview:

The White family was in Israel two years ago for the first time, spending eleven "very full" days in the country. Mr. White, who has developed an important manufacturing business, was shown various projects in Israel. The family was apparently given the VIP treatment. However, to the best of Mrs. W.'s information her husband did not subsequently make any investment in Israel.

The Whites were taken to S'de Boker to meet Ben-Gurion. He asked the boys when they were coming to live in Israel. The second thing he asked them was whether they spoke Hebrew. Receiving a negative response to both questions, he "bawled us out." Ben-Gurion told the Whites that the next time they would meet he wanted the boys to speak to him in Hebrew.

They met "wonderful, wonderful people" in Israel. The study of their home has many framed color photos of their guide, people they had met at kibbutzim, officials of the Histadrut, factory managers, and prominent personalities: Eshkol, Ben-Gurion, Teddy Kollek, Golda Meir. Mrs. W. emphasized again and again the wonderful, wonderful people they met and how very lucky the family was to have these connections. The boys were very impressed with Israel.

From Israel they visited Greece and Italy. They enjoyed these countries, but there are very few pictures in the study about their visit there. The exception is a photo of Mr. and Mrs. W. with Pope Paul. Mr. W. is a generous contributor to a Catholic university located in Lake City.

Mr. and Mrs. White are going to Europe in March for a vacation. After sightseeing and winter sports they have made arrangements to spend several days in Israel. Thus, they will be the first of our respondents to see the country after the awesome events of June, 1967. But even they will not have planned a special trip to Israel—they will jet to Lydda after their European expedition is concluded. But the Whites do want to see what has happened since their first visit, and especially the changes that have occurred since the Six-Day War. Mrs. White looks forward to renewing her acquaintance with the people she met before. She experienced a quality with Israelis that she finds lacking in her friends and neighbors in Lakeville: "they have been making great sacrifices for their country and it is a wonderful place because there is a strong feeling of nationalism and of giving oneself to a cause."

## 2. Shifts in the Level of Pro-Israel Support

In our original study a six-point scale was used to measure the level of pro-Israel support. Interviewees were asked to respond positively or negatively to the following types of support:

Raise money for Israel
Seek to influence U.S. foreign policy in favor of Israel
Belong to Zionist organizations
Give Israeli financial needs priority over local Jewish causes
Encourage their children to immigrate to Israel
Participate personally in the building of Israel through becoming a citizen of Israel

Some 93 percent approved of raising money, 63 percent of influencing foreign policy, 31 percent to belonging to Zionist organizations, 14 percent to giving Israeli needs priority, and 1 percent to both of the items on *aliyah*.

This scale was administered to ten of the eleven respondents who were part of the original sample, with the following results:

Same Response        5
One-Step Increase    2
Two-Step Increase    1
One-Step Decrease    2

Half of our former respondents, then, would extend the same level of support today as a decade ago. These five individuals include two who only go so far as raising money, two who approve raising money and also influencing U.S. foreign policy, and one who approves of belonging to a Zionist organization and giving Israeli needs priority as well. The two individuals who increased by one step were both money approvers who moved up to the influence-foreign-policy level. The single individual who increased by two steps moved from a zero score to approving money and influence. The two individuals who experienced a two-step decline formerly approved of money, influence, and belonging to Zionist organizations; they no longer approve of Zionist organizations.

Very surprisingly, then, the Crisis and War do not appear to have made any real impact on levels of pro-Israel support. Our respondents are not ready to go farther today than they were a decade ago. There are those who have moved up a step, but their example has been balanced by those who have moved down.* Finally, the single case of a two-step increase does not represent a conversion from a medium level of support to a high level. Rather, this individual started out at the zero level and is now at a level that is very close to the average for the community. His life history reveals the story behind this shift. George Mandel was born and raised in a small Iowa town where Jewish influences were minimal. His origins are still manifest in his quiet speech and his reticent manner. Since his marriage to a Jewish girl and his settlement in Lakeville, Mandel has gradually acculturated. This has meant that he has become more "Jewish," including the adoption of normative attitudes toward Israel.

### 3. Shifts in Feeling about Jewishness

If we cannot discern any real increase in the types of support that Lakeville Jews feel compelled to render to Israel, it is possible that there have been subtle shifts in feeling about Jewishness—shifts that have long-range implications of a positive kind for Jewish survival. What these shifts might be we cannot say. But our interview with Rabbi Aaron contains some relevant hints:

Asked about the High Holidays, Aaron said that they were better attended this year than previously. The services were also the best services. He does not know whether

---

*It might be claimed that the meaning of the item "belong to Zionist organizations" is not the same today as it was a decade ago.

this is directly because of Israel, but in his opinion it helped. In general, the Israeli crisis served to bring the congregation closer together. There was an impending crisis in the congregation over Vietnam, but the Israel victory averted any such confrontation. His first sermon for the High Holidays was on Israel. He imagines that every rabbi in the country did the same. The people who were with Aaron on Vietnam (he is a dove) he describes as the better Jews in the congregation. Peculiarly enough, people who followed him on Vietnam were more Zionist-minded than the hawks in the congregation. He thinks that because Vietnam, Jewish identity, Israel, and Hebrew had been presented by him as a package, those who wished to emulate him bought both his Jewish attitudes as well as his general social attitudes. He feels there has been and continues to be a conflict with some over supporting Israel and being against Vietnam. The conflict is sometimes a very subtle one, and in some people there is a conflict, but they are not aware of it. He personally is worried about Moshe Dayan and his image, and there are some people in the congregation who are also worried about Dayan. Aaron is more comfortable with the "Buber image" than with the Dayan image, and he said that for himself and those who follow him in the congregation: "Eshkol is for us a better image than Dayan."

Asked about what residue the Crisis and War have left or what it has meant in addition to the High Holidays, he said that the congregation is in favor of extending its program of sending youngsters to Israel for the summer. This would involve increasing the amount of money they make available—the program now costs the congregation about $3,000 a year. It will escalate, and he feels there is no question but that the congregation will continue to pay for it. The congregation is very proud of its subsidy program in sending some of its young people to Israel each summer. It represents a kind of commitment to Israel. The Reform appeal for Israel, on the other hand, is not attractive; the congregation is not excited about raising money to establish a Reform presence in Israel.

The Israeli Bond dinner that the congregation sponsored raised more money this year than before, and almost everything in the congregation this year has gone somewhat better than before. There is more attendance at Hebrew classes this year.

The impact of the Israeli crisis may be involved perhaps in the new high school department which the congregation has embarked on. Aaron feels the congregation will spend more per pupil in the high school department than any Reform congregation in the country, and that while the groundwork was prepared for this in past years, the issue had to be voted on during the time of the Crisis. He expected much more opposition to the new program than developed. He wonders whether the program received such firm support because of the mood induced by the Crisis.

Aaron finds that Jewish life at the Temple isn't *all* that different this year, however. He expected the change to be sharper than it actually has been.

## The Meaning of the Crisis and the War

We are now prepared to confront the question of what exactly happened to American Jewry during the Israeli Crisis and War. We know that our respondents were shaken by the threat posed by the Crisis, were unambiguously pro-Israel, were tremendously stirred by the victory, felt that they did their duty to bring such victory about through their financial contributions, have not shifted in their level of pro-Israel support, and have not evinced any extraordinary eagerness to visit Israel. We also know that central participants in Lakeville Jewish life, such as Rabbi Aaron, expected "the change to be sharper than it actually has been." And it has occurred to one of our respondents who occupies a much more marginal position in Jewish life, George Mandel, that he no longer feels about Israel the way he did. He recalls how he felt last June:

"If anything had happened to Israel it would have been a catastrophe. People wouldn't have had any place to go. Israel was a symbol of what modern Jews can do." While Mandel did not take any political action, if the war had taken another turn he would have contacted his Congressman and asked for U.S. support. He remembers having a feeling of great pride in what the Israelis had done.

The following excerpt from his interview records his contrasting feelings at the present time:

Mandel does not have as much feeling about Israel at the present time as he thought he would based on his feeling in June. If he was going on a foreign trip, Israel would not be the first place he would visit. He has seen slides taken by one of the people who works at his office. This person brought back an extensive collection and showed them to a group for a whole evening. "When I saw the people and the countryside I didn't relate to it as much as I thought I would. I don't know why, but the people looked very foreign to me." He has no urgent feeling about visiting Israel. He does not know anyone who has changed decidedly in his feelings and his actions about Israel as a result of the Crisis. Since the situation has cooled off he doesn't see much difference. People feel about the same way as they did before.

How then may we explain the sharp difference between present emotions and those of the immediate past, as well as the absence of a revolutionary change in Jewish life?

It seems to us that the response of May–June was not a response to Israel in the conventional sense but rather a response to the events of Jewish history from the 1930's onward. The response in Lakeville must be understood in light of the fact that American Jews, by fortunate circumstance, have been exempt from this cataclysmic history. The Crisis brought to the forefront of consciousness the possibility of a repetition of that history—the possibility of another holocaust. Like the first holocaust—in which American Jewry was exempt not by virtue of any special nobility of its own but rather by pure happenstance—another holocaust would have meant that again the American Jew would miraculously escape harm. If we have the problem of justifying our escape from the first holocaust, the least that we can do is make the gesture of helping to prevent a second one; at the very minimum such a gesture will indicate that some good purpose was served in our being spared. (And the possibility of a second holocaust presents us with an opportunity to cleanse the record of the 1930's and 40's—perhaps we are not entirely sure that we did all we could to avert that holocaust and to succor its victims.) Thus, our support of Israel is intimately connected with our desire to preserve a feeling of our worth as human beings.

Furthermore, we support Israel to protect our sense of meaning. Israel created meaning, for it meant that out of the destruction of the holocaust something new, clean, and good was born. Thus, Israel protected our sense of meaning in a world that assaulted any sense of meaning that the Jew might have. Israel's destruction, then, would involve the destruction of meaning. Hitler, whom we thought to be dead and conquered, would be alive again; the final victory would be his. By upsetting our sense of meaning, a new holocaust would have plunged American Jewry into total *anomie*. From this perspective, Israel *had* to be supported as never before. Her destruction would have meant our end as an American Jewry, for we could not survive such a complete loss of meaning.

These perspectives, tenuous as they are, help us to understand why Mr. Green, who phantasied going to Israel as a soldier, has not taken the first plane and gone there as a tourist; why Mr. Mandel, with his lack of any contact with a meaningful Jewish culture, cannot recapture the enthusiasm of the immediate past; why Mrs. Fried is still as marginal a Jew as before; and why Rabbi Aaron is surprised that Jewish life in Lakeville, although characterized by an aura of good feeling, has seemingly resumed its accustomed tempo.

Those who are disappointed, who feel that an *immediate* and *revolutionary* change in Jewish feeling and behavior should have occurred in Lakeville and throughout the land, might consider that only if events in Israel during May–June 1967 had taken an unfavorable turn might we have expected such a rapid change of values. But such a change would necessarily have been in a negative, rather than a positive, direction; instead of optimism, such a change would have induced the blackest kind of pessimism about the future of being Jewish. Thus for those who are disappointed there is a kind of ironic consolation in the fact that no immediate revolution in Jewish life took place in Lakeville during the aftermath of the Six-Day War. Finally, for students of ethnicity in general and of Jewish life in particular, the response in Lakeville demonstrates that feelings of Jewish identity—albeit on the unconscious level—are more abiding than we had any reason to suspect previously.

# Jews and American Life

# Jews, Ethnics, and the American City

[As Sklare explained in a letter to an editor at the University Press of New England, "The event that occasioned this article was the controversy in the early 1970's in New York City regarding the 'scatter-site' housing program. This effort involved building public housing in middle-class areas rather than in slum neighborhoods. The specific incident that sparked the controversy was the reaction to 'scatter-site' housing in the Forest Hills area of Queens, an area that had many middle-class Jewish residents. The reaction of the Jews to what would be an influx of Blacks and Puerto Ricans in the area was most unusual—formerly Jews had moved from their neighborhoods almost without protest when low-income Blacks and Puerto Ricans appeared on the scene. The unusual Jewish reaction stimulated me to investigate the Jewish relationship to the American city and to compare that relationship with other ethnic groups."—JDS]

At a time when the plight of the American city engages so much of our attention—when scarcely a week can pass without *The New York Times* featuring a story about middle-class New Yorkers fleeing the metropolis to seek contentment in a New England village—it would also seem particularly appropriate to analyze the special relationship of the Jew to the American city. For the Jews, more than any other group, have been among America's most enthusiastic city dwellers, regarding the urban environment not as a problem or a source of pain, but as an opportunity and a place of pleasure. One might even go so far as to say that in their mode of life and occupational patterns American Jews have constituted the perfect urbanites. Furthermore, Jews have played a major role in supplying others with the amenities and graces of urban life (amenities and graces, incidentally, that seem to have lost some of their former attraction).

If Jews have been singularly successful in their accommodation to the American city, their success is not accounted for by anything in their history—East European Jews did not, for instance, merely transfer to an American setting the arts and practices of urban living they had acquired in Warsaw or Kiev or Cracow. In fact, most American Jews are the descendants of villagers. The mass Jewish migrations to the city began only about a century ago, when Jews left their East European hamlets to settle in New York, Philadelphia, Manchester, Johannesburg—*and* in Warsaw. This move followed a precedent set by the German Jews who, half a century or so earlier, had emigrated to New York or Philadelphia, to Berlin or Munich, from their native villages in Bavaria and the Rhineland.

Although they came from villages, Jews never idealized the village experience (the romanticization of the *shtetl* is a rather recent phenomenon). This is not to say that immigrant Jews did not harbor a certain nostalgia for the "old home," as witness the Yiddish stage presentations of the era; but underlying such sentiments there was always a strong element of realism, an awareness that, the warmth of *shtetl* life notwithstanding, the Jews of Eastern Europe occupied a subordinate rung on the ladder of the larger society. (Even in the best of times Jewish security depended on the good will of Czarist officials, who often had to be bribed before they would confer the most elementary rights and opportunities; in less good times the threat of pogroms was constantly in the air.) For the former *shtetl* dwellers there might be shared nostalgia based on happy recollections of family and community experiences, but even the most sentimental realized there was no returning. As for the more sophisticated Jews, the *shtetl* exerted no nostalgic tug whatsoever but was regarded—as in the Hebrew literature of the late nineteenth century—as an abomination, a place of backwardness and bigotry.

For many white American Gentiles, things were different. Whether "ethnics" (the so-called hyphenated Americans: Polish-, German-, Italian-, Greek-, etc.) or "White Anglo-Saxon Protestants," these non-Jewish Americans looked back to a village or rural past to which they remained so strongly attached as to make it difficult for them to become true urbanites. Ethnic Americans, in particular, of whatever origin, even after long residence in America always retained an affection for the village life of their youth, and significant numbers actually returned to the native villages that they had never ceased to regard as their true homes. Of course, the majority of ethnics remained in America, but on their own terms; that is, they sought to recreate the life they had known in the old country. The Italians, for instance, had always lived in close-packed villages rather than in isolated rural cottages or farmhouses, and they moved more aggressively than other immigrant groups to replicate their native patterns in the "Little Italys" that still exist in every large American city. Only with the coming of urban renewal in the 1950's did ambitious planners succeed in destroying some of the weaker Italian-American neighborhoods, though they were scarcely able to touch the main centers.[1]

Whereas many ethnics made poor candidates for urban living, Wasps characteristically turned their backs on the city altogether. For in addition to sharing the yearning of the ethnics for a village past, Wasps often held the city in disdain; to them it was an impersonal place, disorderly, threatening, perilous, corrupt, dehumanizing, unnatural, violent. Of course, Wasps were prepared to grant that the city also had some points in its favor; it was, for example, a place of opportunity as well. But Wasps have often been tempted to lay greater stress on the city's menacing rather than on its beneficent aspects.[2] As soon as electric streetcars, and later commuter rail lines, made it possible to live at a substantial remove from one's place of business, Wasps departed the city in large numbers (though many, of course, stayed on in town houses or luxury apartments). Thus there sprung up around all the major American cities a ring of middle- and upper-class suburbs that sought to reproduce the village habitations of the past. Even today, residents of such suburbs are known to become aroused when improvements—sidewalks or modern street lighting, for instance—are proposed, which would make it more difficult to simulate the atmosphere of an 18th- or 19th-century village.

The late Harold Ickes sought to expose the phoniness of the urban WASP's attachment to the past by characterizing Wendell Willkie, who was born in Elwood, Indiana, and went on to become the head of Commonwealth and Southern, a giant public-utilities corporation headquartered in New York City, as "that barefoot boy from Wall Street." But the fact of the matter is that Willkie constantly sought to maintain his roots in Indiana, at least as much out of a sense of his own identity as out of a wish to present himself to the American public as a simple lad from small-town America. Even before he entered politics, Willkie used his money to buy farms in the area where he and his wife had grown up, and he and Mrs. Willkie returned to Indiana at regular intervals. According to one biographer, Willkie never felt that his plush apartment on Fifth Avenue was his real home.[3]

As for the old-guard Wasp patriciate, it considered its true habitat to be the family country estate. The Roosevelts—both the Oyster Bay and Hyde Park branches—are a case in point. By Gould or Vanderbilt standards perhaps, neither Oyster Bay nor Hyde Park is a particularly grand establishment, but opulence is not the criterion; the point here is that these estates were designed to serve as self-contained units housing a single family and its servants. Life in such establishments was assuredly not "with people" (to use the phrase that has been applied to the society of the *shtetl*). One might, to be sure, politick in the city or come to town for the winter social season, but the real pleasures of life were located in the countryside.

Thus, as Wasps increasingly fled the city and as the ethnics dug into their urban village enclaves, it was left to Jewish immigrants to espouse the liberating possibilities of city life. But not all Jews, of course. There were, for instance, the Hasidim who arrived in the United States during and after World War II and for whom return to their former East European villages was a political and psychological impossibility. These Jews, not unlike so many Wasps, had a deep distrust of the city. One such Hasidic group—the followers of the Skvirer

Rebbe—actually succeeded in establishing their own village (anglicized to "Squaretown" and legally incorporated as "New Square") in New York State's Rockland County, in 1961.

The New Square venture calls to mind an earlier effort at resettling some Jews in the American countryside, an effort prompted by the arrival in the United States, prior to World War I, of a small group of Jewish immigrants from Eastern Europe who had been influenced by the back-to-the-soil movement. Their dream of a Jewish peasantry was aided and abetted by certain European Jewish philanthropists, notably Baron Maurice de Hirsch who subsidized a series of agricultural colonies in the Americas (the best known was in Argentina). The Baron's scheme gained the enthusiastic support of America's German-Jewish patricians—men like Jacob Schiff, Oscar Straus, and Mayer Sulzberger, who had come to share the notion, learned from their Wasp counterparts, of the city as an evil place, and who also wished to give the lie to Gentile charges that Jews were middlemen who lived off the labor of others—and the result was a network of Jewish farm colonies in the Vineland-Bridgeton-Millville triangle of Southern New Jersey.[4] The scheme, however, turned out to be a disaster, leaving a trail of destitution in its wake, and about all that can be said in its favor is that the numbers affected were small. It hardly created a ripple among the mass of American Jews, whose faith in the city as the source of economic and social promise remained undiminished. The failure of the South Jersey scheme was in a sense providential, for had it succeeded America would have been deprived of its perfect urbanites—an irony inasmuch as the German-Jewish elite was much concerned that the Jews make a significant contribution to their newly adopted homeland.

Certainly, the nature of Jewish occupational patterns—partly for reasons of economic necessity—has been uniquely geared to the city. Jews, by and large, engage in economic activities that are most characteristically urban. They are, for instance, prominent in commerce, and those who have gone into manufacturing are specifically concentrated in the manufacture of nondurable goods that are particularly suited to the urban environment. (This is in contrast to the heavy industry pursued by Gentile businessmen; in Pittsburgh, for example, where Gentiles introduced the manufacture of iron and steel, Jews concentrated in the manufacture of inexpensive cigars, stogies.) Thus the historically heavy Jewish representation in the garment industry, especially women's wear.

Jews have also tended to gravitate toward the service professions (law, medicine, accounting, etc.)—a further indication of their affinity for urban modes and manners. It is significant, too, that Jews, in disproportionate numbers, have found their way to the most abstract of the services in question—psychoanalysis, for example. Psychoanalysis might be considered the urban service par excellence, for in its conduct nothing is exchanged but words—and communication is the essence of city existence. This perhaps also may help to explain the large number of Jews who have concentrated professionally in the various media.

An examination of Jewish housing patterns yields additional confirmation of the Jewish predilection for "urbanism as a way of life."[5] Proper urbanism requires a preference for the apartment as against the detached, one-family residence. Of course, most city dwellers must perforce live in apartments; but Jews, it would seem, have been positively ardent in their preference. For non-Jews the one-family house has typically been the preferred mode of residence, boasting as it does a commodity that is abundant in the village but scarce in the urban environment—namely, physical privacy. Jews, however, do not necessarily experience the proximity of neighbors as an invasion of privacy. Accordingly, until the most recent decades, Jews were characteristically apartment renters rather than homeowners. And true to the urban perspective, Jews tended to regard real estate as a commodity to be traded rather than as an economic good to be consumed.

It was only natural, then, that Jews should have achieved prominence in the apartment-building trade, and, indeed, in the years following World War II Jews in many cities in the United States became the leading builders of apartment houses, quickly outdistancing the Italians whose building skills were of long historical standing. (The trend to Jewish primacy in apartment building had in fact been observable as early as the post–World War I real-estate boom.[6]) More recently, Jews have also assumed an important role in the construction of commercial office buildings, a trend most pronounced in New York City, where, as Nathan Glazer has pointed out, Jewish builders have become predominant in the development of what he terms the "Uris brothers–Emery Roth style of space manufacturing."[7]

But it is the apartment house that remains the emblem of the Jews' love affair with the city. Wherever Jews have formed an important segment of the urban American population, they have been the prime developers and prime residents of apartment houses, especially of the so-called "elevator buildings," those bastions of the urban middle class. The phenomenon is best observed in New York City where this type of building has enjoyed its greatest vogue and where the Jewish preference for such housing was less influenced by non-Jewish tastes than elsewhere in the country. The elevator building was designed for people who had moved up from the working class and the walk-up building, and who, though financially able to buy a one-family home in the suburbs, chose to remain in the city. Such construction reached its apogee along the great boulevards of Brooklyn, the Bronx, and more recently, Queens—Eastern Parkway, Ocean Parkway, the Grand Concourse, and Queens Boulevard. These were essentially "Jewish" avenues, built by Jewish developers for a Jewish clientele. (We might note, too, in passing, that New York Jews who have moved from the middle class to the upper class have also tended to resist the appeal of the one-family house and have marked *their* upward passage by moving from elevator buildings to so-called "luxury apartments.")

It was, of course, inevitable that as American Jews became more acculturated, they should also become increasingly attracted to the suburbs. Members of the German-Jewish upper class began to settle in New York's suburban Westchester County as early as the turn of the century (although some who did so also continued to maintain an apartment in the city). Jews of East European background, on the other hand, were relative latecomers to suburbia, making their transfer only after World War II. This move was as much a matter of necessity as of choice. There was, to begin with, the very serious postwar apartment shortage, soon followed by a general decline in the quality of urban life—decaying neighborhoods, mounting crime, and so on. But it was the decline of the urban school system that was the major factor in tipping the balance. To Jewish parents suburban schools, whatever their faults, seemed to offer the promise of better educational opportunities than did the city schools. Newark—that most unhappy of American cities—illustrates the problem. When Weequahic High School (Philip Roth's well-publicized Alma Mater) began to decline, Newark lost whatever hold it still had on the Jewish population. The mass exodus to the suburbs then became inevitable.

The fact of the matter is that when Jews opted for suburbia they did so reluctantly. To large numbers of WASPs and middle- and upper-class ethnics the single-family house in the suburbs seemed like the most natural thing in the world—the only way to live. For Jews it was otherwise. Of course those Jews who moved into the mass-produced Levittown-type suburbs found that though they lived in separate houses their neighbors were still close by. On the other hand, there were no hallways or lobbies, as in apartment houses, for chance meetings, no elevators for quick exchanges of gossip and news, no corner luncheonettes for ready sociability, no street life to speak of. For many the absence of these staples of the Jewish urban scene was a real deprivation. And despite the growing acceptance of suburbia, Jews never became true converts but remained in large measure believers in the old faith of urbanism. Even today Jews tend to be less interested than others in utilizing real estate as a means of establishing distance between themselves and their neighbors. Real-estate dealers have come to know what to stress in showing a suburban house to a prospective Jewish buyer—comfort, modernization, good schools, and easy access to shopping, transportation, and "people." Thus, even when Jews seemingly embrace suburbia, they still look for the urban virtues—convenience, cultural, and social opportunities.

The most telling evidence of the lingering love of suburban Jews for the city is to be found in a Philadelphia study that polled older suburbanites—Jewish and non-Jewish—living in one-family houses, with incomes of $15,000 or more, who either worked in downtown Philadelphia or had retired, and whose children were all eighteen years old or over.[8] With regard to future residential plans, the investigator discovered that "almost all of the suburban non-Jews . . . wished to remain in their single-family homes, whereas the overwhelming majority of Jews either wished or were actually planning to move into new urban high-rise apartments." It may of course be doubted, given the present situation, whether many of these Jews will succeed in returning to the city. Urban crime and decay, the continuing apartment shortage, high rents and poor mainte-nance—all combine to make residence in the suburbs a more pleasing prospect than it was as recently as a decade ago. To accommodate the situation, devel-opers have begun to build high-rise apartment houses in the suburbs, as well as garden apartments,[9] thus affording many elderly Jewish families, who seek out housing of the kind that is reminiscent of the city, the additional advantage of remaining within easy reach of their children and grandchildren.

Jews, then, typically continue to be perfect urbanites (wherever they may live), their positive preference for city life fueled by the social, cultural, and economic predispositions we have been discussing. But how has the Jewish romance with the American city been regarded by outside observers? To begin answering this question we must recall that the so-called ghettos, the areas of settlement where the mass of Jewish immigrants first set down their Ameri-can roots, were in fact slums, with all the dirt and crowding and squalor that the term implies. Today we may congratulate ourselves with the recognition that these slums were remarkably free of social deviance, violence, and despair, but they were hardly recognized as model communities during their heyday. William Dean Howells, for instance, came to inspect the Lower East Side, as did Henry James, and both writers concurred in a strong distaste for the ghetto.

Of course, there were sympathetic observers as well, men like Jacob Riis, Lincoln Steffens, and Hutchins Hapgood, who made earnest attempts to understand the life of the ghetto and were attracted by its vitality.[10] Hapgood, in particular, found in the ghetto a kind of spiritual home. He had grown up in Alton, Illinois, and he came to regard that town very much as the enlight-ened Jews of the 19th century, the *maskilim*, did the *shtetl*—an arid, uncultured, stultifying place. To Hapgood New York represented the vigorous opposite of Alton; and the Lower East Side, the quintessence of the metropolis. In his celebration of the Lower East Side, *The Spirit of the Ghetto*,[11] Hapgood noted that the Jewish neighborhoods were populated by people who accepted rather than rejected the city. He sought to convey to his Wasp readers the message that they should do likewise.

The exceptional quality of Hapgood's understanding of Jewish urbanism can be better appreciated when contrasted with another contemporary ac-count, *The Zone of Emergence: Observations of the Lower Middle Class and Upper Working Class Communities of Boston, 1905–1914*, a series of sociological reports by Robert A. Woods and Albert J. Kennedy.[12] Woods was the director of South End House, Boston's first settlement house, and a leading national figure in the settlement-house movement. Kennedy was his chief lieutenant, later his successor at South End House, and still later the head of the University Settlement in New York. Both were ordained Protestant ministers. Their staff, who assisted in the research, included two ministers' sons, Ordway Tead and George Cary, as well as a minister's daughter, Mrs. Woods, who served as her husband's collaborator. The Protestant factor is not without significance for, as Sam Bass Warner, Jr., the urban historian who edited *The Zone of Emergence* for publication, notes in his preface to the work, the unstated objective of the South End House group was "to help Boston's native and immigrant poor achieve the condition and attitudes of middle-class life"—that is, to turn them into Yankee Protestants of a kind.

One might have expected Woods and Kennedy to have become enamored of the Jews, for of all the groups newly settled in Boston, of whatever origin or background, the Jews came closest to sharing their aspirations. As it happened, they harbored quite different notions on the subject. As Warner puts it, they considered the Jews "altogether a dubious addition to the nation." Given their religious predilections, Woods and Kennedy did admit to enjoying catching glimpses of the Sabbath candles through the windows of the ghetto, and they also professed to admire what they called the "feeling for the ethical values inculcated in the Jewish home-life and hallowed for some at least by the religious observances." But that was as far as they would go in praise of the Jews.

Unaccountably—for no other ethnic minority was more resistant to middle-class Protestant ideals—Woods and Kennedy selected the Italians as the immigrant group that constituted the greatest asset to the American city. "No other body of immigrants of similar quality," they declared, "has made greater and sounder progress." They admired the Italians for their skills as builders—"As a property holder the Italian deserves the highest praise . . . he builds his house of brick rather than wood"—and for their thrift:

A further saving is effected by the use of second-hand brick and stone. Italians frequently take the work of tearing down old buildings, and they sell the used material to their countrymen. Such brick is cheaply cleaned and is probably every whit as solid as new material would be.

As for the Jews:

Every Jew is a born real-estate speculator. Even the poorest among them manage somehow to obtain a house. Having secured title by load[ing] on all the mortgages that the property will stand, the equity is used as a basis for trade. Houses are traded somewhat as the Gypsies swap horses.

Moreover:

In comparison with the . . . Italian districts the Jewish colony seems peculiarly dirty and dismal. . . . The environment is the dirtiest and most noisome on the island. The passage ways of the tenements are dark, filthy, and permeated with fetid odors, while the litter on the floors, the torn wall-paper, and the kicked-out banisters bear witness to the presence of . . . tenants carelessly content with squalor.

Woods and Kennedy were able to discern only one defect in the Italians, their lack of interest in education. The Jewish emphasis on education, however, seemed to them in somewhat bad taste: "Almost any adult Jew grows quite animated in telling of the prowess of his children in High School, or the brilliance of the near relative which he invariably has in Harvard."

Aside from whatever ingrained anti-Semitism may have been involved, the admiration of Woods and Kennedy for the Italians, and their reservations concerning (if not contempt for) the Jews, had a logic of its own. Despite their devotion to Boston's general welfare, Woods and Kennedy were not upholders of urbanism. Rather, they were admirers of the countryside, of the village, of the virtues of an older America. Though they worked in Boston, they were not of Boston. Woods, according to Warner, was "a stranger to the city and its slums." He had been born in a suburb of Pittsburgh and educated at Amherst and at Andover Theological Seminary. "When he moved to Rollins Street in the South End of Boston," Warner writes, "he was as exotic a resident as the latest arrival." Woods's vision of the city was as a village writ large: "[He] never abandoned his hope that the model of the village could be used to build city neighborhoods and thereby bring a regeneration of American urban society." A year before his death, in 1925, "at the urging of his Amherst College friends, Woods went so far as to write a campaign biography of Calvin Coolidge. He saw Coolidge as the example of the best ways of the old rural America, and he hoped that Coolidge's presidency would serve to revive the respect for and use of these ways."

To Woods and Kennedy, then, the Italian immigrants seemed kindred spirits, fellow believers in the virtues of traditional village ways. The Jews, on the other hand, were urban cosmopolites. (Just as Woods and Kennedy overlooked the problems the Italians brought to the city, so too they ignored the ready Jewish acceptance of the virtues of middle-class life.) Their attitude, it should be noted, was shared by some segments of the Jewish community as well. The upper-class German Jews, as we have already seen, busied themselves with schemes for transforming ghetto residents into farmers; and the social and philanthropic institutions that the German Jews established on New York's Lower East Side—the Educational Alliance, for instance—were intended to ease ghetto Jews out of their "inferior" East European culture. Another group that held the ghetto in contempt was, oddly enough, the Jewish Communists. One would have thought the Communists would welcome the existence of the ghetto, finding therein fruitful soil for the implantation of their ideas and programs. Instead, they reviled it in the harshest terms. (The novel, *Jews Without Money*, by Michael Gold,[13] is perhaps the most interesting illustration of the tendency.) Finally, the ghetto was also scorned by the bourgeois, assimilationist sector of the Jewish community, many of whose members charged it with parochialism and intellectual aridity. This attitude found high expression in a volume entitled *The Ghetto*, by Louis Wirth,[14] one of the best-known of the urban studies emanating from the University of Chicago in the 1920's, then the center of research on the American city. What Wirth in effect did (not consciously, to be sure) was to contrast Maxwell Street, Chicago's prime ghetto thoroughfare, which he saw as sterile and anachronistic, with the Midway of the University of Chicago, which he considered as a kind of New Jerusalem. Wirth, given his bias, was unable to appreciate the special Jewish urban qualities. Ghetto Jews won no praise from him for having successfully avoided the social problems that plagued other groups. In fact, in certain passages of *The Ghetto* it is hard to discern any difference in attitude between Wirth on the one hand and Woods and Kennedy on the other.

Nowadays, of course, one would look hard to find anyone—no matter what his ethnic background, attitude to group identity, political persuasion, or class level—willing to say a bad word about the Jewish ghetto. A glow of romance hangs over Maxwell Street and Hester Street, and the ghetto has retroactively been invested with all the virtues—safe streets, a pulsating community life, a sense of "caring"—notably absent from the contemporary urban and suburban scene. The harsh memories of an earlier generation have softened, and for those who never knew the ghetto or who left it decades ago there is a new appreciation, fed by a recent outpouring of books about the Lower East Side, all of them positive and celebratory in tone.[15] The celebration of the ghetto reached a climax of sorts with the Jewish Museum's exhibition, in 1966, entitled *The Lower East Side: Portal to American Life 1870–1924*. The show attracted a great deal of attention and was in fact one of the most successful events in the Museum's history. Alfred Kazin has described the scene:[16]

One saw great crowds of prosperous, well-dressed, extremely sophisticated people —the usual museum crowd—standing in front of enormously blown-up pictures of their parents and grandparents waiting on Ellis Island benches, or standing behind pushcarts on Hester Street while children got some relief at open hydrants from August in New York.

Kazin also noted that there seemed to be two sides to the exhibition. One, of course, was celebration. Look! the prosperous, well-dressed, etc. viewers seemed to be saying, look how far we have come from our humble origins! But the other side of the coin revealed a sadness and an awareness that the beloved city had become a dangerous, bankrupt place:

The most extraordinary photograph taken by Jacob Riis . . . showed a bearded Jew preparing for the Sabbath eve in a coal cellar on Ludlow Street. It is 1900 and he lives in a coal cellar; but there is a Sabbath loaf on the grimy table in front of him, he will not die in a Polish ditch for the greater glory of the master race, and in the 1960's his grandchildren will walk out of the museum, down Fifth Avenue, not even having to say to themselves that the city has been their savior, that it was once a frontier, exciting in anticipation and fact. They have come to these photographs looking for their ancestors, their old selves, their hidden selves. The city is no longer their frontier, and usually they are afraid of it as well as ashamed of it. The city that saved them has by now worn out their expectations of it! "It is impossible to live in New York." That is the first and last thing New Yorkers now say about New York: *it* is impossible.

"It is impossible." The current disillusionment with the city stems from many sources. Perhaps especially problematical for Jews has been the continuing influx into the city of the lower-class migrant groups—Southern blacks, Puerto Ricans, Appalachian poor, and Chicanos—who bring with them a host of social problems lacking in intrinsic solution. Unlike the Jews, these newcomers to the city have no tradition of communal self-help. Urban violence takes its greatest toll on the depressed communities themselves, but it has grown sufficiently in strength and scope to affect all segments of the city. Jews, given their particular occupational and residential patterns, and given too their centuries-old psychological abhorrence of violence, are especially vulnerable victims—to say nothing of the increase in anti-Semitism that has become manifest recently. A further threat to Jewish urban ease and security is the growing demand for community control, a development that has found support among the Wasp upper and middle classes (some of whom voice their sympathy from the suburbs). As for the ethnic middle and working class, who continue to reside in the city, its members are not really urbanites but rather, as we have seen, urban villagers, with few concerns beyond their own neighborhoods. All of which leaves the Jews as possibly the last, lonely defenders of the urban way of life.

Jews were indeed celebrated as such by *Fortune* magazine in a special issue (February 1960) devoted to the future of New York City (the mass media were then just beginning to discover the "urban crisis"). An article entitled "The Jewish Elan" took note of the Jewish contribution to the life of the metropolis:

The great Jewish population gives New York much of the dynamism and vigor that make the city unique among all the cities on earth. And surely it can be said that the Jewish *élan* has contributed mightily to the city's dramatic character, its excitement, its originality, its stridency, its unexpectedness.

The article seemed to imply that Jews were the only group that really cared about the future of the city. While the *Fortune* piece was free of the old Woods-Kennedy type of criticism of the Jews, in its tribute to Jewish urbanity it failed to suggest that the Jews might possibly have their own problems with the city. For the truth of the matter is that, for all their devotion to the city, the Jews, nowadays at any rate, are less than the successful urbanites that so many of them appear to be.

The most striking case in point is the rapid decay—in some instances, the total disappearance—of many of the old urban Jewish neighborhoods. The cycle from non-Jewish to Jewish neighborhood and back to non-Jewish is sometimes a mere thirty years. In communities where blacks form a high proportion of the population, as in Detroit, the cycle has been played out even more quickly. Jewish failure to sustain neighborhood life is in sharp contrast to Italian success. As Nathan Glazer and Daniel P. Moynihan have observed:[17]

The first Italian neighborhoods proved remarkably stable. Areas that were Italian in 1920 remain so, somewhat attenuated, today. . . . While the Jewish map of New York City in 1920 bears almost no relation to that in 1961, the Italian districts, though weakened in some cases and strengthened in others, are still in large measure where they were.

The situation has reached such extreme proportions that there are now books—poignantly similar in tone to the volumes that commemorate the destroyed communities of Western and Eastern Europe—memorializing but-recently-vanished American-Jewish urban neighborhoods such as Brooklyn's Brownsville.[18]

How to account for the corrosion and/or disappearance of the old Jewish neighborhoods? The answer lies in the fact of the Jews' upward mobility, greater than that of many other groups, in their high level of acculturation, and in the peculiarity of the Jewish family structure. As Jews move up the class ladder, they often find themselves outgrowing their old neighborhoods and seeking homes elsewhere, in what they feel to be more suitable surroundings. Italians, on the other hand, including those who have risen in class, tend to acculturate more slowly to American norms than do Jews and thus tend to remain in their old districts even when they can afford better. And while the Jewish family is famous for its closeness, rarely do we find parents and children, especially married children, sharing the same household (unlike the Italians, the Jewish generations also avoid living in the same building and frequently even in the same neighborhood).

There is a further factor, the most important of all, and that is the Jews' lack of commitment to their physical environs. The Jewish neighborhood per se seems to have little symbolic, or even actual, significance for its residents, and its special facilities—synagogues, schools, kosher butchers, delicatessens, etc.—are looked upon as mere conveniences. There is little feeling for the area itself, and hence no overwhelming desire to preserve it from decay. The explanation that first suggests itself for this attitude is that Jewish psychology has been conditioned, by thousands of years of living in Exile, to react to situations of stress by a kind of avoidance behavior. Thus Jews did not feel that Brownsville, say, really belonged to them; when others claimed it, the Jews moved elsewhere.

Most recently, however, we find instances where the impulse to flight has been arrested. This latest development, marked by a new appreciation among Jews of their urban neighborhoods and in some cases even by the conscious attachment to them of symbolic and historical significances, is a consequence in part of the ever-diminishing supply of alternative areas for Jewish settlement, and in part of the persistence of a Jewish working class—including some Hasidic groups—that simply cannot afford to move elsewhere. But there are deeper reasons why Jews are at last taking an urban stand, and these have their roots in two events far removed from the experience of American cities but nevertheless impinging on the consciousness of some of their Jewish inhabitants—namely, the Holocaust and the establishment of the State of Israel. For some years after World War II the tendency of many American Jews was to repress any thought of the Holocaust. But that has now changed—as witness the introduction into Jewish school curriculums of Holocaust studies—and the new openness to the memory of the Holocaust has brought with it a sensitivity to assaults against the Jewish group, from whatever quarter, and a resolve not to yield. The impact of the establishment of the State of Israel, and especially of the Six-Day War, has been even greater in this regard, and has given the American Jew a new sense of ethnic pride; it has made him, ironically, feel more rather than less secure on American soil.

All of this may help to give us a better understanding of what is currently happening in one predominantly Jewish neighborhood, the Forest Hills section of Queens in New York City, where a controversy continues to rage over the construction of a proposed public-housing project, part of the city's "scatter-site" housing program aimed at putting low-income residents, many of them blacks and Puerto Ricans, into middle-income neighborhoods. Local people have expressed fear that the project, in addition to placing a strain on overburdened schools and transportation facilities, will also introduce a host of social problems into an area that has hitherto managed to stay free of the more egregious urban excesses and that, as a result, they will be forced to abandon the neighborhood. Some Jews resolved to resist. Their decision to oppose the low-income project and to fight for the integrity of their neighborhood—their refusal, in effect, to accept the inevitability of another Brownsville—may come to be regarded as a historic event in the relationship of the Jew to the American city. It can be seen from that point of view as an act of affirmation, signifying a desire to keep faith with the city, its possibilities and potential rewards.

But the signs of a new Jewish relationship to the city actually predate the Forest Hills controversy. When crime rates in New York began to rise in the 1960's and the more affluent Jews began to move out of certain Brooklyn neighborhoods, younger Jewish volunteers organized unarmed night patrols. At about the same time one could find instances of synagogues becoming involved with neighborhood conservation efforts, acting as agents or as quasi-agents in real-estate transactions—the most notable example being the Conservative synagogue in the Laurelton section of Queens. In 1969 there was unexpected support in poorer Jewish neighborhoods for Mario Procaccino, the "law-and-order" candidate for Mayor of New York on the Democratic ticket whose message to the Jews was that he would see to it that Jewish neighborhoods remained as Jewish as Italian areas had remained Italian. And, of course, there was the phenomenon of the Jewish Defense League, whose slogan "Never Again!" may be interpreted to mean, among other things, that Jews will not continue passively to accept their fate in the American city, as refugees constantly in search of new neighborhoods.

Of all the groups making their homes in the American city, historically it has been the Jews who best accommodated to the urban ambience. In recent years, their romance with the city has in many cases given way to despair, a change that cannot be attributed entirely to the general urban decline or the impact of new populations. For Jews as a group carry within themselves the seeds of their own urban problem; the Jewish urban crisis, in large part, derives from the insufficient attachment Jews have felt for their own neighborhoods. Now we can see the signs of a new phase in which some Jews are attempting to reshape their relationship to the city by achieving a balance between their traditional attachment to the urban way of life—wherein the city as a whole takes precedence over neighborhood—and loyalty to neighborhood—wherein Jews join with their neighbors in striking roots in the "urban village." If the effort meets with success, it will represent a radically new mode of group adjustment to the American city.

## Notes

1. For an analysis of the destruction of a secondary Italian neighborhood, see Herbert J. Gans, *The Urban Villagers: Group and Class in the Life of Italian-Americans* (Glencoe, Ill.: The Free Press, 1962).

2. For the full range of American attitudes toward the city, see Anselm L. Straus, ed., *The American City: A Sourcebook of Urban Imagery* (Chicago: Aldiné, 1968).

3. Bill Severn, *Toward One World: The Life of Wendell Wilkie* (Ives Washburn, 1967), pp. 90–97.

4. A recent volume gives some of the details of the story: Joseph Brandes, *Immigrants to Freedom: Jewish Communities in Rural New Jersey since 1882* (Philadelphia: University of Pennsylvania Press, 1971). The migrations to New Jersey took place at the same time as the beginning of modern Jewish settlement in Palestine. Pioneering Zionism, of course, took a strongly negative attitude toward the city and stressed the importance of rural and village development. As a consequence a chasm was created between rural and urban development in Palestine and later, in Israel, a disinclination to recognize the inevitability and value of urbanization. These issues are discussed by Erik Cohen in *The City in the Zionist Ideology* (Jerusalem, 1970).

5. The phrase comes from the title of a classic essay on the American city, by Louis Wirth, published in the *American Journal of Sociology* in 1938. Wirth, the leading Jewish sociologist of his time, had immigrated to the United States as a youth from a village in the Rhineland.

6. Jews, one might note, were also active at the time in the field of cooperative housing. Indeed, the leadership in building cooperative-apartment developments came from the so-called "Jewish unions," originating with the Amalgamated Clothing Workers of America.

7. In Nathan Glazer and Daniel P. Moynihan, *Beyond the Melting Pot*, 2d ed. (Cambridge, Mass.: MIT Press, 1970), p. 151.

8. Donald M. Fenmore, "Comment on Hoffman's 'Outlook for Downtown Housing,'" *Journal of the American Institute for Planners* (November 1961), 334.

9. Between 1960–70 housing units overall increased by 18 percent, but suburban apartment units increased by 96 percent.

10. For an anthology of contemporary accounts of the Lower East Side during its heyday, together with an excellent introduction, see Milton Hindus, ed., *The Old East Side* (New York: Jewish Publication Society of America, 1969).

11. Ramsey, N.J.: Funk and Wagnalls, 1902. The work has recently been reissued in two new editions, one edited by Moses Rischin (Cambridge, Mass.: Harvard University Press, 1967) and the other edited by Harry Golden (Ramsey, N.J.: Funk and Wagnalls, 1965).

12. Cambridge, Mass.: MIT Press, Second Edition, 1969. (The manuscript was discovered in 1958 by a Harvard senior in search of material for an honors thesis, in a coal bin in Boston's South End House.)

13. Liveright, 1930. (A new edition, with an introduction by Michael Harrington, was published by Avon Books in 1965.)

14. Chicago: University of Chicago Press, 1928.

15. Of the many volumes, two are of more than routine interest: *The Promised City: New York's Jews, 1870–1914*, by Moses Rischin (Cambridge, Mass.: Harvard University Press, 1962) and *The Downtown Jews*, by Ronald Sanders (New York: Harper & Row, 1969). Concurrently with the new appreciation of the Lower East Side, a more sophisticated understanding of the contemporary slum has emerged among sociologists. See particularly Gerald D. Suttles, *The Social Order of the Slum* (Chicago: University of Chicago Press, 1968). In addition to its general perspectives, the book contains significant material on the Italians.

16. "The Writer and the City," *Harper's* (December 1968). See also Robert Alter, "Exhibiting the Lower East Side," *Commentary*, January 1967.

17. *Beyond the Melting Pot, op. cit.*, p. 187.

18. See Alter F. Landesman, *Brownsville: The Birth, Development and Passing of a Jewish Community* (New York: Bloch, 1969).

# The Bicentennial Spirit:
# Jews, Yankees, and Other Ethnic
# Groups in Boston

[This article, which Sklare re-edited for this volume from his 1988 Sol Feinstone Memorial Lecture at Gratz College entitled "The Bicentennial Spirit: Jews, Ethnics, and the 'Waspim,'" continued his exploration of the contrasts between Jews and other ethnic groups in the United States. "I had not realized previously," Sklare wrote in an introduction prepared for this volume, "that some groups could not rouse themselves to celebrate the Bicentennial with any enthusiasm, and that other groups found the event so distasteful that they disregarded it entirely. . . . When the exceptional nature of the Jewish response became clear to me I sought to answer the question: What forces operated on the Jews to make them such enthusiastic celebrants of the Bicentennial?" As in the previous article, his answer relies on a combination of historical and sociological analysis. Between the lines, the reader may also detect a subtle political agenda. For the group that he described here, "a group that does not take America for granted—a group that comprehends the greatness of America, warts and all," was the group with which he himself proudly identified.—JDS]

## I. Ambivalence about the Bicentennial

Ambivalence about celebrating the American Bicentennial was evident from the time when planning for the event began. Official bodies, as well as voluntary groups whose cooperation was essential, seemed to lack enthusiasm for an all-out celebration of 200 years of American independence. On the one hand there was the feeling that the Bicentennial was indeed a milestone in American history and that since none of us would live to participate in the Tercentennial, we owed it to ourselves and to our children to plan an appropriate celebration. On the other hand there was the feeling that it would be incongruous and rather ridiculous to mark the occasion with anything but the most perfunctory ceremonies. The times were out of joint—there was the debacle of Vietnam, the horrendous story of Watergate, the energy crisis, the threatening spectacle of our crime-ridden and bankrupt cities, and the difficulties that resulted from the simultaneous growth of inflation and unemployment. These developments led even some conservatives to feel that joyous festivities in connection with the Bicentennial should be soft-pedaled. If conservatives had their reservations, radicals were prepared to go much further. They suggested that the Bicentennial should be celebrated as a wake rather than as a wedding.

Boston is perhaps the best place to study these ambivalences. Boston was the place where it all began. Consequently the celebration of the Bicentennial started there a year earlier than in the rest of the nation. The Boston Tea Party and the battles at Lexington, Concord, and Bunker Hill all attest to the fact that the firebrands who promoted the revolution, and who rejected the idea of compromise with England, were concentrated in Boston and its environs.

Given its significant role in the establishment of the nation, Boston seemed less than enthusiastic about celebrating the Bicentennial. The city fathers—confronted as they were with the fact that their revenues did not keep up with their expenditures—seemed more concerned with commercial opportunities that the Bicentennial might create than with a real commemoration of Boston's role in the American revolution. While their initial plans called for an ambitious redevelopment project of sections of Colonial Boston, these plans were soon discarded as too costly.

There were, to be sure, significant public events, most notably the arrival of the Tall Ships. There was also the presentation of a spectacular concert conducted by a local hero named Arthur Fiedler. Nevertheless the mood in Boston—the city where the Tea Party had been held, the city where Paul Revere and Samuel Adams had lived—was rather gloomy. But despite it all, Boston cherished its role in the making of the American Revolution, as became evident when its famous Freedom Trail had been built. The Trail leads the visitor to the many notable sites where significant events occurred during the Revolutionary War period.

The initial disappointment in Boston in connection with the 1976 Bicentennial was financial. The leaders of the city had hoped that the Bicentennial would be a lucrative event. They felt that the Bicentennial would attract hordes of free-spending tourists. To be sure there were tourists. However, businessmen found that the tourists who came to Boston were hesitant to spread the green stuff around. The places where tourists slept were a mystery inasmuch as not a single hotel in Boston attained 100 percent occupancy. It had been hoped that occupancy would reach as high as 120 percent. Hotel managers who had expected that they would have to convert ballrooms and lobbies into temporary dormitories were disappointed at the Bicentennial.

## II. The Bicentennial and the American Indian

The reaction of the American Indian illustrated one end of the spectrum. *The New York Times* of January 31, 1975, carried an article from its Washington Bureau regarding the Indian reaction. The article was headlined "Indians Reject a Role in the Bicentennial, Saying They've Nothing to Celebrate." It is worthwhile quoting the article at length in order to convey the feeling of a group who found the celebration of the Bicentennial meaningless as well as objectionable:

Some of the people who run the Bicentennial sat down with a group of Indian leaders here today to talk about their celebration of the country's 200th anniversary.
   The Indians, however, insisted that . . . they have nothing to celebrate.
   "Indians are already too patriotic," said Robert Burnette, the tribal chairman of the Rosebud Sioux, glancing up at a wall-sized reproduction of the Declaration of Independence.
   "Look at all those words," he said, his voice tense with irritation. "Justice, justice, justice. We've never had any of that justice—and now you people want us to celebrate!"
   The blue-walled conference room in a 19th century mansion near the White House became embarrassingly quiet, and what was to have been just another routine Washington meeting was transformed into a blunt, occasionally bitter and sometimes poignant confrontation between the American bureaucracy and the native Americans.
   One by one, the Indians recited the details of their dissatisfaction and by the time they had finished, John W. Warner, the usually loquacious chief of the Federal Bicentennial Agency, was puffing silently on his pipe, staring occasionally at his subordinates who had planned the meeting.

Warner had no problem inducing Jews and Jewish organizations to participate in the Bicentennial. However for Indians the Bicentennial marked the beginning of the end. It marked the destruction of their tribal culture. It marked the beginning of the hegemony of the white man and his conquest of the Indian. For American Jews, the Bicentennial marked the beginning of a new era in Jewish history—an era characterized by freedom and opportunity, an era in which the history of official discrimination, unequal rights, and the governmentally inspired pogroms that they had known in Europe came to an end.

## III. The Bicentennial and the *Shoah*

If we probe the matter more deeply it becomes apparent that for the American Jew the Bicentennial signified more than just the start of a new era. It signified life itself. Thus the Jewish desire to celebrate the Bicentennial must be understood against the background of the Holocaust. Given the fact of the Holocaust, or to use the more exact Hebrew term *Shoah*, the celebration of the

Bicentennial took on a special significance. The awful truth is that if we, or our ancestors, had not had the good sense to migrate to these shores most of us would not be alive. Our names would be listed in the archives of Yad V'Shem in Jerusalem instead of in our local telephone directories.

## IV. Boston's Ethnic Groups and the Bicentennial

The natural leaders of Boston's festivities should have been the Yankees. However, they seem to cultivate a rather low profile. The reactions of oldline Yankees who resided in the suburbs, particularly in Lexington and Concord, were especially revealing. While they took pride in the role that their communities had played in American history, they did not want to be inconvenienced by visitors to their historic sites. They feared that the visitors would make shopping in their stores more time-consuming, create traffic jams on their streets, and, most important of all, that they would trample the lawns that they had lovingly cultivated. Beneath the surface was the feeling that the visitors would not be "our" kind of people.

Boston's financial disappointments could at least have been borne with Yankee stoicism if there had been a feeling among its inhabitants that they (unlike the American Indians whose reactions we have already analyzed) enjoyed the blessings of liberty. But many groups in Boston during the 1970's felt that their liberty was imperiled. Surprisingly, this included the Yankees. To be sure, the complaints of the Yankees were not as serious as those of the Indians. But the Yankees were not happy with the state of the nation. They felt that the liberty that they had enjoyed was being eroded. Furthermore, for the past 100 years the Boston Yankees have had to contend with the Boston Irish, a powerful influence in the life of the city. And if the Irish were not enough, now power had to be shared with a half dozen new ethnic groups. Thus the Governor of the Commonwealth of Massachusetts in 1976 did not have a proper Yankee name like Endicott Peabody—one of the Commonwealth's former governors. The governor was a Greek-American named Michael Dukakis with a Jewish wife named Kitty. The irony of it all is that the "Duke" was in many ways more Waspish than the Yankees themselves. Dukakis's insistence on frugality in his personal life was legendary.

While the landmarks on Boston's famed Freedom Trail attest to the overriding role of the Yankees in the achievement of American independence, Boston is a city where Catholics—especially Irish Catholics—play an enormous role in the city's public life. For the Irish the Bicentennial could not have come at a worse time. It is they who were the most determined foes of racially integrating the public schools. At the same time the Irish consider themselves the most patriotic of Americans, having participated beyond their numbers in all of the nation's wars, including the struggle in Vietnam. In Boston and in many of our large cities the Irish are the main guardians of domestic order and safety by virtue of their employment on the police force and in the fire department. These facts resulted in a feeling of deep bitterness, for as the Irish see it the reward for their courage and loyalty was that their old neighborhood—South Boston—was to be racially integrated. They interpreted integration to mean that South Boston was being wrested from them and that it would no longer be Irish. And to add insult to injury the judge who issued the court order to desegregate the Boston schools had the name of Garrity. As the Irish pointed out a thousand times, and as the pickets in front of his home made abundantly clear, Judge Garrity did not live in South Boston but in the upper-class and upper-middle-class Yankee suburb of Wellesley where integration was not a problem.

Not only did the Irish feel that Judge Garrity had done them in, but they also felt that one of their very own—a member of a family they had supported and admired for several generations—had deserted them. This man—Senator Ted Kennedy—was viewed by Irish residents of South Boston as a turncoat. He was seen as identifying himself more with the Yankees than with the Irish. Since Kennedy's staff knew how the senator was regarded in South Boston they did not schedule any appearances for him in the area. Kennedy's staff also advised him to stay clear of Italian neighborhoods. In fact the senator was not safe even in downtown Boston's Government Center. He was shouted down, pelted with rotten tomatoes, and forced to seek sanctuary in his office.

Largely because of the integration crisis the Irish (as well as the Italians) could not bring themselves to celebrate the Bicentennial. However, neither group discontinued their traditional festivals. The Italians continued to celebrate their various feast days commemorating Italian saints. The elaborate parades in the city's North End continued as before. The Irish continued the celebration of St. Patrick's Day. However, the St. Patrick's Day parade in 1976 had about it more of a spirit of defiance than of celebration. There were many absentees in the reviewing stand, most notably Boston's Cardinal Medeiros. As a Portugese-American Medeiros's appointment had been accepted by the Irish with the greatest reluctance. When he came out in support of busing, and even permitted priests to ride in school buses in the hope that their presence would discourage Catholic youngsters (as well as adults) from attacking the vehicles, the Irish were infuriated. Their initial opinion of Medeiros was confirmed. Thus when St. Patrick's Day arrived the Cardinal concluded that discretion was the better part of valor. He did not attend the parade. He remained ensconced in his residence on Commonwealth Avenue, far away from South Boston. Since the Cardinal's residence is located in an area that has had an influx of Jews in recent years, he was protected from the fury of the Irish, the Italians, and other Catholic groups.

If the Irish and the Italians could not bring themselves to celebrate the country's founding, their feelings of patriotism and fidelity to the nation inhibited them from deliberately seeking to dishonor the Bicentennial. Not so with the radical youth and the followers of the counterculture. They constituted a noticeable group in Boston, having found the city more hospitable than other Eastern communities such as New York, Philadelphia, and Washington, D.C. Despite high living costs, Cambridge (and the adjoining area of Somerville) became the East Coast headquarters of political and cultural radicals. The radicals had none of the inhibitions of the Irish and the Italians. They were unable to decide whether they should show their disdain of the Bicentennial by disregarding it, or whether they should utilize the occasion to spread the message that "Amerika" is a corrupt and decadent society. Accordingly they did a little of both. Sometimes they boycotted Bicentennial events and at other times they staged counter-Bicentennial events in Lexington, Concord, and on the Boston Common.

That left Boston's smaller ethnic groups—the Jews, the Greeks, and the Armenians (as well as the Chinese)—to take the lead in the commemoration of the Bicentennial. (While Boston had a growing Puerto Rican population their role in the public life of the metropolis was minimal.) With the exception of the Jews none of these groups are cosmopolitan. They lacked individuals who make their living in advertising and public relations. They had very few intellectuals capable of interpreting the implications of the Bicentennial. The Greeks, for example, sponsor an institution of higher learning in Boston—Hellenic College. However, it is an obscure institution. Not only is it unknown to the general public but many of the academicians who teach at such well-known institutions as Boston College, Boston University, Brandeis, Tufts, Harvard, Northeastern, and any one of a dozen other colleges located in the Boston area, are not aware of its existence.

Armenians are another example of unobtrusive ethnicity. While the suburb of Watertown is the capital of Armenian America, Boston Armenians are quite insular. They do not seek to draw non-Armenians to Watertown. While the Italian store owners and restaurateurs of the North End seek to attract a clientele from the entire metropolitan area, the Armenians have never sought to entice the general public into shopping or eating in Watertown. Thus, if the Armenians celebrated the Bicentennial they would be the only people aware of the fact.

## V. The Blacks and the Bicentennial

As for the Blacks, they lacked any enthusiasm for the Bicentennial. The Bicentennial came at a time when Black children in Boston had to be escorted to their classrooms by the police. To be sure, the Boston Police Department acted with admirable discipline during this trying period. The police did their duty despite the fact that many of its members had strong loyalties to South Boston, Charlestown, and other areas of Irish concentration. However, in spite of the best efforts of the police the situation became intolerable. At the height of the disturbances the Boston Police Department barely managed to avoid what promised to become a racial war. At the end of each school day, the police were forced to use diversionary tactics in order to confuse local residents, get Black children from their classrooms into the buses, and return them to the safety of their own neighborhoods.

Even if school integration were not a burning issue the Blacks could not have been expected to muster any enthusiasm for the Bicentennial. The event, with its emphasis on the Colonial period, served to remind them that they had been brought to these shores against their will, that they had once been slaves in America, and that a Civil War had been fought to emancipate them. The Bicentennial also served to underline the fact that the Founding Fathers did not abolish slavery, and that some of the most revered figures of the Colonial period were slave-owners. Furthermore, the establishment of the nation meant that the institution of slavery came to be recognized in public law. Accordingly, the Black community proceeded to disregard the Bicentennial. Their response was somewhat similar to that of the Indians. The Black churches, which normally would have been the backbone of the Black celebration of the Bicentennial, kept silent. The churches knew the mood of their people.

## VI. The Jews and the Bicentennial

Under the circumstances the Jews became the single group both interested in and capable of mounting a significant Bicentennial commemoration. Their celebrations were sophisticated when compared with other groups. They were well publicized and were open to a citywide audience. The attendance of the city's principal religious, ethnic, and racial groups was solicited.

Boston Jewry's first advantage was that it had none of the resentment of the Yankees. Since Boston Jewry had no colonial roots to speak of, it could not feel displaced and dominated by others. To be sure, the Jews of Boston had been compelled to relinquish many Jewish neighborhoods to Blacks—including Dorchester, Roxbury, and Mattapan. Nevertheless, the attitude of Jews toward such changes has not had the fierce bitterness that is evident when the Irish or Italian domination of their ethnic neighborhoods is challenged.[1]

Like other groups, Boston Jews were shaken by Vietnam, by Watergate, by the energy crisis, by urban crime, and by the recession. It is also true that Jews of the New Left abhorred everything American just as fervently as did their Gentile comrades. Despite all of this, the mass of adult Jews had a positive response to the Bicentennial. For them it meant the commemoration of the establishment of a nation that offered them unparalleled opportunities and freedoms. Accordingly, the 4th of July, which celebrates the achievement of American independence and the formation of what has been called the first new nation, is a positive rather than a negative symbol to Jews. Furthermore, those Jews who had any knowledge of American-Jewish history realized that the achievement of American independence and the emergence of a unified nation was advantageous for them. It had the effect of speeding the elimination of anti-Jewish laws that were on the statute books of various states and of local jurisdictions and that dated from the Colonial period.

The feeling of the Jew toward America, however, went deeper than mere gratitude for economic opportunity or for the freedom to express Jewishness without harassment. Until very recently American Jews sought to repress the memory of the Holocaust. Nevertheless, they know very well what would have happened to them if grandfather had not left Poland or if great-great-grandmother had not left Bavaria. As we noted earlier, from this vantage point the Bicentennial had a very special meaning for Jews—a meaning that it could not have for other groups. To be sure, the Irish might have starved if they had remained in Ireland, but starvation is quite different from genocide. And if the Armenians had experiences with Turks that are sometimes referred to as genocidal, Armenians had the alternative of Armenia. Although the expression of Armenian nationalism has been controlled by the Soviets, Russian policy has not called for the genocide of Armenians.

All of this adds up to the fact that paradoxically it was the Jew—historically the outsider—who was able to fathom the meaning of the Bicentennial with its emphasis on the establishment of a new society free of the repression and stratification so characteristic of European nations. It is the Jew who was prepared to celebrate 200 years of American independence without feeling either angry or hypocritical. To be sure America has at times disappointed the Jew. Older American Jews can still remember tuning into the weekly radio broadcast of Father Coughlin during the Great Depression. They listened to Coughlin's rantings about a worldwide Jewish conspiracy with chilling fear. In the intervening years, however, the media have been careful to avoid a repetition of such hate mongering. And of course Coughlin rose to public attention during the Hitler era. This was a time when Jews were understandably fearful of their future.

Jews do feel that eternal vigilance is the price that must be paid for Jewish security. During the 1970's the Recession and especially the energy crisis were seen as engendering anti-Semitism. Nevertheless the Jews had a stake in the Bicentennial that even the Yankees could not appreciate, for in celebrating American independence the Jew also celebrated his escape from the Holocaust. The Holocaust theme is in fact magnified by developments in the Mideast. Without American political and military aid to Israel, the Jews of that country would have been at a loss to defend themselves against Arab might. However critical some American Jews were toward Administration policy in respect to Israel, no responsible observer would deny that American support had been vital to Israel's continued existence. The Bicentennial, then, may be taken to celebrate both American Jewry's escape from genocide and America's role in preventing a Holocaust in the Mideast.

## VII. Temple Mishkan Tefila and the Bicentennial

Boston's Jewish Bicentennial Committee took the Bicentennial seriously. And in addition to the events sponsored by the Jewish Bicentennial Committee, many Jewish groups organized their own Bicentennial events. Thus a large number of synagogues sponsored Bicentennial celebrations. The lead was taken by one of the city's largest and most historic Conservative congregations—Congregation Mishkan Tefila.* They mounted a particularly elaborate program. Mishkan Tefila saw itself as the "mother synagogue" of Conservative Judaism in New England and therefore as the institution that should set the pace for other synagogues.

While it is difficult to single out a particular event there is no doubt that the "Festival on the American Presidency," which took place on April 5–12, 1975, at Temple Mishkan Tefila of Chestnut Hill was the most elaborate and carefully planned Jewish event in commemoration of the Bicentennial. It included exhibits, films, lectures, and a variety of special events. The "Festival on the American Presidency" dealt with the presidencies of Hoover, FDR, Truman, Eisenhower, John F. Kennedy, and Lyndon Johnson. The Festival appeared to be the most elaborate event presented by any of the city's ethnic groups.

Mishkan Tefila could not have produced the Festival without the cooperation of the six presidential libraries. Working through a little-known public official, the Honorable James B. Rhoads, Archivist of the United States, the synagogue was able to obtain permission to borrow material from the various presidential libraries scattered in different parts of the nation. Exhibits from all parts of the country were assembled at the Temple and prepared under an overall plan. As Mishkan Tefila's brochure proudly put it:

The Festival on the American Presidency is made possible through the joint efforts of the nation's Presidential Libraries, which are a part of the National Archives and Records Service, General Services Administration, United States Government, and Temple Mishkan Tefila.

One of the greatest attractions of the Festival was the Kennedy memorabilia that were on display. Not only was Kennedy the only one of the six presidents whose roots were in Boston but at the time the treasures of the Kennedy Library had only been viewed by a small number of scholars. They had been stored in a U.S. Government warehouse pending resolution of the seemingly interminable argument about where the Kennedy Library should be built.

The Festival was no mere rehash of grammar-school civics. The description in the brochure issued by the Temple made the Festival sound like one geared to an audience that had taken a college-level political science course. The purpose of the Festival, according to the brochure issued by Mishkan Tefila, was to

* Mishkan Tefila: Hebrew for "Tabernacle of Prayer"

spread understanding of the functions and role of the American presidency, to show how diverse interest groups pressure the president, and to demonstrate how national leaders seek to unify a nation characterized by such diversity:

The purpose of this Festival is to enable the community at large to observe and understand the complex problems and pressures confronting our Presidents in making decisions which balance the needs and concerns of the various diverse ethnic and religious groups in our society with the national interests of our country.

A hallmark of American democracy has been the maintenance of unity in the midst of diversity. The nature of our pluralistic society is dramatically reflected in the personalities and policies of the American Presidents of the past half-century and in the cultural contributions and political participation of these groups.

Through exhibits, films, lectures, discussions and other special events, the Festival on the American Presidency will present to the Greater Boston community a dramatic panorama of what America has become and a clearer perspective of what may lie ahead. Visitors of all ages and backgrounds will have a unique opportunity to experience history first-hand through photographs, documents, and rarely seen memorabilia assembled from the six Presidential Libraries located throughout the country. This is the first time that material from all the Presidential Libraries has been presented in New England.

If the Festival stressed the political process, particularly as it related to the nation's ethnic and religious groups, there was a bit of Jewish communal politics involved in its promotion. Historically Boston's leading synagogue has been Temple Israel, a Reform institution. As a rule Boston's oldest and most prominent Jewish families joined Temple Israel. During the 1920's and '30's another old-line Reform synagogue, Ohabei Shalom of Brookline, challenged Temple Israel's position, but their effort was unsuccessful. However, during and after World War II, Conservative synagogues grew in numbers, in wealth, and in status, and they began to compete with Reform institutions for preeminence.[2]

Of the many Conservative synagogues in the Boston area, Mishkan Tefila is the oldest and has the most modern and imposing edifice. What Mishkan Tefila was saying in sponsoring the Festival was that it, not Temple Israel, was Number One. In an article in the "Presidential Festival Special Edition" of the *Temple Mishkan Tefila News* the congregation's rabbi, Israel Kazis, emphasized that Mishkan Tefila had been established as early as 1858 in the South End, that Sabato Morais had come from Philadelphia to participate in the dedication of its first sanctuary, and that the synagogue's records show that a long list of notables had delivered lectures at Mishkan Tefila, among them Louis D. Brandeis, Solomon Schechter, Eleanor Roosevelt, and Richard Cardinal Cushing, who had been the favorite Catholic prelate of the Jews of Boston. Rabbi Kazis also pointed out that such famous personalities as Leonard Bernstein received their religious training at Mishkan Tefila.

If some of these subtleties meant for Jewish communal leaders were lost on the large crowds of Jews and Gentiles who came to the Festival, there was no questioning the high degree of professionalism that went into planning the event. The Festival was a multi-media presentation that had something for everybody. Mishkan Tefila's entrance hall became a "Hall of Flags" and its main corridor a "Presidential Gallery." Other parts of the building were devoted to special themes; "See How They Ran," for example, consisted of films of presidential campaigns. There was a special exhibit on "The American President and the Issue of a Jewish State." Since the Festival sought to serve a variety of publics, there was a Senior Citizens Day during which the aged John W. McCormack of the House of Representatives reminisced. Also featured on Senior Citizens Day was David F. Powers, the longtime aide to JFK and the coauthor of *Johnny, We Hardly Knew Ye.*

The Festival made a particular point of attracting high school groups. In addition to the exhibits the students were shown a "decision film" titled "With the Stroke of a Pen." Discussion of the "decision film" took place at the Festival and later in the classroom. Discussion guides were available; they had been prepared with social studies teachers and coordinators representing many city and suburban high schools as well as a number of private schools in the area.

Lectures were given by such nationally known professors and public figures as Daniel P. Moynihan and Arthur M. Schlesinger, Jr. Local Jewish academicians, chiefly professors at Harvard and Brandeis, were also featured in the program. On a lighter note there were presentations by relatives of presidents—most notably Eunice Kennedy Shriver whose subject was "Insights into the Personality of Former Presidents." The first evening of the Festival was devoted to a champagne reception for invited guests. Invitations were extended to important figures in local academic, religious, and business circles and more particularly those who had contributed the necessary funds for the Festival, or had served on the numerous committees formed to ensure the success of the event. Dr. Rhoads was the guest speaker at this event.

The director of the Kennedy Library, Dr. Dan H. Fenn, Jr., pronounced the Festival a success:

We wanted to see whether the Kennedy Library and a distinguished religious society could combine on a program of interest and importance to the general public. We felt that the combined resources and talents of the Library and the Temple could produce a dramatic and unusual collection of events which would appeal to a variety of interests and age levels.

However, the man who had inspired the Festival was not invited; his existence was not even acknowledged in the numerous press releases and brochures that were issued by Mishkan Tefila's public relations committee. The great unseen presence of the Festival was Richard Milhouse Nixon. Nixon had brought the presidency into disrepute, and the unspoken agenda of the Festival was to bring the presidency back into good repute. The Festival seemed to be saying that the faith of the people in the presidency needed to be restored and that the best way to do that was to study Nixon's immediate predecessors. What was suggested was that whatever their shortcomings and however diverse their ideologies and modes of leadership, Hoover, FDR, Truman, Eisenhower, JFK, and Johnson had at least a decent regard for the public interest. Although the presidency had been besmirched by an unscrupulous leader who had surrounded himself with a gang of immoral assistants eager to engage in a host of illegal operations, the Festival seemed to be saying that this was not the real presidency. Dr. John T. Dunlop, a one-time Secretary of Labor, participated at the Festival by presenting what was described as "a case study on decision making in the field of economic policy." His appearance was a way of saying that the system was self-correcting—that under President Ford the presidency was back in the hands of respectable leaders. Thus it was once more entitled to public trust and confidence.

## VIII. An Afterword

When some future historian analyzes the observance of the nation's Bicentennial, judging from the celebration in Boston that person will have to study the Jewish reaction. The Puritans who landed at Plymouth Rock in 1620 saw themselves as fleeing from bondage as did the Israelites when they left Egypt. They had a sense of gratitude because they had miraculously survived and were privileged to reach the haven that was America. They felt that America could become a new Zion and an example to the nations. The descendants of the Puritans seem to be less certain of these ideals: they are unsure of whether these earlier ideals can prevail. Other groups were even more alienated at the time of the Bicentennial in 1975. The Catholics were engaged in battling desegregation. The Blacks fought back although some were not sure of the extent to which desegregation would improve their lot. The smaller ethnic groups, some of which did not have the problems regarding the Bicentennial held by the Irish, Italians, or Blacks, had limited horizons. They lacked academicians and intellectuals who could interpret the significance of the Bicentennial for their group life.

The Jews were special in that they did not have these problems. They possessed a stronger motivation to celebrate the Bicentennial than others. They could therefore serve as an example to the Gentiles though that was not the motivation for their behavior (Jews have been most circumspect in saying anything about how Gentiles have observed [or not observed] the Bicentennial). If indeed it turns out that the Jews are the last Puritans, they will have served American society well. Despite their small numbers they will have provided an example of a group that does not take America for granted—a group that comprehends the greatness of America, warts and all.

## Notes

1. See Marshall Sklare, "Jews, Ethnics, and the American City," *Commentary*, 53, No. 4 (April 1972), 70–77.

2. See Marshall Sklare, *Conservative Judaism: An American Religious Movement* (New York: Schocken Books, 1972), pp. 251–61.

# The Jew in American
# Sociological Thought

Perhaps the most notable fact about the Jew in American sociological thought is that writing and research on Jews has been left so largely in the hands of Jewish scholars.[1] Gentile sociologists do not avoid writing about Jews where it is relevant to a larger interest, but they have not been strongly preoccupied with the study of Jewish life. The reason is, of course, that there has been no "Jewish problem" in American society in the European sense of that term. When during the 1930's and early 1940's it appeared that anti-Semitism was on the increase and that a Jewish problem might be injected into American political life, Gentile social scientists joined with Jewish social scientists to provide scholarly material that could be used to counteract the work of the bigots.[2] But in less threatening times Gentile sociologists tend to leave the study of Jewish life to their Jewish colleagues.

They have done so confident in the knowledge that there were sufficient Jewish sociologists to provide the needed data and interpretation. In fact, the image in academia is that Jews are especially numerous and influential in sociology. This image is not altogether inaccurate, for sociology is one of the fields favored by American-Jewish academicians. Nevertheless, the proportion of academicians in sociology who are Jewish is much lower than in certain other fields. The most obvious examples are medicine and law—the traditional choices of Jews who have wished to go into the professions rather than into business. The survey sponsored in 1969 by the Carnegie Commission on Higher Education, which was based on a sample of 60,000 academicians, discloses that 13 percent of those who teach sociology in American universities are Jewish, but that as many as 25 percent of those who teach law are Jewish, and that 22 percent of those who teach medicine are Jewish.[3]

According to the Carnegie Commission survey Jews constitute some 9 percent of the American professoriat (the Jewish input into the American professoriat is slightly larger, for some of the respondents who claimed "no-religion"

are undoubtedly of Jewish ancestry) (L-L, p. 92).[4] Since 13 percent of the sociological professoriat is Jewish, the field is certainly one that is attractive to Jews.
Actually such attractiveness is characteristic of the social sciences as a whole,
for the Jewish representation in anthropology, economics, political science,
and psychology all exceed the figure of 9 percent of the professoriat that is
Jewish.

Even if 13 percent of the sociological professoriat are Jewish, Jews might be
an insignificant force in a field where 20 percent of the academicians are Catholic and a full 59 percent are Protestant (L-L, p. 95). Furthermore, not only are
American sociologists predominantly Protestant, but Protestant sociologists
are considerably older than their Jewish colleagues and thus might be assumed
to occupy a more strategic position in the field. Since American sociology was
established by Protestant sociologists, the Protestant input might well be even
larger than contemporary statistics indicate. Nevertheless, while Protestants
are predominant in American sociology numerically and are entirely dominant
historically, the image about the Jewish proclivity for sociology is not entirely
mistaken. Given their numbers Jews are extraordinarily influential in American
sociology—though there may be other academic fields where they are similarly
influential.

The Jewish role in sociology is of course related to the overall position of
Jews in American academia. The rise of Jews in the American professoriat is
especially significant because it has been achieved despite the handicap of dis-
criminatory practices that were not substantially modified until after World
War II. The rise has also been achieved without governmental intervention:
Neither preferential treatment nor "affirmative action" has been utilized to
ensure Jewish representation. (In fact rather than being aided by "affirmative action" the influence of Jews may come to be diminished by "affirmative action.") In only three fields of study are Jews less numerous than their
proportion in the American population—namely, in agriculture, religion and
theology, and geography.

The influence of Jews in American academia rests less on their numbers than
on the fact that they have been able to qualify for positions at leading universities and also that they have been extraordinarily productive academicians. In
regard to the type of school with which they are connected the Carnegie Commission data indicate that a much higher proportion of Jewish academicians
are located at the most prestigious universities than is true for Protestants.
Thus some 32 percent of the Jews serve on the faculty of the institutions designated as those of the "highest quality." This is in contrast to only 10 percent of
the Protestants who serve at such institutions (L-L, p. 100). Furthermore, the
publication record of Jewish academicians is outstanding. Despite their youth-
fulness (only 4 percent of faculty 65 years of age-and-over are Jewish while 79
percent of such faculty are Protestants), some 21 percent of Jewish faculty have
already published more than twenty articles in academic or professional jour-

nals. This is in contrast to 9 percent of the Protestant faculty and 6 percent of the Catholic faculty (L-L, p. 101).

It appears, then, that when Gentiles leave the development of sociological thought on Jews to the Jews themselves, they leave it to a group of extraordinarily influential and productive academicians. Viewed from another vantage point, it may be said that Jews are in what may be regarded as the fortunate position of being able to determine how their group is to be portrayed. Rather than be the objects of study by others they can determine for themselves how they are to appear to the larger society. In this respect the Jewish situation has been quite different from that of Blacks, Puerto Ricans, Italians, Poles, and others, where for many decades there were few qualified scholars of minority origin capable of dealing adequately with the groups in which they were reared. In lieu of qualified scholars coming from the in-group it became the obligation of the academic community as a whole to provide needed data and interpretation about particular minority groups.

## The Jewish Ideological Style

Since writing and research on American Jewry have been largely in the hands of Jewish academicians, such writing and research should be influenced by the characteristic ideological style, if any, of Jewish academicians. Even casual observation of the American academic scene suggests that there is a Jewish style: Jewish academicians are more critical of the status quo, are more anti-establishment, are more liberal or radical than Gentile faculty. Attitude studies confirm what casual observation suggests. Thus the Carnegie Commission data indicate that 75 percent of Jewish academicians characterize their politics as either "liberal" or "left" in contrast to 42 percent of the Protestants (L-L, p. 114). The disparity is particularly wide among the minority of faculty who characterize their politics as "left": 12 percent of Jewish faculty consider themselves "left" in contrast to only 4 percent of Protestant faculty.

The degree of "liberalism-leftism" of Jewish academicians varies from discipline to discipline. However, Jewish faculty are more "liberal-left" than Protestant or Catholic faculty whether in the social sciences, the humanities, the natural sciences, or in other fields. Furthermore, the greater affinity of the Jews for the "liberal-left" position is found among Jewish faculty who serve all types of institutions from "highest quality" universities to second-level colleges (L-L, p. 120).

The "liberal-left" position is more pervasive in the social sciences than it is in the humanities or natural sciences (L-L, p. 120). The "liberal-left" position has been strongly represented in sociology, and there has consequently been considerable receptivity to the Jewish "liberal-left" style. While the influence of the Jewish style may be assumed, the dynamics of the process remain unclear, for little if anything is said in standard studies of American academia about

the interaction of Jews and Gentiles. Thus the question of whether Jewish faculty (and perhaps Jewish students as well) have radicalized Gentile faculty or
whether Gentile faculty have made Jews more conservative than they would
otherwise be, has never been adequately studied. In sociology it is entirely
possible that Jewish academicians have had a stronger ideological influence
on Gentile academicians than Gentile academicians have had on Jewish academicians. To be sure, the emergence of aggressive minorities (both ethnic
and nonethnic) on the American academic scene—Blacks, Puerto Ricans, Chicanos, and women—has shifted attention away from what was earlier primarily
a question of the interaction between Jewish and Gentile faculty members and
students.

The emergence of the new minorities, as well as the sharp shift in the political spectrum during the 1960's, has served to complicate the interaction of
Jews and Gentiles in sociology. These changes have resulted in some of the
most prestigious Jewish sociologists assuming the unaccustomed role of being
leaders of establishment sociology. Such Jewish sociologists are liberals in the
older liberal tradition, or leftists in the older leftist tradition. While their earlier
work was considered deviant, daring, or even dangerous, their present work is
considered by some to be in the tradition of establishment sociology. Adherents of the "new sociology" sometimes view it as symptomatic of what they
feel is the corruption of American sociology.

This new development aside, how can the "liberalism-leftism" of the Jewish academician be explained? The simplest explanation is inheritance: Jewish
academicians are "liberal-left" because their parents had "liberal-left" convictions. While there is some evidence for this interpretation (L-L, p. 113) it does
not answer the question of the origin of "liberalism-leftism" among Jews. The
investigation of the origin problem has taken two different approaches. Some
investigators have pursued the line of reasoning that Jewish "liberalism-leftism"
can be explained on the basis of the position that Jews occupy in American
society, while others have taken the position that Jewish "liberal-leftism" can
be traced to the internalization of a Jewish value system. More recent research
has tended to stress the influence of Jewish family structure and child-rearing
patterns.

## The Jewish Identity of the Jewish Sociologist

Whatever implications Jewish "liberalism-leftism" has for American academia as a whole, our special interest is in its effect on Jewish identity, for the
Jewish identity of Jewish sociologists is of crucial significance in determining
how the Jew is portrayed in American sociological thought.

The problem centers on the fact that "liberalism-leftism" should serve to
diminish Jewish identity. As a belief system, "liberalism-leftism" may conflict
with Jewish identity, whether that identity be religious or ethnic in empha-

sis. To be sure the conflict of "liberalism-leftism" with Jewish identity may be moderated in a variety of ways. However, it may also be heightened. The most significant way in which it is heightened is by the individual feeling that he is an intellectual. Intellectuality may lead to a feeling of alienation from existing social structures, including that of the Jewish community. Intellectuality may mean a diminished salience of one's membership in the Jewish community and a heightened feeling of loyalty to membership in the trans-religious, trans-ethnic community of the intelligentsia.

The Carnegie Commission data highlight the proclivity of Jewish academicians to consider themselves intellectuals. In response to the statement "I consider myself an intellectual" 83 percent of the Jews responded "strongly agree" or "agree with reservations." The figure for both Protestants and Catholics was 68 percent. The disparity between Jews and Gentiles is wider than these figures suggest for the crucial group is the one that has a strong image of its intellectuality. We find that while 16 percent of the Protestants and 18 percent of the Catholics "strongly agree" with the statement about intellectuality, some 36 percent of Jewish faculty "strongly agree" (L-L, p. 104).

In theory only in Israel can "liberalism-leftism," in combination with intellectuality, function to supplement more than to supplant Jewish identity. However, even in Israel there are difficulties in building a strong Jewish identity among those simultaneously committed to "liberalism-leftism" and intellectuality. Data are hard to come by since there is only a single important study of Jewish identity in Israel—Simon Herman's *Israelis and Jews*—and furthermore Herman's basic sample is composed of high school youth.[5] Nevertheless, since Herman strongly highlights the fact that being reared in a *secular* Jewish household results in a much weaker Jewish identity than being reared in a religious household, we may infer that the negative relationship in the Diaspora between "liberalism-leftism," intellectuality, and Jewish identity is more characteristic of Israel than traditional Zionist thinking would suggest.

That American-Jewish academicians are more alienated from the Jewish community than other Jews, including Jews with considerable general education, has been documented by both attitude and community studies. Thus, children of academics consider it more likely that they will intermarry than do children of businessmen or professionals, and a larger proportion of them participate in interreligious dating.[6] A study of Champaign-Urbana (Illinois) finds "town" Jews much more strongly identified with the Jewish community than "gown" Jews despite the fact that "town" Jews are descended from families that have been in the United States for a longer period.[7]

The problem of Jewish alienation is particularly evident among social scientists. In a study by Allan Mazur of Jewish social scientists at three major universities in the Boston area it was found that the Jewish identity of such social scientists was considerably weaker than that of Jewish Bostonians generally. While 38 percent of the social scientists have a Gentile spouse, this was true

for only 7 percent of Jewish Bostonians; while only 13 percent of the social
scientists belong to at least one Jewish organization, 50 percent of the Bostonians belong; while only 27 percent of the social scientists attend High Holiday
services, 77 percent of the Bostonians attend. Turning to the area of ritual
observance we find that only in respect to a single ritual—participating in a
Passover seder—are the differences between the two groups somewhat moderated: 59 percent of the social scientists participate in a seder while 87 percent
of the Bostonians do so.[8] All of this adds up to a pervasive alienation from the
Jewish community. According to Mazur:

alienation was reported by a majority of all respondents, but was particularly strong
at Brandeis with 70 percent of the subjects giving alienated responses as opposed
to only 48 percent and 53 percent at Boston University and Harvard respectively.
(Mazur, p. 277)

These findings clue us to the possibility that the result of having the portrait
of American Jewry painted by sociologists who are Jewish may have unanticipated consequences. Instead of the danger that their portrait may involve
a self-serving ethnocentrism, it could involve a critical, alienated, and even
deprecatory view of the Jewish community. The finding about Brandeis social
scientists is particularly significant in giving us insight into the identity problems of Jewish academicians. At first glance the finding appears anomalous.
Presumably social scientists at Brandeis should be less alienated from their
Jewishness than those at Boston University or Harvard. Boston University and
Harvard have a historic relationship with American Protestantism. Despite all
of their secularization, they still train candidates for the Protestant ministry.
Brandeis on the other hand is an institution that to all intents and purposes
is sponsored by the Jewish community. Mazur's explanation for the heightened alienation of Brandeis social scientists is that this sponsorship creates a
psychological conflict for its Jewish faculty members. Brandeis's very connection with the Jewish community serves to motivate its Jewish faculty to deny
any connection with the Jewish community:

The Brandeis faculty orientation can be viewed as an extremely functional adaptation to a potentially conflicting situation. Such close association with a Jewish
institution is difficult to resolve in terms of [the] ego's intellectual set of values. It
would be cognitively dissonant to disapprove of ethnic communalism . . . while
at the same time being intimately associated with an ethnic institution. However,
by a strict compartmentalization of Jews into "them" (the materialistic, the professionals, the new-rich, the Brandeis administration) and "us" (the Jewish intellectual, the ultraliberal, the Brandeis faculty), it is possible for the individual to
very completely dissociate his self concept from most of those characteristics of the
ethnic community that are so distasteful. Academics at Boston University and Harvard are not so closely associated with Jewish communalism, and therefore are not
under as great pressure to dissociate themselves from the Jewish community, and
therefore do not manifest the extremes of . . . alienation found at Brandeis. (Mazur,
p. 278)

The alienation that we have noted in the case of Jewish social scientists would suggest that in some cases attraction to sociology has been at least in part an ideological attraction. Sociology to some Jewish academicians may be a calling as much as a profession—a calling that signifies a break with the ethnic and religious parochialism of the academician's Jewish past. It may signify a refusal to follow in the footsteps of ancestors who made *Jewish* identity a central aspect of their existence. And for some, sociology may signify not only a break with the past but also the desire to replace membership in the Jewish ethnic community with membership in an intellectual subsociety: "the academic community."

The alienation of Jewish sociologists from Jewish communal ties may not be distinguishable from the alienation of Jewish social scientists generally. However, those sociologists who specialize in the study of minority groups confront the problem of Jewish identity in a much more direct way than their colleagues. They must take a position on whether minority groups (especially the Jews) should pursue the goal of self-segregation, acculturation, or assimilation.

Historically the "liberalism-leftism" of the Jewish sociologist, together with his intellectuality, has made assimilation the most attractive alternative. Since ours is an age of ethnicity, however, in recent years there has been greater tolerance for those who prefer to remain within the ethnic community. There has also been greater sentimentalism in regard to the ethnic community than there was at an earlier period. Such sentimentalism is actually part of the alienation from Jewish identity experienced by the Jewish academic, and particularly by the Jewish social scientist. Thus there is rejection of Jews who are on the same class and educational level as oneself and an attraction to Jews who are lower class and uneducated. Mazur quotes one of his respondents as follows:

Well I suppose I feel most alienated not from the European-born pushcart peddlers in New York City—I don't feel as alienated from them as I do from American-born Jews who have been to college, who live in the suburbs, who are fairly well-to-do, and who are afraid to let go. . . . It's interesting. I never thought of that before, but I feel less alienated from the Yiddish-speaking pushcart peddler than I do from people who are closer to me. (Mazur, p. 277)

Of course pushcart peddling exists only in the imagination, having in the 1930's come to an end as an occupation for Jews in New York City. For most Jewish academics pushcart peddling is pure folklore; it is a fair assumption that none of them is personally acquainted with a pushcart peddler.

## The Fourth Community

Given his secularism the Jewish sociologist has not been attracted to the solution of resolving his Jewish alienation by conversion to Protestantism or Catholicism. Indeed he may find Christianity even more unattractive than Judaism. Among leftists the resolution of the problem of Jewish alienation has resulted in the advocacy of a restructuring of society—a restructuring where all old loyalties would be sundered. Among liberals there has been a less drastic resolution of the problem of Jewish alienation—namely the advocacy of a fourth community that would co-exist with the three older communities of Catholics, Protestants, and Jews. The fourth community—composed of ex-Catholics, ex-Protestants, and ex-Jews—would be granted the same legitimacy accorded to the traditional communities.

Appropriately it was a Jewish sociologist specializing in the study of ethnic groups—Milton Gordon—who developed the hypothesis that "intellectuals in the United States interact in such patterned ways as to form at least the elementary structure of a subsociety of their own."[9] While Gordon admired the work of Will Herberg, he could not accept Herberg's conception of America as composed of only three religious communities, each of which had a strong ethnic component. Gordon saw America as composed of four communities (or "subsocieties")—the fourth community consisting of liberal-leftist intellectuals who wished to leave their ancestral religious and ethnic communities. Such intellectuals found in the university a particularly congenial environment.

The most revealing aspect of Gordon's hypothesis was his attempt to legitimate the intellectual subsociety. He viewed American academia as a community more than as an institution, and he made a strong plea for the right of individuals to leave what they saw as the narrow confines of their religious and ethnic groups in favor of the wider horizons of the intellectual subsociety. To be sure, Gentile sociologists such as Robert M. MacIver and S. C. Dodd had been critical of Jewish particularism. Furthermore, an earlier generation of Gentile sociologists—notably Edward A. Ross and Henry Pratt Fairchild—had viewed acculturation and assimilation from a nativistic perspective. They had emphasized the necessity, indeed the obligation, of immigrants to adapt themselves to what would now be called Wasp culture. Gordon, however, views assimilation in terms of the right to assimilate. The "birthright ethnic group," as he termed it, should desist from criticizing its assimilationist academics and intellectuals. Since criticism might provoke guilt, Gordon viewed criticism as constituting unwarranted interference in the right of each individual to determine his ethnic destiny:[10]

the individual, as he matures and reaches the age where rational decision is feasible, should be allowed to choose freely whether to remain within the boundaries of communality created by his birthright ethnic group, to branch out into multiple interethnic contacts, or even to change affiliation to that of another ethnic group should he wish to do so as a result of religious conversion, intermarriage, or simply private wish. If, to the contrary, the ethnic group places such heavy pressures on its birthright members to stay confined to ethnic communality that the individual who consciously wishes to "branch out" or "move away" feels intimidated or subject to major feelings of personal guilt and therefore remains ethnically enclosed, or moves but at considerable psychological cost, then we have, in effect, cultural democracy for groups but not for individuals. (Gordon, p. 263)

## The Sociological Study of American Jewry

Given the alienation that we have noted, it is apparent that Jewish sociologists would tend to concentrate on fields of study other than that of the sociology of the Jews. Concentration on the sociology of the Jews would not serve their identity needs. Since the preference has been to view oneself as a general intellectual rather than as a Jewish sociologist there has been little motivation to involve oneself in the sociological study of American Jewry. Lipset has emphasized that considering their numbers and prominence Jewish sociologists in the United States have done relatively little to advance knowledge about contemporary American Jewry. He traces this situation to the desire to be perceived as an American intellectual rather than as a Jewish sociologist:

The failure of Jewish social scientists to engage in research on the Jews reflects their desire to be perceived as American rather than Jewish intellectuals. To write in depth about the Jewish community would seemingly expose them to being identified as "Jewish Jews," as individuals who are too preoccupied with an ethnic identity, and who lack the universalistic orientation prized by social scientists and American intellectuals generally.[11]

Lipset points out that while Gentile social scientists have "a considerable fascination with Jewish life," they have tended to avoid "studying the Jew precisely because of the large number of Jews in their fields. Sustained contact with Jews suggests to them . . . that Jewish social scientists would do a better job of understanding the Jewish community than an outsider" (Lipset, pp. 162–63).

In the absence of a "Jewish problem" in America, both Gentile sociologists and Jewish sociologists have not experienced any pressure to turn to the study of American Jewry. Both Jewish sociologists and white Gentile sociologists interested in minority groups have tended to concentrate on the study of Blacks—though this has changed in the recent past as Black sociologists have pressed their claims for a Black sociology. The fact that there has been no "Jewish problem" in the United States, combined with the Jewish alienation of the Jewish sociologist, has had the result, then, that sociological research and writing on Jews have been limited and sporadic. Nevertheless, such writing and research have slowly accumulated. Its character has differed from period to period, being affected by changes in sociological thinking as well as by shifts in attitude toward the goals of minority-group living. While these shifts have occurred among members of the dominant group, we are particularly concerned with those shifts that have taken place among minority-group members themselves.

## The Assimilationist Perspective

The most widely known book on the sociology of the American Jew was inspired by a Protestant founder of American sociology, Robert E. Park. A

member of the faculty of the University of Chicago, Park was intensely interested in the sociology of minority groups, including such phenomena as the
marginal man and the clash between the ancestral culture of an immigrant
group and the new culture with which they were in contact. He induced Louis
Wirth (1897–1952)—then a graduate student at the University—to select a Jewish topic for his Ph.D. dissertation. Wirth's research eventuated in *The Ghetto*.
The volume became one of the most popular items in the series of sociological
monographs published by the University of Chicago Press.[12]

Wirth prefigured the present prominence of Jews in American sociology. He
was the first Jew to serve as president of what is now the American Sociological
Association and his worldwide reputation led to his election as the first president of the International Sociological Association. However, he did not make
any substantial contribution to the study of American Jewry after completing
his dissertation. True to Lipset's formulation Wirth desired to be perceived as
an American intellectual rather than as a Jewish sociologist.

Wirth saw the ghetto as a haven from the real world of the metropolis. The
ghetto would die as soon as prejudice diminished, and as soon as its inhabitants
had sufficient opportunity to prepare themselves to participate in the wider
community. The closing pages of *The Ghetto* make clear Wirth's belief that
the Jewish community was an anachronism prolonged by Gentile prejudice
(Wirth, pp. 263–81).[13]

If Wirth's view of the Jewish community was that it was provincial and
retrogressive, his hope for the general community was that ultimately its members would act more rationally, thus permitting the Jews to assimilate. Such
assimilation would involve intermarriage. Despite the fact that Wirth's earliest years were spent in the Orthodox atmosphere of a Rhineland village, he
himself proceeded to marry a Gentile. According to his daughter Wirth was:

the first member of his family to marry a non-Jew . . . [his] assimilationist inclinations and principles, like those of his wife, partly derived from their common
reaction against dogmatism and provincial ethnocentrism. Their two daughters
were to be encouraged in agnosticism with audible atheistic overtones, at the same
time that they were to acquire a generalized minority ethnic identification.[14]

Since Wirth viewed the Jewish community as a dying entity, he did not
continue the research that had eventuated in publication of *The Ghetto*. Rather
he proceeded to direct his attention to the need for social planning, for better
cities, and for improved understanding between racial groups. Nevertheless,
his interest in fighting discrimination and his desire to combat Nazism had the
effect of keeping him in touch with Jewish organizations. It also motivated
him to write once again on a Jewish topic. Thus during World War II Wirth
published an article in the *American Journal of Sociology* that paid homage to
Jewish tenacity in the face of persecution.[15]

## The Critical Intellectual Perspective

Wirth's overtly assimilationist position can still be encountered among Jewish sociologists. However, after World War II a new type emerged: the sociologist who wished to retain his Jewish identity but who at the same time felt alienated from the Jewish community. If Wirth was an "assimilationist intellectual," such sociologists may be termed "critical intellectuals."

The critical intellectual treads a narrow line. On the one hand he wishes in some way to affirm his Jewishness, but he typically finds it difficult to comfortably practice the patterns of Jewishness followed by most of his fellow Jews. Furthermore, despite his desire to affirm Jewishness he may be more strongly affected by the universalistic orientations of the academy than he knows; he may wish to demonstrate that his Jewish interest should not be construed as meaning that he has defected from the academic community. It is immediately apparent that critical academics do not replicate the experience of a Louis Wirth. They have not emerged from the darkness of the European village into the light of the modern world. On the contrary, they were brought up in the metropolis. Since they come from the city, they do not feel compelled to celebrate urbanism as a way of life—they may in fact prefer suburbia or even exurbia. And unlike Wirth who sought to work within the power structure and who never engaged in radical social criticism despite a brief encounter with Marxism, many critical academics are oriented to the left. They pride themselves on their radicalism and on their feeling of alienation from most other Americans. Not only has the increased acceptability of ethnicity in American society made the critical academic a more common phenomenon but it has resulted in the fact that marginal Jews in academia tend to be more "Jewish" than ever before.

It is characteristic of the critical academic that he tends to idealize the immigrant Jew rather than to denigrate him. Instead of viewing the ghetto as retrogressive, the critical academic generally admires it. The ghetto was community. In the ghetto the Jews did their own thing; life was with people. The critical academic reasons that if today's Jews were as authentic as their ancestors he would be able to relate to them and hence he would be able to find meaning in his Jewishness.

A little more than three decades after *The Ghetto* was published, *Children of the Gilded Ghetto* by Judith Kramer and Seymour Leventman appeared.[16] The volume constitutes a kind of sequel to Wirth's book. However, the two volumes stand in sharp contrast. *Children of the Gilded Ghetto* contains much nostalgia for the immigrant era when Jews lived on the margins of society and, according to the authors, were rooted in Jewish culture. Kramer and Leventman infer that although the immigrants were poor and struggling they led a rich and rewarding existence. However, with the rise of Jews into the middle and upper classes American Jewry changed course. Wealthy and successful Jews proceeded to replace the ghetto with a new creation—the gilded ghetto. The inhabitants of gilded ghettos lead sterile lives—prosperity has made them vulgar members of country clubs. Their ostentation extends beyond their extravagant clothes and cars; even charitable giving has become an aspect of their conspicuous consumption. The gilded-ghetto Jews are part of the establishment, or they think that they are. Whatever the limitations of yesterday's immigrant ghetto, it is infinitely preferable to today's gilded ghetto. And, finally, the gilded ghetto cannot long endure—the changing occupational structure of American Jewry will provide the impetus for at least some Jews to turn their backs on the gilded ghetto.

The esteem in which the immigrant community is held is traceable only in part to the supposed authenticity of the Jewish culture that prevailed there. The critical academic is equally attracted by the fact that left-wing movements flourished in first- and second-settlement areas.[17] Accordingly, if the critical academic tends to approve of the "ghetto," he tends to disapprove of Jewish suburbia where Jews seem to conform to regnant American cultural patterns. In suburbia there are no radical orators haranguing a crowd, no proletarian demonstrations, no talk of "the bosses."

The critical academic finds it difficult to relate to that segment of the Jewish community that he is exposed to by virtue of his high acculturation and striking occupational success. He takes no pride in the Jewish middle and upper class: instead of applauding their social mobility he views it critically. Instead of admiration for the desire of Jews to maintain their identity and simultaneously to adapt to American culture, the critical academic—despite his own acculturation—views the desire to acculturate as a compromise unworthy of the descendants of Biblical prophets. Eager to justify his disdain of *bourgeois* Jews the critical academic finds himself highlighting instances of Jewish vulgarity. He views ostentation as proof of the degeneration of the American Jew. As was apparent in the previously cited case of the social scientist interviewed by Mazur, to the critical academic whatever might be said against the pushcart peddler at least he lived a life free of what is felt to be the corruption of the *bourgeoisie*.

Although the critical academic charges the American Jew with vulgarity and ostentation, his most biting criticism is reserved for the politics of the American Jew. As the critical academic sees it the Jewish middle and upper classes are at best conservative and at worst downright reactionary. Instead of carefully weighing the evidence in order to assess the exact degree to which Jewish political attitudes have shifted, the critical academic assumes that successful Jews are conservative. No credence is given to evidence of continuing liberalism among Jews. Furthermore, instead of regarding the growth of conservatism among middle- and upper-class Jews (and now among lower-class and lower-middle-class Jews as well) as inevitable, the critical academic regards it as sinful.

The critical academic is not surprised by the degree of liberalism found among Jews despite their class position (or in the case of less successful Jews, the degree of their liberalism despite the threat that Blacks and Puerto Ricans pose both to their physical security and their occupational position). Rather he seizes upon instances of Jewish conservatism. The strident tone of his criticism suggests that the critical academic is more ethnocentric than he knows: Gentile conservatism is regarded with equanimity while Jewish conservatism is viewed with total disdain.

Melvin Tumin best exemplifies the tendency of the critical academic to charge that the American Jew is a reactionary and hence unworthy of the esteem of honest men.[18] One of the most successful of the post-Wirth generation of Jewish sociologists, Tumin took his doctorate in 1944, and three years later, at the age of twenty-eight, he was offered a professorship at Princeton. Tumin accepted but did not proceed to make himself over in the Princeton image. Rather he continued to espouse the leftism of his radical past. Furthermore, Tumin did not lose touch with Jewish life—during the 1950's and 1960's he was in close contact with Jewish organizations, notably with the Anti-Defamation League. Nevertheless Tumin felt alienated from the Jewish community, as had Louis Wirth at an earlier period. He could barely conceal his contempt for the American Jew:

it would indeed be radical in American politics if there were an identifiable Jewish vote and if that Jewish vote stood for a morally radical position on the political spectrum. And it would be a beautiful challenge to America if the Jewish vote were known as such and worried about as such by all politicians, and known and responded to as such by all non-Jews. Then, you see, the Jews would stand for something, and something vital and alive on the American scene. Then Jewishness would constitute determinate identity. Then to be a Jew would be to be something definite and impressive, however much Jews might be joined in their political position by non-Jews. Short of that, what do Jews stand for in America? For a normal distribution of political opinions along the same spectrum and in the same proportions as non-Jews. However normal, self-protecting and expectable this may be, in effect it is a phenomenon essentially preservative of the status quo. However much this may, in the long run, be the best strategy for self-preservation, it ducks—as it must—the essential question of what is the self that is being preserved. And however much finally—in view of their history—Jews have a right to find their way to life and safety by whatever means they discover or contrive—they ought not to confuse this right and this technique for self-preservation with either a determinate identity or with anything culturally valuable today. (Tumin, p. 138)

Tumin is particularly embittered because he feels that not only has the average Jew sold out to the American establishment but that Jewish intellectuals—of whom more should be expected—have done so as well:

The most distressing aspect of this move into the sphere of all-rightness is the ways in which it is manifested among Jewish intellectuals. In apparent total forgetfulness of the role which radical criticism of American society played in the first half of this century in helping make America less execrable than it might otherwise have been, Jewish intellectuals have increasingly come to play the role of gentlemen of the Establishment. Beguiled by the chance to become influential—in government, education, industry, the mass media—many Jews have rushed in to take advantage of this opportunity to become insiders. (Tumin, p. 139) [19]

## The Survivalist Perspective

We have seen that some sociologists have viewed American Jews as a dying people whose existence is artificially prolonged by Gentile prejudice, while others have viewed American Jews as a reprehensible group that has succumbed to corruptions resulting from newly achieved class position. We are now prepared to consider a third approach to the Jew that exists in American sociological thought: the survivalist perspective.

The survivalist perspective looks for evidence of continuity as well as assimilation. Furthermore, it does not uphold assimilation as a desirable objective. To be sure, adherents of the survivalist perspective differ considerably in the degree to which they are committed to Jewish survival; what they have in common is that they do not uphold assimilation as the goal toward which the minority group should strive. Perhaps the best glimpse into how the survivalist perspective differs from the assimilationist perspective and the critical intellectual perspective is afforded by the closing lines of the first edition of Nathan Glazer's *American Judaism*. This book, which resulted from a series of lectures delivered at the same university where Louis Wirth taught, is by a sociologist who apparently has no religious commitments that could be classified as either Reform, Conservative, or Orthodox Judaism. Furthermore, Glazer does not have the traditional faith in Jewish eternity. But what Glazer does possess— and what he indicates in his own indirect way—is a feeling of unease and regret at the possible end of the Jewish people:

In the Talmud, the voice of God on occasion interrupts or joins the discussions of the sages. With that customary Jewish circumspectness in speaking of God, it is not, in the text, the voice of God that is heard, rather the echo of the voice—not the *kol* but the *bat kol*—for, after the end of the age of prophecy, it was no longer possible to hear the voice of God directly. I have suggested that the Jews are quite a few stages past that. Certainly, they will not hear the voice of the echo, perhaps not even the echo of the echo. But something is still left. What is left is a relation to a tradition in which, from all one can tell, the echo once sounded, and there was a readiness to listen. What can still come of it I do not know.[20]

The range of variation in the survivalist perspective is wide: if Glazer occupies one end of the spectrum, perhaps the individual who best exemplifies the other end is Charles Liebman.[21] Although Liebman is a political scientist by training, his writing on Jewish topics has been heavily sociological. He is an Orthodox Jew who in the final pages of his book *The Ambivalent American*

*Jew* makes clear his commitment to the observance of the *mitzvot* (religious commandments), to the study of Torah, and to the concept of Jewish people-hood.[22] The final lines of Liebman's book differ from those of Glazer's in that Liebman stresses his personal involvement in the struggle for Jewish survival. Furthermore, despite his intellectuality he affirms his readiness to sacrifice participation in the wider society in the interest of preserving Judaism and the Jewish people:

Judaism, as I understand it, is threatened by contemporary currents in American life. Fewer and fewer areas today are even neutral to Jewish values. Literature, theater, art, scholarship, politics—all seem to undermine what I consider to be the essentials of Judaism. More than ever before, the values of integration and survival are mutually contradictory. At least until we enter a postmodern world, it seems to me that Jewish survival requires a turning against the integrationist response. (Liebman, p. 197)

It is clear that those who have adopted a survivalist perspective have quite different visions of what constitutes Jewish survival, of what survival will entail, of what their responsibility as social scientists is to the study of the Jewish community, and of how they should personally participate in Jewish communal affairs. But there are commonalities as well as differences among those who study the American Jew from the survivalist perspective. One such commonality is that they view immigrant life more from a negative than from a positive perspective. They seek to avoid sentimentalism; for them the good old days are also the bad old days. Glazer's examination of the relationship of Jews to American communism is one example of this tendency—Glazer refuses to exalt the involvement of Jews in radical activities as the golden era in American-Jewish life.[23] Liebman's examination of a quite different problem—the religiosity of Jewish immigrants in the pre–World War I period—shows the same unsentimental, perhaps even negative, perspective. Rather than celebrating the immigrants' religiosity Liebman discounts it and marshals impressive evidence to show that such religiosity has been inflated and misunderstood. Liebman's implication is that today is better than yesterday—that is, the Orthodoxy of today is far superior to the Orthodoxy of an earlier period.[24]

Those who write from the survivalist perspective also tend to be distinctive in their approach to the style of life of the Jewish middle and upper classes. The style of life that is so repugnant to those who adopt the critical intellectual perspective, and that is so central to their criticism of Jewish life, does not produce the same reaction in those who write from a survivalist perspective. They tend to take the life-style for granted and instead to focus on identity problems produced by rapid upward class mobility, by sharp rises in educational levels, and by the move from old Jewish neighborhoods in the city to the newer suburbs.

The first volume of the Lakeville Study illustrates the approach. While the book begins with a description of the good life in Lakeville, it proceeds to focus on problems of Jewish identity. It ends by contrasting the poverty of Jewishness in Lakeville with the plushness of life in that community. The inference is that the Jews of Lakeville deserve empathy more than antipathy, particularly since their very success in occupational and educational achievement, and their striking ability to adjust to American life, have produced an abiding problem in regard to their identity as Jews. Despite their desire to remain Jewish and to pass on their identity to their children, they are not very confident of their ability to do so. Their insecurities are particularly poignant considering their mastery of other aspects of their lives. To quote from the final paragraphs of the study:

The meager Jewishness to which the Lakeville youngster falls heir is perhaps the true *bête noire* of Jewish life in Lakeville. Lakeville makes available the abundant life . . . in many aspects it is a model community which fulfills the American dream. But, at the same time it does not provide very rich Jewish experiences for the majority of those who are socialized in its fine homes, winding streets, excellent schools, pleasant beaches, tennis courts, and—let it be said—in its religious schools. Thus many of those who are the product of the Lakeville environment will be faced with the obverse of that which confronted their grandfathers, great-grandfathers, or even more remote ancestors when they arrived on American shores. While the resources of such ancestors—in terms of money, general education, and knowledge of the American way of life—were paltry, their Jewish resources—if not always considerable—were at least sufficient unto the day. Over the generations the families of present-day Lakeville Jews have increased their financial resources, their general level of education, and their mastery of the environment many times over. While some have multiplied their Jewish resources, many have dissipated them to a lesser or greater degree. It is indisputable that the majority of Lakeville Jews would like to conserve their Jewish resources. But unless an aggressive policy of growth is pursued the Jewish resources of a previous generation inevitably decline. The press of the general environment is so compelling that instead of being conserved the inheritance from earlier generations inevitably diminishes. In sum, the long-range viability of the pattern of Jewish adjustment characteristic of Lakeville is in question.[25]

A final aspect of the contrast between the survivalist perspective and other perspectives is that of the politics of American Jews. The critical intellectual perspective emphasizes the growth of Jewish conservatism while the survivalist perspective emphasizes continuing Jewish liberalism. And when those who write from the survivalist perspective discover an increase in Jewish conservatism they are sympathetic, for they trace such conservatism to the collision between liberalism and ethnic loyalty. Nathan Glazer put it best when he said:

Judaism in America had been for a long time not much more than ethnic loyalty on the one hand and "liberalism" on the other. . . . The amalgam that was Judaism in the 1950's in America began to come apart in the 1960's, and after 1967 it came apart even faster. To be "liberal" in 1967 might mean to support Negro interests against

Jewish interests, to support leftists who wished to see Israel destroyed, to oppose American aid to Israel.[26]

If some who write from the survivalist perspective are prepared to view Jewish defections from liberalism-leftism as understandable and in a sense as unavoidable, others have little sympathy for Jewish liberalism. Charles Liebman, for example, views Jewish liberalism as "enlightenment liberalism" produced by an estrangement from Jewish values. Instead of applauding Jewish liberalism he sees it as dangerous inasmuch as it promotes the attenuation of ancestral religious and ethnic traditions. And Liebman also views Jewish liberalism as a threat to the Gentile, for it would promote the estrangement of the Gentile from his own traditions:

The Jewish political quest was for an ethic which could be posed against society's traditions. To this extent, then, the Jew sought to "Judaize" society. But this Judaization does not stem from intrinsic Jewish values. Of course, cosmopolitanism, universalism, liberalism, and even socialism can be found in traditional Judaism. But so can ethnic particularism, nationalism, and political conservatism. The modern Jew chooses that part of the tradition which is compatible with his special interests. He raises these interests to the level of ideology and presses them upon society in universalistic terms. The Jew thus fights for separation of church and state in the name of a secular ideal, not a Jewish ideal. From a parochial traditional Jewish point of view, one must be blind not to see the danger of secularization to Judaism. But the Judaization of society is not the quest to universalize Jewish values: it is the desire to impose the Jewish condition of estrangement upon society. (Liebman, *The Ambivalent American Jew*, p. 158)

What is responsible for the rise of the survivalist perspective? Part of the answer resides in the fact that both Nazism as well as the establishment of the State of Israel strengthened the sense of Jewishness of those sociologists who were not committed to assimilation. Even more significant was the fact that by the 1950's well-identified Jews were becoming sociologists. Put another way, sociology began to attract a much larger number of Jews than before; those who entered the profession constituted a more representative cross-section of the Jewish community than was true for their predecessors. Some of those who became sociologists, including Nathan Glazer, had been strongly influenced by Zionism during their formative years.[27]

Not all of those who entered sociology with Jewish interests succeeded in maintaining them. Furthermore, some proceeded to compartmentalize their concerns—they pursued their Jewishness privately and their sociology publicly. Nevertheless, there were some who sought to pursue sociology and Jewishness simultaneously. Such individuals saw themselves as active members of the Jewish community despite their affiliation with the academic community. The most highly committed not only felt that sociology could be utilized to clarify questions of Jewish communal policy but they also believed that it was essential in furthering Jewish self-understanding. For them the academic community was clearly not a fourth community that would serve as a substitute for the Jewish community.

Several developments in American life generally, and in academia specifically, encouraged these trends. Sometime after World War II there emerged a sense of pluralism that emphasized that minorities could be oppressed by cultural conformity as well as by prejudice and discrimination. Furthermore, some tended to see new value in the survival of minority groups. Such survival would contribute a needed corrective to the cultural blandness that resulted from the impact of the mass media, the rising influence of the corporation and of bureaucracy generally, and the growth of the other-directed personality.

In the academy there was notable lessening of discrimination against Jews. As we have noted, after World War II Jews came to be increasingly accepted as members of university faculties. But of equal significance has been the fact that there has been less pressure to conform to the ideals of assimilation. Many of the better universities—which is another way of saying the universities to which Jews were attracted—espoused the ideal of diversity. To be sure, diversity generally meant a faculty that was diverse in social origin and intellectual interests rather than in ideological conviction. However, the trend toward a more cosmopolitan campus was unmistakable. While such cosmopolitanism provided greater opportunity for those who wished to assimilate to do so, it also made the academy more comfortable for those who wished to pursue their Jewishness. The rise of the Blacks on the campus together with the new appreciation of ethnicity was also important in making possible an affirmation in academia of Jewish interests and Jewish particularism—the qualities that lie at the heart of the survivalist perspective and that differentiate it from the assimilationist perspective as well as from the perspective of the critical intellectual.

## Summary and Conclusions

Jews are unparallelled among American ethnic groups in the number and eminence of the sociologists that they have produced. Such numbers and eminence were impressive enough so that the sociological study of the Jew was left almost entirely to the Jewish academician. However, no rapid expansion of knowledge about American Jewry has resulted, for many Jewish sociologists have been reluctant to study American Jewry. Wishing to be perceived as universalist-oriented intellectuals who are emancipated from parochial loyalties, they have preferred to focus on other sociological topics.

The stress on the value of being emancipated from parochial loyalties is particularly apparent in the work of some Jewish sociologists who have specialized in the study of ethnicity. Valuing such emancipation, they have come to view assimilation more as a right than as a process. They see assimilation as an ideological demand. The ideological demand for the right to assimilate leads to the claim that a new subsociety is emerging—a fourth community that consists of ex-Catholics, ex-Protestants, and ex-Jews. Furthermore, the intellectual subsociety should be granted the same legitimacy accorded to the established religious and ethnic subsocieties. The inference is that the intellectual subsociety may eventually supersede the established subsocieties. If not, the established subsocieties will at least lose their preeminence—they will increasingly be composed of those who lag behind in educational and occupational achievement and who follow a life-style that comes to be regarded as excessively traditionalistic and unfulfilling.

The usual danger of the study of a given ethnic group by members of that group is that their work is influenced by the desire for what Glazer and Moynihan have called "self-celebration and group reassurance."[28] Since the sociological study of American Jewry has been left almost entirely in Jewish hands, it is evident that self-celebration and group reassurance could easily have come to constitute its motifs. But as we have seen, the sociological study of American Jewry has tended in quite a different direction—perhaps even in an opposite direction. This has occurred because of both the political ideology of Jewish sociologists—their liberalism and particularly their leftism—and their alienation from Jewishness. As a consequence they have had no interest in celebration or in providing reassurance: if anything their work has been marred by the conflict between their desire to consider themselves good Jews and their strong feeling of alienation from their fellow Jews.

Those Jewish sociologists who first studied the American Jew viewed him as the prototype of the immigrant. The essence of the immigrant experience was seen as that of coming from a backward and provincial environment into a more advanced and sophisticated culture. The tendency of the immigrant was to build a ghetto in the American society. The hesitancy to leave the ghetto as well as the second-settlement areas in the city was understandable, particularly insofar as it was magnified by the fear of, or the experience with, prejudice and discrimination. Nevertheless, while the immigrant might seek to continue his traditional culture on the new frontier of the American city and to pass his culture on to his children, efforts aimed at ethnic survival would ultimately be futile. The future of the Jew, like that of all ethnics, was to assimilate into the great society. The inference was that the Jews would lead the way—that they would provide other ethnic groups with an example of how a sophisticated culture could be learned and internalized.

The Jewish sociologists who believed that America was the great society— a place that offered the immigrant abundant opportunities including that of assimilation—were followed by Jewish sociologists who were attracted more by alienation than by assimilation. Their alienation took a dual form: alienation from American culture as well as alienation from Jewishness. As a consequence they did not celebrate America. Rather, their alienation, liberalism and leftism, intellectuality, and universalism all conspired to influence them to view the nation as "Amerika"—a power-hungry and brutalized society whose foreign policy was an abomination and whose domestic policy was little better.

America, then, came to be viewed as unworthy of assimilation by Jews. However, at the same time such critical intellectuals have little affinity for Jewish self-segregation. To be sure they have evinced strong sentimentalism about the immigrant era as well as life in the American ghetto. It is assumed that during this period the Jews were fulfilling their sociological destiny of being in, but not of, American society.

There is very little evidence that critical Jewish sociologists uphold the continuing validity of traditional patterns of Jewish culture. What they do uphold is the necessity of the Jew to be a marginal man—an outsider and hence a critic of society. Thus it is that Jewish sociologists who are critical and alienated intellectuals have come to feel that the American Jew is evading his sociological destiny. Instead of being a critic and an outsider, they charge the American Jew with conforming to, if not assimilating into, American society. The Jew who was to be the model of marginality has committed the sin of joining the establishment.

The growth of the survivalist perspective is the latest addition to sociological thinking about American Jewry. The survivalist school is composed of many strands. In its most radical version it would prefer that the Jews serve as the model for the persistence of ethnic and religious loyalties in American society. However, there is a tendency to view the Jews as backsliders. If the members of the critical intellectual school see American Jews as conforming to middle-class life-styles and reactionary politics, the strongest proponents of the survivalist school see American Jews as insufficiently committed to survivalism, insufficiently self-segregated, and excessively cosmopolitan. Furthermore, the Jews are not only a danger to themselves but to others as well—they may influence groups who are more traditionalistic, less exposed to the mass media, and less well educated.

Whatever contribution the survivalist school will eventually make to the sociological study of American Jewry, it has served to introduce an alternative view to that of assimilationist and critical Jewish sociologists. Doubtless a strong commitment to Jewish survival and to self-segregation has its own hazards and pitfalls. However, thus far the survivalist school has avoided the temptation of self-celebration. It has also not been attracted to provide group reassurance—it has in fact been far more interested in warning Jews than in comforting them.

Whether or not they are the wave of the future, followers of the survivalist school are certainly more numerous than would have been predicted a generation or two ago. Despite their advance, hopefully survivalist sociologists will approach their work with a certain humility and self-awareness, and perhaps even self-doubt. The limitations and biases of earlier and competing approaches to sociological thinking on the subject of the American Jew should serve as a warning of the need to control ideology in the interest of better sociology.

## Notes

1. Paper presented at Sixth World Congress of Jewish Studies, Jerusalem, August 12–19, 1973. Further analysis of the development of the sociological study of Jewry can be found in the author's *The Jew in American Society* (New York: Behrman House, 1974), pp. 1–27.

2. See *Jews in a Gentile World*, edited by Isacque Graeber and Steuart Henderson Britt (New York: Macmillan, 1942).

3. See Seymour M. Lipset and Everett Carll Ladd, Jr., "Jewish Academics in the United States: Their Achievements, Culture and Politics," *American Jewish Year Book*, 72 (1971), p. 95. All subsequent citations of the Lipset-Ladd article refer to the Carnegie Commission survey (noted as L-L).

4. According to the estimate in the *American Jewish Year Book* in 1968 Jews constituted 2.9 percent of the American population.

5. See Simon N. Herman, *Israelis and Jews: The Continuity of an Identity* (New York: Random House, 1970).

6. See David Caplowitz and Harry Levy, *Interreligious Dating among College Students* (Processed, Bureau of Applied Social Research, Columbia University, 1965), pp. 41, 53.

7. See Henry Cohen, "Jewish Life and Thought in an Academic Community," *American Jewish Archives* (November 1962), 107–28.

8. Allan Mazur, "The Socialization of Jews into the Academic Subculture," in *The Professors*, edited by Charles H. Anderson and John D. Murray (Cambridge, Mass.: Schenkman, 1971), p. 280.

9. Milton Gordon, *Assimilation in American Life* (New York: Oxford University Press, 1964), p. 224.

10. See Marshall Sklare, "Assimilation and the Sociologists," *Commentary* (May 1965), 63–67.

11. Seymour Martin Lipset, "The Study of Jewish Communities in a Comparative Context," *The Jewish Journal of Sociology*, 5 (December 1963), 163.

12. See Louis Wirth, *The Ghetto* (Chicago: University of Chicago Press, 1928).

13. For a critical evaluation of Wirth's perspectives see Amitai Etzioni, "The Ghetto—A Reevaluation," *Social Forces*, 37 (March 1959), 255–62, and Erich Rosenthal, "Acculturation without Assimilation: The Jewish Community of Chicago, Illinois," *American Journal of Sociology*, 56 (November 1960), 275–88.

14. Elizabeth Wirth Marvick, "Louis Wirth: A Biographical Memorandum," in *Louis Wirth: On Cities and Social Life*, ed. by Albert J. Reiss, Jr. (Chicago: University of Chicago Press, 1964), p. 337.

15. See Louis Wirth, "Education for Survival: The Jews," *American Journal of Sociology*, 48 (May 1943), 682–91.

16. See Judith R. Kramer and Seymour Leventman, *Children of the Gilded Ghetto* (New Haven: Yale University Press, 1961).

17. It is notable that Wirth makes only casual reference to Jewish radical activity in first- and second-settlement areas. It is difficult to believe that he was unaware of such activity. Rather it is a fair supposition that he preferred not to publish data on

Jewish radical activity because of the fear that it would be misused by prejudiced Gentiles.

18. See Melvin M. Tumin, "Conservative Trends in American Jewish Life," *Judaism*, 13, (Spring 1964), 131–42.

19. Some of Tumin's assumptions are analyzed in the discussion that followed the presentation of his paper; see Tumin, pp. 143–53. Milton Himmelfarb has also critically evaluated several of Tumin's assumptions, particularly those relating to Jewish conservatism. See Himmelfarb's article: "How We Are," *Commentary* (January 1965), 69–72.

20. Nathan Glazer, *American Judaism* (Chicago: University of Chicago Press, 1957), p. 149.

21. That Glazer occupies a survivalist position that is minimalist rather than maximalist is perhaps most apparent in his article "City Problems and Jewish Responsibilities," which appeared in *Commentary* (January 1962), 24–30. In this article, Glazer advocates the transformation of many Jewish agencies such as community centers, social work agencies, hospitals into "public or non-Jewish" agencies. His reasoning is that such transformation will benefit less-fortunate minority groups, most notably the Blacks. His justification is not only that Jews are economically well situated but that implementing such transformation would be in the best "interest of the Jewish sub-community." Lucy Dawidowicz maintains that Glazer's blueprint would actually benefit neither Jew nor Black because the transformation of Jewish agencies would "be at the expense of their Jewish educational and survival functions." She also suggests that Blacks would resent such action by Jews. See her comments in *Commentary* (May 1962), 442–43.

22. See Charles S. Liebman, *The Ambivalent American Jew* (Philadelphia: Jewish Publication Society of America, 1973), p. 196.

23. See Nathan Glazer, *The Social Basis of American Communism* (New York: Harcourt, Brace and World, 1961), pp. 130–68.

24. See Charles S. Liebman, "Orthodoxy in American Jewish Life," *American Jewish Year Book*, 66 (1965), 21–97.

25. Marshall Sklare and Joseph Greenblum, *Jewish Identity on the Suburban Frontier: A Study of Group Survival in the Open Society* (New York: Basic Books, 1967), p. 331.

26. Nathan Glazer, *American Judaism*, 2d ed. (Chicago: University of Chicago Press, 1972), pp. 181–82.

27. See Leonard Dinnerstein and Gene Koppel, *Nathan Glazer: A Different Kind of Liberal* (Tucson: The University of Arizona, 1973), p. 54.

28. Nathan Glazer and Daniel P. Moynihan, *Beyond the Melting Pot*, 2d ed. (Cambridge, Mass.: The MIT Press, 1970), p. lxxxiii.

# The Sociology of Contemporary Jewish Studies

## I

Information about contemporary Jewry, and especially information about contemporary American Jewry, is abundant—in sharp contrast to the situation for earlier eras of Jewish history. Because of the insecurity of Jewish life during the Middle Ages, for example, basic documents and archival records concerning medieval Jewry are scant, and historians must frequently rely on documents preserved in church or governmental archives rather than on Jewish sources. Yet such records have decided limitations; chiefly, that they reveal little of the inner life of the Jew. For this the historian must turn to the *responsa* literature—the questions submitted to rabbinical authorities on various matters of Jewish law together with their answers to these questions.

The difference between the study of the Jews of yesterday and the study of the Jews of today is encountered in its most extreme form when it comes to a subject like Marranism. By definition the Marrano was obliged to cover his tracks; secrecy was his only weapon against the Inquisition. Somewhat the same situation characterizes the Jews of the Soviet Union today; the display and promotion of Jewish identity can have grave consequences for an individual's occupational prospects and even for his physical security. As a result scholars confront formidable difficulties in writing about Soviet Jewry; they must rely on indirect indicators and must painfully assemble facts by way of fugitive documents or interviews with those who have managed to leave the country.

If Marranism in medieval times and the situation of Soviet Jewry in the present are located at one end of a spectrum, the study of American Jewry seems to be at the other: the researcher of contemporary American Jewry is inundated with information. He need only consult his daily newspaper for coverage of the multifaceted activities of Jewish organizations, or for feature articles on individual Jews who have distinguished themselves in one or another area. In an election year political pundits discuss at length the voting preferences of city and suburban Jews. And to supplement the information found in the daily newspaper the researcher can consult the *American Jewish Year Book*, which has appeared annually for over seventy years and presents a wealth of authoritative information on American and world Jewry.[1]

The daily press, the Jewish weeklies, the Jewish and general magazines, the yearbooks and commemorative volumes, and the many hundreds—if not thousands—of reports made available annually by national and local Jewish agencies add up to an almost inexhaustible storehouse of facts, and they lend force to Salo Baron's suggestive characterization of the American Jew as an "inverted Marrano," the very opposite of his medieval Iberian predecessor.[2] It is quite apparent, however, that the very large body of information that has accumulated about contemporary American Jewry has on the whole remained just that: information. Very little systematic scholarly work has been done to assemble and analyze this information, draw conclusions from it, and thereby transform it into real knowledge. Indeed, despite the fact that in our age self-confession is a way of life, the display of Jewishness a common occurrence, and information so accessible as to make historians envious, the field of contemporary Jewish studies has yet to attain the stage of scholarly development that has been achieved in other branches of Jewish studies.

In the 1940's Louis Finkelstein (then president of the Jewish Theological Seminary of America), seeking to recruit experts in all branches of Jewish studies to contribute to a two-volume comprehensive survey of Jewish culture, was surprised to discover how few specialists there were in contemporary Jewish studies. Despite the obvious abundance of information about contemporary Jewry, he found that what was actually known on the subject was far inferior to what was known about ancient and medieval Jewry:

There are probably a hundred people, and more, whose profession it is to discover all that can be known about the Jews in Jerusalem in the first century; there does not seem to be one who has the same duty for the Jews of New York in the twentieth century.[3]

Since the 1940's knowledge of contemporary Jewry has increased considerably. Nevertheless, the intriguing problem raised by Dr. Finkelstein persists. To address it adequately we must consider the field of contemporary Jewish studies in relation to the development of Jewish studies generally as a discipline over the past century, as well as the academic development of the social sciences, and specifically of sociology.[4]

## II

The field of Jewish studies as an intellectual discipline emerged in Germany in the first half of the nineteenth century, where it became known as *Wissen-*

*schaft des Judentums*—the science of Judaism. In the United States the field is even more recent, having developed in the twentieth rather than the nineteenth century. *Wissenschaft des Judentums* traced its intellectual origins to the classical tradition of Jewish learning, with its concern for *halachah* (Jewish law) and its emphasis on the mastery of Talmudic texts. But while resembling traditional Jewish learning in that it studied the past, *Wissenschaft des Judentums* viewed the past from quite a different perspective. It not only expanded the content of Jewish learning by going far beyond the study of *halachah*, it also radically shifted the methodology and ideological superstructure of Jewish learning. The net effect was to change the study of Judaism from an exercise in religious piety to an academic and intellectual pursuit. As one historian noted, in speaking of the very first document produced by the movement, it

clearly displays the feature that was to differentiate [the movement] from previous Jewish learning: the assumption of a stand outside of . . . the tradition instead of within it, approaching it with the discerning but cold eye of the scientist.[5]

To be sure there was never a complete break in the link between religious piety and scientific study of Jewish culture. Whatever the public image of Jewish studies in the modern world, some of its adherents continued to conceive of their work in the traditional framework of religious obligation and spiritual exercise. But whether motivated by religious strivings or by a spirit of academic curiosity all modern Jewish scholars were obliged to subscribe to a basic assumption of *Wissenschaft des Judentums*—that priority should be given to scientific evidence in the event that it conflicted with religious dogma. The scholar was of course free to minimize such conflict by concentrating in fields like Jewish history or medieval Hebrew poetry where science and dogma were not on a collision course. He was also free to avoid those fields of study—the most obvious being Bible—where confrontation was inevitable.

Despite their modernism, the founders of *Wissenschaft des Judentums* did not expand the scope of Jewish studies to include research on contemporary Jewry, even though they conceived of their discipline as offering something of great value to the Jews of the time. Indeed they were deeply concerned with contemporary issues, particularly with the relationship of Jewry to the general society. They ardently supported the Jewish struggle for equal rights and wished to assist in this struggle as well as to help combat all forms of anti-Jewish prejudice. Not that they all held a single attitude toward the Jews and the Judaism of their time. Some, believing in the possibility of Jewish survival, sought to utilize the past in order to reconstruct the present. Others harbored doubts over the prospects for Jewish survival. The most pessimistic viewed themselves as morticians charged with giving to the Jewish past the decent, but no less final, burial that had been denied it by prejudiced Gentile theologians and historians. Yet whatever attitude the *Wissenschaft* scholar took toward the importance and likelihood of Jewish survival, he saw his research as centering on the study of the Jews of the past rather than on those of the present.

The proponents of *Wissenschaft des Judentums* prided themselves on the "scientific" spirit with which they approached the history and culture of Jewry. But they were in fact not attracted as a group to the concerns or to the analytical methods of social science, a discipline then in its infancy. They were, first and foremost, humanists, and so may have felt a natural aversion to the social sciences. Then too, Jewish scholars tended to believe that the social sciences involved a denigration of the intrinsic nobility of Jewish culture. Social science seemed to be critical both of traditional Jewish learning, with its belief in Judaism as a unique historical and religious relationship between God and the Jewish people (which it was the duty of the individual Jew both to strengthen and maintain), and of modern Jewish scholarship, with its stress on the broad universal significance of Jewish culture. By highlighting economic relationships, or the significance of social stratification, or the importance of power, social science seemed to imply that the Jews were similar to other groups— though to be sure conceding that the history of the Jews diverged from that of most other ethnic or religious groups. Certainly social science gave no hint that it conceived of the Jews as a kingdom of priests and as a holy people.

The negative attitude of the early Jewish humanists to the social-scientific approach may be seen in its extreme form in an incident that occurred in 1909 at the Academy of Jewish Studies in St. Petersburg. The academy had been established by the preeminent leader of Russian Jewry, Baron David Günzberg, a man of great wealth and of considerable learning, who wished to introduce *Wissenschaft des Judentums* to the Jews of Eastern Europe. The young Zalman Shazar, later to become president of Israel, was at that time a student of the academy; in his autobiography he recounts how he and some other students were dissatisfied with the academy's approach to Jewish history. Led by Shazar, the students confronted the baron with their complaint:

One of the disciplines that we students felt to be lacking and necessary was historical study of the social and economic life of Jews in the lands of the Diaspora. It was not easy to find a specialist in this field, and when [the Russian-Jewish historian Simon] Dubnow, whom we had impressed with our desire for such study, came at last to tell us that there was a fine young scholar available, Dr. M. L. Wischnitzer of Vienna, he added with restrained sadness that he feared the Baron would not agree to open the doors of the Academy to a course stressing the "new-fangled" social and economic approach.

We decided to try to appeal to Baron Günzberg directly. . . . He agreed to receive a delegation. There were three of us, and to this day I remember with absolute clarity the talk between us and the fatherly Baron. I had been charged with opening our case. There in the Baron's study, facing the picture of Maimonides, I spoke of the need for this new discipline and of the young scholar who was available. Excitedly, the Baron rose from his chair, leaned against the doorpost opening onto his great library . . . and said . . . : "Dear ones, I am deeply grieved by this request of yours. I am certain that you have no intention . . . of causing me unhappiness, and it is very difficult for me to say no to you. But how can I hide my concern from you? You have come here to study the nature and destiny of the Jewish people—

and now I hear you asking to be taught what occupations Jews were compelled to engage in. . . . It is as if a scholar had been asked to lecture to you on Kant, and then, instead of teaching you the *Critique of Pure Reason*, spent his time describing the restaurant Kant frequented and the kind of cutlets his wife gave him. And it is not Kant you are studying, but that sublime people God chose for His own! Do you really think it is so important to know exactly when the Gentiles permitted us to engage in trade and when those malicious people forced us to be moneylenders? What good will the information do you? And wouldn't it be a pity to spend your precious time on this when there are still so many rooms in the mansion of Jewish scholarship that are closed to you and so many great books waiting for you?" As he spoke, he pointed to the tens of rooms filled with bookshelves from floor to ceiling, [an] endless, infinite treasure of books. . . .

Walking excitedly across the room between the desk and the books [he] suddenly stood still and went on even more bitingly: "If you do research on horses—there is such a science, too—it is obviously very important to investigate what fodder should be put in the horses' crib: oats or barley. But when the subject of your study is the wisdom of the chosen people, do you think that their fodder . . . should concern you?"[6]

Today, when the utility of the social sciences for the study of the Jewish past is generally conceded, it is almost impossible to imagine a contemporary version of the confrontation between Shazar and Baron Günzberg. While an earlier generation of Jewish humanists could avoid the social sciences, present-day professors of Jewish studies hold posts at universities where the social sciences are firmly established, and the same can be said even of those who teach at the rabbinical seminaries. Yet as recently as the 1930's, when Salo Baron's *A Social and Religious History of the Jews* appeared, the social-scientific emphasis it embodied still seemed daring. By the 1950's and 1960's, of course, when the revised edition began to appear, this approach to the Jewish past had become commonplace.

The current debate concerns instead the status that should be accorded to the social-scientific study of *contemporary* Jewry. Despite his own modernity the Jewish humanist may feel deeply alienated from the contemporary world; he may feel that the study of the present is unworthy, that the present age is debased and brutish in comparison with the past, that its Jewish culture is inferior. The often ambiguous relation of today's humanist to the culture in which he lives cannot be understood without reference to developments in the social sciences—especially to the role of Jewish intellectuals and academicians in that most contemporary of disciplines, sociology.

## III

At virtually no time has there been a lack of Jewish representation in the sociological fraternity. In Europe such preeminent early figures as Emile Durkheim and Georg Simmel were Jewish; in the United States Jews became active in sociology as soon as the field severed its connection with the social-melioration emphasis of liberal Protestantism and established its academic respectability. At present, Jews are strongly represented in American sociology, both as leaders of "establishment" sociology and as active proponents of "new" or "radical" sociology.

Despite their numbers and influence, however, only a handful of Jewish sociologists have been interested in the sociology of the Jews. Until very recently Jewish sociologists hesitated to introduce contemporary Jewish studies into the social-science curriculum. And even those Jewish sociologists who specialized in the study of ethnic groups shied away from the sociology of the Jews. This reluctance to become involved in contemporary Jewish studies has its origin in what sociology as a discipline has traditionally represented to the Jewish academician. More than a profession, sociology has been a calling. For many Jewish academicians it has signified a break with the ethnic and religious parochialism of their past, a way of replacing membership in the Jewish ethnic community with the "universal" community of the academy.

Appropriately, it was a Jewish sociologist, Milton Gordon, who developed the hypothesis that "intellectuals in the United States interact in such patterned ways as to form at least the elementary structure of a subsociety of their own."[7] Furthermore, Gordon developed a rationale for the legitimacy of this intellectual subsociety, pleading for the individual's right to leave behind the narrow confines of the ethnic community for the wider world of academe. Gordon was not alone in his views: Gentile sociologists like Robert M. MacIver and S. C. Dodd had also been critical of Jewish particularism, and an earlier generation of Gentile sociologists—notably Edward A. Ross and Henry Pratt Fairchild— had emphasized the necessity, indeed the obligation, of immigrants to adapt themselves to what is now called Wasp culture. For Gordon, on the other hand, assimilation was a *right*, not a duty. He also wanted the "birthright ethnic group," as he termed it, to desist from criticizing its assimilationist academics and intellectuals:

the individual, as he matures and reaches the age where rational decision is feasible, should be allowed to choose freely whether to remain within the boundaries of communality created by his birthright ethnic group, to branch out into multiple interethnic contacts, or even to change affiliation to that of another ethnic group should he wish to do so as a result of religious conversion, intermarriage, or simply private wish. If, to the contrary, the ethnic group places such heavy pressures on its birthright members to stay confined to ethnic communality that the individual who consciously wishes to "branch out" or "move away" feels intimidated or subject to major feelings of personal guilt and therefore remains ethnically enclosed, or moves but at considerable psychological cost, then we have, in effect, cultural democracy for groups but not for individuals.[8]

Whatever the position of individual Jewish sociologists toward the question of whether Jews should seek group survival or should pursue the goal of assimilation, for most Jewish sociologists a commitment to intellectuality generally and to sociology specifically precluded involvement with contemporary Jewish studies. As Seymour Martin Lipset, a concerned Jew as well as a renowned sociologist, has noted:

The failure of Jewish social scientists to engage in research on the Jews reflects their desire to be perceived as American rather than Jewish intellectuals. To write in depth about the Jewish community would seemingly expose them to being identified as "Jewish Jews," as individuals who are too preoccupied with an ethnic identity, and who lack the universalistic orientation prized by social scientists and American intellectuals generally.[9]

The tendency to avoid contemporary Jewish studies was reinforced by the fact that Jews did not constitute a "problem" for American society. As a consequence neither governmental bodies nor large foundations saw a need to encourage the sociological study of contemporary Jewry. On the contrary, those individuals who were interested in such research found it difficult to locate sources of support. While Jewish organizations occasionally subsidized research, their interest was on the whole sporadic.[10]

The single subject that did excite the imagination of Jewish investigators was the Israeli *kibbutz*. The kibbutz has been written about endlessly; there may already be more books and articles on the kibbutz than there are actual kibbutzim. But the kibbutz is the exception that proves the rule. Most analysts have shown little interest in the kibbutz as an institution in a Jewish society; rather, they have been interested in the kibbutz as an experiment in collective living. Hence the Jewish sociologist, psychologist, or anthropologist who has written about the kibbutz has often continued to perceive himself as an American (or European) intellectual rather than as a specifically Jewish intellectual.

## IV

Contemporary Jewish studies, then, emerged neither out of the interest of the proponents of *Wissenschaft des Judentums* nor out of the concern of Jewish social scientists teaching at European or American universities. The origins of the discipline lie elsewhere, and the movement led by Zalman Shazar at the Academy of Jewish Studies in St. Petersburg to which we have duly alluded—a movement aided and abetted by a "radical" faculty member, Simon Dubnow—provides the clue to these origins.

It was Jewish nationalism, and Zionism in particular, that caused dissatisfaction with the curriculum of *Wissenschaft des Judentums*, a curriculum that had at first dazzled and intoxicated those who—like Shazar—had been steeped in traditional Jewish learning.[11] Students at the academy came to believe that the approach to Jewish history of the scholars whose books they studied did not speak to their situation. They had need of someone who saw Jewish history differently from an Isaac Marcus Jost or a Heinrich Graetz; even so advanced a thinker as Dubnow was not fully satisfactory. Before Shazar came to St.

Petersburg he had carried out missions for the Poale Zion, and he had translated some of Ber Borochov's writings into Yiddish. Other students had been
similarly involved in the Jewish social movements of the time. The result was
dissatisfaction with a curriculum that called for the scientific study of Jewish
culture but placed the emphasis on intellectual history and paid little attention
to the economic life of the Jews and their position in society.

Jewish nationalism saw the Jews as constituting a social "problem," and it
maintained that the solution of the problem lay in the direction of group survival rather than individual assimilation, a course that was neither desirable
nor, some held, possible. Jewish nationalism insisted that the Jewish condition
was an abnormality that had to be corrected, and to that end it advocated the
establishment of a national home.

In addition to its political program, Jewish nationalism stressed the need
for a proper understanding and evaluation of the Jewish condition, a task
that called in turn for accumulating meaningful social and economic data and
analyzing such data in a conceptual framework. This emphasis on understanding and evaluation, combined with nationalism's survivalist thrust, laid the
groundwork for the discipline of contemporary Jewish studies.

Arthur Ruppin (1876–1943), who served as an important official of various
Zionist agencies during much of the time that he was also active on the scholarly scene, may be regarded as the father of the discipline. Ruppin's sociological
work was infused with a Zionist perspective, even as his efforts to establish
settlements in Palestine were filtered through the prism of his sociological
understanding.[12] His methodology called for comparing Jews of one country
with those of another, and he gathered his data not only from library research
and official statistics but also from his contacts and travels as an official of the
Zionist movement. Although he conceived of Jews as a worldwide people, like
many of his contemporaries Ruppin focused almost exclusively on the Jews
of Western and Eastern Europe, as well as upon Jews who had emigrated to
Palestine from European countries.[13]

In 1926 Ruppin began teaching the sociology of the Jews at the Hebrew
University. His lectures subsequently appeared (in 1930–31) in a two-volume
German edition, *Die Soziologie der Juden*. A Hebrew translation followed almost
immediately, as did a condensed version in English. This, however, was not
Ruppin's first scholarly publication in the field, for his book *Die Juden der
Gegenwart* had appeared in 1904. *Die Juden der Gegenwart* became well-known
if only because it was a novelty. As Ruppin wrote in his memoirs:

*Die Juden der Gegenwart* was a new departure in the literature on the Jewish question. People were used to books pleading for or against the Jews, but they did not
know what to do with a book which did not take sides but confined itself to mar-
shaling the facts as objectively as possible. The book was given a mixed reception
in the Jewish press: the assimilationists tended to disapprove of it, the Zionists to
approve.[14]

Two years before the publication of *Die Soziologie der Juden* a significant book in the field of contemporary Jewish studies appeared in the United States: *The Ghetto*, by Louis Wirth (1897–1952).[15] *The Ghetto* had been inspired by Wirth's mentor, Robert E. Park, who was one of the founders of American sociology and was a member of the faculty of the University of Chicago. Park was intensely interested in the sociology of minority groups, and especially in such phenomena as the marginal man and the clash between the ancestral culture of an immigrant group and the new culture with which it came in contact. He persuaded Wirth—then a graduate student at the university—to select a Jewish topic for his Ph.D. dissertation. The resulting volume became one of the most popular items in the series of sociological monographs published by the University of Chicago Press and established itself as a standard source in its field.

The contrast between Arthur Ruppin and Louis Wirth is instructive. One, the founder of contemporary Jewish studies, was a Zionist whose pioneering work is being continued today at the Institute of Contemporary Jewry of the Hebrew University. The other, a non-Zionist if not an anti-Zionist, became the most influential Jew of his time in American sociology and prefigured the present prominence of Jews in American social science. Wirth served as president of what is now the American Sociological Association, and was the first president of the International Sociological Association. As a leading authority on urban sociology and minority groups (as well as in other areas such as the sociology of knowledge), Wirth was a consultant to many official bodies and private agencies. However, he made no effort to establish contemporary Jewish studies as a distinctive field of scholarly inquiry.

Ruppin's work is limited in that his approach to the sociology of the Jews remained the same throughout his life. And since he carried on his scholarly work at the same time that he was engaged in Zionist activity he was not able to realize many of his plans. Nevertheless, his interest and productivity in the field of contemporary Jewish studies extended over more than three decades. He saw the Jewish people as a living organism, constantly growing and ever changing; Jews were an object of continual fascination to him. Wirth, on the other hand, made no substantial contribution to contemporary Jewish studies after completing his dissertation. In his person and in his career he exemplified the very process he described in *The Ghetto*—the transformation undergone by the individual who leaves the traditionalistic world of the European village and starts a new life in the maelstrom of the American city (Wirth came from the Rhineland and arrived in Omaha, Nebraska, at the age of fourteen). According to his daughter, Wirth was

the first member of his family to marry a non-Jew . . . [his] assimilationist inclinations and principles, like those of his wife, partly derived from their common reaction against dogmatism and provincial ethnocentrism. Their two daughters were to be encouraged in agnosticism with audible atheistic overtones, at the same time that they were to acquire a "generalized minority" ethnic identification.[16]

The closing pages of *The Ghetto* make clear Wirth's belief that the Jewish community was an anachronism whose life had been artificially prolonged by Gentile prejudice,[17] and he came to look upon the Jews as a dead—rather than a living—people. He directed his attention to the need for social planning, for better cities, and for improved understanding among racial groups. Nevertheless, his interest in fighting discrimination and his desire to combat Nazism had the effect of keeping him in touch with Jewish organizations, and during World War II he wrote once again on a Jewish topic. In 1943 Wirth published an article in the *American Journal of Sociology* that in effect paid homage to Jewish tenacity in the face of persecution.[18]

## V

With the single exception of a noted social psychologist, for several decades no outstanding personalities in American social science displayed a commitment to contemporary Jewish studies. Despite the lack of leadership, however, by the 1940's and 1950's social science research on the American Jew did begin to accumulate. Occasional studies, subvented by Jewish communal bodies in order to provide a basis for decision making, were often sufficiently wide in scope to constitute more than service research. Other studies were initiated outside of the Jewish community, generally on topics where Jews might serve as a kind of control group, as in research on alcoholism. There were also investigations by political scientists into voting behavior, another area where Jews deviated from the middle-class norm, and there were community studies in places where Jews happened to constitute a significant segment of the population (Park Forest, Illinois, for example, was intensively studied by social scientists from the University of Chicago). Finally, there were dissertations by graduate students as well as investigations resulting from the independent initiative of social scientists who had an interest in the study of contemporary Jewry. By the late 1950's it was possible for the present author to compile a book of social science readings on the contemporary American Jew.[19]

What was responsible for the rise of interest in Jewish research? Part of the answer lies in the strengthened sense of Jewish identity held by Jewish social scientists in the wake of both the Nazi Holocaust and the establishment of the State of Israel. Even more significant was the increase by the 1950's in the number of Jews who were social scientists. To put this development another way, the social sciences had begun to attract a much larger number of Jews than before, and those entering the profession constituted a more representative cross-section of the Jewish community than had been true of their predecessors.

Not all of those who entered sociology with Jewish interests succeeded in maintaining them. Furthermore, some proceeded to compartmentalize their concerns—they pursued their Jewishness privately and their sociology publicly. Yet there were others who saw themselves as belonging simultaneously to the Jewish community and to the academic community, and who sought to integrate the two aspects of their lives. The most highly committed not only felt that social science could be utilized to clarify questions of Jewish communal policy but also believed that it was essential to furthering Jewish self-understanding.

The emergence of an affirmative sense of Jewishness among some social scientists was signaled by the settlement in Israel of a number of rising Jewish academicians, perhaps the most prominent of whom was Louis Guttman. Born in 1916, Guttman, at twenty-five, was invited to join the faculty of Cornell University. His development of the Guttman scalogram method brought him widespread recognition. Despite brilliant prospects in the United States, Guttman settled in Israel in 1947 where he established the Israel Institute of Applied Social Research. Other Jewish social scientists, not prepared to go on *aliyah*, were nevertheless interested in making occasional contributions to contemporary Jewish studies. In a sense Jewish research could serve such individuals as a substitute for a more intense commitment to Jewishness, whether of a religious or nationalist kind. To write on a Jewish topic underlined one's Jewish identity to others and, more importantly, served to allay any tension one might feel between his Jewishness and his commitment to the academic life.

Several developments in American life generally, and in academia specifically, encouraged these trends. After World War II the idea of cultural pluralism began to achieve widespread acceptance, as did the accompanying notion that minorities could be oppressed as much by conformism as by overt prejudice and discrimination. Furthermore, it began to be felt that the presence of distinctive minority groups contributed a necessary corrective to the cultural blandness of the nation that resulted from the impact of the mass media, the rising influence of the corporation and of bureaucracy generally, and of the growth of the "other-directed" personality.

In the academy there was a notable lessening of discrimination against Jews. After World War II not only were Jews widely accepted as faculty members, but less pressure was placed on them to conform to the ideals of assimilation. Many of the better universities espoused the new ideal of diversity, even if diversity meant a faculty diverse in social origin and intellectual interests rather than in ideological conviction. The trend toward a more cosmopolitan campus meant greater opportunity to assimilate for Jews who wished to do so, but it also made the academy a more comfortable place for those who wished to retain their Jewishness. And the new diversity and cosmopolitanism also made it possible to maintain and promote an interest in Jewish research as a valid area of inquiry, particularly if it were pursued as part of a larger interest in such recognized fields as social psychology, the sociology of religion, or racial and ethnic relations.

Kurt Lewin (1890–1947) did not live to see the results of these changes, but he typified the new trend. Lewin was known in the United States even before he arrived as a refugee scholar in 1933, and his reputation as a social psychologist grew rapidly during his American years.[20] Lewin began to write on Jewish topics in 1935; his most influential article, "Self-Hatred among Jews," was published in 1941.[21] In contrast to Wirth, who stressed the negative consequences of ethnic self-segregation, Lewin pointed to the psychological perils that could result when one alienated oneself from the Jewish community, especially the lack of a firm sense of belongingness. His articles emphasized the importance of self-acceptance and of creating a strong Jewish identity in the Jewish child.[22]

Lewin's interest in the study of contemporary Jewry had been stimulated by his personal encounter with Nazism. It came to occupy such a central part of his professional life that he eventually sought to settle in Palestine and made vigorous, though ultimately unsuccessful, efforts to raise funds for a psychological institute, which he wished to establish at the Hebrew University. In the United States, Lewin also sought organizational support for his research into problems of Jewish interest. He conceived of his work as "action research," and he maintained that organizational sponsors could play a vital role in suggesting research problems and in implementing proposed solutions. In 1944 the American Jewish Congress responded to the idea and asked Lewin to set up its new research department, the Commission on Community Interrelations.[23]

## VI

The balance between ethnocentrism on the one hand and self-hatred on the other remains a particularly delicate one for the social scientist of today who rejects assimilation and wishes in some way to affirm his Jewishness. Typically, such an individual is uncomfortable with the patterns of religious and communal practice followed by most of his fellow Jews. Furthermore, he may be more strongly affected by the universalistic orientation of the academy than he knows or can acknowledge, and he may be anxious to show that his Jewish interests do not imply any defection from the world of the academy. The social scientist who wishes to belong to, but at the same time feels alienated from, the Jewish community has become a fairly common type on today's campus. He may be called the "critical academic."

It is apparent that today's critical academic differs from his predecessors; few present-day scholars replicate the experience of a Louis Wirth. They have not emerged from the darkness of the European village into the light of the modern world. Brought up in the metropolis, today's academic does not feel compelled to celebrate urbanism as a way of life—he may in fact prefer suburbia or even exurbia. And unlike Wirth who sought to work within the power structure and who never engaged in radical social criticism despite a brief encounter with Marxism, today's critical academic is typically oriented to the left and prides himself on his feeling of alienation from middle-class America.

The increased acceptability of ethnicity in American society has made the critical academic a more common phenomenon, and it has also brought about a more vocal assertion of Jewishness and a celebration of certain aspects of the Jewish experience. Thus, it is characteristic of the critical academic that he tends to idealize the immigrant Jew of the late nineteenth and early twentieth century. Instead of viewing the Lower East Sides of the nation as retrogressive, as had an earlier generation, the critical academic generally admires them for their embodiment of a sense of "community" and human warmth, for their "authenticity."

A little more than three decades after *The Ghetto* was published, there appeared *Children of the Gilded Ghetto* by Judith Kramer and Seymour Leventman.[24] The volume constitutes a kind of sequel to Wirth's book but also stands in sharp contrast to it. *Children of the Gilded Ghetto* is suffused with nostalgia for the immigrant era when Jews lived on the margins of American society and, according to the authors, were rooted in authentic Jewish culture. Although Jewish immigrants were poor and struggling they led a rich and rewarding existence. Then, with the rise of Jews into the middle and upper classes, American Jewry changed course. Wealthy and successful Jews replaced the ghetto with the gilded ghetto, a new, and worse, environment of their own devising.

The inhabitants of the gilded ghetto lead sterile lives. Prosperity has made them vulgar and ostentatious, conspicuous consumers not only when it comes to clothes and cars but even when it comes to their methods of philanthropy. The gilded-ghetto Jews are part of the American establishment or think that they are. In the authors' view, whatever the limitations of yesterday's immigrant ghetto, it was infinitely preferable to today's suburb. Yet according to the authors the gilded ghetto cannot long endure; the changing occupational structure of the Jewish community, including the attractiveness of employment in academia, will provide the impetus for at least some Jews to turn their backs on the gilded ghetto and enter the larger community.

How can such attitudes as those of the authors of the *Children of the Gilded Ghetto* be explained? Seymour Martin Lipset and Everett Ladd point out that Jewish academics are much more inclined to identify their politics as left or liberal than are their Gentile colleagues. Moreover, Jewish academics do so despite their class interests, for they are also considerably more prosperous on the average than their Gentile counterparts. Liberal and left-wing Jewish academicians are critical of the middle and upper classes, including their Jewish segments—perhaps especially of their Jewish segments. Not even the spectacular success that Jews have achieved in the academy has served to moderate the negative attitudes of the critical academic toward middle-class life; in fact it can serve to intensify them, perhaps as a way of showing that the individual in question, despite his success, has not compromised his integrity.

The critical academic finds it difficult to relate to that segment of the Jewish community which he is exposed to by virtue of his own high acculturation and striking occupational success. He takes no pride in the Jewish middle and upper classes, or in the desire of Jews to maintain their identity while simultaneously adapting to American culture. Despite his own participation in the process, the critical academic tends to view acculturation as a compromise unworthy of descendants of the Biblical prophets. In his work he often finds himself highlighting instances of modern-day Jewish vulgarity and ostentation in contrast to the ghetto Jews who, whatever might be said against them, were in his view at least uncorrupted by bourgeois values.[25] But his most biting criticism is often reserved for the politics of today's American Jew, who is assumed to be conservative (despite continuing evidence to the contrary) if not downright reactionary. Indeed, part of the attraction of the immigrant ghetto community for the critical academic lies in the fact that left-wing movements flourished there, unlike the situation in Jewish suburbia today.[26] In suburbia there are no radical orators haranguing crowds, no talk of the "bosses," no mass demonstrations of "solidarity forever."

The sociologist Melvin Tumin exemplifies the tendency of the critical academic to charge American Jewry with conservatism.[27] One of the most successful of the post-Wirth generation, Tumin took his doctorate in 1944, and three years later, at the age of twenty-eight, was offered a professorship at Princeton. At Princeton Tumin continued to espouse the leftism of his radical past. Nor did he lose touch with Jewish life—during the 1950's and 1960's he was in close contact with Jewish organizations, notably the Anti-Defamation League. Yet though his reasons differed, Tumin came to feel as alienated from the Jewish community as had Louis Wirth at an earlier time. In an address to a Jewish audience Tumin offered his views on what the proper role of the Jewish community should be in American society:

it would indeed be radical in American politics if there were an identifiable Jewish vote and if that Jewish vote stood for a morally radical position on the political spectrum. And it would be a beautiful challenge to America if the Jewish vote were known as such and worried about as such by all politicians, and known and responded to as such by all non-Jews. Then, you see, the Jews would stand for something, and something vital and alive on the American scene. Then Jewishness would constitute determinate identity. Then to be a Jew would be to be something definite and impressive, however much Jews might be joined in their political position by non-Jews. Short of that, what do Jews stand for in America? For a normal distribution of political opinions along the same spectrum and in the same proportions as non-Jews. However normal, self-protecting and expectable this may be, in effect it is a phenomenon essentially preservative of the status quo. However much this may, in the long run, be the best strategy for self-preservation, it ducks—as it must—the essential question of what is the self that is being preserved. And however much finally—in view of their history—Jews have a right to find their way to life and safety by whatever means they discover or contrive—they ought not to confuse this right and this technique for self-preservation with either a determinate identity or with anything culturally valuable today.[28]

Failing a truly radical position, Tumin saw little that was "culturally valuable" in American Jewish life. He was particularly embittered because not only had the average Jew sold out to an American establishment but Jewish intellectuals—of whom more might have been expected—had done so as well:

The most distressing aspect of this move into the sphere of all-rightness is the ways in which it is manifested among Jewish intellectuals. In apparent total forgetfulness of the role which radical criticism of American society played in the first half of this century in helping make America less execrable than it might otherwise have been, Jewish intellectuals have increasingly come to play the role of gentlemen of the Establishment. Beguiled by the chance to become influential—in government, education, industry, the mass media—many Jews have rushed in to take advantage of this opportunity to become insiders.[29]

## VII

The negative stance adopted by the critical academic vis-à-vis contemporary American Jewry has as its corollary, as we have noted, an infatuation with the immigrant Jews of the ghetto generation. But these are not the only Jews to whom the present generation has been invidiously compared: the Jews of the East European *shtetl*, the Jews of the Soviet Union, and the Jews of Israel have at various times and in various hands been singled out for such a purpose. The temptation to regard American Jews as inferior to their progenitors as well as to their contemporaries in other lands is a real one and constitutes a unique problem of bias in contemporary Jewish studies.

Admiration for the *shtetl* Jew was prefigured in the enthusiastic reaction of many writers and intellectuals to the publication in 1952 of *Life Is with People* by Mark Zborowski and Elizabeth Herzog.[30] This book portrayed a world of simple piety in which, despite overwhelming poverty and powerlessness, Jews succeeded in leading a richly human, dignified, and creative existence. The idealized image of the *shtetl* was further refined and elaborated upon some years later in the Broadway musical *Fiddler on the Roof*, which was translated into many languages and performed by innumerable theatrical groups, both amateur and professional, as well as made into a movie. The worldwide success of *Fiddler on the Roof* is a tribute to the appeal of a figure like Tevye, its hero, for people in modern society who feel themselves assailed by rapid change. Whatever Sholom Aleichem may have intended, Tevye has become a prototype of the decent man assailed by forces that would destroy him but who despite all obstacles succeeds not only in keeping body and soul together but in retaining his dignity and humanity.

Judged by the idealized standards of the *shtetl*, the contemporary American Jew may be found wanting. Unless one happens to find social mobility heroic it would be difficult to call American Jews heroes. And among significant numbers of younger Jews there is not even social mobility to admire; born into the middle or upper class, they have little conception of what it means to climb the "greasy pole" of material success. But if the student of contemporary Jewry is to perceive the American Jewish situation in all its dimensions, he must resist the temptation to make invidious comparisons between the American Jew and his *shtetl* forebears, particularly as the latter have been portrayed through the touching affirmations of Zborowski and Herzog, and even of the late Abraham Joshua Heschel.[31] Before he arrives at a judgment he must study the *shtetl* through the eyes of its contemporaries—especially the Hebrew (and Yiddish) writers of the period. These men, themselves the products of the *shtetl* but at the same time exposed to other influences, viewed the *shtetl* as nothing less than an abomination—a place rife with superstition, cursed with a culture that stifled creativity and manliness, and saddled with a class and status system that perpetrated grave injustice. Although it is not incumbent upon the student to render a final judgment on the *shtetl*, he does need to protect himself against uncritical admiration of past generations of Jews, and—a necessary corollary— against unduly harsh evaluations of his own.

If it is possible to devalue the contemporary American Jew by comparing him with his *shtetl* ancestor, it is equally possible to do so by comparing him with the Jew of Israel or of the Soviet Union. Although New Leftists may be critical of Israel, most Jews, including most young Jews, hold the country and its people in the highest possible esteem. In achieving statehood, in successfully defending their nation's sovereignty in the face of concerted attack and continuing acts of terrorism, the Israelis have assumed a truly heroic stature in the minds of the majority of American Jews. Similarly, the courage of a segment of Russian Jewry in asserting its Jewish identity has fired the imagination of many young Jews. But the examples of Israel and of Soviet Jewry may also have the effect of making the American Jew seem drab and uninspiring by comparison.

Now, we can take for granted the fact that present-day American Jews enjoy a standard of living that is incomparably higher than that of their forebears. It is also obvious that most American Jews on the one hand enjoy luxuries that are unavailable to their Israeli or Soviet cousins, and on the other hand seem to lead a less "heroic" existence. But the student of the contemporary Jewish scene must go beyond these differences if he hopes to probe successfully the sociological and psychological situation of today's American Jew. For it is clear that American Jewry's distance from the sweatshop, or from the Arab-Israeli conflict, or from the struggle against Soviet repression, has by no means brought about the elimination of all problems. Even if we were to make the bold assumption that American Jewry has no substantial economic worries, we could not but realize that new anxieties have taken the place of old struggles. There is, to take only one example, the problem faced by many American Jews who wish but do not know how to create a viable Jewish identity for themselves and their children. The crisis of identity—both in its Jewish and in its "universal" aspect—is a problem that the American Jew confronts more starkly than did his forefather in the *shtetl* or in a first-settlement area in the American city, or for that matter, than does his cousin in Israel. It is no exaggeration to say that with each rise in economic level, each advance in educational level, and each move upward in "brow" level, the difficulty has been compounded.

No discussion of the possible sources of bias in the study of contemporary American Jews would be complete without taking into account that those studying the Jewish group are themselves almost invariably Jewish. While this Jewishness is undoubtedly an asset inasmuch as it gives the student both a competence that the outsider would have laboriously to acquire and a rapport that the non-Jew might find difficult to establish, in some sense it is also a handicap. Scholarly training is not culture-free. In the United States, academic training is strongly oriented to western values as well as to the American milieu, and while exposure to western culture brings enormous benefits, it has its characteristic limitations and dangers that are not always perceived as such, especially by members of minority groups. One such possible danger is that of alienation from one's own group. In its most benign form this alienation may be expressed as cultural relativism, a perspective in which the Jews are viewed as merely one of many ethnic groups and in which emphasis is placed on the similarities rather than on the differences among groups.

But socialization in western culture is capable of producing more than simple alienation in the Jewish researcher. There is the deeper alienation of self-hatred, the phenomenon that came to preoccupy Kurt Lewin and other observers of the Jewish personality, in which the individual unwittingly internalizes the anti-Jewish prejudice endemic to western culture. He comes to view the Jews critically; he identifies with the historical aggressor. In its most serious manifestation self-hatred leads to a view of the Jews as retrogressive and reactionary—as clinging to an outmoded identity. As a consequence Jews come to be seen as being in part responsible for the very prejudice from which they suffer. In the final analysis this view of Jewish life constitutes a secularized version of Christianity's traditional stance with regard to the Jews.

Another possible source of bias arising from the Jewishness of most students of contemporary Jewry is the ethnocentrism that can linger even in those who are seemingly cosmopolitan. Ethnocentrism is of course encountered in many areas of a minority community. Among those who are well integrated into the group, ethnocentrism need not create inner conflict—it is congruous with both the individual's ideology and his style of life. The alienated, on the other hand, troubled by their ethnocentrism and finding it incompatible with their ideology and their style of life, tend, as we have seen, to become harshly critical of the Jewish group, and to hold Jews to a standard that others would not be expected to achieve. Since the Jews will necessarily fall short of the arbitrary standard set by the analyst, he comes to feel justified in his alienation from the group.

There is a final temptation that may beset the student of contemporary Jewry—the temptation to view the Jewish group from the vantage point of a tourist. The tourist revels in the exotic, the colorful, the different; only the native finds satisfaction in the ordinary. Even analysts who maintain that Jews are like everyone else—only more so—sometimes find themselves irresistibly drawn to picturesque and unusual aspects of Jewish life: to *hasidim*, to Black Jews, to the *havurot*. The exotic, to be sure, has its undeniable attraction, even its value, but unless such phenomena are placed in perspective, the result for the student will be distortion rather than understanding.

Those who would understand American Jewish life must approach it not in a spirit of tourism, still less in a spirit of preconceived hostility but seriously, sympathetically, and out of a genuine desire to learn. The challenge of comprehending the twentieth-century Jews of New York, Los Angeles, and even of Oshkosh is still very much before us, as difficult a task as that of comprehending the Jews of first-century Jerusalem, and as inviting.

# Notes

1. In recent years the *American Jewish Year Book* has assumed new importance as a source of material for contemporary Jewish studies. In addition to reporting facts and figures about Jewish life, each volume of the *Year Book* contains one or more feature articles dealing with some of the most significant problems of American Jewry. For the most part the *Year Book* relies on data made available by private rather than by official sources. Recently the *Year Book* has published a series of reviews by Daniel J. Elazar of the literature on various aspects of contemporary Jewish studies. See his "The Pursuit of Community: Selections from the Literature of Jewish Public Affairs, 1965–66," *American Jewish Year Book 1967* (Vol. 68), pp. 178–221; "The Rediscovered Polity: Selections from the Literature of Jewish Public Affairs, 1967–68," *American Jewish Year Book 1969* (Vol. 70), pp. 172–237; "Confrontation and Reconstitution: Selections from the Literature of Jewish Public Affairs, 1969–71," *American Jewish Year Book 1972* (Vol. 73), pp. 301–83.

2. In addition to such data there is the additional resource provided by the vast amount of fictional literature produced during the recent "vogue" of American-Jewish writing. While many of these writers—the most familiar names are Bernard Malamud, Saul Bellow, Philip Roth, Herbert Gold, Bruce Jay Friedman—do not seek to create specifically "Jewish" novels, their books do feature Jewish characters and are often intended to reveal one or another facet of American Jewish life. It is difficult to estimate how long this vogue will continue. Calvin Trillin, in a spoof of the New York literary scene, has suggested that the Jewish period is drawing to a close. See his story "Lester Drentluss, a Jewish Boy from Baltimore, Attempts to Make it through the Summer of 1967," *The Atlantic* (November 1968), 71–73.

3. Louis Finkelstein in *Proceedings of the Rabbinical Assembly of America*, Vol. XIII (1949), p. 121.

4. The section that follows is based in part on a paper presented at a colloquium on the teaching of Jewish studies in American universities held at Brandeis University in the fall of 1969. See Marshall Sklare, "The Problem of Contemporary Jewish Studies," *Midstream*, 16, No. 4 (April 1970), 27–35. The paper was also published in the proceedings of the colloquium: *The Teaching of Judaica in American Universities*, ed. by Leon A. Jick (New York: Ktav Publishing House, 1970), pp. 57–70.

5. Michael A. Meyer, *The Origins of the Modern Jew* (Detroit: Wayne State University Press, 1967), p. 162. On the ideology of *Wissenschaft des Judentums* see also Nahum N. Glatzer, "The Beginnings of Modern Jewish Studies," in *Studies in Nineteenth Century Jewish Intellectual History*, ed. by Alexander Altmann (Cambridge, Mass.: Harvard University Press, 1964), pp. 27–45; Gershom Scholem, *The Messianic Idea in Judaism and other Essays on Jewish Spirituality* (New York: Schocken Books, 1971), pp. 304–13; and Max Wiener, "The Ideology of the Founders of Jewish Scientific Research" in *YIVO Annual of Jewish Social Science*, V (1950), 184–96.

However it is a matter of record that at one time Leopold Zunz stressed the importance of statistical research on Jewish life. His memorandum on the subject was published in *Zeitschrift für die Wissenschaft des Judentums*, Vol. I (1823), pp. 523–32. I am grateful to Professor Nahum Glatzer for guiding me to this source.

6. Zalman Shazar, *Morning Stars* (Philadelphia: Jewish Publication Society of America, 1967), pp. 188–90. Surprisingly enough Shazar and his fellow students achieved their objective despite the fact that the baron's hold over the students was absolute. (Not only did he underwrite the budget of the academy, but he bribed the police to arrange residence permits in St. Petersburg for students who lacked them.) Soon after this confrontation the baron invited Wischnitzer to offer a course on "The Economic History of the Jews." A true aristocrat, Baron Günzberg apparently felt, that despite his power, he had no right to deprive students of knowledge that they sought to acquire.

7. Milton Gordon, *Assimilation in American Life* (New York: Oxford University Press, 1964), p. 224.

8. *Ibid.*, p. 263. Cf. Marshall Sklare, "Assimilation and the Sociologists," *Commentary* (May 1965), 63–67.

9. Seymour Martin Lipset, "The Study of Jewish Communities in a Comparative Context," *The Jewish Journal of Sociology*, V, No. 2 (December 1963), p. 163. Interestingly enough, the attraction to a universalistic orientation is observable among Jewish social scientists in Israel as well as in the United States. While Israeli social scientists do study Israeli society, they tend to emphasize its universal aspects rather than its particular ones. Accordingly, they have neglected the study of Jewish identity. The problem is briefly analyzed in my review of Simon Herman's *Israelis and Jews*, which appeared in *Commentary* (January 1972), 84–86.

10. See Marshall Sklare, "The Development and Utilization of Sociological Research: The Case of the American Jewish Community," *Jewish Journal of Sociology*, V, No. 2 (December 1963), 167–86. There are agencies like the Conference on Jewish Social Studies (formerly the Conference on Jewish Relations) whose main objective is that of stimulating and subventing research on topics related to contemporary Jewish studies. However, the Conference has not been able to achieve its objective; in recent years it has been forced to confine itself to the publication of a journal.

11. As the work of the YIVO Institute for Jewish Research demonstrates, Diaspora nationalism and Zionism both gave impetus to the study of contemporary Jewry.

On the tension between Zionism and *Wissenschaft des Judentums* see Alexander Altmann, *Jewish Studies: Their Scope and Meaning Today* (London: Hillel Foundation, 1958), pp. 9–11.

12. For biographical details see *Arthur Ruppin: Memoirs, Diaries, Letters*, ed. by Alex Bein (New York: Herzl Press, 1971). Ruppin's work grew out of the German-Jewish milieu; that of another leading scholar, Jacob Lestschinsky (1876–1966), was a product of the East European scene. Ruppin's books seem to have had the

greater impact, perhaps because they were less specialized than Lestschinsky's, because they integrated data from a large number of countries, because they were
strongly interpretative as well as statistical, and because they were related to German scholarship. Unlike the works of Lestschinsky, most of Ruppin's books were
translated into several languages, and thus his contributions became accessible to a
wide audience. See A. Tartakower, "Jacob Lestschinsky," *Jewish Frontier* (November
1958), 15–17.

13. Isaac Ben-Zvi, who settled in Palestine in 1907 and served as president of
Israel from 1952 until his death in 1963, was one of the few Zionist leaders to become
preoccupied with the situation of the Jews of North Africa and the Middle East.
The research institute in Jerusalem devoted to the study of these communities is
named after him.

14. See *Arthur Ruppin: Memoirs, Diaries, Letters, op. cit.*, p. 74. Although *Die
Juden der Gegenwart* was written before Ruppin committed himself to Zionism,
the direction of his thinking was clear enough. Ruppin's first Zionist article was
published in 1905, and two years later he became an official of the movement.

15. Louis Wirth, *The Ghetto* (Chicago: University of Chicago Press, 1928). *The
Ghetto* had been preceded by an earlier work by an American author: Maurice Fishberg, *The Jews: A Study of Race and Environment* (New York: Charles Scribner's
Sons, 1911). As the title indicates Fishberg's perspective was heavily anthropologi-
cal. Fishberg was convinced that anti-Semitism would soon be eradicated, and he
reasoned that Jews would respond to the new era by intermarrying. His assumptions make interesting reading today: "the differences between Jews and Christians are not everywhere racial, due to anatomical or physiological peculiarities,
but are solely the result of the social and political environment. [This] explains
our optimism as regards the ultimate obliteration of all distinctions between Jews
and Christians in Europe and America. This optimism is confirmed by conditions
in Italy, Scandinavia, and Australia, where anti-Semitism is practically unknown.
When intermarriage between Jews and Christians will reach the same proportions
in other countries, and the facts presented in [this volume] clearly show that the
time is not distant, anti-Semitism will everywhere meet with the same fate as in
Italy, Scandinavia, and Australia. Both Jews and Christians have been contributing
to this end, the former by discarding their separative ritualism, and thus displaying
willingness to bridge the gulf which separated them from others, and the latter by
legalizing civil marriage." (*Ibid.*, pp. vii–viii)

16. Elizabeth Wirth Marvick, "Louis Wirth: A Biographical Memorandum," in
*Louis Wirth: On Cities and Social Life*, ed. by Albert J. Reiss, Jr. (Chicago: University
of Chicago Press, 1964), p. 337.

17. See Louis Wirth, *op. cit.*, esp. pp. 263–81.

18. See Louis Wirth, "Education for Survival: The Jews," *American Journal of
Sociology*, XLVIII, No. 6 (May 1943), 682–91.

19. See *The Jews: Social Patterns of an American Group*, ed. by Marshall Sklare
(Glencoe, Ill.: The Free Press, 1958). For a detailed analysis of the book see Joshua A.
Fishman "American Jewry as a Field of Social Science Research," in *YIVO Annual
of Jewish Social Science*, Vol. XII (1958–59), pp. 70–102.

More than a decade before *The Jews: Social Patterns of an American Group* was
published a volume appeared that contained articles on American Jewry written
by some of the nation's leading social scientists. See *Jews in a Gentile World*, ed.
by Isacque Graeber and Steuart Henderson Britt (New York: Macmillan, 1942).

Despite the fact that this volume contained some significant data and suggestive interpretations, it did not play an important role in advancing contemporary Jewish studies. The primary aim of the book was to serve as a corrective to the various anti-Semitic tracts appearing at the time. Graeber and Britt were at pains to point out that their book was not a Jewish effort, and that more than half of their contributors were Gentile. The first article, which set the tone of the volume, was written by a leading political scientist at Harvard—Carl J. Friedrich—and was entitled "Anti-Semitism: Challenge to Christian Culture."

20. For biographical details see Alfred J. Marrow, *The Practical Theorist: The Life and Work of Kurt Lewin* (New York: Basic Books, 1969).

21. See Kurt Lewin, "Self-Hatred among Jews," *Contemporary Jewish Record*, 4, No. 3 (June 1941), 219–32.

22. While Lewin's views were widely cited in the Jewish community they did not receive universal acclamation among his peers. Bruno Bettelheim, for example, rejected Lewin's theory of group belongingness and the need for a sense of positive Jewish identification in the child. See Bettelheim's article "How to Arm Our Children against Anti-Semitism—A Psychologist's Advice to Jewish Parents," *Commentary* (September 1951), 209–18.

23. At the time of Lewin's death the CCI was in full operation. Later it was gradually phased out, and the researchers whom Lewin had brought together took posts at universities and at other research institutes.

In May 1944, at about the same time the American Jewish Congress was setting up its Commission on Community Interrelations, the American Jewish Committee held a conference on religious and racial prejudice. This conference also eventuated in the establishment of a research department. It was headed by Max Horkheimer, who, like Lewin, had come to the United States from Nazi Germany. Lewin and Horkheimer differed sharply in their approach to social psychology as well as in their attitude to Jewish identification.

24. Judith R. Kramer and Seymour Leventman, *Children of the Gilded Ghetto* (New Haven: Yale University Press, 1961).

25. Allan Mazur, in a study of the attitudes of Jewish social scientists at Brandeis, Harvard, and Boston universities, has found a substantial percentage reporting strong feelings of alienation from Jews who are on the same class level as themselves: "This sort of alienation was reported by a majority of all respondents, but was particularly strong at Brandeis with 70 percent of the subjects giving alienated responses as opposed to only 48 percent and 53 percent at B.U. and Harvard respectively." (Allan Mazur, "The Socialization of Jews into the Academic Subculture," in *The Professors*, ed. by Charles H. Anderson and John D. Murray (Cambridge, Mass.: Schenkman, 1971, p. 277). Mazur quotes one respondent as follows: "Well I suppose I feel most alienated not from the European-born pushcart peddlers in New York City—I don't feel as alienated from them as I do from American-born Jews who have been to college, who live in the suburbs, who are fairly well-to-do, and who are afraid to let go. . . . It's interesting. I never thought of that before, but I feel less alienated from the Yiddish-speaking pushcart peddler than I do from people who are closer to me (*Ibid.*)."

26. It is notable that Louis Wirth made only casual reference to Jewish radical activity in first- and second-settlement areas. It is difficult to believe that he was unaware of it; rather we may suppose that he preferred not to publish data on Jewish radical activity lest it be misused by prejudiced Gentiles.

27. See Melvin M. Tumin, "Conservative Trends in American Jewish Life," *Judaism*, 13, No. 2 (Spring 1964), 131–42.

28. *Ibid.*, p. 138.

29. *Ibid.*, p. 139. Some of Tumin's assumptions were analyzed in the discussion that followed his paper; see *ibid.*, pp. 143–53. Milton Himmelfarb published a critique of several of Tumin's assumptions, particularly those relating to Jewish conservatism, in "How We Are," *Commentary* (January 1965), 69–72.

30. Mark Zborowski and Elizabeth Herzog, *Life Is with People* (New York: International Universities Press, 1952). The volume was dedicated to Ruth Benedict and includes a foreword by Margaret Mead.

31. See Abraham J. Heschel, *The Earth Is the Lord's: The Inner World of the Jew in East Europe* (New York: H. Schuman, 1950).

# Survival of the American Jewish Community

# The Image of the Good Jew
# in Lakeville

["Lakeville" was Sklare's name for a prominent Chicago suburb where, in the late 1950's, he tried to locate "the Jew who would be increasingly encountered in tomorrow's Jewish community." This was the first full-scale sociological study of an American Jewish community in suburbia, and it contains some of Sklare's most original insights, ideas that he returned to again and again in later writings. Two volumes of Lakeville studies eventually appeared, *Jewish Identity on the Suburban Frontier: A Study of Group Survival in the Open Society* by Sklare and Joseph Greenblum, and a parallel study entitled *The Edge of Friendliness: A Study of Jewish-Gentile Relations* by Benjamin R. Ringer. The former, which Nathan Glazer characterized as "the starting-point for all serious discussion of American Judaism for some time to come," closed with this remarkable analysis of "the Image of the Good Jew."

In the mid-1970's, Sklare returned to Lakeville to update his study. His second edition of *Jewish Identity on the Suburban Frontier* (1979) contains a new chapter entitled "Lakeville: A Changing Suburb." There, in his closing pages, he reflects on his earlier work and responds to sociologist Chaim Waxman, who in a perceptive essay on Sklare ("Psalms of a Sober Man: The Sociology of Marshall Sklare," *Contemporary Jewry*, 4 [Fall/Winter 1977–78], 3–11) characterized the book's mood as pessimistic. "Should one be optimistic or pessimistic about the prospects for survival of American Jewry," Sklare asked.

> I confess that I am hesitant to declare myself. I will take my stand with that pious Jew who lived in Jerusalem during the desperate siege of 1947–48. He went through the streets warning the defenders not to rely on miracles to save Jerusalem from the Arab armies that surrounded the city. "Do not rely on miracles," he implored, "say tehillim" (psalms). What has been accomplished in Lakeville in the past twenty years is an encouraging sign of Jewish affirmation. Nevertheless, let us not neglect to say psalms . . . the saying of psalms is a wise precaution when the survival of a Jewish community is at stake.—JDS]

To conclude our study of Jewish identity in Lakeville, we turn to a question that is entirely attitudinal in nature: the conception of the "good Jew."

We assumed that our respondents had a conception of what qualities were necessary for being a good Jew. The assumption seemed to us justified if only by virtue of the fact that exclamations may be heard in Lakeville such as: "X is not a very good Jew," "Y acts like a good Jew should act," "Z thinks he's a good Jew, but as far as I'm concerned he's not." Additionally, inasmuch as being Jewish in the modern world involves self-consciousness, we felt that whatever the *level* of Jewishness, the *problem* of identity was central enough so that our respondents would have a conception of the good Jew. In respect to the evaluation of their answers, we assumed that there would be a strain toward self-legitimation: respondents would identify their own attitudes and behavior patterns as proper for a good Jew. But we assumed that there would be a tendency toward idealization as well: respondents would answer in terms of what the ideal Jew should be like, as well as of the pattern of life that they—the real Jews—had adopted.

In order to study the image of the good Jew we provided our respondents with four alternatives:

In your opinion, for a Jew to be considered a good Jew, which of the following must he do? Which are desirable but not essential that he do? Which have no bearing on whether or not you consider him a good Jew? Which must he not do?

and asked them to respond to twenty-two items:

Accept his being a Jew and not try to hide it
Contribute to Jewish philanthropies
Support Israel
Support Zionism
Support all humanitarian causes
Belong to Jewish organizations
Belong to a synagogue or temple
Attend weekly services
Lead an ethical and moral life
Attend services on High Holidays
Observe the dietary laws
Be well versed in Jewish history and culture
Know the fundamentals of Judaism
Have mostly Jewish friends
Promote the use of Yiddish
Give Jewish candidates for political office preference
Gain respect of Christian neighbors
Promote civic betterment and improvement in the community
Work for equality for Negroes

TABLE I
*The Image of the Good Jew*

| | Percent who believe that to be a "Good Jew" the item is | | | | |
|---|---|---|---|---|---|
| Item | Essential | Desirable | Makes no difference | Essential not to do | N.A. D.K. |
| Accept his being a Jew and not try to hide it | 85 | 13 | 2 | — | — |
| Contribute to Jewish philanthropies | 39 | 49 | 12 | — | — |
| Support Israel | 21 | 47 | 32 | — | — |
| Support Zionism | 7 | 23 | 59 | 9 | 2 |
| Support all humanitarian causes | 67 | 29 | 4 | — | — |
| Belong to Jewish organizations | 17 | 49 | 34 | — | — |
| Belong to a synagogue or temple | 31 | 44 | 25 | — | — |
| Attend weekly services | 4 | 46 | 49 | 1 | — |
| Lead an ethical and moral life | 93 | 6 | 1 | — | — |
| Attend services on High Holidays | 24 | 46 | 30 | — | — |
| Observe the dietary laws | 1 | 11 | 85 | 3 | — |
| Be well versed in Jewish history and culture | 17 | 73 | 10 | — | — |
| Know the fundamentals of Judaism | 48 | 48 | 4 | — | — |
| Have mostly Jewish friends | 1 | 10 | 81 | 8 | — |
| Promote the use of Yiddish | 1 | 6 | 69 | 24 | — |
| Give Jewish candidates for political office preference | 1 | 6 | 39 | 54 | — |
| Gain respect of Christian neighbors | 59 | 32 | 9 | — | — |
| Promote civic betterment and improvement in the community | 67 | 29 | 4 | — | — |
| Work for equality for Negroes | 44 | 39 | 16 | 1 | — |
| Help the underprivileged improve their lot | 58 | 37 | 5 | — | — |
| Be a liberal on political and economic issues | 31 | 32 | 35 | 2 | — |
| Marry within the Jewish faith | 23 | 51 | 26 | — | — |

Help the underprivileged improve their lot
Be a liberal on political and economic issues
Marry within the Jewish faith

Responses are presented in Table 1.

Turning first to an analysis of the "essential" category, we find that the following items receive the highest ranking:

| | |
|---|---|
| Lead an ethical and moral life | 93% |
| Accept his being a Jew and not try to hide it | 85% |
| Support all humanitarian causes | 67% |
| Promote civic betterment and improvement in the community | 67% |
| Gain respect of Christian neighbors | 59% |
| Help the underprivileged improve their lot | 58% |
| Know the fundamentals of Judaism | 48% |
| Work for equality for Negroes | 44% |

This list of essential qualities for being considered a good Jew is indicative of how far conceptions in Lakeville deviate from past models of Jewish religious piety. The list also means that a Jewish nationalistic model is absent as well as that a Jewish cultural model with roots in traditional Jewish life is missing.

At first glance the ideal of Jewishness predominating in Lakeville seems to be that of the practice of good citizenship and an upright life. To be a good Jew means to be an ethical individual; it also means to be kind, helpful, and interested in the welfare of neighbors, fellow Americans, and of humanity-at-large. But further examination leads to the conclusion that Lakeville's ideal of Jewishness is more than a sophisticated version of the Boy Scout who guides the frail old lady across a busy street. It is more than the practice of ethics. There is, for example, the aspect of Jewish self-acceptance: our respondents feel that in order to be a good Jew it is essential to freely and proudly acknowledge one's identity. Does this attitude, we wonder, result from the belief that Jewish existence is a great and wonderful mystery as well as a distinction and obligation which Gentiles are the poorer for not sharing? Or does it have its source in the belief that no honorable person would—either overtly or covertly—lay claim to being anything other than what he is? It is difficult to judge between these alternatives. All that we can say is that in other places and at other times in modern Jewish history it was not always so.

According to our respondents not only is it essential that the good Jew acknowledge his identity, but it is incumbent upon him to lead a life of moral excellence. Their conception appears to be that whatever else Judaism teaches, it teaches such excellence. The true test of being a good Jew is not loyalty to the old sacramentalism but the extent to which the individual actualizes moral ideals. We do not know whether our respondents consider Jewish ethical ideals as superior to those upheld by the religions that their neighbors practice, but it is apparent that they would reject the notion that such ideals are inferior.

Do our respondents, we wonder, locate the source of their belief in moral excellence in the ethic of Judaism, or do they draw upon the ethic common to all American faiths—an ethic that transcends specific religious traditions as it merges into the aspirations characteristic of secular American culture? Our conviction is that by-and-large Lakeville Jews locate the source of their ethic in Judaism, although if pressed they might say that other faiths now share the ethic that Judaism originally proclaimed. But it must also be stated that while the ethic identified by our respondents is certainly intrinsic to Judaism it appears that the motive power for their making such an identification comes from the general culture. Nevertheless, this is less significant than the fact that they identify the source of their ethic as a Jewish one. And we are again reminded that in other places and at other times in the modern history of the Jew it was not always so. Abraham Mendelssohn serves as an example that there have been Jews who felt that Judaism represents a necessary but outmoded stage in the evolution of man's religious thinking—their point of view was that Christianity is characterized by more lofty moral ideals than Judaism.

Some of our respondents introduce an important footnote to the conception of the ethical life as the keystone of being a good Jew: the attitude that the ethical life must not be limited to the personal. It must, rather, be social: the good Jew is a person who works to change the world as well as himself. Thus some feel that the Jew must work for equal rights for Negroes, a greater number believe in the essentiality of aiding the underprivileged, and even more believe that supporting humanitarian causes and working for the betterment of their community is required for being a good Jew.

Another significant theme is that gaining the respect of Gentiles is incumbent upon the good Jew. While it is to his self-interest to do so, more importantly he must make this effort on behalf of his fellow Jews. Gentiles will consider unacceptable behavior to be characteristic of the entire group. Thus the good Jew is under the obligation to conduct himself in an exemplary manner; each Jew represents the Jewish group and is obliged to act accordingly.

We are left with the item "Know the fundamentals of Judaism," which some 48 percent of Lakeville respondents consider essential for being a good Jew. At first glance this would suggest the *mitzvah* of study, an exceedingly important emphasis in the Jewish sacred system. If accepted at face value this item might be considered as contradicting our earlier statements about the absence of traditionalism in Lakeville. We feel, however, that given the lack of importance accorded to other traditional patterns, agreement with this item does not necessarily mean attachment to the Jewish tradition of study as a form of worship. More likely what it suggests is that the intelligent and responsible individual has the obligation to know what he stands for; just as his identification as a citizen makes it obligatory to acquaint himself with American history and current affairs, so identification as a Jew makes it obligatory to acquaint himself with the fundamentals of Judaism. In regard to the reflection of this attitude in the community it is apparent that while Jewish educational programs for adults in Lakeville are not so well attended as their sponsors desire, they are an accepted feature in all of the congregations. While the suprasocial impetus for attendance at such programs must not be denigrated, it appears that the image that the Lakeville Jew has of himself as an intelligent and responsible person is operating in respect to Jewish identity. Adult education flourishes in Lakeville; adult Jewish education is on the increase. Over all, the significant fact is that some apply the concept of intelligence and responsibility to their Jewish as well as to their general identity.

In summary, the essential qualifications for being a good Jew according to Lakeville residents are self-acceptance, moral excellence, good citizenship, and knowledge of Judaism. The acts that the good Jew is obliged to perform include advancing the general welfare, promoting social reform, and increasing intergroup amity.

Turning to the "desirable" category we find that the following items rank highest:

| | |
|---|---|
| Be well versed in Jewish history and culture | 73% |
| Marry within the Jewish faith | 51% |
| Contribute to Jewish philanthropies | 49% |
| Belong to Jewish organizations | 49% |
| Know the fundamentals of Judaism | 48% |
| Support Israel | 47% |
| Attend weekly services | 46% |
| Attend services on High Holidays | 46% |
| Belong to a synagogue or temple | 44% |

In contrast to the essential category, this list is more traditional: it includes items that relate to well-established religious, nationalistic, and cultural models. Thus, such items as attendance at services, support of Israel, and knowledge of Jewish history and culture are listed. A *mitzvah* such as contributing to Jewish philanthropies also occurs. In fact many of the items on the list constitute activities and attitudes ordinarily thought of as characteristic of "survivalist" Jews, such as belonging to a synagogue, joining a Jewish organization, and marrying within the Jewish group.

One of the items ("Know the fundamentals of Judaism") is found both on the desirable and on the essential list. But the significant point is that attitudes and actions directly connected with Jewish survival tend to be thought of more often as desirable rather than essential. It is of course true that if we combine desirable and essential ratings some of these items bulk large: "Contribute to Jewish philanthropies" then scores 88 percent, "Belong to a synagogue or temple" 75 percent, "Marry within the Jewish faith" 74 percent, "Attend services on the High Holidays" 70 percent, and "Support Israel" 68 percent. While these are substantial percentages, they are generally exceeded by a wide margin when we reverse the procedure and add the desirable ratings to the items on the essential list: "Lead an ethical and moral life" then scores 99 percent, "Accept his being a Jew and not try to hide it" 98 percent, "Support all humanitarian causes" 96 percent, "Know the fundamentals of Judaism" 96 percent, "Promote civic betterment and improvement in the community" 96 percent, "Help the underprivileged improve their lot" 95 percent, and "Gain respect of Christian neighbors" 91 percent. Only the item "Work for equality for Negroes" scores less than 90 percent, inasmuch as some 16 percent feel that such efforts make no difference in respect to being a good Jew. All of which is to say that in Lakeville there is greater unanimity in respect to what is essential rather than what is desirable, and if someone does not consider an item essential the chances are that he will consider it desirable. Items considered by some as desirable, on the other hand, will frequently be considered essential but some respondents may also consider them as making no difference in respect to being considered a good Jew.

Turning to the "makes no difference" category, we find that the item "Observe the dietary laws" scores highest. Observance of the dietary laws presents a serious problem to the Jews of Lakeville. It is thus no surprise to find that some 85 percent feel that such observance bears no relationship to being a good Jew; the group that believes that such observance is either essential or desirable constitutes a distinct minority. The next highest item is "Have mostly Jewish friends," about which some 81 percent feel indifferent. The third-ranking item is "Promote the use of Yiddish"; some 69 percent feel that such promotion is irrelevant. This item is followed by "Support Zionism" with 59 percent. The figure is in decided contrast to attitudes about supporting Israel, for most of our respondents believe that such support is either essential or desirable.

The great majority of our twenty-two items draw either an essential, desirable, or makes no difference response, and very few draw any substantial number of respondents who feel that to be considered a good Jew a given action must be proscribed. The exception is "Give Jewish candidates for political office preference." This idea is abhorrent to some 54 percent of our respondents. Their answers could mean devotion to the concept of a political process free from the interest of pressure groups, a sophisticated political orientation where it is felt that Jewish interests can be as easily safeguarded by liberal Gentiles as by Jews, or a defensive reaction based on the fear that Jews will be charged with being more devoted to the advancement of their group than to the common good.

The next highest item on the proscribed list—chosen by 24 percent—is "Promote the use of Yiddish." The fact that a fair-size minority react with vehemence to the idea of promoting Yiddish is significant. It suggests that some Lakeville Jews are highly insecure about Jewish status and acceptance. An interpretation of insecurity is strengthened by the fact that American Jews have the unquestioned right to promote the use of Yiddish, as well as the fact that the item gives no intimation that such promotion would be done through dubious or possibly illegal means, or would involve the use of public funds or facilities. Apparently the idea of promoting Yiddish conjures up an image of a Jewish community less acculturated and accepted than today's community. It may even suggest to some that present-day acceptance could be imperiled. The response to the item on the Yiddish language is especially significant inasmuch as there has never been a problem in the community over this issue, and very few residents belong to organizations that support the dissemination of the language. Furthermore, no organizations exist that are explicitly anti-Yiddish. The response is doubly significant because attitudes in this area are uncontaminated by the operation of processes that ordinarily shape public opinion. This is very much in contrast with Zionism—the Zionist question has been on the agenda of the Jewish community for many decades; pro-Zionist, non-Zionist, and anti-Zionist organizations vie for public support. In spite of efforts to shape Lakeville opinion in an anti-Zionist direction, only 9 percent feel that it is impossible for a good Jew to support Zionism.

How should our findings on the image of the good Jew be evaluated? Some would say that they indicate the hypocrisy of the Lakeville Jew. They would focus on such items as "Work for equality for Negroes" and point out that whereas a total of 83 percent feel such work to be essential or desirable very few lend active support to organizations whose purpose is the advancement of civil rights. Furthermore, there has been no attempt to assist Negroes in purchasing homes in the community. Hypocrisy is not, however, the significant perspective for evaluating the gap between the image that our respondents have of the good Jew and the patterns that they follow in daily life. To stress hypocrisy is to be diverted from the most crucial aspect of these responses: the desire to retain Jewish identity and the simultaneous difficulty that the Lakeville Jew experiences in affirming actions that would help guarantee—or make more meaningful—that survival. Furthermore, it becomes clear that the actions and *mitzvot* that the Lakeville Jew affirms as most essential to being considered a good Jew are actions and *mitzvot* between man and man and that *mitzvot* between man and God assume a distinctly secondary place. Finally, the actions and *mitzvot* that the Lakeville Jew esteems most highly are found in the general culture. In sum, while the Lakeville Jew may be following certain Jewish sources when he formulates his ideals, the lack of distinctiveness inherent in his model of the good Jew is capable of eroding away group boundaries.

At the present moment the Lakeville Jew remains considerably more Jewish in action than in thought. Philanthropy is a good example of this dichotomy. Some 39 percent consider that contributing to Jewish philanthropies is essential, while 67 percent believe that supporting all humanitarian causes is essential. To be sure, almost all Lakeville Jews contribute to both Jewish and non-Jewish philanthropies, but the fact of the matter is that only 19 percent give the bulk of their money to non-Jewish charities. While Jewish campaigns are better organized and set higher sights for givers, the philanthropic behavior of Lakeville Jews is not a result of greater efficiency of the Jewish fund-raising machinery. Rather it results from the Jews' feeling of identity. Leaving aside the fact that fund-raising techniques in the general community are becoming more sophisticated, the question that occurs is how long the present gap between action and thought in the area of philanthropic giving will survive. Will not a sectarianism that is unsupported ideologically wither away when social conditions change? Will future generations be prepared to live with the dichotomy that the Lakeville Jew abides: a universal humanitarianism as the prime value in combination with the practice of giving priority to Jewish causes? Will not future generations attempt to reassess Jewish anguish against the anguish of others, the importance of supporting Jewish institutions against the significance of other institutions? May they not conclude that their humanitarian aspirations dictate that they place the accent on the general rather than the Jewish?

If all of these questions come to mind with respect to philanthropy many more occur with respect to the item on having Jewish friends. One of the most significant responses in Table 1 is the 81 percent who say that having mostly Jewish friends makes no difference to being a good Jew, while only 10 percent consider it desirable to have mostly Jewish friends, and a mere 1 percent feel that it is essential. In actuality some 91 percent of our respondents have an all-Jewish or predominantly Jewish friendship circle, and this pattern is crucial in explaining the cohesion of the Jewish community of Lakeville. Such cohesion, we realize, is supported by its members' social relationships rather than by their attachment to traditional religious, nationalistic, or cultural models. We reason, therefore, that until there is an increase in loyalty to more "positive" aspects of Jewishness, the cultivation and reinforcement of such Jewish social relationships will continue to be required in order to maintain group survival. The threat to such survival is that the Lakeville Jew lacks ideological commitment to his present pattern of friendship ties; he tends also to feel that a mixed neighborhood is desirable, that he should cultivate the friendship and esteem of Christian neighbors, and that he should not be parochial in his social attachments.

The pressure to change social relationships will not be overwhelming in the present generation of Lakeville adults, however. Relevant factors include the following: such relationships are already well structured, the rate of Jews leaving for less dense Jewish areas is small, and Lakeville itself gives every promise of becoming more—not less—Jewish in composition. But the pressure to change should increase in the next generation. The pressure could in fact become overwhelming as highly acculturated Lakeville youngsters—raised in a culture of equalitarianism and taught in a primary and secondary school system that reinforces equalitarian values—venture into college and university settings where today a kind of ethnic liberalism predominates. Particularly if they later practice their occupations in mixed settings those individuals who are products of the Lakeville environment should experience some difficulty in achieving strong Jewish identification. Will their socialization to traditional models and their attachment to Jewish identity—we wonder—be strong enough to assist them in building a viable life pattern that will combine both their Jewish and general identity and thus help to overcome the threat of assimilation?

In spite of the best of intentions, it is our conviction that only a minority of Lakeville parents have been able to provide their children with substantial materials for developing such a pattern. Of course each generation must achieve identity anew. Nevertheless each new generation is in part the product of its inheritance. The meager Jewishness to which the Lakeville youngster falls heir is perhaps the true *bête noire* of Jewish life in Lakeville. Lakeville makes available the abundant life; as we stressed at the beginning of our book, in many respects it is a model community that fulfills the American dream. But, at the same time it does not provide very rich Jewish experiences for the majority of those who are socialized in its fine homes, winding streets, excellent schools, pleasant beaches, tennis courts, and—let it be said—in its religious schools. Thus many of those who are the product of the Lakeville environment will be faced with the obverse of that which confronted their grandfathers, great-grandfathers, or even more remote ancestors when they arrived on American shores. While the resources of such ancestors—in terms of money, general education, and knowledge of the American way of life—were paltry, their Jewish resources—if not always considerable—were at least sufficient unto the day. Over the generations the families of present-day Lakeville Jews have increased their financial resources, their general level of education, and their mastery of the environment many times over. While some have multiplied their Jewish resources, many have dissipated them to a lesser or greater degree. It is indisputable that the majority of Lakeville Jews would like to conserve their Jewish resources. But unless an aggressive policy of growth is pursued the Jewish resources of a previous generation inevitably decline. The press of the general environment is so compelling that instead of being conserved, the inheritance from earlier generations inevitably diminishes. In sum, the long-range viability of the pattern of Jewish adjustment characteristic of Lakeville is in question.

A prayer in the Rosh Hashanah liturgy speaks of the fact that some will die during the months ahead while others will live to greet another year, that some will prosper while others will not, that some will rise while others will be brought low. The Jew is counseled to repentance, prayer, and charity in order to avert the evil decree. If assimilation is an evil decree—as we think it is— the Jews of Lakeville have many favors to be thankful for: pluralistic America not only is permissive in respect to group survival but it also assists such survival in manifold ways. Yet in important ways it also threatens survival—in ways of which Isaac Mayer Wise did not dream and in modes more subtle than Solomon Schechter imagined.

# The Conversion of the Jews

---

[In an introduction prepared for this volume, Sklare recalled that "the impetus for writing 'The Conversion of the Jews,' was the effort by Jewish leaders to have Jews exempted from the conversionist efforts of Key 73, a national campaign in 1973 'to return the nation to Christ.'" Some hoped—vainly as it turned out—that America's leading evangelist, Billy Graham, might be persuaded to speak out on this issue and against the missionizing of Jews.

Sklare's essay provided the historical background for these Jewish countermissionary efforts. "As I began to investigate the Jewish reaction to what Christians called 'Jewish evangelism' (that is, the effort to convert the Jew to Christianity) I realized," Sklare admitted, "how little I knew about the phenomenon. . . . I had been left with the incorrect notion that efforts to convert the Jew were generally confined to the premodern era and that they were certainly not part of the history of the Jew in the United States. Whatever the reason for my misunderstanding, my analysis of Key 73, and of earlier Jewish evangelistic efforts of which I had been unaware, made me realize that Jewish evangelism had a long history in the United States and that it continued to remain on the Christian agenda."

Key 73 was soon forgotten, but Sklare believed that it had an enduring lesson to teach. "The phenomenon of Jewish evangelism represents a fascinating chapter in the relationship of American Jews to the larger society. . . . The irony is that Jewish evangelism continues to exist despite the pervasiveness of good-will movements between Christians and Jews and the seeming acceptance of Judaism as one of the nation's three great religions."—JDS]

Nothing, it would seem, ever goes away; and thus it was that American Jews, living in a society where interreligious friction has been reduced to a minimum and secularism is rampant, recently found themselves again rallying, as in former, less enlightened times, to oppose Christian conversionist efforts. The occasion was the latest resurgence of evangelist proselytizing in the United States—especially the movement known as Key 73, a coalition of 140 Protestant denominational groups and 40-some Roman Catholic dioceses, joined in a year-long campaign to "win the nation for Christ"—

and it evoked a rare display of agreement on the part of organized American Jewry. Religious bodies, Orthodox, Conservative, and Reform, the major community-relations agencies (including those with active interreligious departments whose programmatic success depends on Christian good will)—all were unanimous in condemning the development and in calling for appropriate action to counter the renewed missionary advances.

This outpouring of concern—in some instances, outrage—should not have been surprising. Christian missionizing may not at present pose the greatest threat to American-Jewish survival—it can be argued that secular or political messianist movements have done more damage—but it does strike at the very heart of the Christian-Jewish relationship, reviving for Jews historical memories of the most painful kind. To be sure, American Christianity has in overwhelming part avoided the excesses of the premodern Church, but the persistence of missionary movements in the United States has nevertheless been seen as demeaning by American Jews, imputing a status of inequality that is contrary to the American ideal. For that reason, and despite the fact that American missionaries have been singularly unsuccessful in their conversion attempts—this, as we shall see, applies also to Key 73—Jews have never been able to treat the matter lightly.

Traditionally, of course, Jews have held the Jewish convert to Christianity in utter abhorrence.[1] Centuries of martyrdom are the price that the Jewish people has paid for survival, and the apostate, at one stroke, makes a mockery of Jewish history. But if the convert is contemptible in Jewish eyes, the missionary—all the more, the missionary of Jewish descent—is seen as pernicious, for he forces the Jew to relive the history of his martyrdom, all the while pressing the claim that in approaching the Jew he does so out of love. What kind of love is it, Jews wonder, that would deprive a man of his heritage? Furthermore, given the history of Christian treatment of the Jews, would it not seem time at last to recognize that the Jew has paid his dues and earned the right to be protected from obliteration by Christian love as well as destruction by Christian hate?

It is, moreover, because of the unhappy Jewish experience over the centuries in lands that established religions that American Jews have been among the staunchest defenders of the constitutional principle of separation of church and state. For Jews especially there has been no place in the American scheme of things—to cite the most egregious examples—for the snatching of Jewish children to be brought to the baptismal font, or the offering of inducements to young or gullible Jews. The majority of Americans may be Christians, but America itself, Jews have told themselves confidently, is not a Christian nation;[2] no one faith is preeminent, and the practice (or non-practice) of religion is altogether a private matter. It is a view that has found enthusiastic acceptance among the vast majority of American Jews, religious and secular; and the shared repugnance to Christian evangelism has served to unite the most varied segments of the American-Jewish community.

All these sentiments, keenly felt, have generally gone unvoiced, except under the greatest provocation or by the most exceptional Jewish leaders, for the subject is an exceedingly sensitive one. It forces American religious groups into an unwanted candor with one another on questions whose discussion can generate both anger and fear. Small wonder, then, that American Jews have preferred to concentrate on other, less distressing, aspects of Jewish-Christian relations.

Nevertheless, from time to time American Jews have found it necessary to turn their attention to the question of missionizing. The problem has not been made any easier by the fact of the Jewish commitment to full freedom of religion and strict separation of church and state, a commitment that precludes the advocacy of any legal interference with Christian missionizing. However, there is one tactic that has seemed useful and efficacious, the public exposure of the unsavory character of much missionary work in order to undercut Christian support of the mission centers. Historically the most significant such effort was the Jewish-sponsored republication in the 1920's of a book by an ex-missionary named Samuel Freuder, *A Missionary's Return to Judaism: The Truth about the Christian Missions to the Jews.*[3] Freuder's book came equipped with an introduction by no less an eminence than Rabbi Stephen S. Wise, at the time one of the foremost leaders of American Jewry and a prominent religious liberal.

Freuder had quite a tale to tell. A cantor's son, born in a Hungarian *shtetl*, he was something of a child prodigy. By the age of twelve he had exhausted the local scholarly resources, and was sent to the yeshiva in Pressburg, the home of his uncle, a rabbi. Before long young Freuder began to show signs of liberal tendencies and was packed off to the Hildesheimer Seminary in Berlin, but to no avail. Freuder then decided to start life anew in America as a businessman. Arriving in the United States in 1883, he made his way to Cincinnati, armed with a letter of introduction to a leading Jewish merchant, who made no offer of employment but did introduce him to Isaac Mayer Wise, the dean of American Reform Judaism. Impressed with the young man's yeshiva background, Wise persuaded Freuder to enroll at Hebrew Union College, where he was graduated in 1886. But as a rabbi he did not do well, and after being discharged from several rabbinical posts, he decided to leave the rabbinate and, subsequently, Judaism itself.

In 1891 Freuder was baptized at the Chicago Hebrew Mission and entered the Chicago Theological Seminary where he was ordained as a minister. Supported by the Congregational Church, Freuder started to missionize among Jews as well as to lecture extensively on Judaism before Christian audiences. Then one day—June 3, 1908—he was scheduled to deliver an address, "Christ in the Talmud," at a Hebrew-Christian conference meeting at the historic Park Street Church in Boston. To the consternation of his audience, Freuder proceeded to renounce Christianity, and also his missionary calling:

The Jews stand for pure monotheism, but the Christian does not, for he has set up Christ as a divine object of worship, for which no authority is given in the Bible.

How, then, shall Christianity lead a Jew to be a better man or lead a better life than he would if he had followed his mother instead of running away to his step-mother? . . . From this day forth I will never baptize a Jew or anyone else. If I ever preach in any Christian pulpit again may my right hand forget its cunning and may my tongue cleave to the roof of my mouth.

Freuder was as good as his word; his subsequent career was devoted to an exposure of the Christian missions to the Jews. He told all in his book ("The whole missionary business as conducted by professional converts is steeped in dishonesty and trickery"), where he related tale after lurid tale of cupidity and guile. Missionaries, according to Freuder, made few Jewish converts, but in order to stay in business they engaged in all manner of shady practices.

Even in its own day, Freuder's book could scarcely have been an edifying document, yet the fact that responsible and respected Jewish leaders under-took to disseminate its message underscores the desperation of the Jewish response to the problem of missionizing. Still, on another and perhaps more important publishing front, American Jewry proved less than eager to move decisively. For decades textbooks on American-Jewish history had not a word to say on the subject of missionaries. Thus Lee J. Levinger in *A History of the Jew in America* (1930), the standard textbook for two generations of Reform, Conservative, and to some extent Orthodox youngsters, did not hesitate to dis-cuss anti-Semitism but omitted any mention of Christian missionary activity among American Jews. The young reader was left to infer that such things as the notorious Mortara Affair simply could not happen in America.[4]

Recently a new educational openness to discussing the missionary problem has become evident in Jewish textbooks, as in general it has become more ac-ceptable to hold critical views of American society and as courses in intergroup relations have begun to be introduced into the Jewish school curriculum. Now the question is one of approach: how to present the subject to students in such a way as to clarify Jewish antipathy to missionizing while at the same time not offending Christian sensibilities. (The issue is one of particular delicacy since the Jewish community-relations agencies have been active in stimulating re-search on the anti-Jewish content of Christian religious texts.) The solution that has evolved has been to contrast the Christian and Jewish views of mis-sionizing but not to criticize Christianity directly. Thus, a recent textbook, *Judaism and Christianity: What We Believe*, by William B. Silverman,[5] empha-sizes that Jews believe in "one, universal God for all people and all nations" and that consequently Judaism believes that all men "worship the same God in different ways." From this it follows that

There are no Jewish missionary movements because Judaism does not seek to attract anyone away from his own faith. Judaism does not believe that a man or woman must embrace Judaism to be saved. Judaism claims that the righteous of all peoples, each clinging to the highest ethical ideals of his faith, are equal before God!

The author winds up the discussion by suggesting that if there is any necessity at all for missionary efforts, they should take place within, rather than between, the faith communities. Christians and Jews need only cultivate their own vineyards in order to make their contributions to the spiritual life of the nation.

While Silverman's stress on cultivating one's own vineyard represents the regnant view of generations of American Jews, the fact of the matter is that American Christians have not always been so persuaded. Indeed, missionary activity directed at Jews goes back in America to Colonial times, when the Jewish community numbered a mere 2,000. The most notable conversion of the period took place in Boston in 1722, when Judah Monis, who was later appointed to the Harvard faculty as an instructor in Hebrew, embraced Christianity. Monis's conversion, although an isolated event, must be seen in the context of the Puritan ethos, in which the conversion of the Jews was regarded as a Christian necessity:

Even though they did not go to the full lengths of the Fifth Monarchy Men, the Millenarians or the Judaisers, to the Puritan settlers of America in the 17th and 18th centuries the millennium was something very near and real which every day brought measurably nearer. To them it was possible for any living man not only to have a chance to partake in that great event but personally to hasten its coming. They accepted the words of prophecy literally that as soon as the Jews had been dispersed throughout every land of the earth, there was to be a calling of the Jewish nation and their conversion to Christianity, and then the millennium. It was a subject of active debate whether the conversion of the Jews was to be in the mass or whether individual Jews were to be converted until all had disappeared as Jews. Whichever view was adopted, to be the means of converting a Jew was not merely a matter of personal glory but another step accelerating the establishment of the Kingdom of God on earth.[6]

Nevertheless, it was not until 1816, with the arrival in the United States of a Jewish apostate, Joseph Simon Christian Frederick Frey by name, that organized missionary activity became a significant part of the American scene. Frey, whose original name was Joseph Simon Levi, was born in Franconia in 1770, and prior to his conversion in 1798 had served various communities as a Hebrew teacher, cantor, and *shochet* (ritual slaughterer). He received missionary training in Berlin and then planned to pursue his calling in Africa. Detained in London while awaiting transportation to the Dark Continent, he decided that he would be more of an asset to the movement if he remained in England, spreading the gospel to the Jews. In due course, he founded the London Society for the Promotion of Christianity among Jews, which soon gained widespread support among all levels of British society, including the aristocracy.

After some years, Frey decided to come to the United States—"where though inhabited comparatively by few of my Jewish brethren, yet the harvest is truly great and the labourers comparatively few, and where there is a much brighter prospect for the comfortable support of a growing family."[7] (The fact was that the London Society had dismissed Frey after he seduced the wife of Jacob Josephson, a convert under its protection.) Frey was indeed correct in assuming there would be considerable American interest in his specialty; in short order the American Society for Meliorating the Condition of the Jews, which he promoted, grew to include two hundred branches from Maine to Georgia. Following the London pattern, leading citizens lent their names to the project, among them John Adams and John Quincy Adams. The Society went into decline by the time of the Civil War, but by then it had set the precedents that were to guide all future Christian-Jewish missionary activity in the United States. These included the idea that the best way to approach Jews would be through Jewish converts; that it was justifiable to use Jewish-sounding titles in the literature, like that of the Society's periodical, *Israel's Advocate*; that the convert be given economic assistance; and that interim arrangements, such as special congregations, be devised until the new converts were assimilated into existing denominations.

For all his frenetic activity, Frey actually failed to make a single Jewish convert to Christianity. In the middle years of the 19th century, America's growing population of German Jews was far more interested in reforming Judaism than in becoming Christians. There were, of course, many instances of German Jews who left the fold and even converted, but this was in no way due to the efforts of the American Society for Meliorating the Condition of the Jews. The upwardly mobile German Jews, rapidly entering the ranks of the middle class and beyond, did not avail themselves of Frey's services.

For a while, therefore, the missions lay dormant, but the mass influx of East European Jews, in the 1880's, brought about a renewal of activity and a new crop of missionaries of Jewish descent. The most prominent of these was Leopold Cohn, born in Berenza, Hungary, and a claimant to rabbinical ordination in Europe. After his conversion to Christianity Cohn became a Baptist minister and soon afterward, in 1894, he founded the American Board of Missions to the Jews, to become the most important of the so-called Hebrew-Christian groups.[8] By now there were missions in all of the Jewish immigrant neighborhoods across the land—New York's Lower East Side was dotted with them. These missions all sought to capitalize on the uncertainties of the immigrant situation, but despite their proliferation—from 1920–29, much after the peak of East European immigration, some twenty-five new centers were established—only a handful of Jewish immigrants or their children responded. East European Jews were more attracted to secular political and social movements than to the blandishments of religious messianism.

It was inevitable that sooner or later an inquiry by official Protestant bodies would be made into the effectiveness of the missions to the Jews. In 1939, in anticipation of a Protestant conference on Jewish evangelism to be held in Atlantic City, Charles H. Fahs, of Union Theological Seminary, was commissioned to do a study of the missions. He set about his task with considerable enterprise, collecting data from fifty-four Jewish mission centers, visiting many in person, and sending out scores of questionnaires to converts.[9] Fahs found that the missionaries used a wide variety of techniques to attract their quarry. They published and distributed vast quantities of literature, much of it consisting of Old Testament "proof texts"—that is, texts interpreted as prophesying the coming of Christ and as validating Christianity. They sponsored social clubs and recreational activities; maintained summer camps, schools, and medical dispensaries; made in excess of 100,000 home visits annually; approached hospitals and prisons; sponsored night schools for the study of English and classes for instruction in trades; and broadcast their message over the radio. The most common approach, Fahs discovered, was to play upon the Jewishness of the sought-for converts, seeking to persuade them that by becoming Christians they would, in effect, become better Jews.

Fahs was an experienced student of home missions and was therefore in a position to evaluate the quality of the effort. He concluded that Jewish missions were inferior to the general run of Protestant missions. Their personnel was substandard; talented Gentile missionaries were seldom attracted to the Jewish-mission field, and the training was inadequate. Fahs found none of the bribery or corruption which Freuder had exposed, but he felt that, despite their good intentions, the missionary centers were ineffective instruments for the accomplishment of their purpose. He came to the conclusion that the Jewish missionary effort was a failure, and though he made no specific proposals, Fahs left his sponsors with the clear inference that their funds might be spent to better advantage elsewhere.

The Fahs report came at a propitious moment. This was the time when the interfaith "good-will" movement, later to culminate in the establishment of the National Conference of Christians and Jews, was coming to the fore. "A good-will approach to the Jews seems to some of our people to be more in keeping with Christian ideals than an evangelistic approach that might be interpreted as proselytizing," one Protestant mission board had written to Fahs, in explanation of why it did not sponsor a Jewish mission. It was a notion in which Jews were bound to concur and, indeed, many Jewish leaders were eager to cooperate with the newly founded Committee on Good-Will between Jews and Christians of the Federal Council of the Churches of Christ. However, Jews wondered, did the development represent a genuine shift in Christian sentiment, or was it just another, albeit more sophisticated, missionary effort?

As with all Jewish issues of the time, the question was referred to Louis Marshall, the formidable head of the American Jewish Committee. Marshall decided in favor of the good-will movement, despite the fact that, in addition to its liberal contingent, the Committee on Good-Will also harbored some diehard traditionalists who would not give up the idea of converting the Jews. One of these was the Reverend Alfred Williams Anthony (a founder of the group and its chairman for a time), and Marshall entered into a lengthy correspondence with him, portions of which were published in the Jewish establishment's journal of the time, the *American Hebrew*.[10] It was a remarkable exchange and is worth quoting in some detail.

Marshall was particularly incensed at Anthony's claim that exempting Jews from conversion efforts would constitute a form of discrimination. The reverend had written:

most Christians believe that it is their duty to preach the Gospel, and many of them believe that this means the form of Gospel which they believe in, and that consequently they must preach to others, even to other Christians, and seek to convert them to their way of thinking. Christians really are busily engaged in trying to convert Christians, and are specially engaged in trying to convert all men. Do the Jews wish to have Christians discriminate against them and say, "We have no interest in Jews?" Is such discrimination desirable? Does good-will lie distinctly in that realm? To many Christians such an attitude would mean abandoning Jews to what they would call a "lost" condition, with all the unfavorable implications attached to their theology. I raise the question whether Jews have thought out all the implications of such a policy, and really wish the Christians to adopt it? For certainly in such a policy are some implications very unfavorable to Jews.

To which Marshall indignantly replied:

Your argument is that, when Jews rebel against interference with their most sacred right, that of religious liberty, when Jewish parents seek to protect their children, for whose moral and ethical life they feel a serious responsibility, against the intrusion and trespasses of conversionists, it is the Jews who are interfering with religious liberty, because, forsooth! they are undertaking "to muzzle Christians" and are interfering with free speech. I could scarcely believe the evidence of my own eyes when first I beheld these words in your communication. According to your notion, any conversionist may button-hole me in the street and proceed in his efforts to convert me to his religion. If I refuse to listen and bid him to attend to his own affairs, I am interfering with freedom of speech and am guilty of applying a muzzle. I may not even protect my children or grandchildren against such intrusion.

Anthony was willing to concede some points. "I am confident," he had written, "that Christians as a whole emphatically object to improper methods of proclaiming religious views, and in saying this acknowledge that Christians have used, and still use, improper methods in many places in the advocacy of their doctrine." But Marshall would have none of this:

It seems to be your idea that it shall be recognized as a fundamental right of Christians to enter a Jewish household and to take the children to Christian schools. If you remember the Mortara case you are aware of the fact that there were Christians who carried your theory still further. . . . You "acknowledge that Christians have used and still do use, improper methods." This probably refers to the policies of physical extermination and moral degradation. They have caused untold misery but have not worked, so they are regarded for these days as rather too crude, although 200,000 Jews were massacred in the Ukraine during the present decade. The policy which you advocate is more gentle. It is the employment of the honeyed words of the conversionist. That means to us spiritual annihilation. For the greatest treasure that we possess—our sacred religion, preserved through nearly thirty centuries of unparalleled persecution, oppression, and barbarities—is to be taken from us and to be exchanged, for what? Paulinianism, with all that it implies—the faith of our persecutors. You are entirely frank about it. But why speak of good-will? How can there be good-will "with reservations"? If you have your way good-will toward the Jews would be a mere catch-word, a beautiful figure of speech—for there would be no Jews left. They would be swallowed up by your religion. And then what? *O, sancta simplicitas!*

Marshall's attack had its effect. While Anthony was not forced to resign from the Committee on Good-Will, the secretary of the group, Everett R. Clinchy (later to become the director of the National Conference of Christians and Jews), stated publicly that Anthony's ideas on proselytizing did not represent the Committee's views on the subject.

However, the victory was far from complete. Still to be achieved was a wider understanding of the Jewish position vis-à-vis Christianity beyond the limited circles of the good-will movement. This was not to come about until the 1950's, after a great war had been fought and the Jewish people had undergone one of its profoundest tragedies. America was now entering a new pluralistic age in which Christian triumphalism had no place and in the emerging climate of ecumenicism, missionaries represented a type of spiritual arrogance inimical to unity.

These notions were given striking formulation by the late Abraham Joshua Heschel, whose charismatic presence and eloquent writings on Jewish thought were beginning to have a deep influence on Jews and non-Jews alike. Heschel dedicated himself to the task of convincing Christians that missionary efforts directed at Jews should be discontinued at all levels, and to this end he engaged in a series of extensive negotiations with Christian leaders. The closing of the missions, he argued, would represent the first step in the spiritual rehabilitation of Christians with respect to their Jewish brothers. Such an act would also be salutary inasmuch as it would constitute an acknowledgment of the Jewish contribution to Christianity:

A Christian ought to ponder seriously the tremendous implications of a process begun in early Christian history. I mean the conscious or unconscious dejudaization of Christianity, affecting the Church's way of thinking, its inner life as well as its relationship to the past and present reality of Israel—the father and the mother of the very being of Christianity. The children did not arise to call the mother blessed; instead they called the mother blind. Some theologians continue to act as if they did not know the meaning of "honor your father and mother"; others, anxious to prove the superiority of the Church, speak as if they suffered from a spiritual Oedipus complex.[11]

Christians, he stressed, ought to realize that a world without the people of Israel would be a world without the God of Israel, and hence one more vulnerable to paganism. Would such a world really be to the advantage of Christians?

Heschel's appeal struck a greater chord of response among Catholics than among Protestants, who hewed more closely to the doctrine that the Second Coming made the conversion of the Jews mandatory. He carried his campaign throughout the entire Catholic community and even to the Vatican itself, pressing, along with representatives of the Jewish intergroup-relations agencies, for a favorable statement on the Jews from the Ecumenical Council, Vatican II, then meeting in Rome. The statement, which came to be known as the Schema on the Jews, was indeed forthcoming after protracted negotiations,[12] and though it failed to condemn what Heschel called the "demonic canard of deicide," it was hailed by the Jewish community as an important milestone in Catholic-Jewish relations, ushering in a new era of "fraternal dialogues," in the phrase of the Schema. Perhaps its most gratifying feature was the absence of any plea for mass proselytizing efforts. As Heschel noted:

The Schema on the Jews is the first statement of the Church in history—the first Christian discourse dealing with Judaism—which is devoid of any expression of hope for conversion. This is one of the reasons why I consider this particular Schema to be of great importance in the history of Jewish-Christian relations.[13]

Though Heschel, as noted, was less successful in getting his message across to the Protestants, he did gain one powerful Protestant ally, Reinhold Niebuhr, during his time the most distinguished member of the faculty of Union Theological Seminary. Niebuhr engaged in a thoroughgoing rethinking of the Jewish-Christian symbiosis, and came to believe that, unwelcome as this might be to Christians, they would have to accept the reality of Jewish resistance to Christian messianism. In Niebuhr's view it was the Christian destiny not to convert the Jews but to carry the Jewish prophetic message to the Gentile world; the attempt to proselytize the Jews not only constituted a diversion from the true mission of Christianity but also had a deleterious effect on the Christian's understanding of his own religion. For Niebuhr, missionary activity was ineffective and dangerous as well, constituting theological error at best and at worst justifying persecutions that made a mockery of Christian love.

Niebuhr's views, first expressed at a lecture before a joint faculty meeting of the Jewish Theological Seminary and Union Theological Seminary, were later printed in the journal of the Central Conference of American Rabbis,[14] and had a profound effect on the American-Jewish community. On Niebuhr's fellow Christians the effect was of a different order. His revolutionary restatement of the Protestant position on missionizing evoked an indignant rebuttal (published in the *Christian Century*, the leading Protestant journal) by the Reverend George F. Sweazey, chairman of the General Council of the Presbyterian Church.[15] Sweazey argued that for Protestants to retreat on the missionary question meant surrendering a central point of the Christian doctrine requiring that all men be brought to Christ; for Jews to be exempted would be tantamount to conceding that salvation was possible outside of Christianity.

If normative Protestantism as represented by Sweazey was unwilling to budge on points of doctrine, the fact of the matter was that by the 1950's and early 1960's Jewish missionizing had become an increasingly esoteric activity; the few Christian groups still active in the field were to be found only among fundamentalist sects. The mainstream Christian denominations were willing to live with the thesis then becoming popular—and reflected in the title of Will Herberg's influential book of the period, *Protestant-Catholic-Jew* (1955)— that American society was comprised of three major faith communities, each making a contribution to American society.

These years were the golden age of dialogue. Conferences, institutes, colloquia, brotherhood weeks, interfaith services proliferated. For all practical purposes it seemed that Jewish fears of missionizing were being laid to rest at last and that Jews and Christians could now meet on an equal footing. To be sure, there were Orthodox Jews who continued to maintain that the dialogues were merely a cover for conversionist impulses, and that dialogue was objectionable from the vantage point of Jewish law. Moreover, they contended that in the light of the Holocaust dialogue with Christians was theologically untenable and must await a prolonged period of Christian testing. But such Jews were in a minority. Joint Christian-Jewish efforts proceeded apace, particularly as the civil-rights movement, with its opportunities for "social witness," gathered momentum. Perhaps the climax of this heady period, marking the end of the traditional hostility between the two faiths, occurred on Sunday, November 13, 1966, when the American Jewish Committee feted the American delegates who had returned from Vatican II.

The Middle East crisis of spring 1967 and the ensuing Six-Day War delivered a jolt to the spirit of brotherhood, as Jews discovered to their dismay that there were important Christian spokesmen who were decidedly unfriendly to Israel's cause. Several leading churchmen, during the tense weeks of May and June 1967, remained silent; others betrayed a pro-Arab bias. The Jewish reaction to all this was one of bafflement and hurt. Many Jews felt that participation in the process of dialogue had been a colossal blunder and that further indulgence would not only be futile but would also indicate a lack of self-respect. On the other hand, there were those who felt that the particular letdown was further reason for continuing the dialogue, that to break off now would be to endanger a hard-won victory.

The dialogue resumed; but just as the effects of 1967 were beginning to dissipate, the Jewish community, to its great surprise, found itself confronted by what it had assumed had become an anachronism—an organized missionary campaign directed at Jews. In its latest manifestation, the activity assumed double form, Key 73 and the movement known as Jews for Jesus, a latter-day offshoot of Leopold Cohn's American Board of Missions to the Jews.

The Jews for Jesus movement could be seen as part of the general Jesus phenomenon—variously known as the Jesus Freaks, the Jesus Movement, or Jesus People—that had emerged (via routes too complicated to trace here) from the counterculture. However, the unexpected resurgence of a group like Jews for Jesus also served to remind Jews that the organization that Leopold Cohn had founded in 1894 was still very much alive. As for Key 73, which set out to "win the nation for Christ," this movement seemed to be saying, to Jews and others, that America should be defined as a Christian nation. Further, Key 73 was not some obscure storefront endeavor but a large-scale evangelical effort on an unprecedented national scale, with important backing from major Protestant bodies.

The Jewish architects of interreligious accord were taken aback by these developments. They viewed Key 73 as a breach of contract, a violation of the understandings that had been so painfully arrived at in the 1950's. Rabbi Solomon S. Bernards, director of the Department of Interreligious Cooperation of the Anti-Defamation League, expressed the general disappointment:

All of this threatens a setback for the Jewish-Christian conversation—an enterprise based on mutual respect and trust. Already those sectors of the Jewish community which have been suspicious of Jewish-Christian dialogue from the start are beginning to assert that their suspicions have proved well founded—that the nice things Christians have said to Jews during the past few years were a calculated process intended to "soften up" Jews for the baptismal font. I hope responsible Christian leaders will allay these suspicions by repudiating the effort of Key 73—or for that matter any future evangelical campaign—to proselytize Jews.[16]

Given the wide scope of the Key 73 movement and the broad extent of its ecclesiastical support, the Jewish community, as a matter of tactical procedure, decided to oppose the developments not on the issue of Christian triumphalism but rather on the question of the unseemliness of evangelizing the Jews (on the grounds that Reinhold Niebuhr had elaborated a decade before). However, it soon became clear that there was little chance of persuading the officials of Key 73 to accept the view that the Jewish covenant was as valid as the Christian and hence that Jews had no need of conversion. Indeed, the national officials of Key 73 were quite unyielding to Jewish entreaties and inquiries and in effect warned that Jews had no right to interfere with the activities of Christian evangelism.

To some Jewish leaders, the Reverend Billy Graham was the one person who might save the situation from further deterioration, and he was approached on the question by the American Jewish Committee in March 1973.[17] Graham issued a characteristically friendly statement after the meeting, affirming his regard for Jews and expressing his sympathies with the Jewish concern. "I understood," he noted, "that it is the purpose of Key 73 to call men to Christ without singling out any specific religious or ethnic group." He would not, however, give any specific assurance that Jews would be exempt from the advances of Key 73, though he did promise that no "gimmicks, coercion . . . intimidation" would be used to induce Jews to become Christians. A *Newsweek* report on the meeting concluded thus:

Any change in [Graham's] attitude toward converting Jews would certainly affect morale within the crusade. "Billy would never accept a two-covenant theory," insists the Rev. John Streeter, a close friend of Graham and the Baptist head of Key 73 operations in the San Francisco area. "A Jew is just like everyone else. If he does not accept Jesus as his savior, he cannot be right with God."[18]

So, after forty years of good will and dialogue, to the Christian evangelist Jews were still "like everyone else."

If some Key 73 heads were adamant, and if Billy Graham was statesman-like but noncommital, Jewish leaders found that there were local Key 73 officials more responsive to Jewish sensibilities. Thus the executive committee of the Key 73 Task Force of the Southern California-Arizona Conference of the United Methodist Church disavowed "any efforts on the part of the Christian groups to convert Jews or those of other religious traditions." In Florida, the local Key 73 director, the Reverend Charles L. Eastman, wrote a letter to the rabbis in the Miami area in which he stated: "I, for one, do not consider Jews as 'unchurched.' It is my understanding that the other three ministers [in North Miami] do not consider the Jews as a target for Key 73 either." In Illinois, the chairman of the Chicago-area campaign, the Reverend Henry W. Andersen, pronounced: "Jews are already God's people. God chose them and in His wisdom called them to be His people, and I accept that. I just leave the Jews to God." Such statements were especially forthcoming in communities where there was Catholic cooperation with what was essentially a Protestant-directed crusade. The evangelist tone of the movement was foreign to many Catholics, and in any case they sought to avoid what might be considered a repetition of medieval practice. Thus they were readily agreeable to bringing pressure on the Protestants directing the campaign. (In Detroit, for instance, the Key 73 co-ordinating committee was forced to produce a statement allaying Jewish fears of harassment after the archdiocesan representative threatened to withdraw.)

At the same time, however, there were disturbing reports. Young Jews, it was learned, were being continuously approached by evangelists intent on preaching the Key 73 message. Moving through college dormitories, the Key 73 representatives went from door to door, the less fastidious seeking to gain access to students' rooms on the pretext of conducting an experiment or making a survey. On some campuses the Hillel Foundations were forced to seek aid from university officials in the form of statements assuring students the right to privacy and forbidding door-to-door proselytizing or solicitation of any kind. There was also a rash of incidents in high schools, particularly those with low

Jewish enrollments. The Campus Crusade for Christ and the Fellowship of Christian Athletes induced some principals to allow them into their schools. The usual procedure was to hold an assembly—in contravention of the principle of separation of church and state—where students were compelled to listen to an evangelistic appeal.

If Key 73 officials in some instances proved sensitive to Jewish concerns, the same could not be said of the Hebrew-Christian groups (including Jews for Jesus). As time passed, these groups became increasingly aggressive in their behavior, stressing their Jewish identity more strongly than ever before, and hammering at the theme that one could be a Christian and a Jew simultaneously. They began to display Jewish symbols, such as prayershawls and skullcaps, and to indulge in public observance (in their own fashion) of Jewish holidays. The Hebrew Christians also began to affirm support of such Jewish causes as Soviet Jewry and Israel. Thus, when the Hebrew Christians for the first time made their presence publicly known in Miami, in December 1972, they did so at a "Hanukkah celebration" at the Miami Beach auditorium. They connected the event, which concluded with a call to the audience to decide for Christ, with the celebration of Israel's twenty-fifth anniversary. In other places, Hebrew Christians sponsored "Day of Atonement" services on Yom Kippur.

Altogether, the level of missionary sophistication had risen since the days when Charles Fahs conducted his survey. For instance, the American Board of Missions to the Jews was making effective use of television, preferring that medium to the traditional leaflets and tracts. In 1971 the Board produced a TV film entitled, "The Passover." The film, according to one commentator,

was professionally produced and contained no reference to missions in general or the American Board of Missions to the Jews in particular, but the theme it unfolded was clear. . . . A Christian Jewish "family," composed of persons from ABMJ Beth Sar Shalom in Los Angeles, partook of the Passover Seder and enacted the ancient festival in precise adherence to the Old Testament detail. In the program there was no reference to missions, no appeal for funds. The program concluded by offering (free) *Israel: A Modern Miracle*, a 48-page pamphlet with a color photo of the Wailing Wall on the front cover and photographs of present-day Israel and narratives of fulfillment of Scriptural prophecy inside.[19]

Many Jews found the program objectionable and protested its showing. But perhaps even more offensive was the Board's series of newspaper advertisements, the best known of which appeared on a full page in *The New York Times* (December 10, 1971), with the caption, "So Many Jews Are Wearing 'That Smile' Nowadays!" It featured a striking photograph of a massed group of neatly dressed, respectable-looking individuals, all smiling. The well-written text worked some original and, for Jews, disturbing variations on the old missionary themes:

it is not uncommon at all these days to find many Jewish men and women and children acknowledging the Great Jew [Jesus Christ] as the Messiah.

In doing so, we are not giving up being Jews, we are in fact adding a beautiful dimension to being Jewish. Becoming more so. And the Christian church is being enriched by adding Jewish Christians . . . as Jews, and not causing us to assimilate.

To counter all this activity the American-Jewish community, for the first time in its history, mounted and is still pursuing an organized antimissionary campaign, a procedure altogether different from the random responses of a Louis Marshall or a Stephen S. Wise, and a total departure from the usual policy of silence on the matter. Thus there were set up, under community auspices, telephone "hot lines," where Jews could get information and counsel on how to deal with the missionaries, and "rap sessions" for Jewish young people. The three wings of American Judaism began turning out a body of anti-missionary literature, an endeavor in which their youth affiliates were especially active. (This being the age of "alternate life-styles" and a still-flourishing countercul-ture, it was feared that young Jews, many of whom were already involved with various deviant experimentations, might be more than usually receptive to the lures of Key 73 and Jews for Jesus.) Perhaps the most elaborate of the new publications was *The Missionary at the Door—Our Uniqueness*, prepared by Rabbi Benjamin Segal for the Youth Com-mission of the United Synagogue, an arm of the Conservative movement.[20] The booklet contains an analysis of typical missionary themes, an explanation of "proof texts," and suggestions on how to respond when approached by a missionary. Other materials were prepared and collected by the Union of American Hebrew Congregations (Reform) and distributed to its various af-filiates. On the Orthodox side, the Lubavitcher movement was and continues to be particularly active in antimissionary activity, including the distribution of literature. All in all, this literature looks to become an ongoing feature of the American-Jewish educational scene.

By the summer of 1973, much of the dust had settled and the American-Jewish community was able to engage in an assessment of the effects of the evangelical furor. It appeared that the worst fears had not materialized. Christian-Jewish relations for the greater part had continued in their accus-tomed course despite the new flurry of missionary activity. Key 73 had failed to make any significant breach in the wall between church and state. While numerous incidents of coercion and deception had occurred, these had been disavowed by the mainstream church bodies and steps taken to prevent a repe-tition. No statistics were available on the number of Jews who had been con-verted or who had been in some other way influenced by Key 73, but it did not appear as if the impact had been as serious as originally feared. Some Jews even began to claim that Key 73 had done more good than harm in that it had highlighted the need for more intensive Jewish education and improved community services to Jewish youth.

Thus, at a meeting in June 1973 of the National Jewish Community Relations Advisory Council (NJCRAC), the coordinating body of major and local Jewish community-relations agencies, a policy statement adopted by the delegates noted that concerns on the part of the American-Jewish community that its relations with Christian denominations might be adversely affected by the "aggressive missionizing intent" of Key 73 "appear to have abated." American Jewry, the statement seemed to be saying, could now forget about missionizing and return to the more familiar, less sensitive aspects of Jewish-Christian relations.

Given the human temptation to see a silver lining in every cloud, it is perhaps understandable that American Jews should seek to put the best possible face on the confrontation with Christian evangelism through which they have just passed. But there is no denying that the experience has been a sobering one. The kind of Christianity represented by Key 73 has forced Jews to consider, whether they admit it or not, that a time may yet come when Jews will have to resign themselves to an acceptance of a "traditional" Christianity that retains its links with the past, which cannot be remade in the image of a Heschel or a Niebuhr to accommodate Jewish feelings and necessities, but which can, nonetheless, arrive at an honorable *modus vivendi* with Judaism.

That this may indeed be the case was put to the Jewish community, with considerable delicacy but also with considerable frankness, by Dr. David R. Hunter of the National Council of Churches of Christ, in an address before the above-mentioned NJCRAC conference. Hunter began boldly by stating that evangelizing was an inescapable part of the American heritage "since our nation has always been predominantly Christian in its religious affiliation." Both Protestants and Catholics, he averred, "have always taken seriously, with whatever emendations and qualifications, the Great Commission to 'Go therefore and make disciples of all nations, baptizing them in the name of the Father, and the Son, and the Holy Spirit.'" However, Key 73, he admitted, had raised serious questions about the propriety of certain kinds of evangelizing. What was therefore needed was a set of guidelines that could be used to judge the legitimacy of any given missionizing effort.

Hunter's first guideline indicated how far some mainstream Christians had come in their desire for détente and ultimately rapprochement with Jews. The guideline was what Hunter called the acceptance by Christians of "the living reality of the Covenant Jews have with God." In practical terms, this would mean that any conversionist effort that diminished or obscured Judaism was objectionable. Christianity's proper stance to Judaism, according to Hunter, was to be found in Paul's Epistle to the Romans, where the Church is likened to "wild branches grafted onto the live olive tree of Israel."

A second guideline was the twofold constitutional guarantee of the free exercise of religion and protection from the establishment of a state religion. The constitutional guarantee is a precious part of the American heritage,

Hunter asserted, one whose wisdom was readily apparent when contrasted with the unfortunate experience of lands with state religions, past and present (among his examples, he cited Israel). The third guideline was pluralism, the famous American diversity-within-unity. Evangelism, Hunter stressed, must not become a force to reduce or to minimize the pluralist ideal.

But for all that, in the final analysis Hunter maintained that Christians were still under the obligation to proclaim "the Good News which came to man through the revelation of God to the Jew, Jesus of Nazareth. . . . For Christians this Good News has the feeling-tone of the act of God manifested in the Sinai Covenant with the Hebrews." To be sure, the proclamation of the Good News must be done tactfully. Hunter condemned "the daily hounding of Jews on campuses at the hands of zealous Christians" and termed such behavior "an infringement of human rights and a violation of Christian doctrine of love." Christians, said Hunter, must never forget "the traumatic history of the sufferings of the Jewish people at the hands of Christians, sometimes in the name of conversion and at other times as an act of acknowledged genocide." This awareness must result in making Christians observe restraint in any evangelistic approach to Jews. Yet such understanding, Hunter concluded, must be a two-way street, and Jews for their part would have to surrender their "temptation" to deny a religious group the right to evangelize. In sum, what Hunter was really saying was that his guidelines for Christians would not work unless Jews were prepared to concede the legitimacy of the attempt to convert them.

Hunter's ultimate position is not bound to win enthusiastic endorsement from all segments of American Jewry. Certainly, it will not gain the approval of those who have labored long years at "dialogue" nor of those who hold to a utopian vision of a dramatic restructuring of Christian doctrines toward Judaism, and thus ultimately of Christianity itself. Nevertheless, Hunter's blueprint for achieving a balance between Christian tradition and Jewish rights should prove acceptable to some Jews. His vision of America is not the heavenly city of which some Jews have dreamed, but it does provide them with the possibility of a meaningful and dignified existence, of rearing their children in a culture where religion maintains its importance but where Jews are protected from evangelistic excess. The acceptance of Hunter's position, at its root, means that Jews must make their compromise with Gentile-Christian America. And this, perhaps, is the real lesson to be learned from Key 73, its antecedents, and all its attendant events.

## Notes

1. As the late Maurice Samuel observed: "Perhaps the heaviest and deadliest Yiddish word is *shmad*, deriving from the Hebrew for 'destruction, wiping out,' and having the single meaning of 'apostasy, conversion from Judaism to another religion.' *Zikh shmadn* is to 'apostasize,' and a man who has done that is a *meshumed*, which etymologically would be a 'destroyed one,' but as used in living Yiddish im-

plies something much more hateful than 'self-destruction.' The emotional charge in the word did not spring solely from religious intolerance. Mixed with it was the rage of an embattled minority made more of a minority with every defection; but there was an even stronger motivation. One of the characteristics of the *meshumed* has frequently been the zeal with which he becomes the assistant, or even the renewed inspiration, of the oppressors of his repudiated people" (*In Praise of Yiddish*, Cowles, 1971).

2. However, on certain Protestant ideas of America as a Christian civilization, see Robert T. Handy, *A Christian America: Protestant Hopes and Historical Realities* (New York: Oxford University Press, 1971).

3. The book was originally published by the Sinai Publishing Company in 1915; the third edition was published in 1924 by Bloch.

4. In 1858, Edward Mortara, a six-year-old Jewish child, was seized by Papal guards who invaded the family home in Bologna (the boy had been secretly baptized by his Catholic nurse in infancy). The child was claimed by the Pope as his personal ward, was educated in Catholic schools, and subsequently became a priest. The Mortara Affair, as the whole episode came to be known, gave rise to widespread protest demonstrations in the United States that culminated in the establishment in 1859 of the Board of Delegates of American Israelites (see Bertram W. Korn, *The American Reaction to the Mortara Case*, American Jewish Archives, 1958).

5. New York: Behrman House, 1968. The quotations are from the chapter entitled "Christian Missionaries and the Mission of Israel."

6. Lee M. Friedman, "Cotton Mather and the Jews," *Publication of the American Jewish Historical Society*, XXVI (1918).

7. Quoted in Lee M. Friedman, *The American Society for Meliorating the Condition of the Jews and Joseph S. C. F. Frey Its Missionary* (Boston, 1925).

8. On the phenomenon of Hebrew Christians, see Ira O. Glick, "The Hebrew Christians: A Marginal Religious Group," in *The Jews: Social Patterns of an American Group*, edited by Marshall Sklare (Glencoe, Ill.: The Free Press, 1958); and B. Z. Sobel, "Legitimation and Anti-Semitism as Factors in the Functioning of a Hebrew Christian Mission," *Jewish Social Studies*, 23 (1967). See also Harry Golden, "Hebrew-Christian Evangelist: Southern Style," *Commentary* (December 1950).

9. The report was never published, but the results have been summarized by Max Eisen in an article, "Christian Missions to the Jews in North America and Great Britain," *Jewish Social Studies*, 10 (1948).

10. In the issue of June 28, 1929, under the title "Good-Will between Jews and Christians, and Proselytism; Interchange of Views between Louis Marshall, Esq., President of the American Jewish Committee, and Rev. Dr. Alfred Williams Anthony."

11. Abraham J. Heschel, "From Mission to Dialogue?," *Conservative Judaism*, 21, No. 3 (Spring 1967). The article incorporates portions of Heschel's inaugural address at Union Theological Seminary where he served as Harry Emerson Fosdick Visiting Professor in 1965–66.

12. See Judith Hershcopf, "The Church and the Jews: The Struggle at Vatican Council II," *American Jewish Year Book 1966*, Vol. 67. See also, "Vatican II and the Jews," by F. E. Cartus, *Commentary* (January 1965).

13. Heschel, *op. cit.*

14. Reinhold Niebuhr, "The Relations of Christians and Jews in Western Civilization," *CCAR Journal* (April 1958).

15. "Are Jews Intended to Be Christians?," *Christian Century*, April 29, 1959.

16. Solomon S. Bernards, "Key 73—A Jewish View," *Christian Century*, January 3, 1973.

17. Because his participation in a leadership capacity in Key 73 would have precluded the cooperation of important mainstream Protestant groups, Graham did not serve as chairman of the Key 73 campaign. The Jewish hope of winning his cooperation was apparently based on Graham's reputation for religious statesmanship. In his many crusades, he had carefully avoided denigrating non-Christian groups and, unlike other evangelists, he had never been known to place any special emphasis on converting Jews.

18. March 19, 1973.

19. Wesley Pippert, "Jews with a Smile," *Christian Life* (April 1972).

20. The booklet is accompanied by a discussion guide, also available from the Youth Commission, United Synagogue of America, 1973.

# Intermarriage and the Jewish Future

———————◆———————

[This pathbreaking and highly influential article, published in *Commentary* of April 1964, shattered the American Jewish community's long silence on the subject of intermarriage and rightly predicted that the subject would emerge as a central issue in American Jewish communal life. Sklare challenged the consensus view that held that the intermarriage rate in the United States was "nominal," and argued (correctly) that the real figure for third-generation American Jews was closer to 18 percent—and rising. He also challenged the dominant view that those who intermarried did so in search of higher status, or because of self-hatred, or as a result of some other social or psychological aberration. The real culprits, Sklare understood, were American freedom, the liberalism of Jewish parents, and the ideal of romantic love. In some of his most memorable prose, he warned that Jewish complacency on this issue dared not continue, for the very survival of the American Jewish community was at stake. It was not Gentile hostility that was the problem this time, he insisted, but "Jewish indifference."

Sklare returned to the subject of intermarriage six years later, again in *Commentary* (March 1970), and his tone was even more bleak: "Intermarriage has reached large-scale proportions throughout the country as a whole. Yet, despite the gravity of the problem, the Jewish community, at any rate on the official level, has devoted little attention to the matter." He signalled, once more prophetically, that a turning point was approaching when "individuals may find themselves under a self-generated pressure to redefine the issue from that of combatting intermarriage to that of accommodating to it." He also took note of changing rabbinic attitudes toward intermarriage, especially within the Reform movement.

As a committed survivalist, Sklare found all of these changes alarming; they overshadowed, to his mind, all of the good that was being accomplished on other fronts. "That this should be so is hardly surprising," he explained, "since intermarriage strikes at the very core of Jewish group existence."—JDS]

A merican Jews have always had a reputation for resisting intermarriage, and they still serve as a model in this respect for other ethnic and religious groups who worry about their future in a pluralist society. Just as the Jewish alcoholic or juvenile delinquent is thought to be a rare exception, so the Jewish son who brings home a Gentile bride is generally considered a sport.

Within the Jewish community itself, the danger of intermarriage is always felt to be there, of course, but the prevailing attitude—even among those who are knowledgeable about Jewish matters or professionally concerned with Jewish welfare—is that the threat of the problem has been surprisingly well contained in America.

One result of this complacency is that the Jewish agencies have sponsored or conducted practically no research in the area of intermarriage. Social planning agencies have extensively investigated other community problems as a matter of course—the needs of the aged, the convalescent, the refugee, the maladjusted family, etc.—and the defense agencies have examined anti-Semitism from diverse angles, ranging from studies of the personality of the active bigot to investigations of attitudes toward Jews in rural counties where there are no Jews, merely "images" of them. By contrast, what little hard data we have on the subject of intermarriage comes mainly from the work of independent scholars (often as a by-product of broader projects) and not from the research facilities of the official community.

This surprising lack of interest in a matter more crucial to Jewish survival than any other is not, of course, wholly the product of faith in intuition or of wishful thinking. Actually, the small measure of relevant research that was done in the past has tended to reinforce complacency. The earliest study of intermarriage was Julius Drachsler's *Democracy and Assimilation*, which received a good deal of attention at the time of its publication in 1920. On the basis of an examination of about 100,000 marriage licenses issued in New York City between 1908 and 1912, Drachsler found that of all white groups in the city, the Jews were least prone to marry outsiders. The Jewish intermarriage rate of 1.17 percent was scarcely higher than that of interracial marriages among Negroes, and Drachsler bracketed the two together as a "low-ratio group," as opposed to the "middle-ratio" groups (Italians and Irish) and the "high-ratio" groups (English, Germans, Swedes, and others).

A second investigation that was influential in confirming the Jewish reputation for endogamy was conducted in New Haven by Ruby Jo Reeves Kennedy. Published in the *American Journal of Sociology* in 1944 (a follow-up article appeared in 1952), the Kennedy study was to reach a wide audience through Will Herberg's extensive use of it in *Protestant-Catholic-Jew*. Kennedy's conclusions were in close keeping with those of Drachsler. She found that for all the years investigated—1870, 1900, 1930, and 1940—Jews had the lowest intermarriage rate in the city. The Italians were the only ethnic group that approached them in endogamy, and even their rate of intermarriage was several times higher.

All this must have seemed impressive evidence to the leaders of the Jewish community, just as it did—and does—to the scholars themselves. For example, one sociological investigation of American-Jewish life, C. B. Sherman's *The Jew within American Society*, continues to take a highly optimistic view of the intermarriage problem. Comparing newer statistics with those collected by

Drachsler, Sherman remarks that "considering the degree of acculturation to which the Jewish community has attained during the period, the surprise is not that the increase has been so big, but that it has been so small." Much the same point is made by Nathan Glazer and Daniel P. Moynihan in *Beyond the Melting Pot*. Commenting on the Kennedy study, the authors note that the persisting pattern of endogamy "sharply distinguishes the Jews of the United States from those of other countries in which Jews have achieved wealth and social position, such as Holland, Germany, Austria, and Hungary in the twenties. There the intermarriage rates were phenomenally high." *

But even more influential, perhaps, than the Drachsler and Kennedy studies in establishing the Jewish reputation for continued endogamy was a report by the Bureau of the Census based on its Current Population Survey of March 1957 (the only such survey to include a question on religion). In its sample of 35,000 households, the Bureau found that only 7.2 percent of the husbands or wives of Jews were of a different faith. The comparable figure for Protestants was 8.6 percent, and for Catholics it was 21.6 percent.

These statistics gave many people within the Jewish community reason to believe that the Jews were still doing quite well: after all, the Catholics, who had made a much more conscious effort than Jews to foster separatism, were faced with an intermarriage rate that was almost three times as high. Moreover, the Jewish rate was all the more heartening in view of the absolute size of the group and the insignificant percentage it comprised of the population as a whole. In his annual review of demographic data in the 1959 *American Jewish Year Book*, Alvin Chenkin, statistician for the Council of Jewish Federations and Welfare Funds, described 7.2 as a "nominal" percentage; if marital selection had taken place entirely at random, Chenkin pointed out, the Jewish intermarriage rate would have approached 98 percent.

Since the 7.2 figure has become the most widely quoted statistic in recent discussions of intermarriage and currently provides the main source of reassurance in the Jewish community, it is worth taking a closer look at what it actually means. Quite apart from whether comparisons in this area between majority and minority groups are valid at all (a case could be made that they are not), there remains the fact that almost everyone who has cited the figure has failed to heed the Bureau's *caveat* that its statistics on intermarriage were probably subject to a larger margin of error than would result from normal sampling variation. (In an unusual aside, the Bureau noted that while it had told its personnel not to assume the same religion for all members of a given family and directed them to ask about each adult member of a household separately, some interviewers might have overlooked this instruction.)

Other implications of the 7.2 percent figure have also been ignored. No one has bothered to relate it, for instance, to the well-known fact that consider-

*According to the statistics of Arthur Ruppin, these rates were as high as 20 and 30 percent.

ably more Jewish men intermarry than do Jewish women (at least seven out of every ten Jews who intermarry are men), so that as a consequence some Jewish women must either marry Gentiles or remain single. Spinsterhood does not, to be sure, affect the intermarriage rate, but it does influence another crucial demographic factor: the birth rate. Nor is this the only indirect consequence of intermarriage. For example, all other things being equal, the smaller the size of any group, the higher will be its rate of intermarriage: or to put it the other way around, the higher the proportion of the minority to the total population, the smaller will be the impact of "randomization" upon it. Thus, since the general population in the United States is growing, the Jewish population must also grow in order to escape further attrition by randomization. Should the size of the Jewish population only remain constant, the group's intermarriage rate would inevitably rise.

However, the most crucial point that has been generally overlooked in evaluating the 7.2 figure is that it represented the *ratio* of intermarried to in-married couples and not the *current* rate of intermarriage among Jews. The statistic, in other words, was cumulative—included were people who had taken their vows in Czarist Russia where intermarriage was forbidden, as well as people who had married in the United States; people belonging to the virtually closed community of the immigrant generation, as well as people living in the wide world of the fourth generation. The *current* rate, then, may well be at least double that of the Bureau's cumulative ratio. And even the cumulative ratio is bound to soar in the decades ahead with the thinning-out of the ranks of those who are presently keeping it down—first- and second-generation Jews.

In short, the grounds for the American Jewish community's optimism are by no means as firm as they have been assumed to be by laymen and sociologists alike. Interestingly enough, the present state of Jewish endogamy seems to have been grasped more firmly by the novelists than by the sociologists. Even a hasty rundown of the work of such writers as Bernard Malamud, Saul Bellow, Philip Roth, Leslie Fiedler, Bruce Jay Friedman, Herbert Gold, Jack Ludwig, Myron Kaufmann, Neal Oxenhandler, etc., reveals how much recent American fiction has dealt with marriage or the strong possibility of it between a Jew and a Gentile. That the stance taken toward the question, moreover, is usually not in the least militant or didactic is significant evidence that among those who might be expected to be in closest touch with the climate of the times, the high incidence of intermarriage is no longer a matter of controversy.

Within the organized Jewish community itself, the publication in volume 64 of the *American Jewish Year Book* of Erich Rosenthal's article "Studies of Jewish Intermarriage in the United States," is one of the first signs that this community may at last be preparing to recognize that a problem does exist.*

---

*Another work was also published in 1963, *Intermarriage and Jewish Life*, edited by Werner J. Cahnman (The Herzl Press and the Jewish Reconstructionist Press, 212 pp., $5.00),

(In the sixty-three previous volumes of the *Year Book*, the subject was dealt with only once—in a brief two pages.)

In his pioneering study, Rosenthal provides a sophisticated analysis of statistical data concerning intermarriage in the state of Iowa and in the city of Washington, D.C. According to Rosenthal's findings, during the years 1953–59, only 57.8 percent of the marriage licenses applied for by Jews in Iowa *listed both applicants* as Jewish. (Iowa and Indiana are the two jurisdictions in the United States where the marriage-license form includes a query on religion.) Religion, then, still plays a role in the marital choices of Iowa Jews—42.2 percent, after all, represents a far smaller intermarriage rate than would be produced by randomization. Nevertheless, as Rosenthal suggests, unless the figure drops sharply in the future, the final chapter in the history of Iowa's Jewish community will have been reached by the end of this century.

Of course, the current situation in Des Moines, Davenport, and other Iowa communities is not an accurate reflection of what is happening in the major cities and their suburbs, where the great majority of American Jews still live. But at the very least this section of Rosenthal's study does point up the fact that the problem is most critical where the Jewish population is small both in absolute and relative terms. Moreover, in the other section of his study, Rosenthal reminds us that even in a middle-sized Jewish community like that of Washington, D.C. (with 81,000 members it ranks as the seventh largest Jewish community in the nation), the cumulative ratio is now almost twice the Census Bureau's figure. And since a significant segment of the Jewish population resides in communities of this size, the problem of Jewish survival there cannot be shrugged off as one might be tempted to do with the problem in Iowa.

Rosenthal utilizes a 1956 survey of Washington's Jewish population that was unusually resourceful in locating the unaffiliated Jew. Although the issue of intermarriage was of secondary interest in the design of the study, it was found that in 13.1 percent of the households including a married Jew, either the husband or wife was Gentile. This percentage is probably somewhat higher than the average for middle-size Jewish communities—Washington's Jews not being known for the intensity of their Jewish commitment. But that does not really modify the import of the figure, particularly since there is reason to believe that the current rate of intermarriage in Washington substantially exceeds 13.1 percent. Rosenthal himself does not offer a current rate, but he does provide tabulations on the rate for successive generations: 1.4 percent for the first generation; 10.2 percent for the second; and 17.9 percent for the third. Since it can be assumed that the great majority of Washington's Jews who are marrying in 1964 belong to the third generation, the 17.9 figure is probably very close to the current rate.

Besides offering a sharp corrective to Jewish complacency about the rate of

---

which consists of papers read at a conference organized by the Herzl Institute. This is the first book on the subject sponsored by any American Jewish organization.

intermarriage today, these statistics provide an occasion for calling into question a good many dated notions about the psychological and social conditions under which intermarriage now takes place. One traditional view, for example, holds that the Jew who marries a Gentile often does so to escape the social disabilities of being Jewish (the prototype here is someone like August Belmont). Though this motive was no doubt decisive in the marital choices of a fair number of mobile, *nouveaux riches*, or socially ambitious Jews of an earlier period, it seems to have much less force in the present age when many traditional status distinctions are being swept away and the old-time social arbiters are becoming increasingly ineffective. And as the hospital boards, country clubs, suburbs, and corporations that were once the exclusive preserve of the Protestant upper class become more democratic in their admission policies, we can expect that this reason for intermarriage will become even less significant. One can already observe from Rosenthal's data on Iowa that social climbing is probably not an important element in intermarriage in that state. Lutherans, Methodists, and Presbyterians comprise the three largest Protestant denominations in Iowa, in that order, and in the marriages contracted between Jewish men and Protestant women these three denominations rank in the same order; furthermore, Iowa Jews marry into the plainspun society of the Baptists about as frequently as they do into the prestigious milieu of the Episcopalians. Such inferences are, of course, less than precise, but it seems clear that if social climbing were a leading cause of intermarriage, Jewish men in Iowa would ignore many of the girls they choose to marry.

Along with the habit of interpreting intermarriage as a form of status seeking, there is still a tendency to view it as a form of escape from the burdens of Jewishness and the harassments of anti-Semitism—as, in short, the most effective method of assimilation. This explanation, too, undoubtedly had some relevance at an earlier period in American Jewish history (though never nearly as much as it did among European Jewry), but it is increasingly beside the point at a time when the penalties and risks of being Jewish are obviously on the wane. Indeed, if intermarriage were a response to the threat of anti-Semitism, particularly in a state as remote from the scenes and memories of Jewish persecution as Iowa is, there should currently be less, rather than more, of it.

Other standard explanations of intermarriage take psychological rather than social factors as the governing ones, finding the source of the impulse to intermarriage not in the confrontation of the Jew with Gentile society but in the early relationship between parent and child. Serious conflicts at this stage—so the notion goes—will be expressed later on in the attempt by the child to avoid a marital pattern similar to that of his parents. In its more simplistic form, this theory holds that marriage to an outsider is a gesture of hostility toward the parents, the point being to rob them of the pleasure they would obtain from a "suitable" match, shame them before relatives and friends, and deprive them finally of the consolation of Jewish grandchildren. The more complex form of the same theory regards intermarriage as part of a syndrome of general revolt from the mores and aspirations of the parents, often manifesting itself in bohemianism, political radicalism, or other types of identification with socially alienated and/or dissident groups.

But were this theory particularly pertinent, one would expect Jewish-Gentile marriages to be most prevalent in the second generation, where the trauma of acculturation was most decisively experienced and the generational conflict was at its most intense. However, intermarriage rates, as we have already noted, are clearly higher in the third generation; and in addition, as we shall soon see, Jewish-Gentile marriages are particularly prevalent among certain Jewish groups who are very much at home in the culture.

At best, the existence of a correlation between childhood conflicts and marital choices is easier to assume than it is to demonstrate. In analyzing the data on intermarriage contained in the recent "Midtown Manhattan Study,"* the sociologist Jerold Heiss began with the standard idea that those whose early family life showed marked signs of disruption or had otherwise been unsatisfactory would be more likely to intermarry than those with relatively stable childhoods. But he discovered that this idea could not be sustained. The family backgrounds of the exogamous Jews in the study were not exceptional in terms of conflict, and actually showed fewer cases of parental divorce, separation, and desertion than did the backgrounds of the endogamous Jews surveyed.

In attempting to revise traditional perspectives on the causes of intermarriage, one is even more hampered by the scarcity of research that has been done into the sociological and psychological aspects of the problem than in trying to determine the current rate of intermarriage. The few studies and essays allowing one to draw certain limited inferences about the personal motives and social context that foster exogamy happen to involve professional groups— mainly in the academy—that are marginal to the community life of American Jewry. Therefore, one cannot regard these findings as telling us anything definitive about the "typical" behavior of American Jews who choose to marry outside the faith. On the other hand, there is good reason not to discount them altogether, since most of the people concerned are Jews who grew up in metropolitan Jewish communities, who lead fairly conventional lives, and who practice highly respected professions. It should also be borne in mind that as writers, teachers, scientists, psychoanalysts, and so forth, they serve as models to their younger contemporaries who in increasing numbers are forsaking the Jewish business and community ties of their parents' generation and

---

* It is worth noting that this study found 18.4 percent of all marriages involving Jews to be exogamous.

seeking careers in the professions. Thus, the influence of, say, the exogamous college teacher in legitimizing intermarriage can far outweigh the fact that his importance is statistically very small in relation to the total Jewish population.

According to a recent study conducted by Rabbi Henry Cohen, approximately 20 percent of the Jewish faculty members at the University of Illinois—well over twice the national average—are married to Gentile women. This is a significant figure because Illinois has a reputation for academic and social conservatism, being neither particularly adventurous in its curriculum nor particularly "highbrow" in its faculty. We can therefore assume that the pattern here is more typical than it would be at experimental colleges like Antioch or Reed, or fashionable universities like Yale or Chicago. There is also a comparatively large Jewish student body on the Illinois campus; in contrast to a college such as Swarthmore, for example—which has been described as an "intermarriage mill"—the University of Illinois is a favorite choice of Midwestern parents eager to avoid this peril. (In fact, it was on the Illinois campus that America's first Hillel Foundation was established some forty years ago.)

The Jewish population of Champaign-Urbana numbers about 250 families, which are almost equally divided between town and gown. One of Rabbi Cohen's most suggestive findings on intermarriage was the unexpected disparity between the 20 percent ratio for the faculty members and a 6.5 percent ratio for the Jewish townspeople. The contrast between town and gown is even more striking in view of the respective family backgrounds of both groups, which, if anything, would have led one to expect their respective intermarriage rates to be reversed. Most of the Jewish faculty members (chiefly mathematicians, physicists, psychologists, and sociologists) arrived in Champaign-Urbana during the last few years; they are mainly sons of East European immigrants and grew up in predominantly Jewish neighborhoods; almost all described their parents as affiliated with either Orthodox or Conservative synagogues. The townspeople, on the other hand—chiefly manufacturers, wholesalers, retailers, and professionals—include a group descended from "old" German-Jewish families who are firmly rooted in the community and whose predominant background is Reform.

What lies behind the disparity in the intermarriage rates of these two groups? Rabbi Cohen points out that many of the Jewish teachers and researchers at the University of Illinois (and presumably the overwhelming majority of the intermarried couples) hold to a point of view—"Academic Commitment" he calls it—that fulfills a function analogous to that of religious faith:

How many aspects of religious faith and fellowship we find in the Academic Commitment! There is the dominant philosophy of naturalism. Its method is scientific; its faith, that all being can be explained in terms of a single order of efficient causation in which a supernatural Deity has no place; its morality, the ideals of humanism rooted in finite human experience; its messianic hope, that man—through understanding the consequences of his actions—can build a better world.

As against the case of the Gentile society of Champaign-Urbana, there are a number of Gentile academicians on the Illinois campus who do not consider affiliation with a religious institution to be a necessary sign of respectability. Furthermore, Jewish life in Champaign-Urbana—ethnic, religious, or cultural—depends largely on the town community, most of whose members are attached in one way or another to Jewish organizations. The academicians, on the other hand, range, according to Rabbi Cohen, from "the strongly identified who are trying to preserve Jewish culture in a Midwestern cornfield [to] the cosmopolite who feels that there are enough barriers between people . . . without the clannishness of the Jews." Once the memories of Jewish culture become vague, he writes, the town Jew can still find reasons to remain within the fold: he retains a latent supernatural faith, and the larger community expects him to be Jewish. By contrast, once the faculty Jew ceases to find meaning in the ethnic fellowship or the folkways, he has neither traditional belief nor strong social pressure to help him maintain his commitment.

If intermarriage among academicians on a campus as conservative as the University of Illinois is so high, it should not surprise us that there are cities with larger and more active Jewish communities where intermarriage rates among special segments of the Jewish population are even higher. New Haven is a good example. Champaign-Urbana has many Jewish physicians, but New Haven also has a fairly substantial group of psychoanalysts. In a study that appeared several years ago under the title *Social Class and Mental Illness: A Community Study*, A. B. Hollingshead and Frederick C. Redlich studied the therapists as well as the patients. They found that 83 percent of New Haven analysts "came from Jewish homes," and of these some 64 percent were intermarried. This startling figure exceeds even the current level of the geographically isolated Jewish community of Iowa, and is, of course, many times higher than the general rate in New Haven itself. What accounts for such a high rate of intermarriage among individuals who, like their counterparts in Illinois, were born and raised in communities thickly settled by Jews, whose families were active in Jewish affairs, and who practice a profession second only to the rabbinate in its proportion of Jews? One answer is suggested by Redlich and Hollingshead who point out that the great majority of the New Haven analysts "consider themselves representatives of classical psychoanalysis; when the discussion turns in that direction they look down their classical analytical noses at their colleagues who have a Jungian, Horneyan or Sullivanian orientation." Thus the psychoanalysts of New Haven have an even more sharply defined "commitment" than the academicians of Champaign-Urbana (so much so that they maintain virtually no contact with their psychiatrist colleagues in New Haven who are directive or organic in orientation), and this professional commitment probably is as binding as that of the Illinois professors.

In our context, perhaps the most interesting fact to emerge from the New

Haven study is that apart from marital choice and the lack of religious affiliation, the analysts do not appear to be alienated in any profound sense from the culture in which they live. Far from exhibiting any left-wing political beliefs and sympathies, they tend toward the attitudes of the old-fashioned American who started from humble beginnings and achieved success as a result of hard work. Living in the best residential areas of New Haven, enjoying high incomes that they have earned (unlike many Protestants in the same area) "largely through their own efforts and abilities," their individual social mobility has been such that 73 percent of them have won a higher station in life than their fathers, 79 percent have surpassed their brothers-in-law, and 83 percent have outdistanced their brothers.

Their essential conformity to middle-class ideals is nowhere better shown than in their attitude to their children's education. While denying any desire to impose their own values upon their offspring, their typical response to the question "How much education do you want for your children?" was: "As much as they want; college is the minimum." On the whole, they have no contact with Jewish life, yet as Hollingshead and Redlich put it: "Doubt and confusion is apparent in their response on how they would like to have their children trained religiously." Presumably the rate of intermarriage among the children of these analysts will be very high, although the children's motives will obviously be different from those that led their fathers to intermarry. But even where both parents are Jewish, there will no doubt be a high rate of intermarriage among the children in this group.

Thus far we have concentrated on the behavior of the Jew in relation to intermarriage, but perhaps the newest factor in the situation is the change in the position of the Gentile. Once we shift our focus to the Gentile, it becomes evident that intermarriage is increasing not only because the Jew is moving out into the general society, but also because the tastes, ideas, cultural preferences, and life-styles preferred by many Jews are more and more coming to be shared by non-Jews. In the Herzl Institute volume referred to above, this process is commented upon by Richard Rubenstein, a well-known Hillel rabbi currently at the University of Pittsburgh. As Rubenstein sees it, in the course of "emancipating" themselves, many of the bright middle-class Gentile girls who attend the better colleges are attracted by the political liberalism characteristic of Jewish students or by their equally characteristic avant-gardism in intellectual and aesthetic matters. To the allure of the "Jewish" cultural style is added the fact that Jews are in, but still not completely of, the society. In other words, where Jewish alienation used to inhibit contact with Gentiles (several decades ago, the heavily Jewish radical movements on the college campuses experienced considerable difficulty in appealing to the rest of the student body), it now operates in a subtle way to foster them. For, as Rabbi Rubenstein says, it is precisely this delicate balance between acceptance and marginality that is sought after by girls who do not want Bohemian husbands but rather respectable ones who are somewhat "different." In addition, the marked rise in egalitarianism on the college campuses following World War II has done much to promote a climate in which dating, and in some cases marrying, outside one's social group is no longer regarded as deviant behavior, and on the more "advanced" campuses even confers some degree of status. And finally, these changes in the social atmosphere of the college community run parallel to developments in the occupational world, for to a greater extent than ever before, Jews are now working with Gentiles as colleagues instead of serving them as merchants or free professionals.

What all this suggests is that the old notions about the causes of intermarriage are beginning to look as outmoded as the causes themselves. Both on the folk level and in more sophisticated terms, these notions invariably involved the imputation of some defect in the contracting parties. If a Gentile girl agreed to marry a Jew, it must be because no Christian would have her, or because she had made herself sexually available as no Jewish girl would deign to do. Similarly, if a Jewish man married a Gentile girl, it must be because no Jewish girl would have him, or because he was a self-hater or a social climber. Whatever their applicability to individual cases, it takes no great insight to realize that approaches like these—that stress the deviancy and inferiority of the person who intermarries—serve the dual function of reinforcing the practice of endogamy and allaying fears about the threat of intermarriage. By impugning the motives of exogamous Jews, or by attributing them to dark forces outside the Jewish community, the challenge that intermarriage poses to the prevailing values of the group is vanquished—at least for the moment. The difficulty, however, is that these assumptions of pathology—social or personal—no longer explain either the rate or the reasons for exogamy among Jews. This is not to say that intermarriage can already be considered a routine phenomenon and that the motives that impel Jews to choose Gentile mates are basically no different from those that lead them to marry Jews. Nevertheless, from the evidence that has begun to accumulate, it is becoming impossible to view intermarriage as an indication of either personal aberration or social persecution. In a recent study of middle-class intermarried couples residing in the Boston area, Maria and Daniel Levinson conclude that:

intermarriage is not . . . a unitary phenomenon. It occurs under a variety of psychological and social conditions and has varying consequences. Psychologically it is not purely a neurotic manifestation, although neurotic motives may enter to varying degrees. Nor is it to be seen solely as an "escape" from the Jewish group or as a means of securing social or financial gain, although motives of this kind play a part in some cases.

Heiss's analysis of the Midtown Study supports this conclusion. Surveying the mental-health rating assigned each respondent by a board of psychiatrists, he found that there was no significant difference between the mean rating achieved by those who had intermarried and those who had not.

It is precisely the "healthy" modern intermarriages that raise the most troubling questions of all to the Jewish community in general, and Jewish parents in particular. When his child intermarries, the Jewish parent guiltily feels that in some way he must be responsible. Yet how is he to oppose the match? Chances are that he believes that love is the basis of marriage, that marriage is the uniting of two individuals rather than two families, and that the final determination of a mate is his child's prerogative. This complex of ideas (which constitutes a radical departure from the norm, if not always the practice, of traditional Jewish society) came to be embraced by some of the more advanced members of the first generation in America, by a majority of the second generation, and by an overwhelming proportion of the third. How then can the parent ask his child to renounce what he himself believes in? Moreover, the liberalism of the Jewish parent—his commitment to the idea of equality and his belief in the transitory character of the differences that distinguish people from one another—serves to subvert his sense of moral rectitude in opposing intermarriage. For if he is at all in the habit of personal candor, he must ask himself if the Gentile is any less worthy of the Jew than the Jew is of the Gentile.

The second-generation parent or adviser usually manages to escape this dilemma by falling back on the argument of happiness. Experience, he will say, is the best teacher, and what it teaches is that intermarriage seldom works out well. And he will cite figures to show that exogamous couples have higher divorce rates than those who marry within the fold. Thus the need to confront the painful contradictions in his own position is evaded, and he can oppose his child's intermarriage with a good conscience.

In the writings of such founding fathers of the contemporary American Jewish community as Isaac Mayer Wise or Solomon Schechter, the assumption is that Jewish survival is entirely possible in a free society. But having finally established themselves in such a society, Jews are now coming to realize that their survival is still threatened—not by Gentile hostility but by Jewish indifference. This is what finally makes intermarriage so bitter a dilemma to confront. On the one hand, it signifies the fulfillment of the Jews' demand for acceptance as an individual—a demand he has been making since the Emancipation; on the other hand, it signifies a weakening of Jewish commitment. In short, it casts into doubt American Jewry's dual ideal of full participation in the society and the preservation of Jewish identity. And once the rate of intermarriage is seen to be growing, the contradiction in the basic strategy of American-Jewish adjustment is nakedly exposed.

As the horns of this dilemma sharpen and press closer, the very least one can hope from the Jewish community is that it will eventually surrender the cherished diagnoses and nostrums that have come to obfuscate the true nature of the problem. A more realistic confrontation is necessary, and that requires a much larger body of research than we now possess on the current rate of inter-marriage in the country as a whole. It also requires much more information about the Jews who intermarry and about the causes and consequences of their doing so. So, too, there is a need for studies to evaluate the various methods in use to combat intermarriage, particularly those involving Jewish education. And demographic research will have to be done at regular intervals so that a reliable trend line can be established.

A candid and pertinent discussion of intermarriage will also require a more critical examination of Jewish attitudes than we have had in the past. One im-mediately thinks of the issue of conversion, which many Jews seem to regard as a token, last-gap measure in a developing process of assimilation; but is it? There is also the obvious, but usually ignored, problem of birth rate. One rea-son why a rising rate of intermarriage is of such pressing significance is that the birth rate of native-born Jews has been so low. (This, in part, is why compari-sons between Jewish and Catholic intermarriage rates have helped to confound rather than clarify the issue.) If a greater proportion of second-generation Jew-ish parents had permitted themselves to have even three children rather than one or two, the present situation would be far more hopeful so far as Jewish survival is concerned. But the fact is that the fertility rate of the second gen-eration dropped catastrophically, and with hardly a word of discussion about it among Jewish leaders. Reform and Conservative rabbis decided, for all prac-tical purposes, to exempt the question of contraception from the area of the sacred, implying that a decision about family size was of strictly private con-cern. Orthodox spokesmen were not prepared to go this far in the direction of secularization, but they preferred to concentrate on other issues such as maintaining the practice of *kashrut*.

The threat posed by intermarriage may change all this, and there is a pos-sibility that it will also change the way most Jews think about their Jewish responsibilities. Typically, the American-Jewish notion has been that to be a good Jew means doing something for some other Jew; it means, in short, phi-lanthropy. As the problem of intermarriage grows in urgency, however, the Jewish community in America will for the first time have to face an issue that is highly personal—almost antiphilanthropic—in character. And if the emphasis on philanthropic activism has allowed American Jews to avoid confronting the stark question: "What do you stand for when you wish to remain separate?"—the defense against intermarriage will necessarily involve a coming to terms, sooner or later, with what one is defending.

As the evidence accumulates that Jewish survival in America literally de-pends upon each individual Jew—and in an entirely different way than it did in the past—the answer to the question, "What do you stand for when you remain separate?" may well demand the development of a new consciousness in the community. This will not be the first time in history that social conditions have impelled a people to philosophical discussion and involvement. If the problem of intermarriage should engender such a consciousness—the kind that has been foreign to the activism of American Jewry—it will have had a positive effect on the quality of Jewish life. If it does not, the negative consequences are indeed ominous to contemplate.

# The Future of Jewish Giving

Jewish philanthropy—so high is its reputation—has come to serve as a model for scholars, professional workers, and civic leaders who are concerned with the methods and problems of charitable fund-raising. Just as Jewish sobriety is frequently studied to illuminate the social etiology and cure of alcoholism, so Jewish philanthropy, which combines the twin principles of voluntarily meeting Jewish needs and generously supporting nonsectarian causes, has provided an exemplary case for those who wish to study or improve the state of American philanthropy.

That Jews as a group are extraordinarily generous in their giving we know from many surveys. For example, in a recent study conducted by Dr. James N. Morgan of the Survey Research Center of the University of Michigan, with the cooperation of the National Bureau of Economic Research, it was found that the percentage of Jews donating $50 or more to individuals (chiefly relatives and friends) and to nonreligious charities was higher than that of any other group. Furthermore, the Jewish lead widened in the larger-donation categories, and here the Jewish lag in contributing to churches and church-connected organizations disappeared. Thus, in the category of donations of $250 or more, 25 percent of the Jews gave to individuals, 18 percent to religious or religion-connected organizations, and 17 percent to all other charities. Comparable figures for Episcopalians—whose average income exceeded that of the Jews in the national sample of almost 3,000 households—were 15 percent, 9 percent, and 8 percent, respectively.

Gentile community leaders have long been aware of what researchers like Morgan are presently documenting. Those interviewed in the American Jewish Committee's "Riverton Study," for example, frequently remarked upon Jewish generosity. Samuel Stevenson, a leading local industrialist and an important Episcopalian layman, said about the Jews of Riverton: "In this matter of giving, it's a specific characteristic." A more comprehensive statement was made by Arthur Caruso, a second-generation Italian Catholic and a leading political figure in the community:

The Jews are by far the most highly organized group in Riverton of all the minority groups, and they have the most intelligent leadership. They're the most active. They're the only group that can really raise money. They have a real program. . . . They have the Jewish Federation, a fund-raising group, they have their own social service agency, and . . . they have the YMHA. . . . Theirs is a day-in and day-out program while ours is only for one occasion. They do it with a trained staff that sets up the program and continues it.

Caruso contrasted Jewish behavior in this respect with that of his fellow Italians:

I can call ten Jews on the phone this minute and without giving them any big explanation I can get a hundred dollars from each one. I'd have a tough time with the Gentiles. . . . I'll give you an example. We had a drive among the Italian people to help the people in Italy who suffered from the flood. We raised only $7,000. . . . The same effort that it takes to get ten dollars from an Italian would get a thousand from a Jew.

Perhaps the strongest evidence of the Gentile respect for Jewish generosity has come from the financial community. Year after year some of the nation's largest and most conservative banks—such as the Manufacturers Hanover Trust, the First National City Bank, the Bankers Trust Company, the Chemical Corn Exchange Bank, the Chase Manhattan Bank, to mention only examples from the New York area—have extended sizable loans to Jewish philanthropies. None of these institutions is controlled by Jews, and it is doubtful that their cooperation is given out of guilt over their restrictions on hiring or developing Jewish executives. More likely, they are willing to cooperate solely on the basis of their analysis of the facts of Jewish fund-raising—one of which is that since 1946 Jewish federations in the United States have consistently raised over $100,000,000 per year.*

Jewish philanthropic activity has also succeeded in impressing the Jews themselves: of the many Jewish tributes to Jewish generosity, Harry L. Lurie's *A Heritage Affirmed: The Jewish Federation Movement in America*[†] is the most recent and among the most ardent. The implication of Lurie's title is clear: however far American Jews have strayed from Jewish tradition, however much they may be criticized for irreverence and outright secularism, they have still punctiliously observed one crucial religious commandment—the *mitzvah* of *tsedakah*, or charity—whose force in the Jewish tradition is so great that support of the indigent is defined by the tradition as including the wherewithal for those being supported to observe this *mitzvah* themselves.

---

*The level of such collections has of course fluctuated: in 1948 collections reached a record-breaking $200,000,000, while in 1954 they sank to a low of $107,000,000 (the total for 1960 was $128,000,000). In spite of such fluctuations the record has apparently been consistent enough to convince even the most cautious bankers that they take minimal risks in advancing loans.

[†] Jewish Publication Society of America, 481 pp., $6.00.

The federations described in Lurie's book now exist in all American cities where Jews live in any significant numbers. Each federation raises and allocates funds for local, national, and overseas beneficiaries. Called by a variety of names (in Oakland, California, the "Jewish Welfare Federation"; in Tucson, Arizona, the "Jewish Community Council"; in Lafayette, Indiana, the "Federated Jewish Charities")—the federations also vary in their functions according to the size of the local Jewish population, the particular evolution of the Jewish community, and the structure of the general community. In small cities federations may themselves operate social services. In larger cities they generally serve only as fund-raising, coordinating, and community-planning agencies—each local beneficiary having its own separate board and professional staff. In the large communities the range of services the federations subsidize and coordinate may be wide indeed: care for children who are orphaned, delinquent, or maladjusted; recreational facilities like Y's, day camps, and country camps; Jewish education; psychiatric case work for problem families; employment and vocational guidance agencies; general and specialized hospitals; homes for the aged; and Jewish community relations.

Originally the federations were founded to raise funds for local Jewish institutions; at a later period "welfare funds" were established to help finance agencies that assisted Jews abroad and, to a much lesser extent, the national Jewish agencies. In recent decades amalgamations have led to the creation of one central organization in each city that raises funds for local, national, and overseas needs. The single exception is in New York City where the Federation of Jewish Philanthropies of New York raises funds for local needs, and the United Jewish Appeal of New York—an entirely separate group—runs an annual campaign for overseas agencies and for a small list of national ones. The name of the organization, which Lurie headed until his retirement—the Council of Jewish Federations and Welfare Funds—dates back to the period when separate campaigns were held for local and overseas causes, but today the CJFWF serves as the coordinating body of the many hundreds of integrated federations scattered throughout the nation.

All this is developed at length in Lurie's history, along with his testimonies to the ingenuity of the social engineering and institutional framework of Jewish philanthropy. However, in spite of his highly positive account of the federation movement, as well as the other tributes we have been noting, there is evidence enough on the other side to make it clear that a wide gulf exists between the image and the reality of Jewish philanthropy. The truth of the matter is that Jewish philanthropy in general, and the federations in particular, have a host of serious and unresolved problems, and, further, that many of these problems promise to become more serious in the decades ahead.

The first issue that has frequently been obfuscated concerns the number of Jews who actually make donations. Riverton's Gentile community leaders assumed that all Jews do so, especially to the federation. Even such an acute student of Jewish philanthropy as Lurie reinforces this impression, if only by his failure to discuss the issue. Regrettably, we cannot say precisely how many American-Jewish households fail to contribute, for no one has taken the trouble to gather the necessary data. Nonetheless, the limited research that has been done leads to two conclusions: that there are sharp variations from community to community in the proportion of households that have been enlisted in the campaigns; and secondly, that in some of the largest cities only a minority have been enlisted.

The basic distinction is between the small communities and the large ones. In the former it is not unusual to find 80 percent or more of the potential donors making a contribution. Peoria, Illinois, is a good example: out of an estimated Jewish population of 1,800 there were 615 who gave to the federation's last campaign. Using the rule-of-thumb of 3.5 persons per household, the result suggests that the overwhelming majority of Jewish households in Peoria did contribute and that some of the households had more than one contributor.

But if Peoria does bear out the standard image of Jewish philanthropy, it is necessary to realize that 62 percent of American Jewry is concentrated in four cities: New York, Los Angeles, Philadelphia, and Chicago. Here in the giant urban centers—where it is considerably more difficult to identify and solicit individual donors and where social controls do not operate as strongly—the situation appears to be quite different from the one in Peoria. Again reliable evidence is meager. Next to nothing is known about the most crucial place of all—the New York metropolitan area where over 42 percent of American Jews reside. The data that have been given to the CJFWF by the New York Federation and the New York UJA are slight and of little scientific value.* But such evidence as there is in no way contravenes the standard belief that New York City has the lowest percentage of contributors in the nation.

Useful statistics have, however, been gathered and reported for the three other cities. In Chicago, during 1960, there were 35,326 federation contributors,† including 9,106 donors to the women's division. Estimating the Jewish population of the city as 282,000, figuring that 75 percent of the women's-division contributors do not live in separate households, and calculating house-

---

*At best the New York situation would pose a difficult problem for the analyst: due to an agreement with the Greater New York Fund, the Federation refrains from soliciting donors whose yearly income is under $5,000; also the New York United Jewish Appeal is known to receive many thousands of contributions under $10, which it does not count as individual donations.

†The term "contributors" refers to a gift unit, not to an individual. For example, business partners giving a company rather than a personal contribution would be counted as a single gift unit. It is estimated that even if the totals were adjusted so as to make allowance for such multiple contributions, the percentage of households contributing would not rise by more than 1 percent.

hold size at 3.5 persons, we can conclude that only about 35 percent of the Jewish households of Chicago contributed to the federation.

The case of Los Angeles parallels that of Chicago very closely. The latest available figures are for 1958, when there were 51,881 federation contributors, of whom 15,400 were in the women's division. With an estimated Jewish population for that year of 390,000, and (if anything) a smaller household size than Chicago's, Los Angeles still showed about the same percentage of households contributing to the federation as Chicago—35 percent. Thus, although we cannot say exactly how many Jewish families in America contribute to these central fund-raising organizations, it would be rash to claim that more than 50 percent do, and the evidence we have suggests an even lower figure.

Some observers would undoubtedly argue that this evidence is misleading. Though only a minority may contribute to federations, they would contend, many additional hundreds of thousands of households give to national agencies like Hadassah, the Jewish Theological Seminary of America, The City of Hope, or the Yeshiva Torah V'Daath—which run independent campaigns—as well as to a host of local agencies; hence the number of Jewish households not participating in some campaign or other remains negligible.

It is true that the independent campaigns raise sizable sums of money—enough to make the federations worry about the amount of effort and dollars being diverted from their own campaigns. The CJFWF reports that in 1960 some 75 major national agencies raised $57,000,000; a more inclusive listing might find that the independent campaigns raise well over $100,000,000 annually, or about as much as the federated campaigns.* But professional fund-raisers are aware that those who donate more than token gifts to non-federation causes are more likely than not to be federation donors as well. In any case, the number of those who donate only to the independent campaigns is somewhat beside the point, since the local federation drive is still the basis of American Jewish philanthropy and the most important index of its adequacy.

To be sure, the conclusion that the *mitzvah* of *tsedakah* is practiced in a serious way in only a minority of American Jewish households involves a more complicated picture than I have so far been sketching. Some of the large urban centers, for example, achieve much better results than others; and if some minuscule Jewish communities like Peoria's are "good" fund-raisers, others are notably "bad." Year after year, the federations' standard for the nation as a whole is set by two big cities—Detroit and Cleveland. In the fairly typical year of 1958 the federation in Detroit raised $4,904,000, and the one in Cleveland $4,801,000—from moderately sized Jewish populations of 89,000 and 88,000 respectively. By contrast Chicago, with more than three times as many Jews,

---

* In making such calculations there is the problem of deciding whether to include contributions to synagogues. Should such giving be considered philanthropy? There is also the problem of classifying purchases of Israel Bonds.

raised only $5,340,000 in the same year; while Philadelphia, with nearly four times as many Jews (331,000) was able to raise only $4,031,000.

That the question is not only one of size is further borne out by the fact that in the same year the federation in Newark—a city with 12,000 more Jews than Detroit—raised less than half as much ($1,994,000). Nor is the problem confined to the Eastern seaboard: St. Louis and San Francisco also compare very unfavorably with the Detroit-Cleveland standard.

Whatever the reasons for such striking differentials among Jewish communities, the level of personal income is not a determining one: there is little evidence that Jewish wealth in Detroit or Cleveland is in any way exceptional. What is exceptional is the general prosperity of the Jews in the nation as a whole. Indeed, contemporary American Jewry constitutes one of the few cases in history where the preponderant majority of Jews have the means to practice the *mitzvah* of *tsedakah* seriously and lack only the will to do so.

Again, the data with which to explore this point is meager, and what has been gathered by the local or national agencies is generally either crude or unreliable. None of the leading Jewish fund-raising institutions—for all their sophistication in modern accounting procedures and public relations techniques—has done so much as the most rudimentary market research concerning either the financial status of non-givers or the proportion of disposable income being contributed by donors.*

The only study that we can utilize is the one commissioned recently by the federation in Essex County, New Jersey, an area that includes Newark and its suburbs. Conducted by the National Opinion Research Center of the University of Chicago, this study is well designed, but has limitations for our purposes: for example, it deals only with those who contribute to the federation, and its findings are tabulated by donation categories rather than donor income.

Nevertheless the situation is clear enough. In Essex County those who contribute less than $100 constitute an overwhelming 87 percent of all givers. Furthermore, more than half of these "small givers" contribute under $10. Weighting their sample in favor of those who give $10–$99, the NORC researchers report that the median family income of this group is $13,000 and that approximately one out of four has an income of $20,000 or over. (Since these figures are based upon the respondents' own report of their income, they can be considered minimal estimates.)

---

*The two national studies that have been made are not in any way adequate, though each was conducted by a leading economist—Leon Keyserling and Robert R. Nathan, respectively. Keyserling's—the more recent and thorough of the two—assumes that the median Jewish income is the same as that for the nonfarm population as a whole—his reasoning being that very few Jews are farmers! It is widely known, of course, that Jews have a radically different occupational distribution than the general nonfarm population, which results in a considerably higher average level of income. Local Jewish population studies conducted by some of the federations are usually primitive in the design and presentation of their research, and even the better ones do not gather data on income or relate it to giving.

How typical is Essex County with its 100,000 Jewish population? Can we learn anything from it about cities like Chicago, Philadelphia, and Los Angeles that have three or four times as many Jews, or New York that has over twenty-three times as many? The answer is that we probably can. Campaign results in Newark are proportionally not too dissimilar from those in the giant cities of Chicago, Philadelphia, Los Angeles, and New York, and Essex County Jewry also resembles the Jewish communities in the giant cities demographically. It is apparent, moreover, that the high percentage of small donors in Essex County is far from being peculiar to that area. In Chicago 75 percent of all donors give under $100, in Los Angeles the figure is 82 percent, in Philadelphia 91 percent. It would be difficult to estimate how the average income of small givers in the large cities compares with the findings in Essex County; but even if we assumed it to be lower by $1,000 or $2,000, we would still have to conclude that the bulk of small givers contribute modestly indeed—perhaps 0.5 percent of their yearly earnings. And, as we have seen, they make up the vast majority of the donors.

These small donors, however, are far less significant to the federations than the "big givers"—wealthy families having a much higher percentage of disposable income than those in the middle class. Yet we know as little about the philanthropic behavior of the big givers as we do about the small donors. Our one source—the Essex County study—is of scant assistance because the highest income-category it used was $50,000 and over. Since a majority of those giving $2,500 and over are in this income bracket, along with a sizable group of the $1,000–$2,499 contributors, there is no way of calculating a median-income figure for the big givers. And even if income figures were available, the problem of interpretation would still be considerable—while income may be a good index to net worth among those in modest circumstances, it is less revealing for the rich.

In any case, whether or not the wealthy contribute generously in relation to their income or net worth, the fact is that the drives depend upon them. For example, 2 percent of the contributors to the Los Angeles Federation account for 52 percent of the total money raised; in Philadelphia 2 percent provide 62 percent, and in Chicago 3 percent provide 55 percent.

The reliance upon the big givers has the benefit of containing the ratio of fund-raising expenses to proceeds, but it makes the overall fund-raising operation that much more unpredictable. The big givers tend to watch each other, and in some cities a cut by one may influence the entire group and cause a serious drop in campaign receipts. Then, too, the size of the pledge of the big giver is not so much determined by what he can afford as by his business mood at the time. Any setback in the economy, particularly one affecting paper profits, is a threat to the campaign's success.

Striking evidence of the dependence on the big giver comes from the current

$104,000,000 building fund campaign of the New York Federation. Under the slogan "Let Us Build Us a City of Life" this campaign is developing a new style in centralized Jewish fund-raising—one that is aimed almost entirely at a select group of wealthy donors. Within a few months the unprecedented sum of $68,000,000 has been raised—and this mainly from a mere 137 contributors whose gifts have been in the $50,000–$2,500,000 range and who have also been required to maintain their normal yearly contribution to the Federation.

In the giant cities, then, federations are apparently still capable of enlisting the enthusiastic support of a small group of wealthy philanthropists, even if they have not been too successful with the many who are in more modest circumstances. But the brilliant progress of the "City of Life" campaign also suggests that the New York Federation's annual maintenance campaigns have raised relatively modest sums in terms of the potential now being exhibited. Part of the "City of Life" campaign's success comes from its special aura of present prestige and future immortality. In the medical field, for example, there are opportunities for big givers to name whole buildings or pavilions; or, more modestly, various wings, suites, or floors within buildings; or the donor may, even more modestly, name various laboratory rooms or nursing stations. All of this is very much in contrast to the typical federation campaign in which most of the money goes not into an enduring monument, but toward feeding, clothing, housing, and providing employment opportunities for newly arrived families in Israel; toward paying the rent of local agencies, the salaries of their workers, and so forth.

In general, some special incentive seems to be necessary for a drive to do exceptionally well (the record sum of $200,000,000 raised by the federations in 1948 was unquestionably related to the establishment of the State of Israel). Be that as it may, the best measure of Jewish generosity remains the average campaign. How do such campaigns fare? Ostensibly many do well, frequently coming very near to meeting their goal, sometimes even going slightly beyond it. But does this mean that the drive has actually succeeded? Not invariably, since goals are frequently set with the realities of fund-raising in mind rather than those of needs. There is much resistance to setting "unrealistic" goals: it is feared that if the goal is pegged beyond an attainable figure the morale of campaign workers will suffer and fewer dollars will be raised.

The problem of deciding what constitutes need is far from simple and is necessarily subjective. The Zionist-oriented individual will claim that the problems of the Israeli immigrants are the most urgent ones. A typically modern donor may argue that the need for psychiatric social work in the local community should have first call on funds. One with more traditional Jewish interests can regard both types of need as distinctly secondary to those of his favorite yeshivah.

Nonetheless, the most pressing claims have been those made upon the over-

seas agencies. In spite of heavy taxation in Israel and large reparations payments, along with the vast sums of money raised annually in America, enough
funds have rarely been available to meet the needs of the new settlers. The
only alternative has been to turn to the banks. Far from being a resource used
only in emergencies, borrowing by and for the United Jewish Appeal became
standard operating procedure during the 1950's. Furthermore, new debts were
incurred before old ones could be liquidated. In spite of all recent efforts at
repayment, some $61,000,000 in accumulated debts was still owed to banks at
the end of last year, and a new loan of $65,000,000 had to be arranged to meet
current requirements.

It is true that these overseas needs are the only ones that have seemed pressing enough to prompt such heavy borrowing. Local and national needs are
generally not of the "bread-and-butter" variety, and if unmet, no one will be
deprived of food or shelter. Yet, some national agencies (such as the Yivo Institute for Jewish Research or the Conference on Jewish Social Studies, and
a number of others) receive only token assistance from the federations—perhaps $50 contributions from some of the smaller cities, $500 from the larger
ones. The result is that some agencies receive too much money to die but not
enough to really live and do their work properly. On the other hand, many of
the national agencies with affluent local constituencies have hesitated to become federation beneficiaries, feeling that they can do better for themselves by
running independent campaigns. And it is unedifying but true that an agency
that decides to forgo its own campaign and submit a request for funds must
have a group of "big givers" to back up its request for a subvention. If it does
not, whatever the merits of its case, it is unlikely to get very much assistance.

The problems of need and allocation lead eventually to the more crucial
question of the total amount available for distribution. In recent years the pressure on available funds has been growing because of such developments as
inflation, the demand for more and better services, and the constant increase
of professionalization. But during the last decade the federations have only
once raised more than $130,000,000, in spite of the justifiable assumption that
the amount of income earned by Jews has risen appreciably. When the pie is
no larger than before, the difficulty of meeting the increased demands is great
enough; but when the pie is even smaller, the difficulty becomes enormous.
How should the necessary division be carried out? By giving everyone an appropriately smaller slice—or by selective reapportionment? The argument has
generally reduced itself to the question of "local needs vs. overseas needs"—
the latter signifying mainly the amount of money that should be sent to Israel.

What will the future bring? The few data available indicate that the problems of Jewish philanthropy are likely to become formidable. One reason lies
in the growing influence of American voluntarism, which—except in the case
of certain small sectarian groups—involves a lower standard of generosity than

is customary among Jews. As Jews become more acculturated it is quite possible that they may adopt these general standards, which would considerably diminish the income of their own philanthropies.

The NORC study contains some inferential evidence on this point. While immigrants compose 26 percent of all the contributors, they provide 36 percent of the $2,500-and-over contributors. Furthermore, there is a higher proportion of this group in the $2,500-and-over category than in any other. The question then is whether these proportions reflect the greater prosperity of the immigrant group as against the native-born, or whether the former is more "Jewish" and affirms its Jewish heritage in this respect more strongly. The latter interpretation seems the more likely—particularly when we notice that immigrants constitute only a minor proportion of the small givers—some 18 percent. Thus the small givers do not consist predominantly of an unacculturated element, as is sometimes thought, who sit on their wallets because they are alienated from agencies like the federations that raise funds in ways so different from those of the old country.

The median age of small givers is forty-five, which means that they are neither an elderly group that will soon pass from the scene, nor a group of newly marrieds who cannot as yet be expected to carry their share of the load. In spite of the fact that they are already in their middle years, however, the income of these small givers can be expected to grow beyond the present median of $13,000. Only 5 percent of them are craftsmen or workers; a full 41 percent are proprietors and managers, and 18 percent are lawyers, accountants, and physicians. Will the small givers, we wonder, become more generous as they become more prosperous? Some, of course, will, but the findings indicate that most of them feel complacent about the extent of their present giving, despite the information they receive each week in the federation's newspaper concerning local, national, and overseas Jewish needs. One question asked in the Essex County study was: "From what you've read or heard, do you feel the amount of money raised by the federation is very adequate, moderately adequate, a little inadequate, or very inadequate to meet all needs?" Fifteen percent of the small givers replied that the funds were very adequate, 38 percent that they were adequate, and 18 percent that they were a little inadequate. Only 13 percent said that the funds were very inadequate, while the remainder had no opinion.

Further evidence suggests that not only do many donors, particularly the smaller ones, feel that enough money is being raised, but also that some federation contributors would not be adverse to redistributing their philanthropic dollar—and almost invariably they would do so by decreasing their contribution to Jewish causes. This may be merely a way, in some cases, of justifying a reduction in the total amount of giving, by aligning their standards of generosity with those of the general community. Or it may spring from a conviction that general needs are more pressing today than Jewish needs—a conviction that often accompanies the Jew's thoroughgoing absorption into the general culture. But in either event, the result is the same, one that can have serious consequences for Jewish philanthropies in general and federations in particular.

To be sure, Jewish donors still give the major portion of their philanthropic dollar to Jewish causes. In Essex County it varies from 60 percent for the small givers to 76 percent for the big givers. (These percentages are based on data supplied by the respondents and if anything probably underestimate the amount going to Jewish causes.) Among the host of influences, too complicated for us to unravel at this point, that have created the distribution, must be counted the force of habit ("Put me down for the same as last year"). However, it is questionable that this behavior can be counted on unless it receives relevant ideological reinforcement. In addition there is no longer any Jewish monopoly on hard-hitting campaign techniques, since such techniques are evidently finding their way from the Jewish to the general community. Also of importance is the diminishing incentive that can be expected from the establishment of the State of Israel, whose impact on Jewish consciousness is already noticeably weakening now that the miracle is a decade and a half old.

Other roots of Jewish giving seem also to be withering. In the answers to questions on philanthropy asked of Jewish teenagers in the Riverton Study, there was a remarkable absence of any belief that Jews must take care of their own because they are under a solemn obligation to do so, or because others will not do so, or because it would be bad public relations if Jews were to have Gentiles help them even if they were willing to do so. Such beliefs, characteristic of earlier periods in American Jewish life, seem outdated to those growing up in a culture whose nonsectarian philanthropies extend their aid to all groups, and whose municipal, state, and federal agencies are more than willing to include Jewish agencies in their grants. In fact it is the Jewish institutions rather than the public agencies, that have been holding back. While the federations have accepted community-chest grants (in some of the smaller communities such grants now meet the major portion of the budget for local needs), they have moved cautiously in seeking or accepting aid from public sources.

The responses of Riverton's Jewish teenagers should not lead us to assume that the feeling among Jews that they must be responsible for their own is soon to become extinct. But it does seem clear that in the decades ahead giving to Jewish causes will have to be much more a matter of Jewish affirmation than of Jewish defensiveness, and that it will be less the result of habit than of thoughtful decision.

One trend for which there is abundant evidence is that Jewish givers increasingly resist the image of themselves as being ethnocentric in their choices. For example, in the Essex County study, donors were asked the following question: "Suppose you had $10,000 to donate to charity this year, how much would you give to each of the groups that usually ask you for money?" In comparing the subjects' hypothetical donations to their present ones, the researchers concluded that "Jewish charities generally lose ground among all [donor] groups and non-Jewish [charities] generally gain." This, they said, indicates "the cross-pressures of general citizenship appeals."

Recent studies conducted in a number of cities throughout the country by the American Jewish Committee are also instructive on this point. In the typical community about two-thirds of the respondents said that "supporting all humanitarian causes" was essential to being a good Jew, while only one-third thought that "supporting Jewish philanthropies" was essential to being a good Jew. What we are observing, then, is a marked shift in attitude, if not yet of practice. Many Jews speak in a nonsectarian way but continue to give in a sectarian one.

In all probability the tendency toward supporting nonsectarian aims through sectarian channels will grow more pronounced as time goes on. An elaborate study conducted recently for the St. Louis federation by Social Research, Inc., a leader in the motivation-research field, resulted in findings that led SRI to advise the federation to reduce the proportion of money going overseas, thereby retaining a larger portion for local needs. Their reasoning was that the identification with Israel was weakening. Moreover, none of the overseas beneficiaries conduct nonsectarian programs while some of the beneficiaries in St. Louis do so. The major need—as SRI saw it—was to give the federation a more nonsectarian as well as a more local tone.

But the SRI recommendations went even further. The federation was also advised to look for new local beneficiaries in radically different fields of service, for the motivation researchers inferred that interest in supporting the traditional type of Jewish institution (with its emphasis on welfare) was bound to wane under the influence of the so-called "cultural explosion." In sum, then, the remedy for the federations' problems was to keep more of the money in the local community since givers were coming to feel less solidarity with Jews outside St. Louis—specifically with those in Israel—and to emphasize nonsectarian services, especially in the field of culture ("libraries and symphony orchestras and parks and country clubs").

As much as these recommendations may do violence to the purposes for which federations were established, the SRI researchers may have made a shrewd estimate of the changing values of an increasingly significant number of Jewish donors. The example of Brandeis University, the institution that has enjoyed the most spectacular success in the Jewish fund-raising world in recent years, would seem to support their prognostications. For a variety of plausible reasons, many thought that Brandeis would prove a failure, and yet its great campaigns succeeded far beyond the most ardent expectations. Short of the extended analysis that the subject deserves, we can say that Brandeis has provided donors with the possibility of supporting a nonsectarian cause within a Jewish setting—an inspirational relief from traditional Jewish philanthropies with their stress on clothing the naked and redeeming the captives, as well as their aura of parochialism.

Further evidence suggests that however ethnocentric and "Jewish" a philanthropy remains in practice, it is the better part of fund-raising wisdom to emphasize that it is also nonsectarian and serves general as well as Jewish concerns ("the Jewish community's expression of and contribution to the health and welfare needs of the entire community," as its president recently described the New York Federation). Of course, the reality is that quite a number of the agencies that will benefit from the New York Federation's building-fund campaign (to restrict ourselves to that example) have a policy of taking only Jewish clients, and that some of the agencies that adhere to an open-admissions policy retain a largely Jewish clientele by not locating in neighborhoods that are predominantly Gentile. Thus although the feast is not being served in the same nonsectarian way that it is being cooked, the content of the publicity does demonstrate strong approval of the ideal of nonsectarianism.

This ambiguous orientation is becoming increasingly widespread. It involves a host of significant problems. For now, let us pose only two of them: (1) If nonsectarianism were to be truly practiced as well as preached, in what sense would a federation still be a *Jewish* federation? (2) Assuming that the federations become more nonsectarian, will they become sufficiently so to attract donors whose interests have broadened out from strictly Jewish to a variety of humanitarian concerns?

Such nonsectarian donors could move in a variety of directions. They might seek to transform further those federation beneficiaries, such as hospitals and community centers, which are already nonsectarian in clientele and program, by adding non-Jews, for example, to the staff and later to the board. Next the federation itself might be changed along these lines. Or instead of bothering to reform Jewish institutions, such donors might interest themselves directly in existing agencies that are truly nonsectarian or help to create new ones.

The relatively modest proportion of Jewish households that give to federations and the modest level of most contributions, the reliance upon a small percentage of big givers, the inability of the federations to increase their income in the face of rising needs, the ambiguities suggested by the success of nonsectarian-oriented Jewish causes, the increasing acculturation of the giver and his resistance to conceiving of his philanthropy in traditional ways— these are only some of the problems that confront federations in particular and Jewish philanthropy in general. If few of these obvious issues have received thoroughgoing discussion, even more fundamental problems—such as the secularization of Jewish giving and the gradual weakening of its connection with the belief that *tsedakah* is a God-given commandment—have been noticed by only a handful of sensitive professionals and lay leaders. Even when issues do rise to the surface—currently the federations are agitated by the question of whether to support Jewish day schools—they hardly succeed in modifying the incessant note of positive thinking:

federations have had an eventful and on the whole satisfactory history. They have grown more rather than less important with the years. Given an environment of peace and prosperity, federations will function in the future as a form of Jewish organization adapted to serving Jewish needs according to the requirements of the New World and of democracy. . . .

It would take a radical turn of events, amounting to a revolution in American democratic organization or a world catastrophe, to upset current trends in the development of Jewish federations.

Thus ends Lurie's book. His assurances that the Jewish heritage of *tsedakah* is being affirmed, and that such affirmation is bound to continue short of political revolution or nuclear destruction, is a reflection of the tenor of thinking about American-Jewish philanthropy that is encountered in a variety of circles. Such an approach pays little attention to present difficulties and projects an unduly optimistic view of the future. Reappraisal in this field will have its agonizing aspects, but it is necessary if Jewish philanthropy is to deal constructively with the present realities and future problems that we have attempted to sketch.

# American Jewry:
# The Ever-Dying People

It has been clear for some time that the American Bicentennial comes at a bad moment in the nation's history; the country is not in a holiday mood. The debacle in Vietnam, Watergate, the energy crisis, the problem of crime-ridden and bankrupt cities, the simultaneous growth of unemployment and of inflation, and the yet-to-be resolved question of school integration and the place of Blacks in the American social fabric—all these serve to diminish the urge to celebrate the 200th anniversary of American independence.

Jews of course share in the nation's psychological depression. In addition, they are worried about whether such problems as the energy crisis might be utilized to make them the scapegoat and hence diminish American-Jewish status and security. But most of all, the Bicentennial forces a reconsideration of the internal problem of whether American Jewry will survive as a recognizable and significant community.

As perhaps the most survivalistic of America's major ethnic groups, Jews are not only concerned about the nation's prospects as a whole but about the prospects of their own group as well. It is entirely conceivable that America will survive the travails that have created so much ambivalence in this Bicentennial year, and that when the Tercentennial arrives America will still be a great nation. But it is also conceivable that a hundred years from now American Jewry will be decimated in numbers and in status—with those Jews who survive occupying a beleaguered fortress from which many have departed, opting to join the larger society either out of fear of remaining Jewish or out of a feeling that Jewishness plays no significant role in their life.

Until very recently it seemed that American Jewry was optimistic about its future. Older Jews recall the celebration of the American-Jewish Tercentenary in 1954, honoring the 300th anniversary of the arrival in New Amsterdam of a small band of Jewish refugees from Brazil, as a bright and joyous occasion. The reasons for the festivities are easy to locate: Nazism had been destroyed, the State of Israel had been established, and the enemies of Israel did not seem to pose any immediate threat to its survival. And while the main outlines of the tragedy of the Holocaust were known, American Jewry's illusions had not yet been shattered by the revelations about the Roosevelt Administration's lack of resolve to rescue Jews (first from persecution and later from annihilation).

To be sure, the American-Jewish Tercentenary was not unabashedly self-congratulatory. It was admitted that much more needed to be done if American Jewry was to take its proper place in the long line of Diaspora communities. However, the mood was upbeat. One theme that was reiterated was that if the Jews had managed to survive persecution they would surely be able to survive tolerance and acceptance. Another point was that American Jewry was still young. While it was 300 years old, the great majority of Jews had arrived after 1880. Thus in actuality American Jewry was less than a hundred years old—a mere infant if looked at from the perspective of Jewish history. American Jewry would learn to walk and to talk in good time.

The optimism of this time is perfectly captured in *The American Jew*, a book published in 1964 and edited by Oscar I. Janowsky. Janowsky maintained that "American Jewry is a vital and generous community with good potentialities for the future. Those who condemn it because of its deficiencies betray their own impatience. They expect too much too soon." [1] He went on to say that:

> The great centers of Jewish population of the past did not blossom into cultural communities in a few generations. Jews were in Babylonia in the sixth century B.C.E., but they did not achieve cultural leadership until eight hundred years later. In Spain and in West Germany, Jews lived in considerable numbers for at least six hundred years before cultural life assumed significant proportions in the tenth century C.E. Poland, too, had its Jewish communities for hundreds of years before it became a center of learning in the sixteenth century. [2]

Janowsky concluded his volume with the plea that the pessimists among American Jewry be ignored: "Frustration there is aplenty, but despair is unwarranted. American Jewry is not disintegrating. It is in the process of becoming." [3]

This optimistic attitude appears to us today as pollyannish and insensitive to the contemporary situation of American Jewry. A more appropriate stance might be the one formulated several decades ago by the late Professor Simon Rawidowicz. A volume of his collected writings has recently appeared in English containing the essay, "Israel: The Ever-Dying People." [4]

In this essay Rawidowicz seeks to demonstrate that while the pious Jews of the past ostensibly believed in the doctrine of *netzach yisrael* (the eternity of Israel), in actuality they experienced the very same fears about Jewish survival that we do. Rawidowicz's thesis is that for centuries Jews have feared that theirs would be the last link in the *shalshelet hakabala*, the chain of tradition going from generation to generation. The next generation, it was believed, could not be trusted to forge a new link in the chain.

He who studies Jewish history will readily discover that there was hardly a generation in the Diaspora period which did not consider itself the final link in Israel's chain. . . . Each generation grieved not only for itself but also for the great past which was going to disappear forever, as well as for the future of unborn generations who would never see the light of day.[5]

The relevance of Rawidowicz's thinking to the American Jewish situation is heightened by his claim that pessimism about Jewish survival is not primarily a fear that Jewry would die by the Gentile sword, but rather the feeling that Jews would lose their identity, or in contemporary language, "assimilate."

That Jewish history could cease through assimilation is more threatening than the thought that it could end by persecution. Suicide is more awful than murder. One can accept the existence of enemies outside one's group, but assimilation means that one of our own is defecting. And when this is done out of conviction rather than for material rewards, the defector cannot so easily be dismissed.

It is widely believed that before the Jews came to the United States, the external enemy was the main threat to Jewish survival. With the exception of 19th-century German Jewry, it is generally thought that Jews felt they could take the loyalty of their children and grandchildren for granted. And inasmuch as anti-Semitism before the Hitler era was limited and sporadic in nature rather than genocidal, the common interpretation is that Jews felt much as Janowsky presents the picture—namely, that there was assurance about the fact that Jewish history would extend as far into the future as it had extended back into the remote past.

The facts seem to argue otherwise. If the Jews have been preoccupied with the question of their survival with an intensity unknown to other groups, their preoccupation has not been so much with outside enemies as with ingroup defectors. Even when they conceded that such defectors would not leave the group abruptly, the fear was that the next generation would lack the intensity and the conviction necessary to preserve authentic Jewish culture.

Rawidowicz maintains that instead of seeing themselves as the confident teachers of a generation of successors, for the past two thousand years Jewish teachers have seen themselves as the last of their kind. He reasons that the spate of false Messiahs who arose during the medieval period and who gained ardent followers among seemingly rationalistic Jews resulted from the desire to defeat this fear.

Rawidowicz concedes that the fear of being the last generation is not specifically Jewish; it is encountered in Christianity and Islam, and its origin is traceable to psychological processes that are general rather than specifically Jewish:

> the lamentation of *mi-shi-met* has its psychological origin in man's great admiration for his living masters, in his fear lest the miracle will not occur again, lest there will be no second set of masters—as if genius rises only once, never again to reappear.[6]

Nevertheless, Rawidowicz claims that no group has seen itself "so incessantly dying as the Jews."

The question then arises as to whether the fear of dying does not become a self-fulfilling prophecy. Since the fear of death is potentially immobilizing, Jewish history should be a history of lost opportunities, of despair, of survival based upon exclusion by the dominant group rather than survival based upon the convictions and ideals of a minority people. In answer to this, Rawidowicz maintains that Jewish pessimism served to anticipate catastrophe and in so doing gave the group the ability to withstand events that would have demoralized people who have never faced the possibility of their own mortality:

> In anticipating the end, it [Israel] became its master. Thus no catastrophe could ever take this end-fearing people by surprise, so as to put it off its balance, still less to obliterate it—as if Israel's incessant preparation for the end made this very end absolutely impossible.[7]

If Jews have lived with the ever-present fear of their own extinction, what about the Jewish experience in the United States? As is suggested by Janowsky's statements, American Jews have seemingly shared in the optimism that was characteristic of American culture until our most recent difficulties. But the great emphasis that Janowsky places on retaining an optimistic stance may also be taken to suggest that pessimism has not been unknown in American Jewish life.

From Rawidowicz's perspective pessimism would suggest that American Jews have shared in the feeling that theirs is a dying community. There have of course been a number of commentators who have feared that social change in American society would inevitably result in making Jews into a scapegoat and thus would motivate Jews to disassociate themselves from a group that suffers from social stigma or persecution. Nevertheless, American Jewish anxieties about group continuity have revolved around ingroup defection rather than outgroup hostility. And given the mild character of American anti-Semitism, ingroup defections cannot be explained away by economic necessity or the parental desire to put one's children beyond the reach of anti-Semitism.

A persistent theme of American Reform Judaism has been that Judaism need have no fear of extinction if it reforms itself and embraces a form of Judaism that is in harmony with the real needs and feelings of American Jewry. There is a real question, however, as to whether the Reform elite really believed that their movement possessed the magic formula that would guarantee the loyalty of the future generations.

No individual was ever a greater believer in the future of American Jewry than Isaac Mayer Wise. But even with Wise's belief that America was the new Zion and Cincinnati (of all places) the new Jerusalem, there was still in him a persistent feeling of unease. He could not fully banish the feeling that despite the fact that Jews now live in a new Zion, American Jewry might be a dying people.[8]

If those who were engaged in a drastic reform of Judaism had doubts about Israel's eternity, how much more were such doubts rife in the ranks of the traditionalists? Despite their admiration for America, it was immediately apparent to them that while America was good for Jews it was less good—perhaps even fatal—for Judaism.

In 1900 the famed Slutsker Rov, Jacob David Wilowsky, told an audience of Orthodox Jews in New York City that it was not only home that the Jews had left behind in Europe: "it was their Torah, their Talmud, their *yeshivot*—in a word their *Yiddishkeit*."[9] Accordingly, he urged the immigrants to return to Eastern Europe. With the advantage of hindsight, we may say that in view of the rise of Nazism some three decades later, it was providential that very few of his listeners followed his well-meant advice.

As extreme as he was, the Slutsker Rov would probably have agreed that by and large Jews did not come to America to assimilate. Assimilation might be the by-product of coming to America, but it was not the motivating factor for settling in the United States. This little-noticed observation is one of the factors that must be considered in explaining why continuity has played a larger role in American-Jewish history than has assimilation. In fact the East European Jews who came to America before the Russian Revolution may be characterized as a kind of middle group situated somewhere between the extremes of self-segregation and assimilation. The same is true for the German Jews. Most of the militantly Orthodox German Jews remained in Germany until the rise of Hitler. Furthermore, the opposite groups—those who had decisively broken with Jewish culture and had integrated themselves into the German culture (whether conservative, liberal, or radical German culture)— also tended to remain in Germany itself or in neighboring countries until the Nazis came to power. When the Jews who had integrated most thoroughly into German culture did flee, they maintained that *they* rather than the Nazis represented the true Germany, or the Fourth Reich as they named it.

If the dominant group of both German and East European Jews who came to the United States before World War I were middle-of-the-roaders, they were also Jews who lived with the sentiment that Israel was an ever-dying group. At the same time the bulk of American Jewish immigrants—whether they were German or East European middle-of-the-roaders—appear to have acted in conformity with Rawidowicz's hypothesis that while each generation feared that they were the last of their breed, they were not rendered passive by this thought. The newly arrived immigrants proceeded to take advantage of American freedoms, including the freedom to establish a network of Jewish agencies and organizations. The network which they succeeded in establishing is more intricate than that of any other American group of similar size and resources. In fact so intricate is it that there have been charges of duplication of function and the suggestion that Jewish agencies are in need of consolidation rather than expansion.

The United States, then, offered the Jew the possibility of elaborating a communal structure free from interference by governmental or official bodies. The Jewish response to this opportunity was especially noteworthy given the fact that the United States had no history of Jewish settlement in medieval days. Furthermore, the German and East European Jews who came after the 1830's generally did not look to Jewish pioneers of the Colonial period either for economic assistance, moral support, or models for the building of agencies and communal services.

Despite the energy and ingenuity that went into forming a Jewish communal structure in the virgin territory of America, there were some specifically American factors that reinforced the feeling that assimilation in the United States was inevitable. The overall factor of course was the supposed openness of American society. At least in theory if not in practice America offered the alternative of assimilation in the form of the melting pot. To some the melting pot appeared not as an alternative but as an imperative.

There were also more specific threats that were seen as encouraging assimilation. The first such threat is one that we hear very little about at present although it was brought back to the consciousness of some Jews when Key '73 began its drive to make America what it had supposedly been in the past: a Christian nation.

While little has been written on the subject, the fear that Jews would fall prey to Christian missionaries was a persistent theme in 19th-century American Jewish history. The leaders of the Jewish community came to realize that while the United States offered the Jew freedom both to practice his religion and to establish as many different Jewish organizations and institutions as he was able to support, it also offered free rein to missionaries. The Catholics were not as active as the Protestants in Jewish missionary endeavor—they were occupied with establishing themselves as authentic Americans as well as with coping with those who came from Catholic lands but whose Catholicity could not be taken for granted on American soil.

It was the Protestants who were the most active missionaries—first in respect to home missions and later in respect to overseas missions. While the Jews were only one of a number of groups singled out by Protestant missionary societies, Jews tended to see themselves as almost the sole object of the extensive network of Protestant missionary agencies. Jewish feeling on this issue cannot be discounted simply as a manifestation of ethnocentrism; it is apparent that the conversion of the Jews was seen as having a deeper significance than the conversion of American Indians, or Blacks, or of ethnic groups coming from countries traditionally Catholic.[10]

Protestant missionaries began their activities well before the start of the mass immigration from Eastern Europe. Isaac Mayer Wise was highly concerned about the problem—in this as well as in other matters, he reflected much of what his peers were thinking but not saying. Wise utilized the spoken as well as the printed word to combat missionary influence. He developed a program of fourteen points to destroy their power. Wise was not overly modest—as he viewed his career in retrospect, he felt that he had single-handedly succeeded in defeating the missionaries in all sections of the country except for New York City—an area he did not feel responsible for.

In New York City there were a number of Jewish leaders who took upon themselves the burden of fighting the missionaries, Louis Marshall being perhaps the most notable of these. While Marshall, like Wise, was a Reform Jew, his Reform convictions did not in the least soften his abhorrence—or his fear—of missionaries.

The feeling about the missionary endeavor is evident in the cases of those Jews who converted to Christianity but who subsequently returned to Judaism. Instead of living under a cloud, such individuals were welcomed back into the Jewish community. Samuel Freuder is a case in point. A former *yeshiva bocher* in Pressburg and at the Hildesheimer Seminary in Berlin, Freuder was introduced to Isaac Mayer Wise when he arrived in Cincinnati. Wise proceeded to admit him to Hebrew Union College where he graduated in the class of 1886. After failing in the rabbinate, Freuder converted to Christianity and became a Protestant clergyman.

When Freuder wanted to return to Judaism, he was not only welcomed back but was provided with a job that was in effect a sinecure. More importantly he was extravagantly praised for his book, *My Return to Judaism*. The appeal of the book for Jews resided in the fact that it portrayed Christian missionaries in a most unfavorable light: they were characterized as charlatans who preyed on innocent Jews and were masters at extracting money from their Christian sponsors—money that they proceeded to divert to their own uses.

The possibility of Jewish conversion to Christianity was only one fear shared by the leading Jews of an earlier period; there was a second—the fear that Jews would find secular religions more attractive than Judaism. For East European Jews such secular religions took the form of one or more variants of Marxism. For the German Jews the comparable secular religion was Ethical Culture. This movement, the creation of Felix Adler, was designed to supersede Judaism as well as Christianity.

Ethical Culture asks both the Jew and the Christian to give up their religions.[11] It was attractive to German Jews but had little appeal to East European Jews. For them the radical movements of the time served the function of promising that a new world was about to be born—a world without the old divisions such as Judaism and Christianity. The strong appeal of these movements to East European Jews was neatly formulated by Nathan Glazer in his volume, *The Social Basis of American Communism*: while most Jews were not Communists, most Communists were Jews.

While some leading German Jews feared the appeal of radicalism because it could be used by Gentiles to prove that Jews were not good Americans, survivalist-oriented leaders were more concerned about what it might portend for the American Jewish future. Solomon Schechter, for example, who arrived in New York City in 1902 after living in England for some years, clearly perceived the effect of radical movements on the Jews of the Lower East Side: the ultimate effect of adherence to radical social movements would be assimilation—group continuity would be undermined despite the seeming Jewishness of a radicalism that employed the Yiddish language and was almost entirely carried on within the framework of a Jewish milieu. Schechter's subsequent adherence to Zionism was not unconnected with the need he felt for a movement that was capable of appealing to idealistic and secularly oriented spirits but that at the same time would eventuate in Jewish survival.

In our day fears about Jewish survival are centering on somewhat different problems—namely, the problem of Jewish youth, especially Jewish college youth.

The first study on the subject was published in 1932: Marvin Nathan's *The Attitude of the Jewish College Student in the Colleges and the Universities toward His Religion*. Nathan concentrated on both the breakdown of faith that ensued as a result of encountering science and relativism as well as on the withering away of ingroup loyalties, which resulted from being part of an environment that disvalued parochialism.

What was to be done about this unforeseen menace? Interestingly enough the approach of the Jewish community was neither that of solving the problem by discouraging college attendance nor that of embarking on the establishment of a network of Jewish-sponsored colleges. Rather, emphasis was placed on the establishment of campus agencies.

The first Hillel Foundation was opened at the University of Illinois in 1923. A year later the idea of establishing a nationwide chain of such foundations was adopted by B'nai B'rith. Not only was B'nai B'rith the leading Jewish fraternal order of the time; it also saw itself as a neutral meeting place where Jews who had differing conceptions of Jewish survival could come together.

By the late 1950's even those who were highly committed to the Hillel Foundation idea had doubts about the ability of the agency to cope with the alienation of Jewish college youth. Innumerable articles, conferences, and sermons were devoted to the topic. The most common way of expressing anxiety about the American-Jewish future was to focus on what was happening on the campus.

That the campus was seen as the enemy of Jewish identification was indeed an irony—from 1910 on Jewish community relations agencies had struggled to get Jews admitted into private universities. They sought to abolish the geographical quotas that placed a severe limitation on the number of Jews who could be admitted to the more prestigious universities.

Soon after World War II the quotas began to be liberalized and even to disappear. It was said that as many as 40 percent of Harvard College and Columbia College students were Jewish. Nevertheless, satisfaction with the withering away of the quotas quickly dissolved as concern about the Jewish identity of young people escalated. It appeared that the Jewish community was not being given a chance to enjoy its newly won opportunities. Why the fear about Jewish survival? Despite quotas, large numbers of Jews had been attending American colleges and universities for several decades, and the Jewish community seemed to have survived. Worried Jewish leaders, however, took no consolation in the lessons of the past, for they perceived the campus as having changed. They saw two movements that centered in the American campus as a challenge to Jewish survival.

The first was radicalism. The radicalism of the 60's, or the New Left, was felt by Jewish leaders to be more threatening than that of the Old Left. There was indeed evidence to suggest that the New Left, in its extremism and in its demand for total commitment, would substitute itself for Jewish identity. Furthermore, the New Left was seen as having anti-Jewish aspects, including a deep enmity to Israel and an abiding sympathy for the Arab countries and for Palestinian liberation groups.

The second movement feared by Jewish leaders that found its center on the campus was the youth culture, or the "counterculture." Again, it was not as if the meeting of a different culture was a new phenomenon—the Jewish community was thoroughly familiar with the Wasp culture that pervaded even as "Jewish" a campus as City College. While Wasp culture might influence Jews to be less Jewish, the counterculture was seen as threatening Jewish identity itself. Here again confirmatory evidence seemed available. Although Wasp culture might make Jewish youth less Jewish, the counterculture appeared to say that all ethnic or religious loyalties were outdated by loyalty to the "Woodstock Nation." Like political radicalism, cultural radicalism seemed to demand total commitment. As a consequence it was feared that those who succumbed to the counterculture would never again be seen in a synagogue; they were beyond the reach of conventional Jewish student groups such as the Hillel Foundation.

Many Reform Jewish leaders were attracted to some aspects of campus radicalism and the counterculture: for example, its stand on racial equality and its demands for American withdrawal from Vietnam. But they were also suspicious, for they saw their youngsters as particularly vulnerable to campus extremism given the fact that Reform young people had been reared to believe in "prophetic Judaism" and the affinity of the Jew for social justice. Furthermore, since so many Reform youngsters were from the upper reaches of the middle class and in the upper class, they would naturally be deeply touched by a phenomenon such as the counterculture, which appealed almost entirely to youths from prosperous homes.

Conservative and particularly Orthodox leaders also harbored strong fears regarding the loyalties of students coming from their own circles. The anxiety of the Conservative movement was observable by the constant repetition of the request that parents provide the synagogue office with the campus address of their offspring. At a minimum Conservative congregational leaders (as well as Reform) wanted to try to remain in touch with their young people by sending them congregational bulletins as well as mailing them occasional special messages from the rabbi. More ambitious spiritual leaders felt that only personal contact could be effective, and they began to make regular tours of the campuses.

Part of the fear of Orthodox leaders stemmed from their concern for the children of the non-Orthodox, whom they saw as more vulnerable than their offspring. But in truth, they were not all that confident of the loyalties of their own children. Orthodox leaders stressed the advisability of enrolling boys in Yeshiva College and girls in Stern College, where students would presumably be insulated from both radicalism and the counterculture, as well as be exposed to a rich program of Jewish studies. But Orthodox leaders were realistic enough to realize that the pull of the general universities, and specifically of the Ivy League schools, was irresistible. All they could hope for was that Yavneh, the newly founded organization of Orthodox collegians, would be able to prevent at least some traditionally trained young people from defecting to campus radicalism and to the counterculture.

A left-wing Orthodox leader, Rabbi Irving Greenberg, who made the college issue his own, made this stark formulation: "All of the studies we have point to one fact. By and large, college is a disaster area for Judaism, Jewish loyalty and Jewish identity."[12] If college was a disaster area, it would mean that the American Jewish community was slated for suicide, ironically, as a result of the emphasis that Jewish culture places on the value of learning. In the 1960's it was estimated that some 80–90 percent of eligible Jewish youth were attending college compared to less than 30 percent in the general population. Thus the thrust of Jewish culture (in combination with the emphasis in American culture on obtaining a higher education) was generating near-universal attendance at college, which in turn was seen as undermining Jewish identity.

Centrist Orthodox leaders were also concerned. Rabbi Ralph Pelcovitz, spiritual leader of Congregation Knesset Israel of Far Rockaway, New York, was as worried as Greenberg despite the fact that his congregation—unlike that of Greenberg who at the time was the rabbi of Riverdale Jewish Center—was located in a bastion of Orthodoxy, the so-called "Torah Suburb-by-the-Sea." [13] In fact the only Orthodox group that took any satisfaction in the existence of the campus problem were those ultra-Orthodox leaders who had long advised against exposure to what they saw as the inevitable secularism of higher education. They felt that if avoiding college meant that Jewish youth would be closed out of many desirable occupations, it was a sacrifice that American Jewry should be glad to make in the interests of its own survival. But even some *roshe yeshivot* were aware that their students were taking courses at Brooklyn College at the same time that they were pursuing their Talmudic studies. Most of the *roshe yeshivot* decided that discretion was the better part of valor and did not expel such students. Thus college attendance was silently tolerated even in the ultra-Orthodox camp.

The fear of what was happening on the campus permeated not only the religious agencies of American Jewry but reached the highest echelons of the Council of Jewish Federations and Welfare Funds, the national association of the federations that are found in every city in the nation where there is a significant Jewish population. Local pressures were so strong that the CJF felt that if it did not do something about the campus it would open itself to the charge of conducting business as usual while the Jewish community was burning. In June 1968 the CJF established a special "Committee on College Students and Faculty" and retained the services of a leading civil servant of the American Jewish community, John Slawson. The Jewish community had scored a brilliant victory in abolishing quotas on college admission, or at least in having them liberalized to the extent that it would be unwise and even slightly ludicrous to press for more, given the fact that Jewish youth constituted well under 3 percent of the young people of the nation. What would it profit the Jewish community, Slawson reasoned, if this giant step forward resulted in the alienation and ultimate assimilation of those who benefited from these new opportunities? [14]

The anxieties of the CJF, of the local federations themselves, of the religious bodies, and of a wide spectrum of Jewish agencies resulted in the raising of significantly larger sums for work on the college campus. However, the philanthropic impulse was more a type of Jewish kinetic response than anything else; the problem was obviously one that would not be solved by philanthropy.

There seemed to be no treatment for the alienation that was seen as running rampant among the campus population.

At the present time one hears less about the campus problem. That is because the campus has changed and appears less threatening as well as because the Jewish community has learned to live with alienation stemming from the campus. Suffice it to say while American Jewry may be an ever-dying people, at the time of the Bicentennial, American Jewry still lives. The fact that American Jewry has survived the appeal of the New Left and the counterculture, the appeal of the Old Left to East European Jews and of the Ethical Culture Movement to German Jews, the importunings of Christian missionaries (as well as dozens of other perils) will be taken by some as proof that the idea of *netzach yisrael* is valid and that its validity stems from a covenant between God and Israel. Those who find such reasoning unconvincing will look to historical and to sociological factors to explain Jewish persistence. But both will agree with Rawidowicz who pointed out that while Jews might believe that theirs is a dying people, they have refused to take the responsibility for hastening the end. Rather, they have gone about implementing heroic and extraordinary measures to prolong Jewish life. Rawidowicz himself offers us some hope:

A nation dying for thousands of years means a living nation. Our incessant dying means uninterrupted living, rising, standing up, beginning anew. We, the last Jews! Yes, in many respects it seems to us as if we are the last links in a particular chain of tradition and development. But if we are the last—let us be the last as our fathers and forefathers were. Let us prepare the ground for the last Jews who will come after us, and for the last Jews who will rise after them, and so on until the end of days.[15]

## Notes

1. *The American Jew: A Reappraisal*, ed. by Oscar I. Janowsky (Philadelphia: Jewish Publication Society of America, 1964), p. 396.

2. *Ibid.*

3. *Ibid.*, p. 399.

4. Simon Rawidowicz, *Studies in Jewish Thought*, ed. by Nahum N. Glatzer (Philadelphia: Jewish Publication Society of America, 1974), pp. 210–224.

5. *Ibid.*, p. 211.

6. *Ibid.*, p. 220.

7. *Ibid.*, pp. 220–221.

8. See Marshall Sklare, "Judaism at the Bicentennial," *Midstream*, 21, No. 9 (November 1975), p. 25, for the optimistic side of Wise's views on the future of the American Jew.

9. See Moshe Davis, *The Emergence of Conservative Judaism* (Philadelphia: Jewish Publication Society of America, 1963), p. 318.

10. See Marshall Sklare, "The Conversion of the Jews," *Commentary*, 56, No. 3 (September 1973), pp. 44–53.

11. See Michael A. Meyer, "Beyond Particularism: On Ethical Culture and the Reconstructionists," *Commentary*, 51, No. 3 (March 1971), pp. 71–76. For a detailed analysis of the relationships between Ethical Culture and Reform Judaism and Reform Jews, see Benny Kraut, *From Reform Judaism to Ethical Culture: The Religious Evolution of Felix Adler* (Cincinnati: Hebrew Union College Press, 1979).

12. See Irving Greenberg, "Jewish Survival and the College Campus," *Judaism*, 17, No. 3 (Summer 1968), p. 260.

13. See Ralph Pelcovitz, "The Challenge of College," *Jewish Life*, 30, No. 5 (July–August 1963), pp. 18–23.

14. Some believed that the quotas were abolished or liberalized as a result of the inner reform of the universities themselves rather than as a result of the pressure from the Jewish community.

15. Rawidowicz, *op. cit.*, p. 223.

# Marshall Sklare: An Assessment

## Charles S. Liebman

Marshall Sklare shaped the field of American Jewish sociology in its formative years and his work continues to play a central role in the discipline. It seems appropriate to begin an assessment of Sklare by looking at some of the forces that shaped his work. The autobiographical remarks that introduce this volume are most instructive.

## Sociological Observations on Sklare's Autobiographical Remarks

There are four aspects of Sklare's autobiography that I think merit special attention: the intellectual role models present at early stages of his intellectual career; his study of history as background to his subsequent studies in Jewish sociology; the fact that after completing his doctorate in 1953 Sklare was employed by the American Jewish Committee (AJC) for thirteen years; and his continued career in a Jewish milieu.

Sklare lists some of the faculty members at the College of Jewish Studies of Chicago. He mentions Simon Rawidowicz, Shimon Halkin, Nahum Glatzer, and Fritz Bamberger. Any department of Jewish studies in the world would take pride in this gallery of stars. Sklare was exposed, at an early stage of his student life, to keen intellectuals who not only swam in the vast ocean of Jewish knowledge but were productive scholars whose formulations of the Jewish historical, philosophical, and literary traditions must have set standards for Sklare and instilled a sense of the responsibility he bore as a Judaic scholar.

I deliberately use the term Judaic rather than Jewish. Virtually everything Sklare wrote emerged out of a context of Jewish history and tradition. This was the way in which he viewed North American Jewish life, and this is the way in which he described North American Jews. Sklare took it for granted that the study of American Jewish behavior had to be located in the context of Jewish history and tradition. It stood to reason, therefore, that the student of American Jewish life had to become familiar with that history and tradition.[1] So Glatzer, Rawidowicz, Halkin, and others like them not only provided models of intellectual distinction but starting points in Sklare's own scholarly pursuits. Nevertheless, despite Sklare's identification with the field of Judaic studies and his admiration for its practitioners, he was unsparing in his criticism of their slighting treatment of contemporary Jewish studies.

In addition to his college and university mentors, Sklare singles out two of his American Jewish Committee colleagues—Milton Himmelfarb and Lucy Dawidowicz. I have vivid memories of those halcyon days when Sklare, Dawidowicz, and Himmelfarb shared adjoining offices on the fifth floor of the AJC. I still recall the pleasure I derived from my visits there, generally though not always occasioned by something I was writing for the *American Jewish Year Book*. I remember thinking how unfair it was that the magnificent AJC library was a few steps away from their offices. After all, Sklare knew all there was to know about North American Jews, Dawidowicz all there was to know about East European Jews, and Himmelfarb all there was to know about everything else. Why, I wondered, did they also need a library at their fingertips. The three of them were marvelous talkers and even better listeners. Sklare's intellectual acumen must have been sharpened in their presence.

My second observation is related to the first. Sklare's undergraduate major was history. His first serious academic interest was modern Jewish history. History requires an attentiveness to text, an ear to what is being said. Answers to questions that the historian poses are culled from a mass of material that requires thought and reflection. This is a distinct advantage, perhaps almost requisite training to one who ultimately enters the field of sociology where so much evidence is based on survey research and the temptation to make facile assumptions about the meaning that the questions have for respondents and the legitimacy of treating responses outside the context in which they are offered is always present.

My third observation brings us back to Sklare's employment at the AJC. Sklare mentions the difficulties in working as a professional in a Jewish organization, albeit as study director and later director of the Division of Scientific Research. ("The Division of Unscientific Research is not my responsibility," he used to quip.) No doubt there were all kinds of administrative tasks as well as trivial kinds of programs that Sklare was expected to undertake, and there were always additional and seemingly unrelated responsibilities that any senior member of a professional organization is expected to share. Nonetheless, over a period of thirteen years, most of Sklare's time was spent in learning about American Jewish life whether it was in formal research efforts, in traveling and speaking with Jews all over the continent, in perusing the material that crossed his desk as a matter of course, in listening to the variety of Jews who came through the offices of the AJC, or in his and his family's own intense participation in Jewish life. There is no university position today, and there certainly was none thirty years ago, that would have allowed its incumbent the amount of time and access that Sklare had to the raw materials of Jewish life. Sklare was probably the most perceptive and best trained sociologist the American Jewish community has ever had; he was surely the best informed. It is unlikely that anyone will ever know as much as he did about American Jews, and his knowledge was critical in those formative years of the discipline.

There is also a minor point about Sklare's AJC association that deserves mention. I was always surprised at his sensitivity to differences of class and origin among Jews. He was conscious of status differences between Eastern European and German Jews in the United States and to class differences among all kinds of Jews. This was less noticeable in his own publications though he devoted a number of articles to the topic in his first reader, *The Jews*.[2] It also emerged in his public speeches, his classroom lectures, and most frequently in private conversation. It was an important component in his conceptions of North American Jews. He was also extremely sensitive to class consciousness and snobbery among other Jews. His private comments in this regard always surprised me, as I tended to be rather insensitive in such matters. The differences between us might have been a matter of generation, but I always thought it was attributable to his years of association and the nature of his relationships with the lay leaders of the AJC.

The final point in Sklare's autobiography that casts important light upon his work is his continued employment, even after he left the AJC within a Jewish milieu. Sklare was employed on a full-time basis by Yeshiva University for three years. In 1970 he accepted a full-time position in the Department of Near Eastern and Judaic Studies at Brandeis University. In both locations, as at the AJC, Sklare was located among Jewishly committed colleagues who never called upon him to justify his research preferences or his presumptions in favor of Judaism and Jewish survival. One has only to compare the first reader that Sklare prepared, *The Jews: Social Patterns of an American Group* with the next important reader to appear on the same topic, Peter Rose's *The Ghetto and Beyond*[3] published in 1969. That volume contained an article (written especially for the volume by a colleague of Rose's at Smith College) on the benefits of the demise of Judaism.[4] The articles on political topics in that reader assumed a radical-liberal stance, reflecting the academic consensus of the period. Not only was Sklare freed, relatively speaking, of the need to project his research as "value-free," he was under fewer constraints than those that normally adhere among scholars to satisfy the political and cultural biases within academia. In addition, he was under no pressure to publish in scholarly journals rather than in journals under Jewish sponsorship. Indeed, as his bibliography indicates, almost none of his publications are in journals of a non-Jewish nature, and most of the few that were, I would guess, by invitation.

There are advantages and disadvantages for any scholar who works under such conditions, and they are important to note. Sklare never felt obliged to explicate the theoretical assumptions that guided his work. On the contrary, the editors of the Jewish journals in which he published, *Commentary* more than any other, would have found such an elaboration distracting. He never had to justify the validity of his studies in relationship to the broad field of sociology, nor did he have to answer to referees who might have required him to justify his topic in terms of its applicability to non-Jewish groups. Finally, he didn't have to legitimate his assumptions about the value of group identity and the desirability of Jewish survival, nor did he have to assume a nonjudgmental posture. The topics Sklare chose to research, the manner in which he presented his material, and the conclusions he drew stemmed from his own scholarly Jewish agenda. The fact that Sklare was able to distance himself as thoroughly as he did from the material he researched is a tribute to his own professionalism—he was under no pressure to do so. The institutional settings in which Sklare was located freed him from constraints to which most other students of American Jewish sociology are subject. I should add that many such sociologists do not view these constraints as impediments in their work. They have so internalized the values and the cultural ethos of the social science discipline that they operate more easily in this Jewishly neutral context. I don't know if that makes them better sociologists. There are certainly temptations that someone in Sklare's position faces, temptations to be less than strictly analytical about the data and to impose one's hidden agenda on the material. I think that even Sklare succumbed once. On the other hand, there is no question in my mind that the kind of research that sociologists who are located in Jewishly neutral situations produce is far less valuable to the Jewish community than anything Sklare did. What I find striking is that even when such sociologists are employed by the Jewish community they refuse or are unable to abandon their professional, value neutral, and nonjudgmental *persona*. In refusing, ostensibly, to adopt a stance, what they really do is impose the hidden assumptions of their discipline or of academic culture on their work and indirectly on the Jewish community that employs them—the assumptions of personalism, voluntarism, universalism, and pluralism.[5]

## Sklare's Role in Shaping the Discipline

Sklare influenced the field of American Jewish Sociology in a number of ways: through key conceptions that he introduced; through his methodology; through the readers that he edited; and finally through his explicit statements about the nature of the field culminating in the establishment of the Center for Modern Jewish Studies at Brandeis University.

No individual has introduced as many core conceptions to the study of American Jewish sociology as did Marshall Sklare. I will note a few concepts that appear most frequently in studies by other scholars. Sklare identified the characteristics of rituals that North American Jews were most likely to adopt, what Sklare called "criteria for ritual retention."[6] He defined them as rituals capable of effective redefinition in modern terms; rituals that do not demand social isolation and the following of a unique life-style; rituals that accord with the religious culture of the larger community and provide an alternative when one is felt to be needed; rituals that center on the child; and, finally, rituals that are performed annually or infrequently.

Sklare was not the first to study immigrant culture through successive areas of settlement; the notion derives from the Chicago school of urban studies. But Sklare's application of the notion to studies of Jewish immigrants, especially to the development of the Conservative synagogue[7] brought it to the attention of American Jewish historians and sociologists, in whose fields it has become a major research tool. *Conservative Judaism*, in my opinion the best book ever written on American Jews, describes the subtle transformation of Jewish religious life as a consequence of acculturation, a theme that has become standard in the study of North American Jews. The same volume also demonstrates the importance of observing the religious behavior of the masses as well as the ideological predispositions of the elite. The cooperation and tension between mass and elite was critical in the formation of Jewish religious institutions in general and Conservative Judaism in particular. Although it was I who introduced the terms "folk" and "elite religion" in an *American Jewish Year Book* article, parts of which Sklare subsequently reprinted with his own three-page introduction,[8] it was Sklare's study of Conservative Judaism that provided the inspiration for these concepts. Similarly, I introduced the terms "public" and "private" Judaism to distinguish collective, ethnic orientations of Jews from personal, self-fulfilling, more religiously oriented tendencies,[9] but the conceptions are inherent in Sklare's article "The Greening of Judaism."[10] Finally, it was Sklare who introduced the instrument that measured "images of the good Jew" by listing a whole series of characteristics or behavior patterns and asking respondents whether each such characteristic or behavior was *essential, desirable, made no difference*, or was *inimicable* to being a good Jew.[11] That instrument, which was subsequently incorporated in a variety of community surveys, is, in my opinion the best single measure we have for testing through survey research what Jewishness means to North American Jews.

Sklare focused his studies on Jewish identity. He did not exclude the study of religious institutions—they play an important part in both *Conservative Judaism* and *Jewish Identity on the Suburban Frontier*—but he generally ignored studies of other communal institutions, though he was as fully informed about them as he was about every other aspect of North American Jewish life. His methods of data collection were eclectic. He utilized survey data where it was available and did his own attitude surveys when there were no other materials at hand. But he was primarily an ethnographer. He observed Jews in a variety of settings, he listened to them as they spoke, he read all that they produced but always appreciated the value of a single anecdote as paradigmatic for a general condition. He employed archival material when it was available, and above all else, he empathized with American Jews. His empathy was really a research tool, for it enabled him, as it does the best of the ethnographers and cultural anthropologists, to imagine himself in the place of a variety of types of Jews and thereby understand how they respond to a variety of situations. I was and remain awe-struck by his capacity to empathize with so many types of Jews—perhaps this is connected to *ahavat yisrael* mentioned in his autobiography. I never could comprehend his ability, given his own commitments, to move comfortably in Reform circles and with a variety of Reform leaders. I don't think he became quite comfortable with the ultra-Orthodox until family circumstances propelled him into their company. But he surprised even himself at how easily he was able to relate to them. It was a source of satisfaction to him.

I don't mean to suggest that Sklare loved, sympathized with, or even empathized with all Jews. He did not. There were many Jews whom he could not abide. The distinguished professor of Jewish studies whom he mentions in his autobiographical remarks was only one of them. But as far as I know the only group of committed Jews with whom Sklare was unable to empathize was the Ramah-*havurah* type of young Jew to whom he refers in his article "The Greening of Judaism." Oddly enough, they are the sons and daughters, nieces and nephews of people whom he genuinely liked. I read the article when it first appeared, and I recall thinking at that time that it had a grumpy tone to it. Upon rereading it, there can be no doubt that Sklare was absolutely correct in pointing to a malaise that was reflected in *The Jewish Catalog*, a malaise that increasingly characterizes central tendencies within the "committed" segment of American Jewish life. But because I believe Sklare allowed his irritation to overcome his empathy (the only occasion in which I recall his doing so), he missed the opportunity to analyze the ubiquity of the important phenomenon he was describing—the rise of personalism and personal autonomy and the decline of heteronomous authority—a phenomenon that has become critical in the transformation of religion among North American Jews.

Despite his distrust for that group of young Jews whom he felt were Jewishly irresponsible, he was not alienated from the young. Sklare looked to students to exert pressure on faculty and administration to introduce courses in contemporary Jewish studies:

if Jewish studies in the American university are to have a vital future it will be because they fulfill a need which the young Jew experiences. Thus the push to the study of Judaica must originate in the desire to explore personal identity. It follows then that the future of Jewish studies in the American university will be abortive if they move too far in the direction of becoming a pure and impersonal science . . . in order to plumb his identity the young Jew will not only have to be familiar with the Jewish classics and the history of his remote ancestors but he will have to study himself and his immediate forebears.[12]

There is an autobiographical flavor to these lines, and they may constitute the best explanation of Sklare's own devotion to Jewish identity as the controlling concept in the study of North American Jewry.

The readers that Sklare edited represent, independently of his own publications, an important contribution to the field. The first reader represents a major contribution. His autobiographical remarks suggest the importance and sense of responsibility with which he viewed that particular work, *The Jews: Social Patterns of an American Group*, which he prepared for The Free Press. Sklare mentions the significance of The Free Press, but younger colleagues may not appreciate the important role that this publisher played among graduate students in the social sciences in the 1950's and 1960's. In the two fields in which I was most involved, sociology and political science, The Free Press was by far and away the most significant publisher. I remember the feeling that in order to keep current with important new developments in the field, all one really had to do was read the Free Press list. Sklare's reader, even more than his book *Conservative Judaism*, was a statement that the sociological study of the Jews was intellectually respectable. The articles in the reader were magnificent. Without slighting their uniform excellence, the ones by Nathan Glazer, Fred Strodtbeck, Herbert Gans, Jerome Carlin and Saul Mendlovitz, Martha Wolfenstein and Charles Snyder became topics of conversation among Jewishly interested graduate students and were frequently cited in the subsequent literature. (Ben Halpern's "America Is Different" had, as I recall, already achieved the status of a minor classic.) They demonstrated that study of Jews fit into the range of subjects to which sociology addressed itself and that these studies could be carried on without the least sacrifice of the highest academic standards. I never realized, until I read Sklare's autobiographical remarks, that the vast majority of articles were not reprinted from academic journals. Sklare's remarks led me to look once again at the origins of the thirty-three articles. Seventeen were written specifically for the volume. An additional five articles were revisions, some undertaken by Sklare himself, of research reports or in one case of a series of articles previously published in the *American Jewish Year Book*, which Sklare molded into one piece. Contrary to what I had thought, only six of the articles had appeared or had originally been written for publications or as reports that were not specifically Jewish. In other words, Sklare did not find a mass of superior articles on topics of Jewish interest from which he could pick and choose those most suitable for a reader. He had to persuade others to prepare them or produce the articles himself or a bit of both. His next readers, two volumes titled *The Jew In American Society and The Jewish Community in America*, published by Behrman House in 1974, contained twenty-six articles, only two of which had appeared in The Free Press edition, and only one of which was an original article written for the reader. These two volumes, published seventeen years after the first edition, reflected the growing maturity of the field, in no small measure a tribute to Sklare's pioneering endeavors.[13]

The final category of contribution that Sklare made to the discipline was in articles on the nature of the field of contemporary Jewish studies and in the establishment of the Center for Modern Jewish Studies at Brandeis University. In his early articles, Sklare pointed to the need for courses in the field and to the question of where such courses might be best located—in social science departments or departments of Jewish studies.[14] (He seemed to favor the latter.) By 1984 Sklare was able to describe the problems that those who teach contemporary Jewish studies and those who enroll in such courses must face.[15] Evidence, once again, of the rapid development of the field.

The establishment of the Center for Modern Jewish Studies was made possible by a Revson Foundation grant. The grant was made in anticipation of Sklare's central role in the projected development of the Center. Prior to issuing the substantial grant and as a condition therefor, the Revson Foundation offered Sklare a smaller sum to commission a series of papers surveying the state of the field. The authors were invited to describe different areas of American Jewish studies including the kinds of knowledge available and some research projects that ought to be undertaken in each of these areas. The papers were then discussed before a larger meeting of scholars in October 1979. Sklare chose ten areas of American Jewish life: demography, identity, religious life, education, families and family policy, the Jewish polity, relations between Jews and non-Jews, Jewish organizations, local Jewish communities and Jewish organizations.[16] There was an additional paper on the genesis and organization of research centers. Sklare himself wrote an essay that urged the Center to sponsor a synthetic or interpretive volume on the sociology of American Jewry.[17] He believed that such a work would be an important stimulant to the growth of the field, would encourage publishers to solicit other such works, would lead to the introduction of college-level courses in the subject, and by suggesting new problems would inevitably lead to new works of synthesis and interpretation. Sklare made no secret of the fact that he intended writing such a volume, and it is indeed unfortunate that he never did so.

## Sklare's Influence on American Jews

Sklare was a popular figure on the Jewish lecture circuit. His presentations, like his essays, were carefully crafted, yet entertaining. Whether in print or behind a podium, whatever he had to say had a point. He never used the lecture hall or the classroom simply as a forum to display his erudition or his wit or to appeal to popular prejudices. He bitterly resented those of his colleagues who did. In the 1960's I sat through two of his courses on American Jews at Yeshiva University's Wurzweiler School of Social Work in anticipation of my substituting for him the following year. His course lectures, if anything, were even more stimulating and entertaining than his popular lectures. Almost all his classroom lectures followed the same structure. He would begin with a brief survey of the institution he was describing, whether it was the family, or the synagogue, or education, or communal leadership, or the rabbi, as it developed through Jewish history, noting its condition in Eastern Europe in particular. He would then describe its evolution in the United States from the immigrant generation until the contemporary period, accompanying his description with a plethora of anecdotes and statistics when the latter were available. His listeners, classroom students, or popular audiences never failed to feel stimulated as well as informed. He touched their Jewish nerve and allowed them to integrate their own Jewish experiences with the Jewish historical experience and the life of the world Jewish community. I can't imagine many figures in the rabbinate, much less in academia, who did more than Sklare to stimulate Jewish awareness and sensitivity.

The topic upon which he was asked to speak most frequently and upon which he wrote such important essays in *Commentary*, a topic that he increasingly saw as a threat to Jewish life in the United States, was that of intermarriage. Sklare wrote and spoke about intermarriage before it had assumed its present proportions and before it had affected so many Jewish families in the United States that one had to be very careful about how one addressed the topic for fear of offending the majority of one's audience. I would like to think that if not for Sklare the situation would be even worse than it is. I may be fooling myself.

This essay affords me an opportunity to comment upon the charge that Sklare overlooked the resurgence of Orthodoxy in American Jewish life until the revised edition of *Conservative Judaism* was published by Schocken in 1972. It is true that Sklare belittled Orthodox prospects in North America in the first (1955) edition of the book. It is also true that in his study of Riverton [18] (Riverton was, as I recall, a pseudonym for Trenton, New Jersey), he found Orthodoxy in precipitous decline. One cannot fault a researcher for reporting what he uncovers. Furthermore, I'm not sure that the emergence of Orthodox Judaism as a new force in American Jewish life could have been apparent to anybody short of a prophet or someone intimately involved in the ultra-Orthodox world at the time Sklare gathered the data for *Conservative Judaism*. But I can certainly correct the impression that Sklare was insensitive to these developments until he prepared the augmented edition of his book in the early 1970's. In 1963 I prepared an article on Orthodox Judaism. [19] I only knew Sklare by reputation, but I sent him a draft of the article and asked him for his comments. He invited me to his office, and that is how our association began. He had many comments to make about the article, and it was clear to me that he was well informed about Orthodoxy. A year later Milton Himmelfarb, who was then coeditor along with Morris Fine, invited me to write an essay on Orthodoxy for the *American Jewish Year Book*. The need for such an essay, Himmelfarb explained to me, stemmed from the fact that whereas observers of American Jewish life had tended, in the past, to dismiss Orthodoxy, its recent resurgence required the *Year Book* to take a new look at it. Two points deserve mention here. First, it is stretching credulity to believe that Himmelfarb would have decided upon a lead article in the *American Jewish Year Book*, especially one that concerned religion in American life, without first consulting with Sklare. Indeed, the original idea might well have been Sklare's. Secondly, although Himmelfarb approached me some time in early 1964, I know that someone else had been approached as early as 1962 and had submitted a manuscript on the same topic, which Himmelfarb rejected as inadequate. The timing indicates that Sklare was no less if not more sensitive to the resurgence of Orthodoxy than I, although this was the area in which I presumably possessed more detailed knowledge.

I spent quite a bit of time with Sklare from the middle to the late 1960s, but after that time I was in Israel and our meetings may have averaged one a year. However, when we did meet we spent many hours in conversation, and he shared many thoughts with me. Sklare had little regard for Jews in academia who sought to mask their Jewishness or who felt apologetic about being Jewish. He had no patience for sociologists who happened to be Jewish and who evidenced sympathy for every minority group in the world except their own. But he had least patience of all for those Jews who sought to exploit their Jewishness, and what little knowledge they had about Judaism to further their own agendas, whether personal or public. Sklare not only loved the Jewish people, he loved Judaism—though I'm not sure he would have recognized the distinction. For as Chaim Waxman quotes him as saying:

there cannot be an authentic Jewish people without the continuity of Jewish tradition, even as there cannot be meaningful continuity of Jewish tradition without the maintenance of the integrity of the Jewish group.[20]

## Notes

1. As Sklare noted in his catalogue of problems in the teaching of contemporary Jewish studies:
the teaching of contemporary Jewish studies proceeds without much attention to interrelationships with Jewish studies generally. The tendency in contemporary Jewish studies is to see every problem as new. Thus, the Jewish family is not treated against the backdrop of *halachah* or even against the backdrop of medieval and modern Jewish history. It is our impression that whether it is the family, Jewish political behavior, or Jewish religious behavior, the framework of teaching tends to be contemporary American society rather than the framework of historic Jewish society or of Jewish tradition. (Marshall Sklare, "Problems in the Teaching of Contemporary Jewish Studies," *American Jewish Historical Quarterly*, 63 [June 1974], p. 365.)
2. Marshall Sklare, *The Jews: Social Patterns of An American Group* (Glencoe, Ill.: The Free Press, 1957).
3. Peter Rose (ed.), *The Ghetto and Beyond: Essays on Jewish Life in America* (New York: Random House, 1969).

4. Kenneth Stern, "Is Religion Necessary," *ibid.*, pp. 190–200. Stern concludes his articles as follows:

Let me say in conclusion that I recognize that along with the prospective demise of Jewishness, there will be a concomitant loss of values, or, at least, things I hold valuable. Most of these will be aesthetic. On the other hand, perhaps an important good will arise out of this loss. Perhaps the demise of Judaism will be the first in the demise of all the racial and national separateness that has caused the world so much havoc throughout its history. If this is the price, the loss of Jewish community, shall anyone say it is not worth paying? (p. 200.)

5. Sklare introduced these concepts in his Lakeville study: Marshall Sklare with Joseph Greenblum, *Jewish Identity on the Suburban Frontier: A Study of Group Survival in the Open Society* (New York: Basic Books, 1967, second edition, University of Chicago Press, 1979). Steven M. Cohen and I try to show how they undermine traditional Jewish life. See our book, *Two Worlds of Judaism: The Israeli and American Experience* (New Haven: Yale University Press, 1990) and my article "Ritual and Ceremonial in the Reconstruction of American Judaism," Ezra Mendelson (ed.), *Studies in Contemporary Jewry* VI (New York: Oxford University Press, 1990), pp. 272–283.

6. *Jewish Identity on the Suburban Frontier*, 2d ed. (Chicago: University of Chicago Press, 1979), pp. 57–59.

7. Marshall Sklare, *Conservative Judaism: An American Religious Movement* (Glencoe, Ill.: The Free Press, 1955).

8. "The Religion of American Jews by Charles S. Liebman," in Marshall Sklare (ed.), *The Jew in American Society* (New York: Behrman House, 1974), pp. 223–52, reprinted in Marshall Sklare (ed.), *American Jews: A Reader* (New York: Behrman House, 1983), pp. 245–274.

9. If I'm not mistaken I first introduced these terms in my article "Changing Conception of Political Life and Their Implications for American Judaism," Sam Lehman-Wilzig and Bernard Susser (eds.), *Comparative Jewish Politics* (Ramat-Gan, Israel: Bar-Ilan University Press, 1981), pp. 91–100, republished in revised form under the title "American Jews and the 'Modern Mind'" *Midstream*, 27 (April 1981), 8–12.

10. Marshall Sklare, "The Greening of Judaism," *Commentary*, 58 (December 1974), pp. 51–57.

11. The table appears in *Jewish Identity on the Suburban Frontier*, p. 322 and is described on pp. 321–32 but was developed earlier. If my memory serves me correctly, it was first utilized in the early 1960's, if not before, in surveys sponsored by local AJC chapters in four large Jewish communities.

12. Marshall Sklare, "The Problem of Contemporary Jewish Studies," *Midstream*, 16 (April 1970), pp. 27–35.

13. Another edition of the Behrman House readers, this time in one edition, was published nine years later, and all but four of the fourteen articles were reprinted from earlier editions.

14. "The Problem of Contemporary Jewish Studies," *op. cit.*, pp. 27–35.

15. "Problems in the Teaching of Contemporary Jewish Studies," *op. cit.*, pp. 361–68.

16. The papers were revised and published under the title Marshall Sklare (ed.), *Understanding American Jewry* (New Brunswick, N.J.: Transaction Books, 1982).

17. "On the Preparation of a Sociology of American Jewry," *ibid.*, pp. 261–71.

18. Marshall Sklare and Marc Vosk, *The Riverton Study: How Jews Look at Themselves and Their Neighbors* (New York: The American Jewish Committee, 1957).

19. Charles S. Liebman, "A Sociological Analysis of Contemporary Orthodoxy," *Judaism*, 13 (Summer 1964), 285–304.

20. Chaim Waxman, "Psalms of a Sober Man: The Sociology of Marshall Sklare," *Contemporary Jewry*, *ibid.*, p. 9. The citation is from the second edition of *Conservative Judaism*, p. 282.

# Chronological Bibliography of the Writings of Marshall Sklare

*Conservative Judaism: An American Religious Movement*, Glencoe, Ill.: The Free Press, 1955.

"Forms and Expressions of Jewish Identification (with M. Vosk and M. Zborowski), *Jewish Social Studies*, XVII, No. 3 (July 1955), 205–18.

*The Riverton Study: How Jews Look at Themselves and Their Neighbors* (with M. Vosk), New York: The American Jewish Committee, 1957.

*The Jews: Social Patterns of an American Group*, Glencoe, Ill.: The Free Press, 1958.

"A Study of Jewish Attitudes toward the State of Israel" (with B. B. Ringer), in *The Jews: Social Patterns of an American Group*, Glencoe, Ill.: The Free Press, 1958, pp. 288–303.

"Some Socio-Psychological Aspects of the Jew in America," in *Changing Patterns in American Jewish Life*, ed. by Leon A. Feldman, New York: Jewish Education Committee Press, 1958, pp. 9–24.

"Ethnic-Religious Groups and Subsidized Pluralism," *School and Society*, May 23, 1959, pp. 16–19.

"Church and Laity among Jews," *The Annals*, 332 (November 1960), 60–69.

"The Values of East European Jewry and of American Society," *Jewish Frontier*, XXVIII, No. 7 (July 1961), 7–11.

"American Jews and American Jewish Life: Observations of a Sociologist," *Central Conference of American Rabbis Yearbook*, Vol. LXXI (1961), pp. 229–44.

"The Future of Jewish Giving," *Commentary*, 34, No. 5 (November 1962), 416–26.

"The Development and Utilization of Sociological Research: The Case of the American Jewish Community," *The Jewish Journal of Sociology*, 5, No. 2 (December 1963), 167–86.

"Intermarriage and the Jewish Future," *Commentary*, 37, No. 4 (April 1964), 46–52.

"Assimilation and the Sociologists," *Commentary*, 39, No. 5 (May 1965), 63–67.

Discussion of papers on "Acculturation and Identity in American Society," *American Jewish Historical Quarterly*, LV, No. 1 (September 1965), 32–36.

"Introduction" (with T. Solotaroff) in C. H. Stember and others, *Jews in the Mind of America*, New York: Basic Books, 1966, pp. 3–28.

*Jewish Identity on the Suburban Frontier: A Study of Group Survival in the Open Society* (with J. Greenblum), New York: Basic Books, 1967.

"The Trouble with 'Our Crowd,'" *Commentary*, 45, No. 1 (January 1968), 57–62.

"Introduction" in P. Y. Medding, *From Assimilation to Group Survival: A Political and Sociological Study of an Australian Jewish Community*, Melbourne: F. W. Chesire, 1968, pp. XVII–XXII.

"Lakeville and Israel: The Six-Day War and Its Aftermath," *Midstream*, 14, No. 8 (October 1968), 3–21.

"Synagogue Organizations," *Encyclopedia Britannica*, 1968.

*Not Quite at Home: How an American Jewish Community Lives with Itself and Its Neighbors* (with J. Greenblum and B. B. Ringer), New York: Institute of Human Relations Press, 1969.

"The New American Jewish Parent and Jewish Education," in *The Parent and Jewish Education*, ed. by Jay B. Stern, New York: Educators Assembly of the United Synagogue of America, 1969, pp. 77–82.

"The Impact of Israel," in *The Impact of Israel on American Jewry: Twenty Years Later*, New York: American Histadrut Cultural Exchange Institute, 1969, pp. 55–59.

"The Forces Shaping American Jewry," *Jewish Frontier*, XXXVI, No. 5 (May 1969), 21–24.

"Intermarriage and Jewish Survival," *Commentary*, 49, No. 3 (March 1970), 51–58.

"The Problem of Contemporary Jewish Studies," *Midstream*, 16, No. 4 (April 1970), 27–35. Reprinted in Leon A. Jick (ed.), *The Teaching of Judaica in American Universities*, New York: Ktav Publishing House, 1970, pp. 57–70.

*America's Jews*, New York: Random House, 1971.

"Where Are We—Where Are We Going?" in *When Yesterday Becomes Tomorrow*, New York: Congregation Emanu-El of the City of New York, 1971, pp. 47–63.

"The Sociology of the American Synagogue," *Social Compass*, 18, No. 3 (1971–73), 375–84.

*Conservative Judaism: An American Religious Movement*, rev. ed., New York: Schocken Books, 1972.

"Recent Developments in Conservative Judaism," *Midstream*, 18, No. 1 (January 1972), 3–19.

"Jews, Ethnics, and the American City," *Commentary*, 53, No. 4 (April 1972), 70–77.

"The Conversion of the Jews," *Commentary*, 56, No. 3 (September 1972), 44–53.

*The Jew in American Society*, New York: Behrman House, 1974.

*The Jewish Community in America*, New York: Behrman House, 1974.

"Problems in the Teaching of Contemporary Jewish Studies," *American Jewish Historical Quarterly*, 63, No. 4 (June 1974), 361–68.

"The Jew in American Sociological Thought," *Ethnicity*, 1, No. 2 (1974), 151–73.

"The Greening of Judaism," *Commentary*, 58, No. 6 (December 1974), 51–57.

"Jewish Religion and Ethnicity at the Bicentennial," *Midstream*, 21, No. 9 (November 1975), 19–28. Reprinted in Jacob Katz (ed.), *The Role of Religion in Modern Jewish History*, Cambridge: Association for Jewish Studies, 1975, pp. 147–59.

"The American Synagogue," *Proceedings of the Rabbinical Assembly*, Vol. 37 (1975), pp. 30–39.

"American Jewry—The Ever-Dying People," *Midstream*, 22, No. 6 (June–July 1976), 17–27.

"The Social Background of American Jewish Education—A Commentary," in *Colloquium Papers* of The American Jewish Committee's Colloquium on Jewish Education and Jewish Identity, New York: American Jewish Committee, n.d., pp. 12–26.

"Our Future Responsibility: What Lies Ahead for Boston Jewry?," *Jewish Perspective*, 2, Nos. 5–6 (May–June 1977), 1–3.

"The Symposiasts: A Response," *Contemporary Jewry*, 4, No. 1 (Fall–Winter 1977–78), Special issue entitled, "The Sociology of Marshall Sklare," 37–45.

"Foreword" to *Mishpokhe: A Study of New York City Family Clubs* by William E. Mitchell, The Hague: Mouton (1978), pp. 7–10.

"Jewish Acculturation and American Jewish Identity," in *Jewish Life in America: Historical Perspectives*, edited by Gladys Rosen, New York: Ktav Publishing House, 1978, pp. 167–88.

*Jewish Identity on the Suburban Frontier: A Study of Group Survival in the Open Society* (with J. Greenblum), 2d ed., Chicago: University of Chicago Press, 1979.

*Understanding American Jewry*, New Brunswick, N.J.: Transaction Books, 1982.

"On the Preparation of a Sociology of American Jewry," in *Understanding American Jewry*, edited by Marshall Sklare, New Brunswick, N.J.: Transaction Books, 1982, pp. 261–71.

*American Jews: A Reader*, New York: Behrman House, 1983.

"Foreword" to *Perspectives in Jewish Population Research*, edited by Steven M. Cohen et al., Boulder, Colo.: Westview Press, 1984, pp. IX–XII.

"Jewish Demography: The Unanswered Questions," delivered at Colloquium on Jewish Population Studies, Sugar Loaf Conference Center, Philadelphia, March 18, 1984.

*Conservative Judaism: An American Religious Movement*, repr. ed. with new foreword, Lanham, Md.: University Press of America, 1985.

"The Bicentennial Spirit: Jews, Ethnics, and the 'Waspim,'" Sol Feinstone Memorial Lecture delivered at Gratz College, Philadelphia, January 10, 1988.

# *Acknowledgments*

"Jewish Acculturation and American Jewish Identity," in *Jewish Life in America: Historical Perspectives*, edited by Gladys Rosen (New York: Institute of Human Relations Press/KTAV, 1978), pp. 167–88.

"The Jewish Religion in America," in *America's Jews*, by Marshall Sklare (New York: Random House, 1971), pp. 110–35.

"The Conservative Movement: Achievements and Problems," published as "Recent Developments in Conservative Judaism," in *Midstream*, 18 (January 1972), pp. 3–19; and in *Conservative Judaism*, by Marshall Sklare (New York: Schocken Books, 1972), pp. 253–82.

"The Greening of Judaism," *Commentary* 58, No. 6 (December 1974), 51–57.

"A Study of Jewish Attitudes toward the State of Israel," with Benjamin R. Ringer, in *The Jews: Social Patterns of an American Group*, edited by Marshall Sklare (New York: Free Press, 1958), pp. 437–50.

"Lakeville and Israel: The Six-Day War and Its Aftermath," *Midstream* 14, No. 8 (October 1968), 1–19.

"Jews, Ethnics, and the American City," *Commentary* 53, No. 4 (April 1972), 70–77.

"The Bicentennial Spirit: Jews, Yankees, and Other Ethnic Groups in Boston," originally published in somewhat different form as *The Bicentennial Spirit: Jews, Ethnics, and the 'Waspim,'* Annual Sol Feinstone Memorial Lecture, Gratz College, January 10, 1988 (Philadelphia: Gratz College, 1988).

"The Jew in American Sociological Thought," *Ethnicity* 1, No. 2 (1974), 151–73.

"The Sociology of Contemporary Jewish Studies," in *The Jew in American Society*, edited by Marshall Sklare (New York: Behrman House, 1974), pp. 1–27.

"The Image of the Good Jew in Lakeville," in *Jewish Identity on the Suburban Frontier*, by Marshall Sklare and Joseph Greenblum (New York: Basic Books, 1967), pp. 321–32.

"The Conversion of the Jews," *Commentary* 56, No. 3 (September 1973), 44–53.

"Intermarriage and the Jewish Future," *Commentary* 37, No. 4 (April 1964), 46–52.

"The Future of Jewish Giving," *Commentary* 34, No. 5 (November 1962), 416–26.

"American Jewry: The Ever-Dying People," *Midstream* 22, No. 6 (June–July 1976), 17–27.

# Index

Aaron, Rabbi Samuel, 114–15, 120–21, 124–25
Academia: alienation of youth in, 269–73; intermarriage in, 163–64, 241–42; Jews in, 159–67, 175–76; political-cultural pressures in, 277–78
Academy of Jewish Studies, St. Petersburg, 184–85, 187–88, 199(n 6)
Acculturation: of American Jews, 23–28, 34–35 (*see also* Survival); effect on residential preferences, 142; effect on ritual observances, 40–41; in Jewish sociology, 170, 194, 279; theory, 21–22. *See also* Assimilation; Secularism
Adams, John, 24, 220
Adams, John Quincy, 24, 220
Addams, Jane, 30
Adler, Felix, 269
Affiliation: group, 56–60; synagogue, 45–46. *See also* Conservatism; Orthodoxy; Reformism
AJC. *See* American Jewish Committee
Alienation: critical intellectualists and, 169, 171, 177–78, 192–95; of Jewish academics, 163–66, 185, 197, 201(n 25); of Jewish college youth, 269–73; leadership fears about, 85; among psychoanalysts, 243
*Aliyah*, 123
*Ambivalent American Jew, The* (Liebman), 173
America: Jewish attitudes toward, 25, 28, 33–34, 152–53, 157, 177–78; separation of church and state, 216, 230–31

American Board of Missions to the Jews, 220, 228
American Council for Judaism, 104(n 12), 108, 109
*American Hebrew*, 222
American Indians, 148
*American Jew, The* (Janowsky), 263
American Jewish Committee (AJC), 103(n 1), 201(n 23), 259; interfaith relations, 221, 225, 226–27; Sklare's work for, 10–11, 275, 276–77; survey on reactions to Israel, 89–103, 103(nn 2, 3), 104(nn 4, 5, 6, 7, 9, 12), 105(n 14), 105–106(n 18)
American Jewish Congress, 192
*American Jewish History*, 55
American-Jewish Tercentennary, 262–63
*American Jewish Year Book*, 63, 70, 182, 198(n 1), 236, 237, 279, 283–84
*American Jews: A Reader* (Sklare), 13
*American Journal of Sociology*, 168, 190, 235
*American Judaism* (Glazer), 172
American Society for Meliorating the Condition of the Jews, 220
American Sociological Association, 168, 189
*America's Jews* (Sklare), 11–12
Andersen, Rev. Henry W., 227
Anthony, Rev. Alfred Williams, 222–23
Anti-Defamation League, 171, 194, 226
Antin, Mary, 30
Anti-Semitism: AJC work on, 10; during Hitler era, 153, 159; increases in,